Asset-Building Policies and Innovations in Asia

Asia has long been a testing ground for efforts to augment financial and social security by developing assets that may support individuals and households and contribute to long-term social development. Rapid growth in the number and breadth of asset-based social policies has prompted Asian scholars, practitioners, and policymakers to share lessons from current efforts and chart future directions.

This book offers a unique collection of macro- and micro-level analyses on asset-based social development and compares and contrasts national social policies across the Asia Pacific region. Many asset-building policies and programmes have been undertaken in Asia, and innovative proposals continue to emerge. The contributions in this book present and assess this broad, often nuanced, and evolving landscape, and offer an insightful analysis of the evolution of asset-building policies, innovative programmes in rural populations, asset-based interventions to facilitate the development and well-being of children, as well as case studies on new, ground-breaking asset-building projects.

Asset-Building Policies and Innovation in Asia will be an invaluable resource for students and scholars of Asian social policy, social welfare, social development, and social work.

Michael Sherraden is George Warren Brown Distinguished University Professor, George Warren Brown School of Social Work and Director, Center for Social Development at Washington University in St. Louis, USA.

Li Zou is International Director and Director of the Global Assets Project, Center for Social Development at Washington University in St. Louis, USA.

Hok-bun Ku is Associate Professor, Department of Applied Social Sciences, Hong Kong Polytechnic University.

Suo Deng is Assistant Professor, Department of Sociology, Peking University, China.

Sibin Wang is Professor, Department of Sociology, Peking University, China.

Routledge research on social work, social policy and social development in Greater China
Series editors: Angelina Woon-ki Yuen-Tsang, Hok-bun Ku, and Ngai Pun
Hong Kong Polytechnic University

This series focuses on issues related to the rapid social change in contemporary Mainland China, Hong Kong, Macao, and Taiwan. Comprising contributions from diverse disciplines, the series will explore and respond to the impacts of marketization, globalization, urbanization, modernization, migration, technological change, consumerism, dualism and disasters on people's livelihoods, well-being, and social life in Chinese societies.

Asset-Building Policies and Innovations in Asia

Edited by
Michael Sherraden, Li Zou,
Hok-bun Ku, Suo Deng, and
Sibin Wang

Routledge
Taylor & Francis Group

LONDON AND NEW YORK

First published 2015 by Routledge

2 Park Square, Milton Park, Abingdon, Oxon OX14 4RN
711 Third Avenue, New York, NY 10017, USA

Routledge is an imprint of the Taylor & Francis Group, an informa business

First issued in paperback 2017

British Library Cataloguing in Publication Data
A catalogue record for this book is available from the British Library

Library of Congress Cataloging in Publication Data
A catalog record for this book has been requested

ISBN: 978-1-138-82581-9 (hbk)
ISBN: 978-1-138-10408-2 (pbk)

Typeset in Times New Roman
by Wearset Ltd, Boldon, Tyne and Wear

Contents

Figures

Tables

Contributors and editors

Toivgoo Aira, Executive Director, Wellspring NGO.

Charles C. Chan, Associate Professor, Department of Applied Social Sciences, Hong Kong Polytechnic University.

Chun-yi Chen, Doctoral Student, Department of Social Work, National Taiwan University.

Li-Chen Cheng, Professor, Department of Social Work, National Taiwan University.

Ho Kong Chong, Associate Professor, Department of Sociology, National University of Singapore.

Ross Clare, Director of Research, Association of Superannuation Funds of Australia (ASFA).

Suo Deng, Assistant Professor, Department of Sociology, Peking University.

Baorong Guo, Associate Professor, University of Missouri–St. Louis School of Social Work.

Xincai Guo, Former Director, Hutubi County Rural Retirement Social Insurance Office, Xinjiang, China.

Chang-Keun Han, Associate Professor, Department of Social Welfare, Sungkyunkwan University.

Jin Huang, Assistant Professor, School of Social Work, St. Louis University.

Minchao Jin, Doctoral Student, George Warren Brown School of Social Work at Washington University in St. Louis.

Lissa Johnson, Director of Administration, Center for Social Development at Washington University in St. Louis.

Youngmi Kim, Assistant Professor, School of Social Work, Virginia Commonwealth University.

Hok-Bun Ku, Associate Professor, Department of Applied Social Sciences, Hong Kong Polytechnic University.

Simon M. K. Lai, Research Associate, Department of Applied Social Sciences, Hong Kong Polytechnic University.

Gyanesh Lama, Assistant Professor, Department of Social Work, California State University, Fresno.

Wendy S. Y. Lau, Research Associate, Department of Applied Social Sciences, Hong Kong Polytechnic University.

Eunlye Lee, Doctoral Student, Mandel School of Applied Social Sciences, Case Western Reserve University.

James Lee, Professor, Department of Applied Social Sciences, Hong Kong Polytechnic University.

YungSoo Lee, Assistant Professor, Incheon National University, Department of Social Welfare.

Yu Meng, Postdoctoral Fellow, School of Humanities and Social Sciences, Nanyang Technical University of Singapore.

Eddie C. W. Ng, Research Associate, Department of Applied Social Sciences, Hong Kong Polytechnic University.

Kok-Hoe Ng, Assistant Professor, Lee Kuan Yew School of Public Policy, National University of Singapore.

Marion Riedel, Associate Professor of Professional Practice, Columbia University School of Social Work.

Sharad Sharma, Research Team Leader for the YouthSave Project, New ERA.

Michael Sherraden, George Warren Brown Distinguished University Professor, George Warren Brown School of Social Work; Director, Center for Social Development at Washington University in St. Louis.

Sung Suk Song, Director General for Strategic Planning & Coordination, Seoul Welfare Foundation.

Wimonmat Srichamroen, Nonprofit Organization Management, Thailand.

Fred M. Ssewamala, Associate Professor, Columbia University, School of Social Work.

Ciwang Teyra, Doctoral Student, School of Social Work, University of Washington.

Wai-fong Ting, Associate Professor, Department of Applied Social Sciences, Hong Kong Polytechnic University.

Laura Cordisco Tsai, Doctoral Student, School of Social Work, Columbia University.

Parichart Valaisathien, Associate Professor, Department of Community Development, Thammasat University.

Sibin Wang, Professor, Department of Sociology, Peking University.

Susan S. Witte, Associate Professor, Columbia University School of Social Work.

Siew-Yong Yew, Director, the Social Security Research Centre, Faculty of Economics and Administration, University of Malaya.

Tan Tai Yong, Vice Provost (Student Life) and Director of Institute of South Asian Studies, National University of Singapore.

Deyu Zhao, Professor, School of Social Development and Public Policy, Fudan University.

Li Zou, International Director and Director of the Global Assets Project, Center for Social Development at Washington University in St. Louis.

Acknowledgements

The editors express our sincere gratitude to each of the authors of the chapters in this book for their excellent contributions, first during the conference on Life-long Asset Building: Strategies and Innovations in Asia, held at Peking University in November 2012, and then in following up to refine their papers for this publication. The editors also acknowledge the work of Chris Leiker, editor at the Center for Social Development at Washington University in St. Louis, for his expertise and commitment to making each of the chapters clear and informative. We would like to thank John Gabbert, also an editor at the Center for Social Development, for seeing this project through to completion.

We extend our deep appreciation to the main organizers of the 2012 conference – Peking University–Hong Kong Polytechnic University China Social Work Research Centre and the Center for Social Development of Washington University in St. Louis – for their close collaboration over the past 15 years and for organizing such a successful first-of-its-kind conference. In addition, we are grateful to the conference co-organizers: the Department of Sociology of Peking University, Centre for Social Development (Asia) of the National University of Singapore, and the Chinese Association for Social Work Education. The editors are indebted to the following sponsors for their generous support of the 2012 conference: the Levi Strauss Foundation, the Keswick Foundation, the Ford Foundation, and the McDonnell International Scholars Academy of Washington University in St. Louis. Finally, we thank the Lee Foundation in Singapore for supporting the publication and distribution of this book.

Abbreviations

ABP	asset-based policy
ADD	American Dream Demonstration
AFI	Assets for Independence Act of 1998
AIDS	acquired immunodeficiency syndrome
AMNS	average monthly net savings
ASEAN	Association of South East Asian Nations
ASFA	Association of Superannuation Funds of Australia
ATM	automated teller machine
AUD	Australian dollar
BOK	Bank of Kathmandu
CAD	Canadian dollar
CDA	Child Development Account
CDF	Child Development Fund
CHIP	China Household Income Project
CNY	Chinese Yuan renminbi
CODI	Community Organizations Development Institute
COP	Commission on Poverty
CPF	Central Provident Fund
CYBY	*Chetanshil Yuva Bachat Yojana* (Conscientious Youth Savings Scheme)
DOSM	Department of Statistics Malaysia
EPF	Employees Provident Fund
FGD	focus-group discussion
GDP	gross domestic product
GHLC	Government Housing Loan Corporation
HBA	Hope Building Accounts
HDA	Hope Development Account
HDB	Housing Development Board
HIV	human immunodeficiency virus
HKD	Hong Kong dollar
HKSAR	Hong Kong Special Administrative Region
HOH	head of household
IDA	Individual Development Account

KRW	Korean won
LG U+	LG Telecommunication Company
MHW	Ministry of Health and Welfare (Korea)
MOHP	Ministry of Health and Population (Nepal)
MRQ	mentoring relationship quality
MYR	Malaysian ringgit
NBS	National Bureau of Statistics (China)
NGO	non-governmental organization
NPC	National People's Congress (China)
NPR	Nepalese rupee
OECD	Organization for Economic Co-operation and Development
OLS	ordinary least squares regression
PAP	People's Action Party
PDP	personal development plan
RM	reverse mortgage
SCDA	Seoul Child Development Accounts
SD	standard deviation
SEED OK	SEED for Oklahoma Kids
SG	superannuation guarantee
SGD	Singapore dollar
SIDA	Seoul Individual Development Accounts
SOCSO	Social Security Organisation (Malaysia)
SRR	sexual risk-reduction condition
SRR-plus	sexual risk-reduction plus microsavings condition
THB	Thai baht
TWD	New Taiwan dollar
USD	US dollar

Introduction

Michael Sherraden, Li Zou, Hok-Bun Ku,
Suo Deng, and Sibin Wang

'Why are assets important to us?' This is one of the most frequently asked questions in research and policy discussions related to asset building in social policy and programmes. There is growing evidence that assets – distinct from income – contribute positively to people's overall well-being. If this is the case, then it may be desirable for everyone to accumulate resources invested for their long-term social and economic development. To achieve the long-term goal of universal and inclusive asset building, a growing number of countries and regions have tested related policies and programmes.

Asia has long been a testing ground for efforts to augment financial and social security by developing assets that may support individuals and households and contribute to long-term social development. Rapid growth in the number and breadth of asset-based social policies has prompted Asian scholars, practitioners, and policymakers to share lessons from current efforts and chart future directions. Regional collaborations and knowledge exchange can be an important contribution to these efforts.

This book is published at an opportune moment for those interested in asset-based social and economic development. Many asset-building policies and programmes have been undertaken in Asia, and innovative proposals continue to emerge. The contributions in this book present and assess a broad, often nuanced, and evolving landscape. Together, the chapters offer an insightful overall analysis of asset-building policies and programmes in Asia.

This collection emerges from the November 2012 conference on Lifelong Asset Building: Strategies and Innovations in Asia held at Peking University in Beijing. The conference organizers include Peking University–Hong Kong Polytechnic University China Social Work Research Centre; the Center for Social Development at the George Warren Brown School of Social Work at Washington University in St. Louis; the Department of Sociology at Peking University; the Centre for Social Development (Asia) at the National University of Singapore; and the China Association for Social Work Education. The conference was a great success thanks to the organizers and generous support from the Levi Strauss Foundation, the Keswick Foundation, the Ford Foundation, and the McDonnell International Scholars Academy at Washington University in St. Louis.

We have arranged the book's contents in two broad themes: asset-building policy and asset-building strategies among diverse populations. We recognize that such arrangements are inevitably imperfect but hope that juxtapositions will enhance the whole by suggesting interrelationships and spurring discussion on points of common ground. The seven chapters in Part I discuss asset-building policies in Singapore, Hong Kong, Japan, Australia, Malaysia, Korea, and Taiwan. James Lee opens the section with an analysis of housing policy and home ownership in Singapore, Hong Kong, and Japan. He focuses particularly on efforts to achieve economic security through home ownership and the value of home equity. In Chapter 2, Ross Clare considers the history and features of Australia's superannuation (i.e. private pension) system, examining the system's effectiveness in enabling Australians to accumulate assets. Chapter 3 by Siew-Yong Yew traces the evolution of Malaysia's Employees Provident Fund and compares its effects with those of Singapore's Central Provident Fund. In Chapter 4, Chang-Keun Han and Youngmi Kim survey the proliferation of asset-building initiatives in Korea over the last decade, assessing whether the offerings can be considered inclusive and identifying challenges faced by those pro-grammes. In Chapter 5, Li Zou and colleagues analyse the rapid expansion of asset-building policies in Korea and Taiwan, documenting the policy diffusion process and suggesting pathways to shape such policy through collaboration among multiple stakeholders. In Chapter 6, Tan Tai Yong and Ho Kong Chong trace the development of Singapore and the city-state's Central Provident Fund, suggesting that this history reveals the elements needed to craft and implement a national system of social security. The Central Provident Fund also lies at the centre of Kok-Hoe Ng's contribution (Chapter 7), which asks whether the fund provides sufficient income security for retirees or offers security as the size of Singapore's elder population grows.

Part II turns to asset-building strategies among diverse populations. The first three chapters focus primarily on children and youth. In Chapter 8, Charles C. Chan and colleagues detail results from research on Pioneer Projects of the Hong Kong Child Development Fund. Chapter 9, by Sharad Sharma and colleagues, presents early research results from YouthSave's *Chetanshil Yuwa Bachat Yojana* (Conscientious Youth Savings Scheme) in Nepal. In Chapter 10, Suo Deng and Yu Meng examine the depth and breadth of access to mainstream fin-ancial services among youth with disabilities in Beijing.

Using data from the Chinese Household Income Project, Jin Huang investi-gates in Chapter 11 the influence of asset poverty on the happiness of urban households in China and identifies several mediating factors. In Chapter 12, Baorong Guo, Xincai Guo, and Li Zou re-examine the Hutubi Model, which allowed famers in western China to use their assets in rural retirement savings accounts for agricultural and household development in Hutubi County, the Xin-jiang Uygur Autonomous Region.

The next three chapters highlight asset-building efforts and perspectives among ethnic minority women, earthquake survivors, and land-deprived rural dwellers. In Chapter 13, Hok-Bun Ku details an action research project to preserve traditional culture and mitigate rural poverty through the creation of a women's handicraft group in Pingzhai, an administrative village of Yunnan Province. In Chapter 14, Wai-fong Ting focuses on a project to rebuild financial, social, cultural, and human assets in the aftermath of a severe earthquake that struck Sichuan province in 2008. She uses that context to analyse and broaden the conceptual framework that underpins asset building. In Chapter 15, Deyu Zhao and Minchao Jin introduce a probing discussion of land policy in China. Reviewing current land policy, they detail several local innovations in land use, considering the advantages and disadvantages of each.

Chapter 16 presents three case studies of innovative approaches to social development. The study by Toivgoo Aira and colleagues describes the features of Undarga, a microfinance intervention for female sex workers in Ulaanbaatar, Mongolia, and presents insights from an asset-building intervention. In the second case study, Wimonmat Srichamroen reports on the Light of Hope Saving Program, an asset-building effort to provide resources for the education and development of vulnerable children in Thailand, and outlines a continuing study of the programme. Parichart Valaisathien contributes the third case study, which details implementation of the Thai government's *Baan Mankong* (Secure Housing) programme in Nong Kaem, a poor community that originated as a squatter's camp for garbage pickers on the outskirts of Bangkok's municipal dump. Focusing on the role played by the Nong Kaem Housing Cooperative, Valaisathien emphasizes the organic, community-driven nature of development efforts in Nong Kaem.

The Conclusion, by Michael Sherraden, shifts to a broader view of asset-based social policy in Asia and beyond, with observations on policy innovations and research outcomes. Although they are relatively recent developments in the evolution of social policy, asset-building strategies are emerging in many parts of the world. Whether and to what extent asset-based policies will become part of renewed social contracts in Asia remains to be seen. This book may play a small part in that inquiry and deliberation.

Part I
Asset-building policies

1 Housing policy and asset building

Exploring the role of home ownership in East Asian social policy

James Lee

Home ownership is not a new socio-economic policy in Western industrial economies. In the United Kingdom, the Right to Buy was the backbone of Margaret Thatcher's conservative economic policy in the early 1980s (Jones and Murie 2006). Through the discount sales of council housing, the United Kingdom has successfully sold part of the post-war welfare state to the public. As a result, wealth for many households has grown, albeit in a fragmented way (Forrest, Murie, and Williams 1999). Nonetheless, there is a new consensus in the West that owner-occupied housing provides a means to build individual economic security and thereby offsets shortfalls in the pension system (Doling and Ronald 2010; Malpass 2008; Smith, Searle, and Cook 2009).

A debate has emerged regarding the notion that asset building could augment the wealth portfolios of homeowners to supplement income protection and offset diminishing welfare state provision (Regan and Paxton 2001; Sherraden 2003). Many governments acknowledge that home ownership represents a means to build assets in the face of current challenges to pension provision (Watson 2009). However, the volatility of the global economy in the last two decades has subjected home ownership policies to serious challenges. On one hand, many assert that mammoth lending to home buyers was a major determinant of the 1997 Asian economic crisis and the 2008 subprime crisis in the United States. On the other hand, huge debts assumed by many governments during financial crises suggest that the neoliberal orientation in housing and other welfare policies might persist (Brenner, Peck, and Theodore 2010).

In his latest attempt to expose the perils of neoliberal urbanization, David Harvey (2012) observes the strange connection between the degree of indebtedness by ordinary households – mainly indebtedness incurred through mortgage borrowing – and the occurrence of urban economic crises in modern capitalism of the last century (e.g. the 2008 subprime crisis in the United States). The purpose of this chapter is to explore the role of home ownership as an institutional arrangement for asset building within the broad domain of social policy in East Asia, using examples from Singapore, Hong Kong, and Japan.

Productivism, developmentalism, and the welfare state in East Asia

A key dimension of welfare states in East Asia is an intriguing connection between development and social policy. Social policy serves an important economic development purpose in this part of the world, where two related conceptual debates emerged: productivism and developmentalism. Championed by Holliday (2000), *productivism* describes a central feature of East Asian social welfare that emphasizes work, productivity, and growth. In addition to cultivating export-led economic policies, high-growth East Asian economies such as Japan, Singapore, and Hong Kong fostered the integration and innovation of well-structured social policies to support economic growth.

Holliday (2000) elaborated on three modes of productivism – facilitative, developmental-universalist, and developmental-particularist – to explain the connection between social policy and development. Central is the idea that social policy in East Asia is subordinate to economic policy, which explains why social expenditures often rise when economies grow. However, an opposite perspective – developmentalism – emphasizes the alternate idea of integration. According to Midgley (1997), the integration of social policy to economic growth was the key institutional innovation behind the East Asian miracle. Midgley and Tang (2001) suggest that a very important symbiotic relationship exists between social policy institutions and economic development in countries like Singapore and Japan: 'Social development cannot take place without economic development and economic development is meaningless if it fails to bring about significant improvements in the well-being of the population as a whole' (246).

Housing and welfare

What, then, is the connection between social welfare and housing? The answer lies in the dual nature of owner-occupied housing. Because housing involves human welfare and investment, it intricately links economic and social dimensions. This relationship is sometimes harmonious and sometimes conflicting. After two decades of housing booms in the West, markets crumbled. A 2012 report by the Federal Reserve in the United States (Mullaney 2012) suggests that the average US household lost nearly 39 per cent of its wealth between 2007 and 2010, while the richest 10 per cent of households gained 2 per cent. These estimates show the effect of home ownership on income inequality when housing policy runs on a free-market model.

Peter Malpass (2008) suggests two ways to consider the relationship between housing and welfare. The first is to understand housing as a feature within the welfare state and recognize that there is a need for the state to intervene if the housing market cannot provide affordable housing. This is a *weak* formulation of the relationship because the state normally plays a remedial and passive role in the housing market, responding passively to local and global house price fluctuations. As a result, the market tends to be volatile and easily fall prey to speculative market forces. Malpass's second suggestion is to view housing policy as an integrated part of social policy. This represents a case of *strong* connection because the state takes an active role in setting up institutional frameworks to capture the economic and social policy advantages of home ownership. It also seeks to minimize the role of housing market adversaries through regulations. From this perspective, housing consumption is a core activity of socio-economic policies, not purely a matter of private consumption. Individual home ownership and national housing policy are part of a wider framework to promote economic development through asset building (Groves, Murie, and Watson 2007). The expansion of home ownership expands the economic capacity of households and empowers them to meet retirement needs (Doling and Ronald 2010).

During the last two decades, home ownership rates have increased globally. Schwartz and Seabrooke (2008) assert that wealth accumulates more rapidly among homeowners than among renters. Michael Sherraden (2003) notes that households increasingly see the positive potential of home ownership, including minimized dependence on social security in old age. Sherraden champions the idea that home-owning households tend to accept personal responsibility in accumulating assets for the future. Although a home is not the only asset that has accumulative functions, home ownership is an effective vehicle by which house-holds accumulate the largest pool of assets. As fiscal pressure rises and political trends favour market-oriented solutions, support for the use of housing as a basis of welfare provision grows (Brenner, Peck, and Theodore 2010).

Singapore: a strong case of institutionalism

Public housing started in Singapore to address a post-Second World War housing shortage and urban slums. In 1947, the colonial government appointed a Housing Committee to investigate the problem. They discovered that one-third of the population inhabited the heart of the city, which was highly overcrowded. Noting that only 8.8 per cent of the population could access public housing, the committee pressed for a large-scale development plan (Castells, Goh, and Kwok 1990). In 1960, Singapore set up the first and most important institution on housing: the Housing Development Board (HDB), which soon embarked on an enormous building programme. It began with a goal to build 110,000 public housing units within a decade and exceeded this goal by 10 per cent. While the HDB built only rental flats in the beginning, it decided to sell these flats to sitting tenants in 1964. Lee Kuan Yew, the first prime minister, explains his perspective on Singapore's housing initiative:

> My primary preoccupation was to give every citizen a stake in the country and its future. I wanted a home-owning society. I had seen the contrast between the blocks of low-cost rental apartments, badly misused and poorly maintained, and those of house-proud owners, and was convinced that if every family owned its home, the country would be more stable.
>
> (Lee 2000, 96)

From the outset, home ownership in Singapore was and is about political stability, not simply meeting residential needs. Underlying housing policy is an intention to create a sense of stakeholdership (Chua 2002). However, when the HDB offered to sell flats to tenants at the early stage, they were too poor to afford the 20 per cent down-payment. Dr Goh Keng Swee, an economist minister, proposed to adopt and expand a colonial saving institution called the Central Provident Fund (CPF). Lee and Goh decided to expand the colonial scheme to include both an income maintenance function for old age and funding for home purchase. In 1968, the CPF allowed account holders to access their savings for home purchases. Such a policy shift succeeded in what Peter Evans (2005) describes as an institutional turn – a point at which development is no longer primarily a process of capital accumulation but rather a process of institutional change.

Under this framework, household savings are directed collectively towards home purchase while the HDB acts as a mortgage bank (Chua 1997). Households accumulate savings in the CPF, which in turn buys government bonds, providing the government with financial resources for housing investment. The HDB then acts as a developer and mortgage provider. Households can deduct funds from their CPF accounts to pay their mortgages, storing equity value in their flats until old age. In operational terms, this circuit of capital is created through the mobilization of CPF savings for capital formation. The government then provides development loans and grants to support housing development, which explains why Singapore had a relatively high ratio of government debt to gross domestic product (GDP) – an average of 85.45 – even during periods of positive economic growth (Fiscal Monitor Database 2012). The essence of this first circuit lies in the integration of the individual saving function with the collective housing investment function. This enables the mass mobilization for designated consumption – an essential condition for growth. Thus, housing provides mass satisfaction of both housing and investment needs (DiPasquale and Wheaton 1996).

The HDB mortgage interest rate is pegged at 0.1 per cent above the CPF interest rate, which is generally about 2 per cent below the market mortgage interest rate (or a minimum of 2.5 per cent) provided by commercial banks. The advantage of the first circuit is that it addresses the problem of market failure in low-income housing finance – a common problem in developed and developing countries.

Collaboration between the CPF and the HDB also affects the housing loan market. For a long time, the HDB provided mortgage loans at both concessionary interest rates, which accounted for 63 per cent of all loans granted by the HDB in 2001, and at market rates. Assuming the role played by a commercial lender, the HDB made market-rate loans to private borrowers who were not eligible for ordinary HDB loans. During the peak of the HDB's mortgage business, it took up 66 per cent of the market (Phang 2001). In January 2003, the HDB stopped issuing market-rate mortgage loans because the government decided that such loans are more appropriately provided by commercial banks. In a 2002 speech, the Minister for National Development indicated that the HDB should not engage in the private mortgage business but concentrate on providing housing loans only to eligible Singaporeans (Tan 2002).

In sum, Singapore succeeded in creating a developmental state by using public home ownership to drive economic development and providing its citizens with an important opportunity to amass capital through their own housing assets. This highly regulated housing regime epitomizes the power of appropriate institutional arrangement to meet social and economic objectives. It provides the state with growth from housing investment and an important institutional arrangement in which the state effectively distributes capital gains from home ownership among its senior citizens. The latest development in Singapore is the establishment of the Lease Buyback System, which allows elderly people to receive a monthly income through a reverse mortgage (RM), thus realizing the ultimate goal of using housing asset as a form of supplementary social security.

Hong Kong: a weak case of institutionalism

Hong Kong has the second largest public housing sector in East Asia after Singapore. Roughly half of the population lives in public housing, mostly rental flats. Only a small percentage (18 per cent) of the population enjoys subsidized home ownership. The other half of the population, mainly middle-class people, must contend with one of the world's most expensive and speculative housing markets. Housing cost has created enormous pressure on the government and the people.

Many argue that high housing costs in Hong Kong are a direct consequence of land shortage. On the contrary, Raymond Tse (1998) suggests that land supply is more 'a consequence rather than a cause of house-price inflation in Hong Kong'. He suggests that the land price regime is a component of the government's strategy to maximize revenue. Inflation in Hong Kong's housing market has provided the government with substantial and reliable revenue for many years. Between 1970 and 2000, land revenue amounted to USD 71 billion (in 2000 constant US dollars) (Lee 2012). Four sources provide this revenue: auction of land, rental of land, modification of leases, and renewal of leases. If revenues from property tax are included, total revenues were USD 96.1 billion (Hong 2003).

Between 1996 and 2000, land revenue accounted for 17 per cent of total government income and was the second largest source of revenue in Hong Kong after personal and corporate taxes. Between 1970 and 1995, 75 per cent of land revenue came from auction, and 20 per cent came from fees associated with modification of leases (Lee 2012). Why was there such a distribution? Some research results suggest that Hong Kong's leasehold system imposes institutional constraints on people's ability to derive value from land (Hong 1998, 2003). The system forces the government away from a long-term approach (e.g. land rental) and favours land auctions for maximizing land value. However, auctions encourage inflation and drive overinvestment in real estate. Because of such auctions, commercial and residential developments have peaked along with the government's land premium collection (Lee 2012).

House prices rose along with land prices. From the 1960s to the 1980s, the government sought to offset inflation in house prices by subsidizing public housing, but subsidies became ineffective as prices exceeded affordable levels. The Special Administrative Region's first government proposed housing production to target inflation, but strong opposition arose from developers and homeowners who feared that increasing production would harm property values (Lee 2012).

The influence of Hong Kong's powerful developers is evident in remarks by Chris Patten, the last colonial governor of Hong Kong:

> Our ability to apply the radical free market solutions that were required was limited by proximity to the transition. Any convincing attack on the monopoly effectively enjoyed by a few extremely rich property developers in Hong Kong, making grotesquely large profits, could have had a serious effect on market confidence at a sensitive time.
>
> (Patten 1998, 51)

When the new government attempted to correct such influence by increasing land supply, developers and homeowners strongly opposed the initiative, which led to political disaster and the termination of the Home Ownership Scheme in 2003 (Lee 2012).

Land sales and the leasehold system provide the government with substantial opportunities to generate revenue for the public housing programme, implement a low-tax regime, and offer a wide range of social welfare services. However, Hong (2003) notes that land leasing in Hong Kong may produce public revenue but impede efforts to stabilize the cost of housing. Beginning in the 1950s, Hong Kong has met this dilemma by building East Asia's second largest public housing system, the primary goal of which is to meet the housing needs of low-income households and correct market failure in the provision of affordable housing.

This background suggests that the Hong Kong government depends and survives well on a continuing stream of revenue from land sale. One can use asset-building terms to characterize the problem: the state realizes substantial asset benefits from land sale but also is responsible for pushing up house prices. As Hong Kong is an international city with a small, open economy, residential and commercial properties are heavily exposed to global speculative interests. I suggest elsewhere that there are two major motivations for home ownership: 'use-value' and 'exchange-value' (Lee 2012, 179). Hong Kong clearly has developed a mass culture that favours the exchange-value of housing much more than its use-value. Over the last three decades, this has continued unfailingly to fuel speculative activities and housing price inflation.

One question remains unanswered: how can the state guarantee that home ownership is a stable way to build household assets in a relatively open housing market? The answer is that it cannot. For individuals and families, the key to building household assets through equity lies in the 'cohort effect', in which the wealth effect differs tremendously depending on the timing of the household's entry into the housing market (Forrest and Lee 2004). A long history of volatility and speculation in the housing market suggests that only a handful of middle-class households enter the market at the right time to experience asset appreciation and building. Many middle-class households suffered from negative equities and were trapped by heavy mortgage payments after the Asian financial crisis.

Facing immense political pressure due to the lack of income protection for older people, the government asked the Hong Kong Mortgage Corporation – a public agency responsible for mortgage securitization and insurance – to introduce a pilot RM scheme in 2011. Six private banks participate in the scheme, which currently is run on a commercial basis. Although RMs are often seen in the West as a form of equity release for low-income elderly people who lack liquidity but possess housing assets, Hong Kong emphasizes that the RM is a loan scheme. Borrowers receive monthly payments over a fixed payment term of 10, 15, or 20 years, or for the rest of their lives. They also may borrow lump-sum loans for specific purposes.

Since its inception, the scheme has received a lukewarm response from elderly homeowners. One study estimates that there are 67,168 people in Hong Kong who are aged 65 years or older, living alone, and cash poor (Business and Professionals Federation of Hong Kong 2008). However, fewer than 300 have registered for RMs since the scheme's inception in 2011, which suggests that either a small number of elderly people own a home or the RM scheme is not attractive to them. Recent data from the Hong Kong Mortgage Corporation further suggest that only middle-class elderly homeowners have registered for the scheme thus far. These registrants have average home assets of HKD 3.7 million (Hong Kong Mortgage Corporation 2012). Low-income elderly homeowners with property valued at less than HKD 2 million are much less interested in the scheme. Although it is still early to gauge the success of Hong Kong's RM scheme, it is run on a commercial basis and charges a market interest rate with competitive administration costs. Its benefits to low-income homeowners will be limited.

In sum, social policy in Hong Kong represents a weak connection between housing and welfare because only a small portion of the population with housing assets can enjoy the benefits of home ownership. Homeowners easily could spend 60–70 per cent of their monthly incomes on housing-related debt. That level of obligation imposes an enormous financial burden on middle-class families and creates a heavily skewed pattern of consumption. The situation has worsened as the global economy has fluctuated in recent years, creating further hardship for homeowners who face rising unemployment during economic downturns.

Japan: from strong to weak connection

Japan has a home-ownership rate of about 60 per cent. After the Second World War, a strong state policy facilitated home ownership through the state monopoly of housing finance and provided robust impetus for the growth of owner occupation in post-war Japan. The Japanese government sought to provide long-term, low-interest loans through a state agency, the Government Housing Loan Corporation (GHLC). The GHLC regulates the housing market through housing finance and the promotion of owner-occupied housing (Hirayama 2007).

Although home-ownership rates accelerated in the post-war decades, they began to diminish in the 1980s. In the 1990s the intensification of loan provision and the extension and improvement of loan criteria helped expand gross national mortgage debt but not the ratio of homeowners, particularly in places like Tokyo (Hirayama 2007). In the late 1990s, the GHLC set interest rates on its loans at 2 per cent for 10 years and reduced the 20 per cent down payment requirement to 10 per cent. This triggered growth in housing loans to around JPY 180 trillion by 2006. There is a clear intention by the government to boost home ownership again after the economic bubble of the early 1990s (Japan Housing Finance Agency 2007).

The relative ease of access to state housing finance provided the greatest impetus for home ownership in Japan, as it did in Singapore and Hong Kong. Over the past two decades, however, the traditional framework of the Japanese housing system has lost its effectiveness. A robust economy gave way to economic uncertainty, capital gains became capital losses, and a cohesive society became increasingly marked by social fragmentation (Hirayama 2007). The bubble economy, which started with an abnormal rise in land and housing prices during the latter half of the 1980s, collapsed at the beginning of the 1990s. Since the bubble burst, Japan has experienced a deep and prolonged recession. It has been one of the longest periods of economic stagnancy in modern times. Land and house prices, which plummeted sharply for the first time in the 1990s, remained stagnant until 2010. Owner-occupied housing has come to generate capital losses. For many households, the security of home ownership has been replaced by the burden of debt and negative equity. The government has begun to retreat from housing policy, entrusting it and its related financing to an increasingly deregulated market. In 2001, the government finally abolished GHLC loans. Looking back on the 1990s, Hirayama and Ronald (2007, 3) are among several who dub it the 'lost decade' of housing policy in Japan.

Given a bleak global economic outlook and a highly volatile Japanese political system, the real estate sector likely will remain stagnant for some time. Since the government suspended GHLC loans, more and more young people find home ownership inaccessible because of the rising cost of home financing.

This case clearly illustrates state orchestration of housing investment in post-war economic construction. The dual purpose of Japan's post-war housing policy – to boost the economy through housing investment and help households build individual assets – is clear from the outset. Nonetheless, economic deregulation and political failures rendered the asset-based housing offerings unsustainable. It remains an institutional arrangement badly in need of transformation.

Of the three East Asian economies, Japan was the first to start RMs, but the benefits of home ownership now apply more to the older generation than the younger. Doling and Ronald (2012) suggest that homeowners account for 86 per cent of Japanese people aged 65 years and older. For the elderly with limited incomes who wish to extract equity value from their homes, RMs are likely to be an attractive option. To capitalize the equity value of the assets held by elders, Musashino municipality in the Tokyo metropolitan area launched an RM programme in 1981 (Doling and Ronald 2012). In 2002, Japan's Ministry of Health, Labour and Welfare began providing RMs to elderly homeowners with low incomes. Private banks and housing corporations began operating RM schemes in the early 2000s. For private banks, the expansion of RMs represents a new financial market bolstered by the change in the GHLC's loan policy.

Nevertheless, the Japanese RM market remains stagnant for various reasons. Since the bubble burst, many homeowners have experienced a tremendous devaluation in their residential properties. Economic uncertainty, property values, and interest rates limit the value of RMs. Unlike many Western countries, Japan deals with housing and land separately. The market values of buildings are very low because the structures have short lifespans. This means that RM borrowers can take out a mortgage only on the land. Thus, the RM market excludes most condominium owners.

Discussion and conclusion

As I have noted elsewhere:

> Housing encompasses two unique characteristics: first, the *use-value*, which suggests that housing provides a household with residence and second, the *exchange-value*, which suggests that housing represents an asset capable of capitalization from time to time. Henceforth housing satisfies both a need for space and an asset for investment.
>
> (Lee 2012, 179)

Some have argued that a housing system inclined heavily towards exchange-value generally generates an unstable housing market, while one that emphasizes use-value normally engenders a more stable housing market (Lee 2012). Recognizing this dual nature of housing and its ensuing contradictions is fundamental to understanding why many housing systems become unstable if left entirely to the market.

While it is in the interest of the state to promote use-value, thereby maximizing the chances of market stability and sustainability, 'capitalists and real estate developers hold a different view' (Lee 2012, 179). They apparently are more interested in the maximization of exchange-value and often prevail in struggles with housing consumers. Developers wield much greater power and influence in capitalist economies, such as Hong Kong, South Korea, and Taiwan, and in transforming economies, such as China. In the literature of governance, research results suggest the importance of state autonomy and the need to balance developers' interests with those of the public (Lee 2012). However, land scarcity and rapid urbanization increase capitalists' chances to extend their power in the housing market and limit the state's power to intervene.

Political tension is a central characteristic of housing policy in Hong Kong, where pressure to expand state housing for low-income households and strengthen regulations for the real estate sector is constant. On the contrary, enormous political pressure to curtail state intervention and expand market freedom for developers also exists. Housing price fluctuations and severe afford-ability problems are consequences of this tension. On an affordability index – in which higher scores indicate lower affordability – most industrial economies have average scores between three and four. Hong Kong's affordability score, known as the price-to-income ratio, was 17.6 in 2012. This means that an average household requires 17.6 years of total income to purchase a medium-priced flat (Lam 2012). Former colonial Hong Kong Governor Patten (1998) succinctly characterizes the situation:

> A great deal of politics had been channeled into housing activities, and since elected politicians were responsible for so little from left to right, they tended to articulate tenant grievances rather than apply themselves to the fundamental causes of these problems. The construction of public housing has been regarded as substitute for the introduction of democratic politics.
>
> (41)

Given this context, how do we gauge the success of asset-building policies in East Asia? What causes one housing system to succeed while others fail? From a brief examination of three economies, we have seen different institutional attempts to promote asset building through home ownership. While home owning builds a household's assets and augments social security systems to some extent, any housing system has inherent risks. The relative success of these systems depends heavily on whether one can avert the inherent risk of home ownership: exposure of an investment asset to the turbulence of the global economy. In other words, success depends on whether appropriate institutional arrangements are present. This is particularly true of systems in countries where the economy depends heavily on the performance of the real estate sector. I argue elsewhere (Smart and Lee 2003) that some financialization of the real estate sector in a post-Fordist regime like Hong Kong might produce stabilizing effects on income and employment, but the complexity of such relationships demands more rigorous research.

One conclusion to be drawn from this brief analysis is that institutional arrangement still matters if housing policy is designed primarily as a pillar of social policy and asset building. In Singapore, where a semi-closed housing system and strong state capacity to integrate social security with housing policy exist, the resulting asset-building effect is strong. In Japan, the monopolization of the mortgage market and heavy state subsidies in housing finance provided great impetus and effective institutional promotion of home ownership and asset building in post-war years. However, the collapse of the housing bubble in the early 1990s and the lasting impact of that collapse on the Japanese economy limit the asset potential of home ownership somewhat. Even when housing price inflation was at its historical peak before the 1990s, affordability severely limited access among many working-class Japanese. In Hong Kong, where home ownership is largely facilitated by land sale and an institutional arrangement that encourages housing market development, only those who enter the market at the right time are able to build assets through equity. Thus, limited housing affordability severely limits access to home ownership. Although Hong Kong established a rather successful state-subsidized home ownership scheme between 1980 and 2000, it was terminated because of political pressure from powerful real-estate interests. Undoubtedly, the political economy of housing dictates scarcity of housing resources in Hong Kong.

Singapore's success in building an asset-based social policy and Hong Kong's and Japan's failures to sustain theirs prompts a different question: what exactly is the role of the state? Perhaps the answer lies in Michael Sandel's (2012) book *What Money Can't Buy*. In it, he asserts that the sustainability of certain public policies depends on one's choice of society and economy. In Singapore, the government decided at the outset to play a monopolistic role and provide 85 per cent of all housing to ensure a lasting effect on price stability. This reflects the state's value choice to ensure housing affordability for the majority of citizens. Hong Kong and Mainland China largely leave housing to the open market, and price inflations and market volatilities are the apparent result. This also reflects a value choice to allow the market free rein. Once a housing market is open to global investment and financialization, few governments have the capacity to regulate it effectively. China's housing market now suffers as the government contemplates high-level regulation measures. In sum, effective housing-asset social policy requires a high level of social organization, corporatist practices, and protection from the fluctuations of the global economy. In the final analysis, these institutional arrangements, if proven effective, should reflect a set of value choices, including equitable distribution of wealth through wider access to publicly subsidized home ownership.

References

Brenner, Neil, Jamie Peck, and Nik Theodore. 2010. 'After Neoliberalization?' *Globalizations* 7 (3): 327–345. doi:10.1080/14747731003669669.

Business and Professionals Federation of Hong Kong. 2008. *Asset Rich? Income Poor? Is Reverse Mortgage a Solution?* Report, December. Hong Kong: Business and Professionals Federation of Hong Kong. www.bpf.org.hk/data/uploads/93a07fca89a0c5d46df 287ce89d8a3e5/editor/file/0902061541388727584pf8tv.pdf.

Castells, Manuel, Lee Goh, and Reginald Yin-Wang Kwok. 1990. *The Shek Kip Mei Syndrome: Economic Development and Public Housing in Hong Kong and Singapore*. London: Pion Press.

Chua, Beng-Huat. 1997. *Political Legitimacy and Housing: Stake Holding in Singapore*. Abingdon, England: Routledge.

Chua, Beng-Huat. 2002. *Political Legitimacy and Housing: Singapore's Stakeholder Society*. London: Routledge.

DiPasquale, Denise, and William C. Wheaton. 1996. *Urban Economics and Real Estate Markets*. New York: Prentice Hall.

Doling, John, and Richard Ronald. 2010. 'Home Ownership and Asset-Based Welfare,' in *Home Ownership and Asset-Based Welfare*, edited by John Doling and Richard Ronald, special issue, *Journal of Housing and the Built Environment* 25 (2): 165–173. doi:10.1007/s10901-009-9177-6.

Doling, John, and Richard Ronald. 2012. 'Meeting the Income Needs of Older People in East Asia: Using Housing Equity.' *Ageing and Society* 32 (3): 471–490. doi:10.1017/S0144686X11000298.

Evans, Peter. 2005. 'The Challenges of the "Institutional Turn": New Interdisciplinary Opportunities in Development Theory.' In *The Economic Sociology of Capitalism*, edited by Victor Nee and Richard Swedberg, 90–118. Princeton, NJ: Princeton University Press.

Fiscal Monitor Database (International Monetary Fund, October 2012; accessed 23 April 2013). www.imf.org/external/pubs/ft/fm/2012/02/app/FiscalMonitoring.html.

Forrest, Ray, and James Lee. 2004. 'Cohort Effects, Differential Accumulation and Hong Kong's Volatile Housing Market.' *Urban Studies* 41 (11): 2181–2196. doi:10.1080/0042098042000268401.

Forrest, Ray, Alan Murie, and Peter Williams. 1999. *Home Ownership: Differentiation and Fragmentation*. London: Uwin Hyman.

Groves, Richard, Alan Murie, and Christopher Watson. 2007. *Housing and the New Welfare State: Perspectives from East Asia and Europe*. Aldershot: Ashgate.

Harvey, David. 2012. *Rebel Cities: From the Right to the City to the Urban Revolution*. New York: Verso Books.

Hirayama, Yosuke. 2007. 'Reshaping the Housing System: Home Ownership as a Catalyst for Social Transformation.' In *Housing and Social Transition in Japan*, edited by Yosuke Hirayama and Richard Ronald, 15–46. Abingdon: Routledge.

Hirayama, Yosuke, and Richard Ronald. 2007. 'Introduction: Does the Housing System Matter?' In *Housing and Social Transition in Japan*, edited by Yosuke Hirayama and Richard Ronald, 1–14. Abingdon: Routledge.

Holliday, Ian. 2000. 'Productivist Welfare Capitalism: Social Policy in East Asia.' *Political Studies* 48 (4): 706–723. doi:10.1111/1467-9248.00279.

Hong, Yu-Hung. 1998. 'Transaction Costs of Allocating Increased Land Value under Public Leasehold Systems: Hong Kong.' *Urban Studies* 35 (9): 1577–1595. doi:10.1080/0042098984295.

Hong, Yu-Hung. 2003. 'Policy Dilemma of Capturing Land Value under the Hong Kong Public Leasehold System.' In *Leasing Public Land: Policy Debates and International Experiences*, edited by Steven C. Bourassa and Yu-Hung Hong, 151–176. Cambridge, MA: Lincoln Institute of Land Policy.

Hong Kong Mortgage Corporation. 2012. 'Our Business: Reverse Mortgage Programme.' Hong Kong Mortgage Corporation. Accessed 27 March 2014. www.hkmc.com.hk/eng/pcrm/ourbusiness/rm.html.

Japan Housing Finance Agency. 2007. *Overview of Housing Market in Japan*. Japan Housing Finance Agency. www.jhf.go.jp/files/100012578.pdf.

Jones, Colin, and Alan Murie. 2006. *The Right to Buy: Analysis and Evaluation of a Housing Policy*. London: Blackwell Publishing.

Lam, Thomas. 2012. 'Housing Affordability Ratio Alarming for Hong Kong, Guangzhou, Shanghai.' *South China Morning Post*, 22 August. www.scmp.com/property/hong-kong-china/article/1020230/housing-affordability-ratio-alarming-hong-kong-guangzhou.

Lee, James. 2012. 'Housing Policy at a Crossroad? Re-examining the Role of the Hong Kong Government in the Context of a Volatile Housing Market.' In *Repositioning the Hong Kong Government: Social Foundations and Political Challenges*, edited by Stephen Wing-kai Chiu and Siu-lun Wong, 165–186. Hong Kong: Hong Kong University Press.

Lee, Kuan Yew. 2000. *From Third World to First: The Singapore Story: 1965–2000*. New York: HarperCollins.

Malpass, Peter. 2008. 'Housing and the New Welfare State: Wobbly Pillar or Cornerstone?' *Housing Studies* 23 (1): 1–19. doi:10.1080/02673030701731100.

Midgley, James. 1997. *Social Welfare in Global Context*. London: Sage.

Midgley, James, and Kwong-Leung Tang. 2001. 'Social Policy, Economic Growth and Developmental Welfare.' *International Journal of Social Welfare* 10 (4): 244–252. doi:10.1111/1468-2397.00180.

Mullaney, Tim. 2012. 'Fed: Recession Kicked Median Household Wealth to 1992 Level.' *USA Today*, 13 June. http://usatoday30.usatoday.com/money/economy/story/2012-06-11/wealth-shrank-in-recession-fed-says/55528036/1.

Patten, Chris. 1998. *East and West: China, Power and the Future of Asia*. London: Macmillan.

Phang, Sock-Yong. 2001. 'Housing Policy, Wealth Formation and the Singapore Economy.' *Housing Studies* 16 (4): 443–459. doi:10.1080/02673030120066545.

Regan, Sue, and Will Paxton. 2001. *Asset-Based Welfare: International Experiences*. London: Institute for Public Policy Research.

Sandel, Michael J. 2012. *What Money Can't Buy: The Moral Limits of Markets*. New York: Farrar, Straus, and Giroux.

Schwartz, Herman, and Leonard Seabrooke. 2008. 'Varieties of Residential Capitalism in the International Political Economy: Old Welfare States and the New Politics of Housing.' *Comparative European Politics* 6: 237–261. doi:10.1057/cep. 2008.10.

Sherraden, Michael. 2003. 'Assets and the Social Investment State.' In *Equal Shares: Building a Progressive and Coherent Asset-Based Welfare Policy*, edited by Will Paxton, 28–41. London: Institute for Public Policy Research.

Smart, Alan, and James Lee. 2003. 'Financialization and the Role of Real Estate in Hong Kong's Regime of Accumulation.' *Economic Geography* 79 (2): 153–171. doi:10.1111/j. 1944-8287.2003.tb00206.x.

Smith, Susan J., Beverley A. Searle, and Nicole Cook. 2009. 'Rethinking the Risks of Home Ownership.' *Journal of Social Policy* 38 (1): 83–102. doi:10.1017/S0047279408002560.

Tan, Mah Bow. 2002. Speech by minister for national development, Real Estate Developers' Association of Singapore 43rd Annual Dinner 2002, Singapore.

Tse, Raymond Y.C. 1998. 'Housing Price, Land Supply and Revenue from Land Sale.' *Urban Studies* 35 (8): 1377–1392. doi:10.1080/0042098984411.

Watson, Matthew. 2009. 'Planning for the Future of Asset-Based Welfare? New Labour, Financialized Economic Agency and the Housing Market.' *Planning Practice and Research* 24 (1): 41–56. doi:10.1080/02697450902742148.

2 Australian superannuation

An example of asset building in practice

Ross Clare

Individuals' economic well-being is determined largely by their command over economic resources. People's income and wealth provide access to many of the goods and services consumed in daily life. Reserves of wealth can be used to support current consumption and smooth consumption over people's lifetimes.

Over the last two decades, many countries have adopted what could be described as inclusive asset-building policies (Organization for Economic Co-operation and Development 2003). These policies seek to assist and empower low-income earners to save and develop their financial and human capital. Although such policies do not necessarily effect marked reductions in aggregate asset inequality, advocates for inclusive asset-building policies claim that opportunities for saving and asset accumulation should be universal, progressive, life-long, and adequate (Sherraden 2005).

Australia is an interesting case study in that its asset-building policies are close to universal, not particularly regressive, apply for most of life, and are approaching adequacy – adequacy, at least, in regard to the asset building needed for retirement. Although there remains scope and need for further improvements, advocates have made considerable progress in introducing such policies. In particular, successive Australian governments over recent decades have actively encouraged the accumulation of superannuation wealth; maintained tax incentives for investment outside of superannuation by allowing full deductions for interest payments used to purchase an asset while providing tax concessions for the capital-gain assets held for more than 12 months; maintained the tax-free status of capital gains on the family home; and financially assisted first-time home buyers.

Superannuation arrangements have been by far the most important of these measures with the broadest impact across the population and the biggest impact per individual. Such policies aim to smooth levels of consumption over the life course, build wealth during pre-retirement years, and help people fund their retirement living.

Household wealth in Australia

In the 2009–2010 fiscal year, the average Australian household held assets valued at AUD 839,000 and had liabilities of AUD 120,000 (Australian Bureau of Statistics 2011).[1] In June 2013, the Australian dollar was equivalent to around USD 0.95. If the average assets figure is adjusted for changes in the Australian consumer price index, the average household net worth in 2009–2010 was approximately AUD 720,000, which was 14 per cent higher than in 2005–2006 and 30 per cent higher than in 2003–2004 (see Table 2.1).

Household wealth is more unequally distributed than household income in Australia. People in the three lowest equivalized income deciles share 13 per cent of all income, and those in the three lowest equivalized wealth deciles share only 3 per cent of all wealth (Australian Bureau of Statistics 2011). However, within the lowest income decile, large differences in household net worth exist. Although one-quarter of people in the lowest income decile are also in the lowest net worth decile, a substantial proportion is in much higher wealth deciles. The top five deciles include more than 40 per cent of Australians. People with low incomes but high levels of net worth are unlikely to be at risk of experiencing economic hardship, despite their incomes. An age-related pattern also is associated with both income and wealth: older persons are more likely to be asset rich but income poor, particularly after retiring from the paid labour force.

Most Australians aspire to own their homes, and home-ownership rates are relatively high. In the 2009–2010 fiscal year, one-third of Australian households owned their homes without a mortgage, and 36 per cent owned their homes with a mortgage (Australian Bureau of Statistics 2011). As Table 2.1 suggests, the average value of these homes in 2009–2010 was AUD 530,000, up 15 per cent from the inflation-adjusted average in 2005–2006 and up 26 per cent from the value in 2003–2004. Over the last few years, average house prices have been fairly static.

After the family home, superannuation – the Australian term for private pension – is the largest component of household wealth in Australia. In 2009–2010, 75 per cent of households had some superannuation assets, and the average value of superannuation assets held by those households was AUD 154,000 (see Table 2.1). That figure is up 50 per cent in real terms from the average value held by the 73 per cent of households that had superannuation assets in 2003–2004. However, just under half (49 per cent) of the households with superannuation in 2009–2010 had less than AUD 60,000 in superannuation assets (Australian Bureau of Statistics 2011).

In 2009–2010, the vast majority (95 per cent) of Australian households had some money in passbook, checking, or term deposit accounts. Such accounts usually are held with banks or other financial institutions (e.g. credit unions, building societies, insurance companies, finance companies). The average balance across all households was about AUD 34,500 in 2009–2010 (see Table 2.1).

Direct ownership of stock shares grew during the 1990s, in part as a response to numerous, well-subscribed public floats, including some by businesses previously in public ownership (e.g. the telecommunications carrier Telstra). In 2009–2010, 27 per cent of households owned shares, and the average value of shares held by those households was approximately AUD 82,000 (see Table 2.1).

Table 2.1 Average value of the components of household wealth

Components of household wealth	Average value among households with the particular component (AUD in 1000s)		Percentage of households with the particular component		Average value among all Australian households (AUD in 1000s)	
	2003–2004	2009–2010	2003–2004	2009–2010	2003–2004	2009–2010
Assets					637.4	839.4
Accounts held with financial institutions	36.8	34.5	68.1	95.3	25.1	32.9
Shares (excluding own incorporated businesses)	69.7	82.3	31.0	27.1	21.6	22.3
Public unit trusts	NA	90.7	NA	4.1	NA	3.7
Private trusts	150.7	572.2	7.2	3.1	NA	17.8
Debentures and bonds	65.1	54.5	1.7	.8	1.1	.4
Own incorporated businesses (net of liabilities)	678.4	811.8	4.0	4.9	27.1	39.5
Superannuation	103.1	154.2	73.0	75.2	75.3	115.9
Owner-occupied dwelling	421.5	530.3	70.1	68.8	295.5	364.9
Other property	445.3	660.7	18.9	20.6	84.0	136.4
Own unincorporated businesses (net of liabilities)	265.4	338.1	7.0	6.7	18.5	22.7
Contents of dwelling	56.2	60.8	100.0	100.0	56.2	60.8
Private vehicles	23.1	22.7	88.5	90.1	20.4	20.5
Liabilities					82.4	119.8
Loans for owner-occupied dwelling	144.8	204.6	32.8	33.4	47.5	68.4
Other property loans	226.3	312.3	10.4	11.7	23.6	36.6
Study loans	13.2	16.4	10.9	12.2	1.4	2.0
Credit card debt	3.2	3.8	70.0	70.3	2.2	2.6
Loans for private vehicle purchases	17.8	17.3	17.8	13.2	3.2	2.3
Investment loans (excluding business and rental property)	121.2	222.4	2.3	3.1	2.8	6.9
Loans for other purposes (excluding business and investment)	14.4	14.9	11.9	6.8	1.7	1.0
Net worth					555.0	719.6

Source: Australian Bureau of Statistics (2011).

Note
AUD = Australian dollars; NA = not applicable.

Providing retirement support in Australia

Although other forms of assets, particularly housing, are important to the wealth of Australians, this chapter focuses on the role of compulsory and voluntary contributions to superannuation in lifelong asset building. Australia has a classic three-pillar retirement system (Australian Treasury 2001; World Bank 1994), which includes:

- a mandatory employer contribution of 9.25 per cent of wages at the time of this writing, scheduled to increase gradually to 12 per cent by July 2019;[2]
- voluntary contributions, many of which attract tax concessions; and
- a government means-tested Age Pension that commences at age 65 for male civilians, age 64 for female civilians, age 60 for male veterans, and age 59 for female veterans.[3]

Voluntary contributions to superannuation accounts come from a number of sources (Australian Prudential Regulation Authority 2007), including:

- employers (usually large companies and governments) that contribute more to employees' retirement than the law requires;
- members who make pre-tax contributions – which are eligible for tax concessions that have been reduced significantly in recent years – from their salary packages;
- members who make after-tax contributions, which are subject to a contribution cap of AUD 150,000 per year or AUD 450,000 over a three-year period; and
- the government through co-contributions, which supplement after-tax contributions for low-income earners.

The taxation structure for superannuation is relatively complicated but can be discussed in broad terms. Most members of defined contribution funds are taxed at a flat rate of 15 per cent on contributions and investment earnings rather than at their marginal tax rate, which can be as high as 46.5 per cent. Benefits, both lump-sum and those disbursed in income stream form, are tax free if received at age 60 or later. Despite regular changes made by governments for fiscal or equity reasons, the broad structure is robust and supported by voters, politicians, and industry.

The Age Pension is funded by general Australian government tax revenue. It does not require pensioners to have a history of social security contributions. Eligibility is determined by whether one meets the eligibility age, has been a resident in Australia for 20 years, and qualifies under the applicable asset and income tests. The Age Pension is taxable, but those receiving the maximum rate generally do not pay any income tax because they receive a variety of rebates.

Table 2.2 shows recent budget standards for modest and comfortable lifestyle as indicated by the retirement standard of the Association of Superannuation

Table 2.2 The age pension compared to the ASFA retirement standards (Australian dollars)

	Modest lifestyle		Comfortable lifestyle	
	Single	Couple	Single	Couple
Yearly total	22,641	32,603	41,169	56,317
Age Pension	21,076	31,775	21,076	31,775
Difference from Age Pension	1565	828	20,093	24,552

Source: ASFA (2013a).

Note
For definitions of 'Modest' and 'Comfortable' lifestyles, see ASFA (2013a).

Funds of Australia (ASFA). The budget standards are based on a typical retiree at age 65 and are widely used in Australia as an indicator of adequacy of retirement income. They are updated regularly on the ASFA web site.[4] Although these values do not reflect the situation of every retiree, they allow us to gauge the average needs for different lifestyle expectations given costs of living in Australia. The *modest* retirement budget allows the retiree to afford fairly basic activities. In contrast, the *comfortable* retirement budget enables a healthy retiree to be involved in a broad range of leisure and recreational activities and purchase household goods, private health insurance, a reasonable car, good clothes, a range of electronic equipment, and domestic – and occasionally international – holiday travel.

The Age Pension comes close to meeting the modest lifestyle needs of retirees. The ASFA adjusts the retirement standard for changes in prices every quarter and every four or five years makes more substantive adjustments for changes in the pattern of expenditure by retirees and increases in the general living standard of the community.

Because the Age Pension by itself will be inadequate for a comfortable lifestyle in retirement, individuals need to build their own superannuation. A high level of home ownership among retirees is also important for their living standards, as is government funding on a means-tested basis for residential aged care and some other aged care.

A brief history of superannuation in Australia

In most other countries, the term 'private pension' tends to be used to describe what is known as superannuation in Australia and New Zealand. Occupational superannuation in Australia first emerged in the mid nineteenth century.

From its earliest days until the 1940s, superannuation was available only to a select group of salaried employees, mostly male, in the public sector and some large companies. Contributions were not compulsory. By 1974 superannuation covered 32.2 per cent of wage and salary earners. Most superannuation assets were in defined-benefit funds (Australian Treasury 2001).

In 1983, the newly elected Labor government expressed support for the principles of employee superannuation and initiated discussions with the Australian Council of Trade Unions on the possibility of broadening access to superannuation as part of the government's prices and incomes accord with the unions. The process of making employee superannuation a more or less universal entitlement began in September 1985. With the support of the government, the Australian Council of Trade Unions sought to require employers to make a 3 per cent superannuation contribution to industry funds specified in relevant, legally enforceable, industrial awards and in collective agreements, which set the minimum wages and conditions for many, but not all, employees (Australian Prudential Regulation Authority 2007).

Proponents of this so-called award superannuation noted the implications of the trend towards an ageing population, including the work-force. They also noted the effects of the trend towards earlier retirement and the existing dependence on the Age Pension (Australian Conciliation and Arbitration Commission 1986). The government estimated significant increases in the cost of the Age Pension and pensioners' dependence on the working population. At the time, there were wide disparities in superannuation coverage, which varied according to sex, industry, occupation, and income level. In particular, women, manual workers, and those with low incomes were less adequately covered than others.

In effect, the trade unions, and then the government, recognized the role that concessionally taxed superannuation contributions and investment earnings played in building the assets of white-collar and professional workers with high salaries. Extending the benefits of this asset building for retirement to a wider group of Australians, particularly low-income earners, was an important social objective.

In addition to compulsory employer contributions came requirements that contributions be fully vested and in most cases portable between regulated superannuation funds. Once a discretionary benefit is provided by employers to selected long-standing employees, superannuation accounts in effect become the property of the employee. However, it is a form of property that is accessible only when a condition of release is satisfied (e.g. preservation age is reached or permanent disability occurs). As I will describe below, hardship and compassionate grounds provisions allow Australians to access superannuation funds under certain circumstances.

As new industrial awards and agreements were negotiated according to the guidelines in the national wage case decision (Australian Conciliation and Arbitration Commission 1986), superannuation coverage increased rapidly. In the four years after the introduction of award superannuation, coverage grew from around 40 per cent of employees to 79 per cent. In the private sector, coverage grew from 32 per cent in 1987 to 68 per cent in 1991 (Bateman and Piggott 1998).

This was a major achievement for award superannuation, but more coverage and an increased rate of contribution were needed. Accordingly, the government announced in the 1991–1992 budget that it would introduce a mandatory superannuation system through the implementation of the superannuation guarantee (SG). The SG system uses the taxation power of the Australian government to provide a very powerful incentive for employers to make superannuation contributions of the required amount.

The SG system, which came into effect on 1 July 1992, required employers to contribute a minimum of 3 per cent of the employee's income. Beginning on 1 July 2002, the system required employees to contribute 9 per cent of earnings (Australian Treasury 2001). The SG did not require employers to make additional payments if they already made contributions to an account that met the SG's requirements.

While it covers most employees, the SG does not cover those earning less than AUD 450 in a calendar month, part-time employees younger than 18 years, or employees older than 65 years. Also, the SG does not apply to the self-employed with the exception of owner-managers who receive wages and technically are employees of a company they control (Australian Treasury 2001). Around 30 per cent of self-employed workers make contributions. In part, tax concessions drive such contributions (Clare 2012a).

In May 2010, the Australian treasurer announced that compulsory employer superannuation contributions would increase gradually to 12 per cent by July 2019. A .25 per cent increase was introduced in the 2013–2014 financial year, and another .25 per cent increase is scheduled for 2014–2015. In each of the five years after the 2014–2015 financial year, the SG rate is scheduled (as currently legislated) to increase by .5 per cent. It will reach 12 per cent in July 2019 (Australian Taxation Office 2013a).

Tax concessions and other assistance for superannuation contributions

The government provides several tax concessions and subsidies related to superannuation. These provisions have the following purposes:

- To encourage voluntary contributions.
- To provide workers with compensation for the measure that limits their access to savings for a very extended period of time (up to 30 or 40 years in many cases).
- To put in place what is in effect a partnership between the individual and the government.
- To boost retirement savings, including savings for low-income earners.

Given that employer contributions generally are concessionally taxed at a flat rate of 15 per cent for all employees, tax concessions are larger in percentage and absolute terms for upper income earners than for those with lower income. However, the government provides vertical equity through other subsidies for low-income earners and the means-tested Age Pension. Also, the government recently introduced a 30 per cent flat-rate tax on contributions made on behalf of the 130,000 or so individuals whose earnings, including superannuation contributions, exceed AUD 300,000 per year (Shorten 2012).

The low-income superannuation contribution

To improve the equity of superannuation taxation arrangements, the state provides a superannuation contribution of up to AUD 500 annually for individuals on adjusted taxable incomes of up to AUD 37,000. The amount payable under this measure is calculated by applying a 15 per cent matching rate to the concessional contributions made by or for individuals with incomes below the limit (Australian Taxation Office 2013b). Self-employed workers who satisfy a legislative test for self-employment can claim tax deductions for concessional contributions that they make themselves and claim a deduction in their tax return.

Before the introduction of the government contribution, low-income earners received little or no tax concession because the rate of tax on their contributions was about the same as the rate of tax on their personal income. The low-income superannuation contribution measure improves the equity of superannuation taxation arrangements by effectively returning to low-income earners the tax they pay on SG contributions (Clare 2012b).

Projections indicate that the measure will boost the superannuation savings of 3.5 million low-income earners (Shorten 2012).

The superannuation co-contribution

The government is also encouraging non-concessional contributions by individuals. Such contributions can be made in addition to the concessional contributions referred to above. This assistance is called the co-contribution. Individuals can qualify for a government co-contribution by meeting several eligibility requirements. A person who earns AUD 31,920 or less per year and makes a voluntary contribution of AUD 1000 or more can receive a co-contribution of AUD 500 from the government. The amount phases down for those earning more than AUD 31,920, but less than AUD 46,920 (Australian Taxation Office 2013c). In 2010–2011, approximately 655,000 females and 440,000 males received co-contributions. In total, these co-contributions amount to AUD 680 million.

Access to superannuation benefits

The rules for superannuation in Australia largely restrict access to benefits until retirement (after at least age 55) but permit access in some cases where there is disability or death. Provisions also allow limited access to benefits on certain strictly defined compassionate grounds or in strictly defined circumstances related to financial hardship.

Superannuation does not allow an individual to access the account for assistance with housing purchase, medical expenses, or financial needs associated with unemployment. Some endorse amending the rules to allow access for such purposes, but successive governments have taken the position that current and prospective rates of contributions will not provide superannuation savings sufficient to cover retirement and other expenditure needs. Also, other measures are in place to assist individuals with their first home purchase, and a universal system covers most medical and hospital expenses.

Financial hardship release

Individuals who have received social security payments (i.e. unemployment benefits or sickness or disability income support) from the government for six months or more may receive a lump-sum of up to AUD 10,000 for a one-off financial problem (e.g. outstanding bills). The funds cannot be used to pay day-to-day expenses or cover debts not currently due (e.g. the full balance of a credit card or personal loan).

Compassionate release

The very strictly defined cases in which an individual can access superannuation chiefly relate to medical and related expenses not met by the public health system, palliative care expenses for a terminally ill fund member or dependent, mortgage assistance in cases of impending foreclosure, and funeral expenses for a family member. The number of applications for early release of superannuation benefits on compassionate grounds rose strongly in earlier years but has fallen recently. The 2010–2011 fiscal year marked the third consecutive year of decline.

Anecdotal evidence suggests that some secondary lenders and medical practitioners exploit this release mechanism. Lenders require borrowers to grant access to the superannuation account in the case of a mortgage default, and certain medical practitioners recommend that individuals access their accounts to cover the costs of cosmetic and certain other discretionary surgery.

Despite provisions allowing individuals to access funds under the circumstances discussed above, serious consequences are associated with accessing superannuation funds before retirement:

- Funds released prior to retirement are taxed at a higher rate.
- Less superannuation is available to the individual in retirement or during another period of financial hardship.
- Funds lose protection from creditors when released early.

Equity and government assistance for superannuation savings

Equity clearly is a key issue in the debate about superannuation and retirement income reform. The government and communities argue that assistance should be spread fairly according to need, and there is a strong tradition in Australia of support for what we call a 'fair go'. In the context of superannuation, this means that no group should face barriers to participation in the retirement income system.

The cost of tax concessions for superannuation is also an issue when governments look for ways to reduce budget deficits. Contribution caps (i.e. caps on contributions eligible for tax benefits) have been tightened several times, and the latest set permitted annual contributions of no more than AUD 25,000 per year for those younger than age 50 and AUD 50,000 per year for those aged 50 and older. However, the AUD 50,000 per year cap was transitional and expired on 30 June 2012. A new measure increases the cap to AUD 35,000 initially for those aged 60 and older, and on 1 July 2014 the cap will extend to those aged 50 and older (Australian Taxation Office 2013d).

Clear empirical evidence indicates that the contribution caps have reduced concessional contributions from upper income earners. Table 2.3 reflects estimates of the proportion of concessional superannuation contributions made on behalf of wage earners in the various marginal income tax bands applying in 2009–2010. These estimates are based on data extracted for the ASFA from the Household, Income and Labour Dynamics in Australia Survey of Australian households.

As is shown in the table, employers' superannuation contributions are not spread evenly across all taxpayers or income ranges because a basic characteristic of superannuation is that contributions are linked to employment, particularly full-time employment.

Individuals with low incomes in any given year will not necessarily be on a low taxable income for all of their lives. Many of these individuals work part-time positions because they are enrolled in school or have family responsibilities that prevent them from undertaking full-time employment. However, they will complete many years, usually decades, of full-time work. Also, wages often increase in real terms over the course of a career. The distribution of taxable incomes and tax concessions for superannuation contributions in any given year is not a good indicator of assistance delivered over a lifetime. However, Table 2.3 indicates that around 90 per cent of employer contributions are made on

Table 2.3 Employer contributions by employee income range, 2009–2010

Taxable income (AUD)	Marginal income tax rate (percentage)	% of wage earners	Employer contributions	
			Value (AUD)[a]	%[a]
0–6000	0	5.4	54	.1
6001–37,000	15	31.5	4255	7.9
37,001–80,000	30	42.7	23,120	43.0
80,001–180,000	38	18.0	20,280	37.7
180,001+	47	2.4	6050	11.3

Source: Clare (2012b).

Notes
AUD = Australian dollars.
a Based on data extracted for the ASFA from wave 10 of the Household, Income and Labour Dynamics in Australia survey.

behalf of individuals taxed at less than the top marginal rate. Over 50 per cent of employer contributions are made on behalf of individuals taxed at a marginal rate of 30 per cent or less. The top 5 per cent of employees in terms of income accounted for less than 20 per cent of the total superannuation contributions in 2009–2010.

The trends concerning individual, discretionary contributions differ somewhat from those related to employer contributions. Although superannuation contributions by upper income earners are typically higher than those of lower income earners, the amount of discretionary contributions of upper income earners is now much lower than in previous years, largely due to a reduction in contribution caps.

Table 2.4 provides estimates of the amount of tax concession by personal income. It also factors in the state's co-contribution, which is available only to low-income earners making personal contributions. The results indicate that less than 15 per cent of government assistance for superannuation contributions (i.e. tax concessions and co-contributions) flows to those paying the top marginal rate. In comparison, this group of taxpayers pays around 30 per cent of aggregate personal income tax collections. Although upper-income earners receive assistance for their superannuation contributions, the overall personal tax system imposes a substantially higher tax burden on them than on those with lower incomes. Table 2.4 also indicates that the bulk of government assistance for superannuation flows to those in the groups paying marginal tax rates of 30 per cent and 38 per cent. Such taxpayers make up a very large part of the full-time work-force in Australia.

In addition, the new low-income superannuation contribution – up to AUD 500 annually for eligible low-income earners making concessional contributions

Table 2.4 Employee tax concessions on contributions by income range, 2009–2010

Taxable income (AUD)	Marginal income tax rate (percentage)	Tax concession		Tax concession and co-contribution	
		Value[a]	% of total for employer contributions	Value (AUD 1,000,000s)	% of total
0–6000	0	−8	−.1	192	1.5
6001–37,000	15	68	.6	1068	8.3
37,001–80,000	30	4462	39.2	4662	36.4
80,001–180,000	38	4968	43.6	4968	38.8
180,001+	47	1906	16.7	1905	14.9
All employees		11,397	100	12,797	100

Source: Clare (2012b).

Notes
AUD = Australian dollars.
a Takes into account the Medicare levy, the phasing out of the Low Income Tax Offset, and the phasing in of the Medicare liability. Results are in AUD 1,000,000s.

in the 2012–2013 income year – now applies. The phased increase in the rate of compulsory superannuation to 12 per cent will have its greatest impact on low- and middle-income earners because those with higher incomes are more likely to already receive the benefit of contributions in excess of 9 per cent of wages.

Had the proposed measures applied in 2009–2010, the combined effect would have increased the state's total retirement-savings assistance for employees earning less than AUD 80,000 per year from AUD 5920 million to around AUD 7580 million (Clare 2012b).

The real equity challenge

Evidence from surveys of balances held in individual superannuation accounts indicates that compulsory superannuation has been very effective in lifting coverage rates and average superannuation balances (Table 2.5). However, it will be 40 or 50 years before the system is fully mature.

Although the superannuation co-contribution has been effective in lifting personal contributions of low-income individuals, the design parameters of the co-contribution and recent changes (i.e. cut-backs) have made the co-contribution less effective than it could be. There is a case to be made for encouraging additional contributions by both increasing the maximum co-contribution and reducing the matching rate.

Table 2.5 Superannuation coverage and holdings of men and women not yet retired, by annual wage and salary income, 2006 and 2010

Annual wage and salary income	Those with superannuation 2006 (balance (AUD))			Those with superannuation 2010 (balance (AUD))		
	%	Mean	Median	%	Mean	Median
Men						
<28,000	75.1	37,312	5700	79.9	43,553	5000
28,000 to <58,000	96.7	70,698	30,000	96.8	62,853	25,000
58,000 to <80,000	98.1	134,981	65,000	98.7	108,092	50,000
80,000+	97.8	207,801	110,000	98.6	212,025	110,000
Total	91.4	99,506	35,000	93.9	109,609	40,000
Women						
<28,000	80.7	32,807	9000	80.9	37,622	8500
28,000 to <58,000	96.8	56,253	25,000	96.6	52,885	29,000
58,000 to <80,000	98.6	102,844	55,000	98.2	98,071	50,000
80,000+	97.7	158,652	88,000	98.9	142,855	75,000
Total	89.4	55,433	21,000	90.9	63,412	26,000

Source: ASFA (2013a).

Note
AUD = Australian dollars.
Results weighted to be representative of the population of Australia.

The AUD 450 threshold for receiving the SG

Employers are not required to make SG contributions for employees earning less than AUD 450 per month. Removal of the threshold would increase the eventual retirement savings of around 250,000 individuals, the majority of them women (Clare 2012a). If the threshold were eliminated, employers and the common-wealth's budget would absorb a very modest cost.

The self-employed

Nearly 10 per cent of the Australian labour-force is self-employed. Although tax concessions have led some self-employed workers to save for retirement through superannuation, average balances and coverage remain relatively low. Around 29 per cent of the self-employed have no superannuation, which is more common for males than females (Clare 2012a). There is a strong case to be made for extending compulsory superannuation to include the self-employed.

Individuals on paid parental leave

For the purposes of income taxation, the government considers income received during paid parental leave to be equivalent to wages. Requiring employers to pay SG on parental-leave compensation would help to reduce the average differ-ence between women and men in entitlements in superannuation. The effects of compound interest also would be very favourable; many women take parental leave in their twenties and thirties.

Indigenous Australians

On average, coverage and balances are lower among indigenous Australians than among the general population. Again, these disparities are largely related to dif-ferences in paid labour-force experience. As Table 2.6 suggests, superannuation

Table 2.6 Superannuation coverage and holdings of Aboriginal and Torres Strait Islander men and women not yet retired, 2006 and 2010

Group	Those with superannuation in 2006 (balance (AUD))			Those with superannuation in 2010 (balance (AUD))		
	%	Mean	Median	%	Mean	Median
Men	68.3	49,589	9000	70.7	55,743	14,000
Women	52.1	42,109	10,000	60.6	39,909	15,000
Individuals	59.5	46,069	10,000	65.3	47,863	15,000

Source: Clare (2012a).

Note
AUD = Australian dollars.
Results are weighted to be representative of the population of Australia.

covers about 70 per cent of indigenous men and 60 per cent of indigenous women. In comparison, superannuation covers 85 per cent of men in the general population of Australia and 80 per cent of women. Average (mean) balances are also lower for indigenous Australians than for the equivalent Australian population as a whole (Clare 2012a).

Increases in superannuation coverage and average superannuation balances among indigenous Australians would indicate improvements in involvement with paid work and in wages. Current superannuation arrangements and administrative requirements do not always mesh well with the circumstances and needs of indigenous Australians. In particular, those who live in remote areas may have difficulty communicating with their superannuation funds, claiming benefits, and identifying lost accounts. There is scope for the superannuation industry and the regulators to work towards a regulatory framework and administrative arrangements that better address the special needs of indigenous Australians.

Exposure to investment risk

A critical element of Australia's retirement system is that members generally carry all the investment risks themselves. In the long term, almost all members will hold accumulation (defined contribution) accounts. Table 2.7 shows that investment returns in Australia – like in many countries – have not been favourable in recent years after the global financial crisis.

Exposing assets to relatively high levels of risk could provide members with high retirement benefits. Most individuals will be members of a superannuation fund for a period of 40 years or more, and such exposure should be sustained throughout a member's career. Of course, that argument should be subject to individual decisions concerning exposure to investment risk and volatility. Because of the volatility of markets, at least some members will wish to avoid 'sequencing risk' by shifting assets into cash over the five years before retirement. This will allow them to cater for any required lump-sum benefit and their

Table 2.7 Average annual fund investment returns to 30 June 2013 (%)

	Fund returns
1 year	16.7
5 years	4.1
10 years	6.8
15 years	6.0
20 years	7.2
25 years	7.9
30 years	9.7
35 years	10.8
40 years	10.3

Source: ASFA (2013b).

initial pension draw-downs. Life-cycle investment options can accommodate such an investment strategy. Also, this may not be a good time to switch allocations from equities to bonds, as returns on bonds are at historic lows, and recent returns from equities, especially Australian equities, have been relatively strong, with double-digit returns in 2012–2013.

Income streams in retirement

Some contend that the objective of superannuation should be to provide income during the whole of retirement. However, a number of issues make it difficult to structure the Australian system around regular reliable pension payments:

- The state introduced award superannuation in 1986 as deferred pay. Fund members consider superannuation savings to be their own money, and they expect flexibility in disbursal of those funds.
- Because of low average incomes and various tax rebates, most older Australians are also subject to low personal-income tax rates or to no tax at all (Australian Taxation Office 2013d). As a result, there is only a limited incentive for individuals to leave money in the system during retirement.
- No one is forced to draw benefits over time, and some individuals use superannuation for estate planning purposes.
- Members can buy lifetime annuities from the private sector (albeit from a small number of suppliers), but current sales are not large in number or aggregate dollar terms (Plan for Life 2013). Consumer research indicates that most Australians are unrealistic about the pricing of an indexed lifetime annuity and expect much more than fair value. Without compulsion or incentives, most fund members in Australia will not buy these products.
- Many members retire with small benefits, and they appear comfortable with leaving the money in an interest-bearing bank account rather than in superannuation.
- Many people today retire with debt, including mortgages. It is rational to clear such debts at retirement.

That said, the evidence indicates that many Australians take an income stream from their superannuation in retirement, albeit an account-based stream that allows access to lump-sum payments for up to the entire account balance.

As Table 2.8 shows, superannuation covers around 70 per cent of recently retired males aged 60–64. In 2010, the average balance among these men was around AUD 380,000. For women, coverage of superannuation in the same age group was around 60 per cent. The average balance among those women was around AUD 255,000.

These figures strongly suggest that the great majority of recent retirees keep the bulk of their retirement savings in superannuation and draw-down an income stream. In Australia, these income streams almost invariably are phased draw-down income streams rather than life annuities. Phased draw-down income

Table 2.8 Superannuation coverage and holdings of men and women recently retired, 2006 and 2010

Age group	Those with superannuation in 2006 (balance [AUD])			Those with superannuation in 2010 (balance [AUD])		
	%	Mean	Median	%	Mean	Median
Men						
<60	70.2	283,430	200,000	89.8	528,105	386,000
60–64	76.7	573,228	500,000	68.8	381,703	250,000
65–69	48.1	421,618	200,000	65.7	299,161	164,000
70+	41.6	283,938*	162,000*	32.3	273,218*	90,000*
Total	60.7	419,841	280,000	60.8	367,336	245,000
Women						
<60	62.1	322,945	100,000	63.7	135,501	53,000
60–64	53.1	273,135	195,000	58.6	255,485	120,000
65–69	46.4	129,491	90,000	41.7	205,855	70,000
70+	41.6*	48,358*	15,000*	7.1*	184,000*	184,00*
Total	54.5	254,647	100,000	53.0	191,474	102,000

Source: ASFA (2013a).

Notes
AUD = Australian dollars.
Results are weighted to be representative of the population of Australia. 'Recently retired' if 'currently retired and observed not retired (i.e. employed) at some stage in the last three years'.
* Estimate not reliable.

streams have a minimum draw-down requirement related to the age of the retiree, and the account can be exhausted if investment returns are lower than expected or if a person lives beyond the average life expectancy. Even for this minority, however, there is no evidence that the superannuation savings are used primarily for immediate consumption purposes, such as an overseas trip. Survey data indicate that lump sums are used mainly to make investments that generate income over retirement or pay off debt (Australian Bureau of Statistics 2009, 92 [Table 31]).

Conclusion

The Australian superannuation system is not without shortcomings. It is too complex, particularly in regard to the taxation of contributions and fund earnings. Also, the system is not yet mature enough to provide most with a comfortable standard of living in retirement. Finally, the system does not deal well with the financial consequences of longevity for the large majority of members who are in defined-contribution schemes.

However, the system also has several advantages. It is sustainable; respective burdens on governments, employers, and individuals are and will continue to be manageable. The system also is comprehensive and equitable. If one considers all the elements of the system, the amount of government assistance is broadly

comparable across the income distribution. Superannuation is particularly beneficial for the financial system; assets in the pension system are invested in the
real economy rather than in national securities issued by a central government.
Finally, the system is advantageous because it provides an asset-building mechanism for the great majority of Australians. It is a particularly effective instrument for assisting and empowering individuals with low incomes.

Notes

1 The Australian dollar (AUD) is the primary unit of currency in Australia. One US
  dollar (USD) is equivalent to approximately AUD 1.03.
2 The recently elected government has proposed a two-year pause in the phased
  increases.
3 Age limits are scheduled to increase over the next decade.
4 www.superannuation.asn.au.

References

ASFA (Association of Superannuation Funds of Australia). 2013a. *Super System Evolution: Achieving Consensus Through a Shared Vision*, ASFA White Paper – Part 4
www.superannuation.asn.au/policy/reports.
ASFA (Association of Superannuation Funds of Australia). 2013b. 'Record returns.'
Superfunds Magazine, September 2013 issue.
Australian Bureau of Statistics. 2009. *Employment Arrangements, Retirement and Superannuation, Australia: April to July 2007*. Canberra: Australian Bureau of Statistics.
www.abs.gov.au/ausstats/abs@.nsf/mf/6361.0.
Australian Bureau of Statistics. 2011. *Australian Social Trends, December 2011*. Canberra: Australian Bureau of Statistics. www.abs.gov.au/AUSSTATS/abs@.nsf/Lookup
/4102.0Main+Features10Dec+2011#Contents1.
Australian Conciliation and Arbitration Commission. 1986. National Wage Case decision. Mis 360/86 MD Print G3600. Accessed June 2013. www.airc.gov.au/safetynet_
review/decisions/G3600.htm.
Australian Prudential Regulation Authority. 2007. 'A Recent History of Superannuation
in Australia.' *APRA Insight* 2: 3–10. www.apra.gov.au/Insight/documents/History-of-
superannuation.pdf.
Australian Taxation Office. 2013a. 'Key Superannuation Rates and Thresholds.' Australian Taxation Office. Accessed 14 October 2013. www.ato.gov.au/Rates/Key-
superannuation-rates-and-thresholds/?page=20.
Australian Taxation Office. 2013b. 'Low Income Super Contribution.' Australian Taxation Office. Accessed 14 October 2013. www.ato.gov.au/Individuals/Super/In-detail/
Contributions/Low-income-super-contribution.
Australian Taxation Office. 2013c. 'Super Co-contribution Thresholds.' Australian Taxation Office. Last modified 10 July. www.ato.gov.au/General/New-legislation/In-detail/
Super/Super-co-contribution-thresholds.
Australian Taxation Office. 2013d. 'The Superannuation System.' In *Taxation Statistics
2010–11*. Australian Taxation Office, 124–128. Canberra: Australian Taxation Office.
www.ato.gov.au/uploadedFiles/Content/CR/Research_and_statistics/In_detail/Down-
loads/cor00345977_2011CH15SPR.pdf.

Australian Treasury. 2001. 'Towards Higher Retirement Incomes for Australians: A History of the Australian Retirement Income System since Federation.' *Economic Roundup*, Centenary Edition, 2001: 65–92. http://archive.treasury.gov.au/documents/110/HTML/docshell.asp?URL=4round.asp.

Bateman, Hazel, and John Piggott. 1998. 'Mandatory Retirement Saving in Australia.' *Annals of Public and Cooperative Economics* 69 (4): 547–569. doi:10.1111/1467-8292.00094.

Clare, Ross. 2012a. *Equity and Superannuation: The Real Issues*. ASFA Research Paper, September. Sydney: Association of Superannuation Funds of Australia. www.superannuation.asn.au/policy/reports.

Clare, Ross. 2012b. *The Equity of Government Assistance for Retirement Income in Australia*. ASFA Research Paper, February. Sydney: Association of Superannuation Funds of Australia. www.superannuation.asn.au/policy/reports.

Organization for Economic Cooperation and Development. 2003. *Asset Building and the Escape from Poverty: A New Welfare Policy Debate*. Paris: Organization for Economic Cooperation and Development. http://browse.oecdbookshop.org/oecd/pdfs/free/8403051e.pdf.

Plan for Life. 2013. 'Back to Life: Surge in Lifetime Annuity Sales Following Product Innovation.' Press release, January. Plan for Life. www.planforlife.com.au/pdf/Release%20-%20Lifetime%20Annuities.pdf.

Sherraden, Michael, ed. 2005. *Inclusion in the American Dream: Assets, Poverty, and Public Policy*. New York: Oxford University Press.

Shorten, Bill. 2012. '2012–13 Budget: Superannuation Reforms.' Press release, 8 May. http://ministers.treasury.gov.au/DisplayDocs.aspx?doc=pressreleases/2012/024.htm&pageID=003&min=brs&Year=&DocType.

World Bank. 1994. *Averting the Old Age Crisis: Policies to Protect the Old and Promote Growth*. Policy Research Report. Washington, DC: World Bank.

3 Malaysia's Employees Provident Fund and social security

Siew-Yong Yew

Malaysia is a member of the 10-nation Association of South East Asian Nations (ASEAN). Previously ruled by the British, Malaysia gained independence in 1957. Adopting an export-oriented strategy to encourage manufacturing, Malaysia developed an open economy and is one of the largest trading nations in the world. Over the past 50 years the economy has evolved to become more diversified, outward oriented, and globally integrated. The per-capita gross domestic product (GDP) in 2011 was USD 9656 (World Bank 2012) (Table 3.1).

Demographic trends

In 2012 Malaysia's multi-ethnic population reached 29.5 million. According to the Department of Statistics Malaysia (DOSM) (2012a), half (51.4 per cent) of the population is male, and 8.3 per cent is older than age 60. Life expectancy at birth is 71.9 years for males and 77.0 years for females. The average expectancy was 58 years in 1957 but rose by more than 10 years between 1970 and 2012. In 2012 the life expectancy at age 60 was 17.6 years for males and 20.2 years for

Table 3.1 Key Malaysian economic indicators

Indicators	1991	2000	2011
GDP (billion, current USD)	49.1	93.8	278.7
GDP growth (annual %)	9.5	8.9	5.1
GDP per capita (current USD)	2642	4029.9	9656
Gross capital formation (% of GDP)	37.8	26.9	20.31[a]
Gross domestic savings (% of GDP)	34.1	46.1	39.23[a]
Inflation (CPI, annual %)	4.4	1.5	5.9
Stock market capitalization (USD billions)	56.7	113.2	408.69[a]
% of GDP	115.5	120.7	141.77

Source: author's calculation based on data from the World Bank (2012); World Federation of Exchanges Monthly Reports database (www.world-exchanges.org/statistics/monthly-reports, accessed 5 August 2013).

Notes
GDP = gross domestic product; CPI = Consumer Price Index.
a Refers to 2010.

females. Figure 3.1 shows the statistics of older persons in Malaysia between 1950 and 2011 and projections to 2100. Figure 3.2 shows the population pyramid for 1980, and Figure 3.3 shows the pyramids for 2000 and 2010 (DOSM 2012b).

A comparison of the trends shown in Figures 3.2 and 3.3 indicates that the 2000 and 2010 pyramids are wider and less steep than that for 1980. Older people represent a larger percentage of the population, and the proportion of people aged 40 to 59 has also increased, reflecting a shift towards an aged population. Projections indicate that the percentage of elderly persons in Malaysia will reach 11.9 per cent in 2020 and 23 per cent in 2050, when about one in four Malaysians will be above age 60 (United Nations 2011).

Increasing life expectancy and a declining birth rate have accelerated the ageing of Malaysia's population. The total birth rate declined from 4.9 per cent in 1970 to 2.4 per cent in 2005, and the number of children dropped from six per woman in the 1960s to 2.2 in 2010 (Tay and Diener 2011). As the proportion of aged people grows, productivity and tax revenues decline while health care expenditures increase. Malaysia must deal with these factors properly through social security systems. Is the nation ready to address the issues that will arise as the population continues to age?

Labour market trends

Malaysia remains heavily reliant on foreign workers from neighbouring countries, especially Indonesia. On 1 January 2012, Malaysia extended the retirement age to 60 for public sector workers. Later that year, the parliament passed the

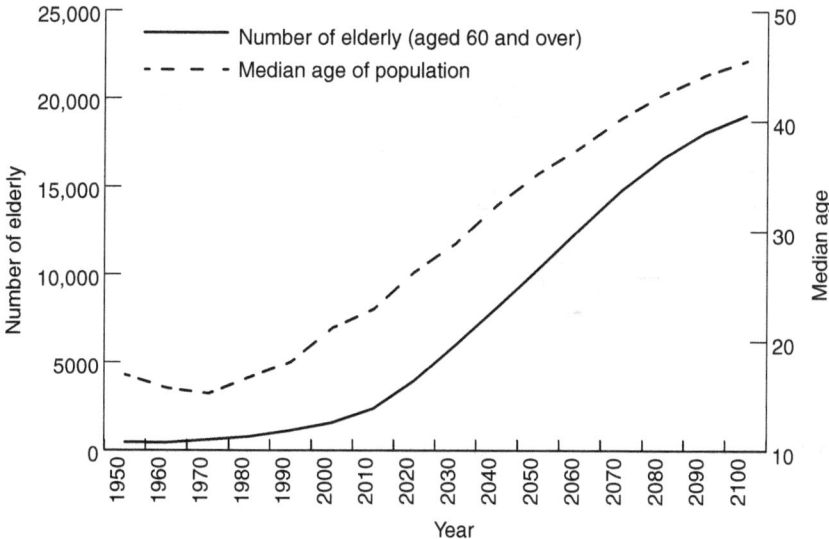

Figure 3.1 Number of elderly (aged 60 or over) and median age of population, 1950–2100 (source: author's calculations based on United Nations 2011).

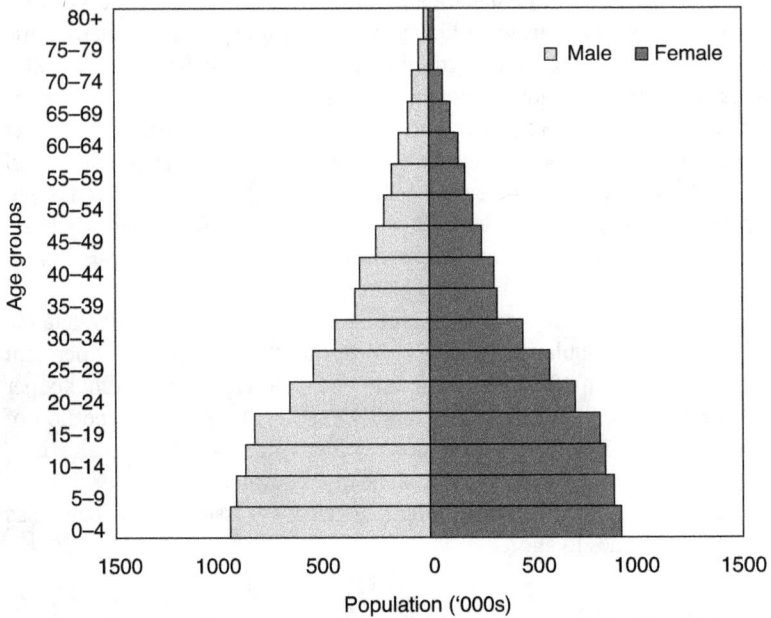

Figure 3.2 Malaysian population pyramids, 1980 (source: DOSM [n.d.a]).

Note
Population figures in thousands.

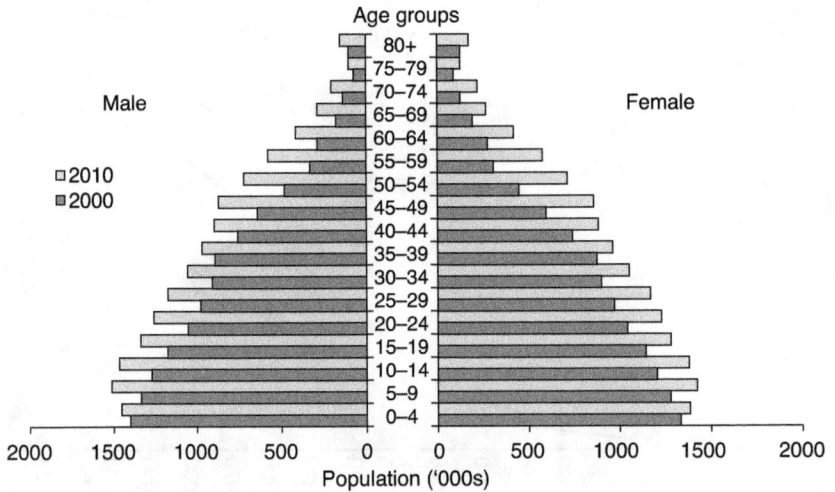

Figure 3.3 Malaysian population pyramids, 2000 and 2010 (source: DOSM [n.d.b]).

Note
Population figures in thousands.

Minimum Retirement Age Act 2012 (Act 753), extending the retirement age for private sector workers as well. In coming years, the labour-force participation rate for those in the 55–59 and 60–64 age groups should grow as public and private sector workers extend employment until the new mandatory retirement age of 60. Those extensions will have positive economic impacts on the retirement savings of the Malaysian population as a whole.

Elements of social security

Although social insecurity exists among all age groups, the aged are most affected. The World Bank's multi-pillar system for old-age income support provides a model for categorizing the elements of social security systems, and Malaysia's supports can be aligned to the five pillars.

Pillar 0: welfare as the minimum level of protection

Malaysia's social security policies share common roots with Britain. The Department of Community Welfare focuses on protection, rehabilitation, prevention, development, and integration services and serves a broad base of target groups. Social welfare services are often temporary and minimal but cover the broadest spectrum of the population, focusing on meeting needs after other avenues are exhausted. The Department of Social Welfare (n.d.) serves the elderly through the *Bantuan Orang Tua* (Assistance for the Aged) scheme, which includes a MYR 300 per month payout,[1] assisted-living homes for the elderly, and senior day-care centres. In June 2008, the department began Program Cari, an active campaign to locate those in need of aid. As of February 2011, *Bantuan Orang Tua* had about 128,000 beneficiaries, and its 2010 annual disbursement amounted to .06 per cent of Malaysia's GDP (DOSM 2012d). To qualify for benefits, applicants must be older than age 60 and lack support or income. The Department of Social Welfare's officers verify eligibility in the field, but their workload limits the department's ability to recertify the eligibility of beneficiaries.

The programmes and measures under this pillar lack a consistent policy framework, and there is a strong need for a comprehensive review and a good, targeted, means-tested programme. The poor require support if they are to grow out of their needs, and eligibility for benefits must be recertified diligently and often. However, implementation is bogged down by bureaucratic, and sometimes political, ineffectiveness.

Pillar 1: defined-benefit pension schemes

Unlike its ASEAN neighbours – the Philippines, Thailand, and Vietnam – Malaysia does not have a defined-benefit pension scheme. In most pension reforms, a basic, universal, defined-benefit scheme is recommended, but such schemes tax the budgetary system and do not encourage personal responsibility.

In 2012, Malaysia's budget deficit amounted to 4.5 per cent of its GDP, and the outstanding debt stood at MYR 503.2 billion, an unhealthy 54.8 per cent of the GDP (Ministry of Finance Malaysia 2012). Malaysia's current debt levels indicate that such a defined-benefit pension scheme is not advisable for the coming years.

Pillar 2: mandatory direct-contribution pension schemes

Under this pillar fall Malaysia's main social security policies, including the Employees Provident Fund (EPF), the civil service pension scheme, the Employment Injury Insurance Scheme, and the Invalidity Pension Scheme managed by the Social Security Organisation (SOCSO). The Armed Forces Fund is also a major component of the nation's social security policy.

The EPF

The EPF is a trust fund established under the Employees Provident Fund Act 1951 (Act 272), which was later replaced by the Employees Provident Fund Act 1991 (Act 452). Members of the EPF and their employers contributed a combined fixed rate of 10 per cent of wages between 1952 and 1975. The rate rose to 23 per cent in 1996 but has since remained roughly stable (EPF 2011). (See below for additional details about the EPF.)

The civil service pension scheme

The Public Service Pension Scheme Act (Act 227) serves to convey appreciation for public service, retain valuable manpower, provide resources for the pensioner after retirement, and extend pension benefits to dependants of deceased officers and pensioners (the dependants receive a derivative gratuity or pension). The scheme's benefits include:

- a monthly service pension at 1/600 of the number of months of eligible service and the last-drawn pay capped at 60 per cent maximum of the last salary;
- a lump-sum service gratuity amounting to 7.5 per cent of the number of months of eligible service at the last salary;
- a lump-sum cash award paid in lieu of unused leave amounting to a maximum of five months of last salary;
- a disability pension up to half the last salary paid to civil servants who take health retirement arising from travelling for or performing public duty except for negligence; and
- a dependants' pension for the dependants of public servants who die while on duty, from work-related disease, or during travel for work and pays benefits to dependants of deceased retired pensioners.

Since the enactment of the Pensions Trust Fund Act 1991 (Act 454), the government has fully borne the liability for civil service pension benefits. The Act provided a MYR 500 million federal grant and entrusted the Pensions Trust Fund Council with the scheme's administration. In 2007, the government set up the *Kumpulan Wang Persaraan* (Retirement Fund) to handle contributions from employers (i.e. the federal government, local authorities, statutory bodies, and government agencies). The contributions amount to 5 per cent of the budgeted emolument from the federal government and 17.5 per cent of the basic salaries paid to pensionable employees of statutory bodies, local authorities, and government agencies contributed on a monthly basis. In 2011, the Malaysian government contributed MYR 1.5 billion, and statutory bodies, local authorities, and government agencies contributed MYR 2.51 billion. The objective of *Kumpulan Wang Persaraan* is to ensure that pension benefits are sustainable. The fund grew from MYR 48.1 billion in 2007 to MYR 78.9 billion in 2011. The return on investment has ranged from 5.62 per cent to 9.21 per cent since 2007, exceeding the fund's target of 5.5 per cent (Retirement Fund 2011).

The civil service pension scheme covers only a limited share of the population and is designed to smooth consumption, prevent poverty in old age, and continue to provide benefits for the duration of the retiree's life. The scheme has good replacement rates of 50–60 per cent of basic salaries and provides protection against inflation risk. The primary challenge for the Pensions Trust Fund Council is to meet future pension liabilities and to contain the fiscal burden.

SOCSO

Established in 1971 under the Ministry of Human Resources, SOCSO implements and administers social security schemes under authority afforded by the Employees' Social Security Act 1969 (Act 4). The organization oversees the Employment Injury Insurance Scheme and the Invalidity Pension Scheme (SOCSO 2013).

In addition to the two schemes, SOCSO also provides medical, physical, and vocational rehabilitation benefits and facilities to help injured employee members return to work and daily life. SOCSO also administers accident prevention activities, providing safety and health awareness programmes for employees.

All employers with one or more employees must register with and contribute to SOCSO to fund the schemes and services above. Employees who earn less than MYR 3000 are required to contribute, but those earning more than MYR 3000 can obtain coverage only if they and their employer agree to contribute. Coverage begins when an employee makes the first contribution and never ends once it begins. The required contribution is currently 2.25 per cent of the employee's salary. The employer contributes 1.75 per cent, and the employee contributes .5 per cent (SOCSO 2013).

In 2011, 5.76 million employees actively contributed to SOCSO, and the organization paid benefits in 59,897 cases (SOCSO 2013). In total, there were 378,377 beneficiaries receiving benefits totalling MYR 1.73 billion, or an average of MYR 4519 per beneficiary. The organization disbursed MYR 111 million for physical and vocational rehabilitation programmes and MYR 93 million for dialysis treatment. In 2011, SOCSO received an income of MYR 3.23 billion and paid out MYR 2.01 billion: MYR 1.73 billion in benefits and MYR 280 million for administrative expenditures.

On average, the organization's continuous net income exceeded MYR 1 billion per year during the 2007–2011 period. As such, the organization's sustainability is not in question. The focus on accident prevention, training programmes, and return-to-work programmes will benefit SOCSO, enhancing long-term sustainability while improving workplace safety (SOCSO 2013).

The Armed Forces Fund

Another defined-contribution scheme is the Armed Forces Fund established in 1973 under Act 101. The scheme is mandatory for military personnel in the ranks below commissioned officers. Service members contribute 10 per cent of their salaries, and the government contributes 15 per cent. Members can withdraw their contributions at age 50. Those who opt for pensionable schemes are entitled to withdraw only their portion of the contribution.

Pillar 3: voluntary savings

This complementary pillar includes support accumulated through unit trusts, insurance saving schemes, bank deposits, private retirement schemes, and other assets. The typical insurance products include long-term care policies, reverse mortgages, and annuities. The public lack of awareness and understanding of annuity products means that insurers should invest more in public education for long-term retirement products.

In 2012, the Securities Commission Malaysia established the guidelines for private retirement schemes under the Capital Market Masterplan 2, with the objective of improving living standards for retired Malaysians by facilitating accumulation of additional savings. The schemes offer long-term vehicles, complement existing mandatory schemes, and are entirely voluntary in nature. Contributions come from individuals or from employers that offer the products to employees as a way to retain manpower. The commission approved eight private retirement scheme providers, and sales of the scheme commenced at the end of 2012. Risk in these private retirement schemes is regulated by measures that vary with the investor's age. Returns are credited into the investor's account. As an incentive, the Malaysian government offers tax relief to individuals and contributing employers that participate in the private schemes. The entire private retirement scheme system is regulated under the Capital Markets and Services Act 2007 (Act 671).

Pillar 4: non-financial aid

This pillar includes a variety of informal, non-governmental support, including family support, health care, housing, and support not classified elsewhere. Filial piety, the traditional notion that children support their parents, is prevalent in Malaysia, so this is a particularly important pillar. Members protect each other from social risks through intergenerational and intragenerational measures, including income pooling and transfers of personal income. This holds true despite growth in life expectancy and the portion of members for whom EPF funds provide inadequate retirement security. Many aged Malaysians co-reside with and receive financial assistance from their adult children. The fourth Malaysian Population and Family Survey, conducted by the National Population and Family Development Board (2004), shows that 61–73 per cent of women who have ever been married and their spouses provide parents with regular assistance in the form of money and goods.

Malaysia's EPF

The 1991 EPF Act specifies the governance of the fund. The board of directors oversees the fund and its operations. The EPF's investment function is controlled by the Investment Panel.

Between 2001 and 2004, contribution rates changed almost annually, but the combined rate has remained at 23 per cent since 2004. Employees are required to contribute 11 per cent of their gross wages, and employers contribute 12 per cent.

Table 3.2 presents results from a comparison of contribution rates in countries with defined-contribution schemes. The contribution rate of EPF members is one of the highest among countries with defined-contribution schemes. Before the 2012 extension of the retirement age to 60, the main issue was the low retirement age. This significantly affected the sustainability of the member's fund. By extending the retirement age to 60, Malaysia increased the replacement rate of members' pensions. In a tight labour market like the current one, this move is deemed effective.

Members' EPF accounts are in fact two accounts: Account 1 comprises 70 per cent of the total contribution and Account 2 holds the other 30 per cent. Members can withdraw from Account 1 only under the following terms:

- When they reach age 55, all Account 1 savings can be withdrawn in a lump sum or as a portion of those savings.
- If the member is physically or mentally incapacitated and unable to work, the full lump sum can be withdrawn.
- Members may withdraw all Account 1 savings if they are permanently migrating out of the country.
- Pensionable employees in the civil service may withdraw from Account 1 after returning the government's portion of contributions paid into the account or after optional retirement.
- Members may withdraw up to 20 per cent of Account 1 savings to invest in approved funds.

Table 3.2 Contribution rates in selected countries

Country	2010 per-capita GDP (USD)	Statutory retirement age	Employee %	Employer %	Total %
Malaysia	8373	55	11	12	23
Singapore	43,867	62	20	16	36
China	4393	60	8	20	28
Brazil	10,710	65	7.7	20	27.7
United Kingdom	36,100	68	11	12.8	23.8
Argentina	9124	65	11	10.2	21.2
Poland	12,271	65	9.5	9.8	19.3
Vietnam	1191	60	6	12	18
Japan	43,137	65	7.7	7.7	15.4
Mongolia	2207	60	7	7	14
United States	47,184	67	6.2	6.2	12.4
Chile	11,888	65	10	1.2	11.2
Philippines	1836	65	3.3	7.1	10.4
Hong Kong	31,758	65	5	5	10
Lao PDR	1208	60	4.5	5	9.5
Korea	20,757	65	4.5	4.5	9
Mexico	9166	65	1.7	6.9	8.6
Thailand	3838	55	3	3	6
Indonesia	2946	55	2	3.7	5.7

Source: World Bank (2012).

- Members may withdraw funds from Account 1 if it exceeds MYR 1.05 million.
- Nominees, administrators, or the next of kin may withdraw Account 1 funds if the account holder dies.

The withdrawal options are more varied for Account 2:

- At age 50, members may withdraw Account 2 funds to plan for retirement.
- Account 2 funds may be withdrawn to reduce or redeem or pay instalments on a housing loan.
- Members may withdraw from the account to finance their own or their children's education.
- Through the Flexible Housing Withdrawal initiative, members set aside Account 2 funds for use in determining housing loan eligibility. One's income determines the size of the loan for which one qualifies, and funds saved monthly via the Flexible Housing Withdrawal help increase the size of a housing loan.
- Members may withdraw funds for medical expenses associated with treatment of critical illnesses and to buy medical aid equipment approved by the EPF.

The EPF requires members to maintain a minimum balance. Regardless of the withdrawal options mentioned above, the member's EPF must hold at least

56 per cent of the total contribution. Most members do not invest heavily or even consider investing in other funds because the EPF pays high dividend rates, which crowd out other investment options. Other than retirement withdrawals from Account 1, the most common withdrawals are for the purchase of a house. Withdrawals for education are not common, as undergraduates in Malaysia commonly secure funding for tertiary education through a government loan scheme at a 3 per cent interest rate (National Higher Education Fund Corporation n.d.). In January 2010, the government extended EPF coverage to self-employed workers and individuals without fixed monthly income by voluntarily contributing to the 1 Malaysia Retirement Savings Scheme at a minimum of MYR 50 to the EPF. The government will contribute a maximum of 5 per cent of the member's contribution or a maximum of MYR 60 per year.

The EPF and Singapore's Central Provident Fund

The EPF and Singapore's Central Provident Fund (CPF) both have British colonial roots, but the CPF expanded coverage and benefits at a faster pace. Membership in the CPF is restricted to citizens and permanent residents of Singapore. Throughout the life course, savings in CPF can be used for health care, education, social insurance, home ownership, retirement, and investment. The division of accounts is very different from the EPF. Contributions to the CPF are channelled into three accounts: the ordinary account that receives two-thirds of contributions and is reserved for housing and investment schemes; the Medisave account that receives 19 per cent of contributions for hospitalization expenses and catastrophic health insurance; and the special account that receives 14 per cent of contributions for retirement and other purposes (Asher and Nandy 2011).

A unique feature of CPF is CPF Life, which provides a monthly payment to members who were born in or after 1958 and have more than SGD 40,000 in their retirement accounts at age 55 or have at least SGD 60,000 when they reach the draw-down age. The monthly payout continues as long as the member lives (Central Provident Fund Board 2013a). The CPF and EPF differ on another feature: the CPF does not make investment decisions. Monies transferred from the CPF into government reserves could be managed by the Monetary Authority of Singapore, Temasek, or the Singapore Government Investment Corporation (Singapore Government Investment Corporation 2013). The comparisons below identify the shortcomings and strengths of both. A discussion of policy implications follows the comparison.

Coverage

In 2011, the EPF covered 6.3 million members actively contributing to their EPF accounts (EPF 2011) or 50.4 per cent of the 12.92 million people in Malaysia's labour-force (DOSM 2012c), making EPF the scheme with the broadest coverage in Malaysia. The coverage includes the 54,000 self-employed individuals through the 1 Malaysia Retirement Savings (*New Straits Times* 2012).

The small contribution figure should be monitored closely to see how the self-employed respond to this voluntary savings scheme and whether additional incentives are required to improve the number contributing. Figure 3.4 shows the coverage of the EPF scheme.

In contrast, Singapore's CPF covers fewer members at 3.4 million, of which 1.74 million were active as of 2011. Although both the EPF and CPF are mandatory defined-contribution savings schemes, the CPF covers a high 83.6 per cent of the 2.08 million people in Singapore's resident labour-force and 53.7 per cent of the 3.24 million people in the total labour-force. Both the EPF and CPF cover slightly more than half the work-force of their respective countries. However, the CPF covers a larger percentage of the resident work-force because its members include most of the civil servants employed after 1986. Most Malaysian civil servants, except those who have opted to continue contributing to the EPF, are covered under the civil service pension scheme. It is significant to note that the CPF's 83.6 per cent coverage of the resident work-force is tantamount to universal coverage for Singaporeans, making the CPF the principal social security scheme in the city-state.

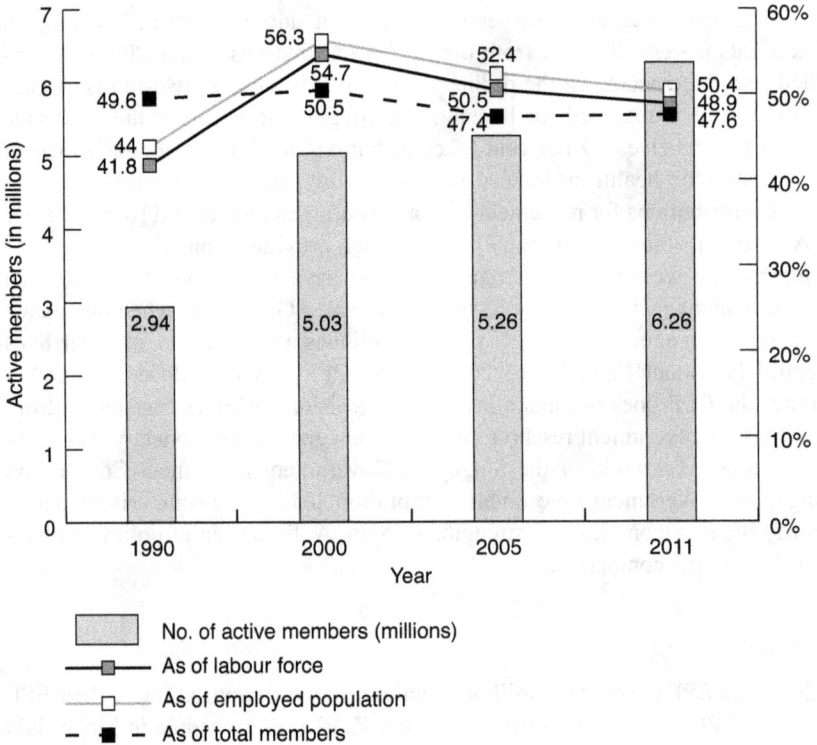

Figure 3.4 Coverage of the EPF scheme, 1990–2011 (source: author's calculation based on EPF (1994, 2001, 2006, 2012); DOSM [2012b]).

Replacement rate and adequacy

A survey conducted by the EPF in 2003 indicates that 14 per cent of EPF retirees use their entire retirement savings within three years, 50 per cent spend it within five years, and 70 per cent exhaust it within 10 years (Huzaime 2012). At the time of the survey, Malaysia's retirement age was 55, and the average life expectancy was 74 years (DOSM 2012b). Thus, individuals who retired at age 55 in 2003 would have to survive a period of 20 years with the support provided by the EPF.

The available EPF data do not allow a detailed review of the scheme's adequacy or replacement rate. At the end of 2011, the average savings among 54-year-old active members was MYR 149,217 (EPF 2012). By permitting full lump-sum withdrawals at age 55, the EPF members take full risk of adequacy and sustainability. With the 2012 extension of the retirement age to 60 years, members who begin drawing down at age 60 and live to age 74 (the average expectancy) will need to distribute their funds over a 14-year period. The estimated monthly income stream at a 2 per cent compounded adjusted return is MYR 1172. In 2011, the estimated per capita GDP was USD 9656 (MYR 2504) per month, so the EPF's replacement rate is about 47 per cent (Bank Negara Malaysia 2012; World Bank 2012). However, only 83.6 per cent of retirees in Malaysia have EPF balances exceeding MYR 100,000 (Huzaime 2012), and 72.5 per cent have balances of less than MYR 50,000 at age 54. Although the average balance (MYR 149,217) appears adequate, most retirees have lower balances in their accounts and will fare far worse. This is a major issue of concern in elderly retirement planning in Malaysia and among EPF members.

An assessment of the CPF's replacement rate and adequacy must recognize a key difference between the schemes. Singapore's CPF does not allow members to take their own risks and planned actions in managing their retirement savings and provides several schemes to smooth retirement payouts over time. The scheme requires members to retain minimum sums in both the CPF account (SGD 120,000 in 2013) and the Medisave account (SGD 25,000 in 2013) (Central Provident Fund Board 2013b). If the remaining balance is less than the sum of these two amounts, members are not permitted to withdraw their savings.

After reaching age 62, the CPF encourages them to purchase annuities or deposit their CPF savings into fixed-deposit accounts. This encouragement is designed to convert members' savings into monthly payouts. The average balance of 55-year-old CPF members, SGD 94,100, suggests that members who begin withdrawing their savings at age 55 will have low replacement rates. However, members who start the monthly payouts at age 62 would receive SGD 669 per month. Data on median wages in 2011 indicate that the average wage level is SGD 3317 per month (Ministry of Manpower Singapore 2013). A monthly retirement payout of SGD 669 replaces about 20 per cent of the average wages. This does not consider the effect of converting part of the savings to assets such as homes and property.

If one compares the EPF and CPF on the adequacy of savings for retirement, it is apparent that the EPF leaves the risk of sustainability to members, but the CPF has taken mandatory steps to ensure that income is sustainable for the duration of retirement. The income stream from each scheme and the life expectancies in the two countries suggest that EPF members will be able to live more comfortably in retirement. As mentioned, the Malaysian scheme's replacement rate is 47 per cent, but the CPF replaces only 20 per cent of members' pre-retirement wages. However, EPF members remain exposed to risk associated with managing their own retirement incomes. The CPF's planned scheme, if applied to the EPF, should improve the EPF's outcomes.

Dividend rates

Figure 3.5 presents the dividend rates and net dividend rates (after deducting inflation) for each scheme and the inflation rates in each country. Except when it dropped from 5.80 per cent in 2007 to 4.50 per cent in 2008, the EPF dividend rate generally rose between 2002 and 2011. Because of this drop and high inflation rate (5.7 per cent), EPF members suffered a negative net dividend rate of 1.2 per cent in 2008. The EPF dividend rate rose again after 2008 to 6 per cent in 2011.

The CPF's dividend rates differ across the scheme's several accounts. Instead of paying out dividends based on fund performance, the CPF has paid out dividends at the same rates for the past 10 years: 2.5 per cent for the ordinary account and 4.0 per cent for the Medisave, special, and retirement accounts. Estimates in Figure 3.5 presume this 4 per cent dividend rate is adjusted for inflation.

Overall, the dividend rates are higher for the EPF than the CPF. If the schemes are compared on the fund's performance, the question of sustainability arises. As mentioned above, the CPF's conservative approach provides the more sustainable support.

Types of withdrawals

The previous discussion summarizes the various types of pre-retirement withdrawals allowed by the EPF. Table 3.3 summarizes pre-retirement withdrawals from the EPF for the period from 2001 through 2011.

The CPF's withdrawal options, methods, and limits are not comparable to those in the EPF. The CPF scheme is more complex; its retirement provision focuses on meeting basic needs in old age and ensuring that levels of relative poverty are low, not limiting absolute poverty (Beddoes 2012).

In both schemes, sustainability depends on the number and level of individual contributions, interest earned, the extent of pre-retirement withdrawals, and the outcomes of efforts to convert accumulated balances into a retirement income stream. Individual members bear investment and macroeconomic risks (e.g. unemployment, relatively stagnant wages, inflation).[2] The CPF system is obli-

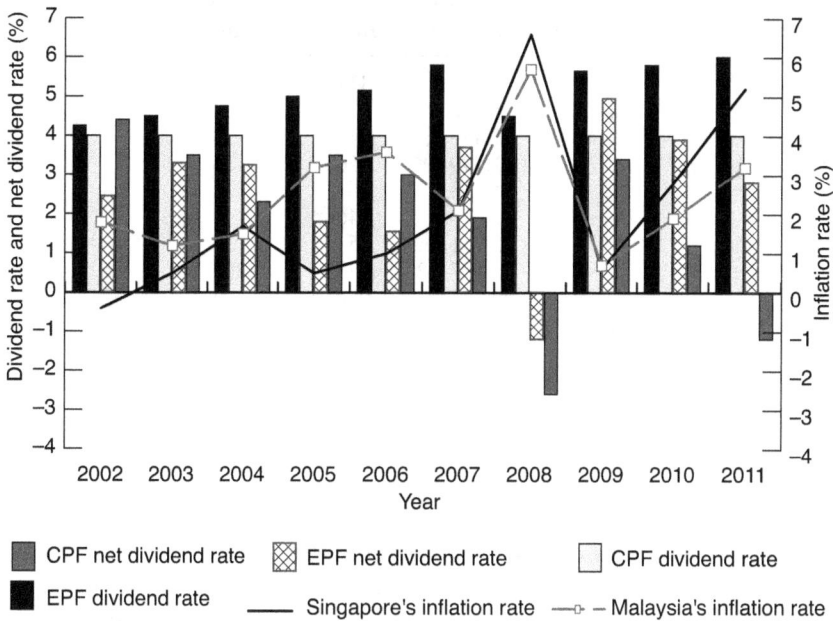

Figure 3.5 EPF and CPF: divided rate, inflation rate, and net dividend rate, 2002–2011 (source: EPF [2012]; DOSM [2012b]; Central Provident Fund Board [2012]; Department of Statistics Singapore [2013]).

gated to return only the accumulated balances and interest at a nominal, government-guaranteed, 2.5 per cent rate. The government also implicitly guarantees that it will honour the balances and CPF Life obligations.[3]

Investment performance

For EPF members, investment performance is the key factor that determines the dividend rate and whether members' funds are sustainable. Global uncertainties suggest that the EPF will face challenges in maintaining returns and declaring high dividend rates. Table 3.4 summarizes the distribution and growth and returns of EPF investments.

The EPF's investments were centred in low-risk options such as government securities, loans, and bonds. However, investments in equities are growing at a fast pace. In 2011, they represented the largest class of EPF investments. The returns on EPF investments suggest the reason for the turn towards equities, without which the continued declaration of a 6 per cent return will have a negative impact on the quantum of funds.

There is a strong need for the EPF to review the quality of its assets and long-term returns to sustain the high dividend rates declared. Otherwise, regardless of

Table 3.3 Pre-retirement withdrawals from the EPF, 2001–2011 (MYR billions)

Year of withdrawal	Housing	50 years	Health	Education	>1 million
2001	2.417	1.046	.317	.093	
2002	2.387	1.132	.036	.120	
2003	2.441	1.430	.042	.118	
2004	2.710	1.599	.056	.136	
2005	2.571	1.598	.061	.116	
2006	3.296	1.718	.046	.140	
2007	5.938	2.711	.051	.256	.083
2008	5.395	2.827	.048	.264	.362
2009	4.770	3.151	.040	.266	.323
2010	4.310	3.207	.035	.270	.362
2011	4.350	3.606	.039	.278	.482

Source: EPF (2004, 2008, 2012).

electoral promises made by the government, the EPF will be forced to lower dividend rates to ensure sustainability.

The CPF's investment performance is difficult to assess. Asher and Nandy (2011) state that the CPF system lacks transparency and accountability. As an example, they note that the Government of Singapore Investment Corporation is not required to disclose the performance of CPF investments. They estimate that the real rate of return on the CPF balance from 1987 to 2009 was 1.3 per cent. Because members lack freedom to invest their CPF funds, and policy ties interest declarations to the return from government securities, the CPF return is unattractive to CPF members. Table 3.5 presents returns on CPF investments for 2010 and 2011. Future returns and interest paid to CPF members will not increase unless substantial changes are made in investment policies and disclosure regimes.

The returns achieved by the EPF are higher than those of the CPF. The EPF's future performance depends very much on the actions of the Investment Panel, which has been granted more freedom to invest in overseas securities.

Administrative efficiency

The EPF was managed by a staff of 5162 as of 2011. In 2011, the ratio of staff to active members was 1:679 (EPF 2011). Examining the 2009 ratios in Singapore, Asher and Nandy (2011) point out that the ratio of CPF staff to active members was 1:1217. The CPF's staffing efficiency is twice that of the EPF, and the CPF's 2011 *Annual Report* notes a 98 per cent level of satisfaction among members and employers who use CPF services (Central Provident Fund Board 2012). There is little information on satisfaction with EPF services. To reduce administrative costs, the EPF could further upgrade information technology applications and make corresponding reductions in staffing levels. Another measure of administrative efficiency is the ratio of operating expenses to the

Table 3.4 Investment fund and growth and returns of EPF, 2007–2011

Type of investment	2007		2008		2009		2010		2011	
	MYR millions	% growth	MYR millions	% growth	MYR millions	% growth	MYR millions	% growth	MYR millions	% growth
Malaysian government securities	112,932 (36.08)	10.1	110,642 (32.35)	−2.0	114,098 (30.73)	3.1	118,517 (26.90)	3.9 4.6*	124,569 (26.55)	5.1 4.7*
Loans and bonds	112,722 (36.01)	17.0	122,776 (35.90)	8.9	131,977 (35.55)	7.5	142,614 (32.37)	8.1 5.3*	160,686 (34.25)	12.7 5.1*
Equity	66,275 (21.17)	20.7	87,948 (25.71)	32.7	100,426 (27.05)	14.2	153,531 (34.85)	52.9 10.6*	167,207 (35.64)	8.9 11.0*
Money market instruments	19,259 (6.15)	−36.7	19,026 (5.56)	−1.2	23,208 (6.25)	22.0	23,987 (5.45)	3.4 3.0*	14,937 (3.18)	−37.7 3.4*
Properties	1776 (.57)	7.6	1622 (.47)	−8.7	1554 (.42)	−4.2	1867 (.424)	20.2 6.1*	1821 (.39)	−2.5 6.4*
Total	313,013 (100.0)	9.5	342,014 (100.0)	9.3	371,263 (100.0)	8.6	440,527 (100.0)	18.7 6.4*	469,220 (100.0)	6.5 6.7*

Source: Adapted from EPF (2011, 152).

Notes
Numbers in parentheses show percentages of the types of investment.
* Percentage returns on investments
Total investment return (income) as above does not include MYR 1.66 million miscellaneous investment income for 2011 (MYR 2.48 million in 2010).

Table 3.5 Central Provident Fund investments and returns, 2010 and 2011

Type of investment	2010		2011	
	Investment (SGD)	% return	Investment (SGD)	% return
Special issue of Singapore government securities	176,141,998	3.8	197,245,527	3.7
Advance deposits	8,041,446	1.3	8,407,067	1.3
Singapore government securities	532,122	2.9	605,640	2.9
Statutory board bonds	462,164	3.2	491,556	3.3
Corporate bonds	199,506	3.2	314,215	3.0
Equity securities Singapore	45,282	1.8	79,545	3.5

Source: adapted from Central Provident Fund Board (2011).

fund size. In 2011, these were .187 for the EPF and .090 for the CPF (Central Provident Fund Board 2012). This again suggests that the CPF operates at a higher level of efficiency.

Future options

The EPF, which covers 50 per cent of the total work-force, is still the dominant retirement scheme for Malaysians. It plays an important role in ensuring that funds are available for the elderly in retirement. However, the retirement account allows only full or partial lump-sum withdrawal. The EPF lacks a mandatory phased withdrawal option or an annuitized payment scheme and limits withdrawals for investment to 20 per cent of the total contribution. The effect of these provisions is that retirees bear the full burden of risks associated with investment and longevity. As the 2003 EPF survey (Huzaime 2012) indicates, lack of discipline and poor financial planning skills often lead retirees to exhaust retirement savings within a short period of time. Despite the recent extension of the retirement age to 60 years, there is very high resistance to moving the mandatory full withdrawal age to 60 from 55 years. Withdrawal conditions remain unchanged. To be more effective in maintaining retirement security, the EPF should introduce voluntary top-up options, which would allow members to deposit additional contributions into their accounts when they have excess funds. A retiree's account could receive these contributions from the individual's own holdings, from kin, and from others. They would increase the likelihood that members' accounts hold sufficient funds to meet expenses for medical care. The EPF also could introduce annuitized schemes that provide regular payments based on basic minimum savings specified in the same manner as the CPF Life scheme. The implementation of such measures will take time and strong political will.

The coverage of self-employed workers remains low in Malaysia. Incentives offered by the 1 Malaysia Retirement Savings Scheme to attract self-employed workers are not generous enough, despite the savings benefit from EPF's high dividend rate. There is no proactive effort to pull in retirement contributions from such workers, and mandatory measures may be necessary. Examples of possible measures include licensing controls, compulsory contributions based on income tax declarations, and increases in tax relief.

To ensure higher levels of adequacy than those offered at present, the EPF should encourage members to delay withdrawals and extend their working lives. Such adjustments would increase the balance of savings when the individual decides to retire. Active engagement in work will also keep older workers on a healthy footing, possibly reducing or delaying the need for wealth-sapping medical treatments.

If one takes the CPF as the benchmark, the EPF will need to adopt operational efficiencies by improving its technological infrastructure. There is always a need to monitor the service level of EPF staff. In addition, the EPF should further study the behaviours of members, especially the rate of savings use after retirement. An open attitude in allowing information to be used for study purposes will stimulate suggestions and proposals, enabling continuous improvements to the fund. At this moment, the EPF is not very forthcoming in the release of data.

Notes

1 The Malaysian ringgit (MYR) is a unit of currency. One US dollar (USD) is equivalent to approximately MYR 3. The currency code SGD refers to Singapore dollars.
2 In a defined-contribution system, rapid growth in the aged population is felt when net contributions to the system decline and eventually become negative; it also is felt when asset prices change because the elderly sell physical and financial assets to finance consumption.
3 Individual members can benefit from government guarantees of individual retirement accounts because such guarantees have a market value (Lachance and Mitchell 2003). Since CPF members benefit from government guarantees, this benefit must be included in full analysis of the implicit tax. However, it is not included here.

References

Asher, Mukul G., and Amarendu Nandy. 2011. 'Singapore: Pension System Overview and Reform Directions.' In *Pension Systems and Old-Age Income Support in East and Southeast Asia: Overview and Reform Directions*, edited by Donghyun Park, 152–175. Abingdon: Routledge.

Bank Negara Malaysia. 2012. *Annual Report 2012*. Putrajaya, Malaysia: Bank Negara Malaysia. www.bnm.gov.my/files/publication/ar/en/2012/ar2012_book.pdf.

Beddoes, Zanny Minton. 2012. 'For Richer, for Poorer.' *Economist*, 13 October. www.economist.com/node/21564414.

Central Provident Fund Board. 2012. 'Annexes.' In *Annual Report 2012*. Singapore: Central Provident Fund Board. http://mycpf.cpf.gov.sg/NR/rdonlyres/0F1D08A4-B10F-4F4E-A969-9EDAABC526F2/0/Annexes.pdf.

Central Provident Fund Board. 2013a. 'CPF Life.' Central Provident Fund Board. Last updated 4 July. http://mycpf.cpf.gov.sg/Members/Gen-Info/CPF_LIFE/CPF_LIFE.htm.

Central Provident Fund Board. 2013b. 'Your Retirement Savings and Withdrawals.' Central Provident Fund Board. Accessed 23 September 2013. http://mycpf.cpf.gov.sg/Members/Gen-Info/Sch-Svc/S-and-S.

Department of Social Welfare. n.d. 'Criteria and Schemes for Social Welfare.' Accessed 20 September 2013. www.jkm.gov.my.

DOSM. 2012a. *Population Projections Malaysia: 2010–2040*. Report, November. Putrajaya, Malaysia: DOSM. http://statistics.gov.my/portal/download_Population/files/population_projections/Population_Projection_2010-2040.pdf.

DOSM. 2012b. *Malaysia Economic Statistics: Time Series 2011*. Putrajaya, Malaysia: DOSM. www.statistics.gov.my/portal/download_Economics/files/DATA_SERIES/2011/Penerbitan_Time_Series_2011.pdf.

DOSM. 2012c. *Labour Force Survey Report: Malaysia 2012*. Putrajaya, Malaysia: DOSM. http://statistics.gov.my/portal/download_Labour/files/labour_force/Labour_Force_Survey_Report_Malaysia_2012.pdf.

DOSM. 2012d. *Social Statistics Bulletin: Malaysia 2012*. Report. Putrajaya, Malaysia: DOSM. www.statistics.gov.my/portal/download_Labour/files/BPS/Buletin_Perangkaan_Sosial_2012.pdf.

EPF. 2004. *Annual Report 2004*. Kuala Lumpur: EPF. www.kwsp.gov.my/portal/en/web/kwsp/annual-report-2004.

EPF. 2008. *Annual Report 2008*. Kuala Lumpur: EPF. www.kwsp.gov.my/portal/en/web/kwsp/annual-report-2008.

EPF. 2011. *Annual Report 2011*. Kuala Lumpur: EPF. www.kwsp.gov.my/portal/en/web/kwsp/annual-report-2011.

EPF. 2012. *Annual Report 2012*. Kuala Lumpur: EPF. www.kwsp.gov.my/portal/en/web/kwsp/annual-report-2012.

Huzaime, A. Hamid. 2012. 'The World Bank's 5 Pillars Pension System and Its Refinements for Application in Malaysia.' Paper presented at Dynamic Evolution of the Pensions World, international conference organized by Employees Provident Fund, Kuala Lumpur, 2–3 April.

Lachance, Marie-Eve, and Olivia S. Mitchell. 2003. 'Guaranteeing Individual Accounts.' *American Economic Review* 93 (2): 257–260. doi:10.1257/000282803321947155.

Ministry of Finance Malaysia. 2012. *Economic Report 2012/2013*. Putrajaya, Malaysia: Ministry of Finance Malaysia. www.treasury.gov.my/index.php?option=com_content&view=article&id=2281%3Alaporan-ekonomi-20122013&catid=73%3Asenarai-laporan-ekonomi&Itemid=174&lang=en.

Ministry of Manpower Singapore. 2013. 'Income.' Labour market statistical information. Singapore: Ministry of Manpower Singapore. Accessed 23 September 2013. Updated 31 May 2014. www.mom.gov.sg/statistics-publications/national-labour-market-information/statistics/Pages/earnings-wages.aspx.

National Higher Education Fund Corporation (Perbadanan Tabung Pendidikan Tinggi Nasional). n.d. 'Repayment.' National Higher Education Fund Corporation. www.ptptn.gov.my/web/english/loan-repayment.

National Population and Family Development Board. 2004. *4th Malaysian Population & Family Survey*. Kuala Lumpur: Ministry of Women, Family and Community Development.

New Straits Times. 2012. 'Self-employed Urged to Join EPF 1 Malaysia Retirement Savings Scheme.' 2 July. www.nst.com.my/nation/general/self-employed-urged-to-join-epf-1malaysia-retirement-savings-scheme-1.101365.

Retirement Fund (Kumpulan Wang Persaraan). 2011. *Limitless Possibilities: Annual Report 2011*. Kuala Lampur: Retirement Fund. www.kwap.gov.my/En/Reports/ KWAP%20Annual%20Report%202011.pdf.

Singapore Government Investment Corporation. 2013. 'Does GIC Invest CPF Monies?' FAQ 47. Singapore Government Investment Corporation. Accessed 23 September 2013. www.gic.com.sg/en/faqs#47.

SOCSO (Social Security Organisation). 2013. *Annual Report 2011*. Kuala Lampur: SOCSO. www.perkeso.gov.my/en/component/rsfiles/download.html?path=Laporan+T ahunan%2Flaporan+tahunan+2011.rar.

Tay, Louis, and Ed Diener. 2011. 'Needs and Subjective Well-Being around the World.' *Journal of Personality and Social Psychology* 101 (2): 354–365. doi:10.1037/ a0023779.

United Nations, Department of Economic and Social Affairs, Population Division. 2011. *Comprehensive Tables*. Vol. 1 of *World Population Prospects: The 2010 Revision*. New York: United Nations. http://esa.un.org/unpd/wpp/Documentation/pdf/WPP2010_ Volume-I_Comprehensive-Tables.pdf.

World Bank. 2012. *World Development Indicators 2012*. CD-ROM. Washington, DC: World Bank.

4   Asset-based policies in Korea

Expansion, challenges, and future directions

Chang-Keun Han and Youngmi Kim

In the last decade, there have been notable expansions of asset-based policies (ABPs) in South Korea (hereafter Korea). The Korean government started Child Development Accounts (CDAs) in April 2007 and Hope Building Accounts in October 2010. The Seoul city government launched Hope Plus Accounts in December 2007 and Seoul Child Development Accounts in March 2009. In addition, small-scale ABPs have been developed in several regions.

These developments suggest a growing interest in programmes and policies that promote the accumulation of assets by disadvantaged populations in Korea. They also reflect a keen desire among policymakers to develop new strategies for addressing poverty and inequality. As most Korean social policies are oriented towards income maintenance efforts, ABPs can be attractive to policymakers, policy consumers, and citizens, regardless of political ideology.

This chapter aims to introduce and explain the key features of ABPs in Korea. It employs the notion of inclusive ABPs – defined by the principles of universality, progressiveness, lifelong process, and adequacy – as a theoretical framework (Clancy *et al.* 2006; Han 2013). This chapter also discusses several critical challenges facing current ABPs and suggests future directions for inclusive ABPs.

Background

Asset poverty and inequality in Korea

The rising interest in ABPs for low- and moderate-income households is related to growth in inequality of income and assets. Kim and Kim (2013) estimate the prevalence of asset poverty in Korea using data collected in 2007 for the Korea Welfare Panel Study. They employ two measures of asset poverty grounded in Wolff's (2001) definition of asset poverty: net worth and liquid assets. Kim and Kim (2013) find that about 12.7 per cent of the population has net worth at or below 120 per cent of the poverty line, and about 13.2 per cent has net worth at or below 150 per cent of that line. If asset poverty in Korea is measured as holdings of liquid assets, 32.8 per cent of the population lives at or below 120 per cent of the poverty line, and 36.5 per cent lives at or below 150 per cent of that line. According to 한국부자의 소비지출과 노후준비 보고서 (*The Report on*

Expenditures and Retirement Planning of the Korean Rich) published by Kookmin Bank Research Center (2012), the rich comprise .28 per cent of Korea's total population but own 13.8 per cent of the total financial assets. The report identifies people as rich if they have financial assets of KRW 1 billion or more (including savings deposits, bonds, stocks, and other holdings).[1] On average, Korea's wealthy own financial assets worth about KRW 2.2 billion and real estate assets worth about KRW 12.2 billion. Their portfolios indicate preferences among types of assets: 58 per cent of the total assets are held in real estate, 19.8 per cent are held in stocks, and 12.3 per cent are held in savings deposits.

Asset inequality may explain income inequality. Wealthy households in Korea have an average annual income of KRW .4 billion, of which 36.5 per cent comes in returns from assets. In comparison, the average total annual income of other Korean households is KRW 45 million, and only .4 per cent of that comes in returns from assets.

Household debts also provide some indication of asset inequality. According to estimates from Statistics Korea (2011), the government agency that produces national statistical information, the ratio of household debt to disposable income is 1.585 among households in Korea's lowest income quintile. Households in the group had average debts of KRW 14 million in 2011, an increase from KRW 12 million in 2010. The increase in debt is related to declines in disposable income, and the debt threatens household financial security among the lowest income group (Han and Hong 2011).

Home-ownership rates among poor households also serve as an indicator of asset inequality. The number of households with income below the poverty line increased from 698,075 in 2001 to 882,925 in 2009, and a significant portion of the poor lost owned housing. The number of poor homeowners decreased from 172,715 in 2001 to 125,590 in 2009. In 2001, 24.74 per cent of poor households owned their housing, but the percentage decreased to 14.22 per cent in 2009 (Ministry of Health and Welfare [MHW] and Korea Institute of Health and Social Affairs 2010). Although the general population's home-ownership rate fluctuates around 55 per cent in Korea, the significant decrease in home ownership among the poor suggests that asset inequality has worsened.

Key features of inclusive ABP

Michael Sherraden (1991) initiated and has promoted inclusive ABPs. Claiming that asset ownership can spark positive development on individual, family, and community levels, he endorses ABPs even for low- and moderate-income households. Indeed, asset accumulation is a promising way for families to improve their well-being over time and across generations (Han and Hong 2011; Lerman and McKernan 2008; Rothwell and Han 2010). There is increasing recognition that the best social policy alternatives move beyond the idea of defining well-being with measures of income and consumption. Building people's assets is one policy pathway to increasing capabilities and reducing the pressure to choose between economic growth and social development (Sherraden 1991).

Four principles guide inclusive ABPs. (For a summary, see Clancy *et al.* [2006] and Han [2013].) First is universality. Asset-accumulation opportunities should be open to all people, regardless of income, age, race/ethnicity, and gender. Policies should decrease barriers to saving and expand low-income households' access to saving opportunities (Schreiner and Sherraden 2007; Sherraden 1991). Second is progressivity. Policies should provide greater incentives and benefits to low-income households and minorities than to high-income households and people in the racial or ethnic majority. Progressive mechanisms include financial incentives such as tax-free earnings, matched savings, and tax rebates (Clancy *et al.* 2006). Third, asset building should be a lifelong process. The earlier people begin to save, the more likely their chances for economic and social development. Many studies find that children are more likely to have positive outcomes if their households own the home and other assets than if they live in asset-poor households (Chowa, Ansong, and Masa 2010; Kim and Sherraden 2011; Williams Shanks *et al.* 2010). These findings support efforts to develop ABPs that offer CDAs. The principle that asset accumulation is a life-long process also suggests that saving continues from birth to death and that assets should be portable across the life course (Rank 2008). Fourth, ABPs should take adequacy of assets into account. It is not easy to determine how much savings are adequate for the saver's purpose. Thus, saving programmes should provide institutional mechanisms that help people save enough to achieve self-determined goals (Han 2013).

Expansion of asset-based policies in Korea

Child Development Accounts

The Korean central government has tested a number of ABPs (Table 4.1). In 2007, it began to offer CDAs as part of an effort to help at-risk children achieve self-reliance in adulthood (Nam and Han 2010).[2] The project started with about 30,000 children and serves youth aged 0 to 17 who live in disadvantage (i.e. those in the child-welfare system, group homes, and child-headed households and those with a disability or who live with a person with a disability). The number of children participating in CDA programmes has steadily increased since 2007. In 2012, the government expanded the project, offering accounts to children born in 2010 who live in poor households that receive welfare benefits (about 10,000 children). As of 2012, about 52,500 children had CDAs. The savings in a CDA may be accessed after the youth reaches age 17 and used only to meet costs associated with education, occupational training, housing, small business investment, health care, and marriage (Han 2013). The last two savings goals were added recently because some youth may experience health problems and wish to prepare for costs related to marriage.

Several other key features are noteworthy. First, the project offers a 1-to-1 matching rate with a match cap of KRW 30,000 per month. That is, the government provides a matching *won* for each *won* saved by a participant, and

Table 4.1 Comparison of asset-based policies in Korea

Characteristic	National		Seoul city	
	CDA	HBA	SIDA	SCDA
Target population	Children at risk	Welfare recipients	Working poor	Children of working poor
Goal	Self-reliance in adulthood	Welfare exit	Self-reliance	Human capital enhancement
Matching rate	1:1	1:1	1:1	1:1
Matching cap	30,000			
Matching obligation (KRW/month)		50,000 or 100,000	50,000, 100,000, or 200,000	30,000, 50,000, 70,000, or 100,000
Financial education	Required	Offered	Required	Required
Years of saving	18	3	3	5 or 7
Saving purposes	Housing, education, small business, marriage, medical cost	Welfare exit	Housing, education, small business	Child's education
Additional incentives	High interest rate to the account	Work incentive	High interest rate to the account	High interest rate to the account

Notes
CDA = Child Development Accounts; HBA = Hope Building Accounts; SIDA = Seoul Individual Development Accounts; SCDA = Seoul Child Development Accounts.

participants may receive up to KRW 30,000 in matches per month. Savings above this cap are not eligible for matching, but CDAs with less than KRW 50,000 in participant savings earn interest at a special high rate. Youth can save until they reach age 24, but savings deposited after the age of 17 are not eligible for matching (Korean National Consortium of Social Welfare 2012).

Second, although children can save voluntarily in their CDAs, sponsorship helps disadvantaged children accumulate savings. Two types of sponsorship are offered: designated and general. A designated sponsorship provides funds that go directly into the sponsored children's CDAs. In general sponsorship, the Community Chest of Korea raises funds and distributes donations to children, who voluntarily save some portion of the gift. The government incorporated the sponsorship component to lower the public's financial burden and invite contributions from the private sector.

Third, the project developed a financial education programme with curricula appropriate for children's education levels: one for elementary school-aged children and another for youth in middle and high schools. The programme is designed to increase knowledge and understanding of CDAs, proper management of pocket money, saving habits, and long-term goal setting.

Fourth, the successful launch of CDAs is due in part to collaboration among stakeholders. The MHW led the project's implementation in close partnership with sponsors, the Korean National Consortium of Social Welfare, local governments, and Shinhan Bank (Han 2013).

Despite the expansion of CDAs, the project's scope remains small. The government planned to eventually cover about half of all children in Korea (Nam and Han 2010), but present budgetary constraints force it to maintain selective coverage and prevent a large expansion. Another issue related to policy implementation is the coverage of the financial education programme in CDAs. It began with 600 children in 2008 and had been offered to only 6000 children as of 2012 (Korean National Consortium of Social Welfare 2012). Most children have no access to a financial education programme, which should be provided to all participating children as they accumulate savings in CDAs.

Hope Building Accounts

To help the working poor exit welfare, Korea offers an Earned Income Tax Credit, tax relief, workfare, employment-related services, and other supports. As the number of working poor increased from 1.9 million in 2008 to 2.1 million in 2009 (Choi *et al.* 2011), some proposed ABPs. Assuming that ABPs mobilize the working poor to save, the proposal seeks to maximize the chances that, with seed money and additional work effort, they will leave welfare. Thus, the government implemented Hope Building Accounts (HBAs) in 2010 to encourage self-reliance among the working poor.

These accounts target welfare recipients whose family income is 60 per cent of the poverty line or higher. The initiative presumes that these recipients are highly likely to exit welfare if they continue to work and receive financial incentives. About 15,000 participants opened HBAs in 2010 and 5000 in 2011. Approximately 3000 participants are estimated to have opened accounts in 2012. Participants choose one of two monthly savings amounts – KRW 50,000 or KRW 100,000 – and agree to save that fixed amount each month for three years. Participants' savings are matched at a 1:1 rate, and participants are offered an incentive to encourage them to keep working. The incentive formula is as follows: work incentive = [total household income − (poverty line × 0.6)] × 1.05. The poverty line depends on household size: KRW .55 million for a one-member household, KRW .94 million for a two-member household, KRW 1.22 million for a three-member household, KRW 1.49 million for a four-member household, KRW 1.77 million for a five-member household, and KRW 2.04 million for a six-member household. For example, a worker with monthly income of KRW 1.10 million who lives in a four-member household, agrees to exit welfare, and saves for three years in a HBA can receive a monthly work incentive of KRW 250,000, or KRW 19.93 million over three years. Although the matching funds come from the Community Chest in Korea and the private sector, the government provides the work incentives (Choi, Han, and Choi 2011).

In addition, the HBA project provides financial education and counselling programmes. The education programmes are designed to teach financial literacy, retirement planning, and retirement pension planning. The project offers each educational component two to four times annually. To help the poor achieve self-reliance, the project provides various supportive services to participants. For instance, participants may receive priority in applying for public housing, housing vouchers, job training, and microcredit (Choi, Han, and Choi 2011).

An evaluation study of HBAs is underway. Commissioned by the MHW and conducted by the Korea Institute of Health and Social Affairs, the evaluation has collected panel data from 3168 households, about 28.8 per cent of the 11,014 participants who opened HBAs in 2010 (Choi *et al.* 2011). The evaluation conducted a baseline survey twice in 2010: once for the first two cohorts ($n = 1861$) and again in 2010 for four additional cohorts ($n = 1307$). It also conducted a follow-up survey every six months (six follow-ups in total). Additional follow-up surveys, scheduled for 2014 and 2015, will examine whether HBA participants remain off of welfare (Choi, Han, and Choi 2011).

Results from the baseline survey indicate that 89 per cent of the participants, who could choose to save either KRW 50,000 or KRW 100,000 every month, chose to save KRW 100,000 (Choi, Han, and Choi 2011). This suggests that most participants try to maximize the benefits from HBAs by depositing as much as they are able and receiving as many incentives as possible. However, the drop-out rate appears to be high. Monitoring data show that 14.2 per cent of programme participants dropped out during the programme's first 10 months (October 2010–August 2011). The number of drop-outs grew from 200 in October 2010 to 1573 in August 2011. Those who dropped out are not eligible for the matching incentives. Last, estimates from a simulation of project participation indicate that about 42.3 per cent of participants (4720 households) will drop out by the end of the three-year participation period (Choi, Han, and Choi 2011).

One noteworthy finding is related to the main savings goal of the HBAs. The data indicate that 1738 participants moved out of welfare within the first 10 months. The early leavers can continue saving in the HBAs, and a high percentage (86 per cent; $n=1495$) of them did so. They are given matching incentives for saving during the participation period (Choi, Han, and Choi 2011).

Seoul Individual Development Accounts and Hope Plus Accounts

Adapting lessons learned from research on Individual Development Accounts in the United States, the city of Seoul and the Seoul Welfare Foundation started the Seoul Individual Development Accounts (SIDA) demonstration project in 2007 with 100 households across the Seoul metropolitan area.[3] After the pilot demonstration, Seoul launched a citywide programme called Hope Plus Accounts. The programme recruited seven cohorts of participants, and 14,139 individuals received Hope Plus Accounts by May 2012 (Kim, Kim, and Ryu 2011). The programme is designed to help Seoul's working poor. To be eligible, one must have a residence in Seoul, household income below 150 per cent of the poverty line, been employed for at least 10 months prior to completing the programme application, a low level of debt (i.e. no more than KRW 50 million), and a good credit history. Also, individuals may not participate in other ABPs during their time in the Hope Plus Account programme (Kim, Lee, and Sherraden 2012).

The programme is designed to promote saving among employed workers strongly motivated to achieve self-reliance with seed money. Upon opening the account, programme participants set their savings goal and the amount of monthly savings for three years. By programme design, welfare recipients agree to save at one of two levels: KRW 50,000 or KRW 100,000 per month. Working-poor individuals (i.e. those with household income below 150 per cent of the poverty line) who do not receive public assistance benefits agree to save either KRW 100,000 or KRW 200,000 per month. Participants' savings are matched at a 1:1 rate, and they must use all savings in the account for the savings goal they specify when they open the account. The goals must be related to housing, education, training, or business start-up. Most (65.8 per cent) of participants save for housing, but sizable portions save for education (27.2 per cent) and small business (7.1 per cent). Participants can choose to save towards two or more goals and withdraw the deposits plus matching incentives after graduation from the programme (Kim, Kim, and Ryu 2011).

Every Hope Plus Account participant must take part in financial education classes held at least three times per year and nine times before graduation from the programme. The classes are designed to promote financial knowledge, capability in asset management, and understanding of economic consumption. In addition, the programme offers various supportive services, including individual financial consultation, self-help group meetings (both offline and online), case management, and invitations to cultural events (Kim, Lee, and Sherraden 2012). Participants who opt out of the programme or withdraw the accumulated savings before the end of the programme can receive their own deposits and interest earnings, but not savings matches (Kim *et al.* 2010).

An evaluation study (Kim, Lee, and Sherraden 2012) suggests that Hope Plus Accounts have positive effects on savings, financial behaviour (e.g. whether to educate their child about how to save and spend money, whether to make a plan about how to spend money, the extent to which they discuss income and spending with household members), and attitudes towards saving. Despite having low incomes and low economic status, as measured by material hardship and debt holding, programme participants show that they can save if offered a structured, asset-based programme that provides financial incentives and supports.

Participants report that they made efforts to save the agreed-upon monthly sum and developed various saving strategies. For instance, they report increasing their work efforts or reallocating expenditures to meet the monthly obligation. The evaluation also finds that participation increases the likelihood of planning ahead before spending money. Although some indicate that they felt economic pressure to meet the monthly commitment, most participants express a strong feeling of achievement that they can make regular savings deposits and say that they would like to continue the Hope Plus Accounts for more than three years. Thus, the programme appears to facilitate financial capability among low- and moderate-income families by encouraging efforts toward savings and financial planning.

Recently, there have been several noteworthy changes in the operation of the Hope Plus Accounts. As the early cohorts have graduated from the programme, regulation concerning the use of the savings has been changed. First, the programme has adopted two types of matching rates: a 1:1 rate for the poor and a .5:1 rate for working poor. Second, participants can withdraw their savings immediately after terminating the programme and may do so without any condition. However, the matching incentives remain tied to the savings goals and are paid only with the approval of the operation committee, which consists of seven members (two internal members in the Seoul City Foundation and five external members). Third, the programme now emphasizes the role of case management. For example, participants who want to withdraw matching incentives must submit official forms and documents through case management offices. Last, paying debts is included as a possible savings goal. However, the history of debts must be certified by financial institutions. It means that resolving personal debts from friends and relatives is not an allowable savings goal.

Seoul Child Development Accounts

Shortly after the start of Hope Plus Accounts, the Seoul city government began to implement the Seoul Child Development Accounts (SCDAs) programme for poor families with children.[4] A household with income below 150 per cent of the poverty line in which no member has a CDA from the MHW is eligible to open one account for one child aged 12 or older. As of May 2012, 14,066 households held an SCDA. Participants agree to save a fixed amount (KRW 30,000, 50,000, or 70,000) every month for five or seven years. Households with three or more children can agree to save KRW 100,000 for five years. These monthly deposits are matched at a 1:1 rate with funds from the city government and the Community Chest. Therefore, if a household with three children opens one SCDA for the oldest child and saves KRW 100,000 every month for five years, the child can receive KRW 12 million plus interest upon completion of the saving programme.

Savings may be used only for children's educational expenses. In addition, the programme provides financial education (annually), personalized financial consultation, and other support activities (e.g. art and cultural experiences for children, education for parents on involvement in their child's education). Those support activities are provided to parents and children together. Children's participation in the financial education programme is mandatory to receive matching incentives. These offerings are designed to increase parents' interest in and knowledge about their child's education (Kim, Kim, and Ryu 2011). No evaluation study has been developed to examine savings outcomes and behaviours of participants in the SCDAs.

Other local saving programmes

The popularity of saving programmes has prompted other local governments to launch several ABPs, and additional ABPs are supported by large corporations (Kim, Kim, and Ryu 2011) (Table 4.2). All of these efforts follow the Individual Development Account model. Some features are noteworthy. First, the scale of ABPs is small. Most are sized as demonstrations, and the largest includes 500 households. Limited funding may prevent local governments from developing large-scale ABPs. Second, local ABPs may face sustainability challenges, since many local governments in Korea depend financially on the central government. Third, local governments can develop ABPs that target more specifically than do the programmes mentioned above. For example, the Sungdonggu district in Seoul developed a programme that targets district children who drop out of school. Last, large corporations have implemented saving programmes. For instance, LG Telecommunication Company (LG U+) has raised funds to support asset accumulation by children with disabilities. This suggests that the idea of asset building can be expanded by partnering with private corporations.

Challenges

In a strict sense, ABPs in Korea do not meet the criteria for inclusive ABPs. This section briefly explains the challenges that existing ABPs face, and we provide some suggestions to enhance the inclusiveness of those policies.

Table 4.2 Other asset-based policies in Korea

Location	Target population	Size (household)	Matching rate	Funding
Kyunggi Province	Working poor; families with children	500	1:1	Public and private funding
Incheon city		500	1:1	
Chumbook Province		500	1:1	
Pusan city		250	1:1	
Changwon city	Working poor; single-parent families	50	1:1	City government funding
Pyungtak city	Working poor	100	1:1	City government, and city welfare foundation
Namyangjoo city	Working poor with children	70	1:1	Private funding
Sungdonggu district in Seoul	Poor families with children leaving school	10	2:1	Community bank and foundation
LG U+	Children with disability	100	4:1	Corporate funding

Source: Kim, Kim, and Ryu (2011, 66).

Universality

Existing ABPs in Korea have critical limitations, and policies fall short of universality. Because of high costs for matching grants, operations, and case management, ABPs are expensive. However, gradual progress has been made in expanding the coverage of ABPs, and two examples illustrate this progress. First, the original CDAs were open only to children in poor families. Few individuals were covered, but the accounts for poor children could lead to further expansion of ABPs. Second, Hope Plus Accounts in Seoul have increased coverage by broadening the income eligibility threshold to 170 per cent of the poverty line. In addition, the programme reduced the length of the required work period before applying for an account from 10 months to six months. Hope Plus Accounts also have opened the door to the poor working for a shorter duration than 10 months if they submit documentation of their work history.

Progressiveness

Income level and other requirements indicate that ABPs target disadvantaged populations and are progressive. For example, eligibility features target services toward people with disabilities, single-parent families, and at-risk children. However, a critical issue is that the poorest are relatively excluded. For example, only 18.2 per cent of the participants in Hope Plus Accounts and SCDAs are welfare recipients. Working-poor individuals with income between 100 per cent and 120 per cent of the poverty line comprise 36 per cent of ABP participants, and those with an income level between 121 per cent and 150 per cent of the poverty line comprise 45.8 per cent of participants (Kim, Kim, and Ryu 2011). These features suggest that strict work requirements may hamper participation among the poorest. Although strict eligibility rules may increase the success (matched withdrawal) rate and decrease the drop-out rate, they exclude a disadvantaged income group from the institutional opportunities to save. Recently, the programme revised Hope Plus Accounts so that two matching rates are available: a 1:1 rate for welfare recipients and a .5:1 rate for those with household income between 101 per cent and 150 per cent of the poverty line. This change may increase progressiveness within the programme. However, the change decreases the matching rate for the higher income group, which may threaten the adequacy of the savings for future investment.

Lifelong process

Asset accumulation is a lifelong process. Policies to help the disadvantaged accumulate assets may enable them to break through the obstacles that prevent them from saving. Experience of saving through an ABP may encourage them to develop good saving habits and teach them how to save (i.e. how to budget, how to track the balance in the account) after graduating from the saving programme.

However, it would be challenging to institutionalize lifelong asset building in Korea. Singapore's ABPs provide good examples of how savings policies can be interlinked institutionally to increase transferability of assets. For example, savings left over in CDAs can be transferred into a Post-Secondary Education Account, and funds left over in the account after graduation can be transferred to the individual's Central Provident Fund account. All residents in Singapore have such an account and are required to save a portion of earnings for retirement and other expenses (Han and Chia 2012). In Korea, ABPs could facilitate lifelong saving if they were altered to allow individuals to transfer unused savings into individual retirement or national pension accounts. For example, about 25 per cent of graduates from the Seoul Hope Plus Account programme could not withdraw matching incentives because they could not identify a future investment approved by the operation committee (personal communications with staff of the Seoul Welfare Foundation). It would be ideal to allow individuals to transfer the unused matching incentives into the National Pension and/or individual retirement accounts. This change can facilitate the lifelong asset accumulation.

Adequacy

Adequacy of savings in ABPs depends on the duration of saving and on the purposes for which individual participants save. For example, by saving for three years in a Hope Plus Account, one may amass adequate funds to cover a job-training expenditure but not enough for a housing purchase or a small business. It is true that small amounts of seed money in saving programmes can achieve social and economic development. However, it will take time to evaluate whether the existing saving programmes can achieve adequacy in the long run. To address the adequacy problem, it is necessary to link graduates of ABPs to other existing policies such as public housing and microcredit programmes. However, longitudinal data are needed to examine adequacy over the long run.

Future directions

In the last decade, we have seen the expansion of ABPs in Korea: CDAs for disadvantaged children and Individual Development Accounts for low-income families. Central and local governments have implemented policies. We expect that expansion will continue in the future. However, the preceding discussion identifies many challenges to expansion, and ABPs in Korea have a long way to go before they are actually inclusive. This section suggests a path forward.

The coexistence of centralized and decentralized ABPs is a distinguishing feature of ABPs in Korea. Although CDAs and Hope Building Accounts are examples of centralized ABPs, the other ABPs are decentralized (i.e. local governments have more responsibility for budgets, recruitment of participants, and implementation of the programme than does the central government). Decentralized ABPs can meet local needs and develop new asset-building initiatives for local residents, but local efforts may face difficulties. Seoul's

Hope Plus Accounts are an example of the decentralized process of ABPs. Recently, the Seoul city government tried to transfer the unit governing Hope Plus Accounts to local county-level control. Although the city provides 50 per cent of the budget for the accounts, local counties may have difficulty raising the remaining funds. The funding issue is one of several critical challenges confronting locally initiated ABPs in Korea, and budget shortages may threaten their sustainability.

Furthermore, inequality is a problem in a decentralized policy environment. Centralized ABPs cover a large population of eligible individuals. Although decentralized ABPs offer some people the opportunity to accumulate assets, annual budget struggles leave many local governments no capacity to implement ABPs. Without the central government's budgetary support, decentralized ABPs may lead to inequality in asset building because opportunities offered in some locales will be absent in others.

In examining Korean ABPs, we have come to believe that case management is a key factor in efforts to maintain participation and support participants' efforts to save. Most ABPs employ case managers who provide services through local welfare centres and community centres. The managers are responsible for keeping participants' account records, encouraging savings, leading financial education sessions, counselling, and co-ordinating with other agencies. Thus, relationships between programme participants and case managers may determine saving performance. Despite the importance of case management, there is no empirical evidence on the performance of case managers. We also believe that policymakers should provide case managers with regular on-the-job training on how to manage counselling, consultation, and referral to other social services.

We conclude by calling for additional research to examine the operation and performance of ABPs in Korea. The Seoul Welfare Foundation has conducted quantitative and qualitative studies to evaluate Hope Plus Accounts. The Korea Institute of Health and Social Affairs has initiated a longitudinal evaluation to examine the effectiveness of HBAs. Although these evaluations are not free from design limitations (e.g. the absence of a comparison group), the efforts are commendable. Research findings can provide strong evidence to support further expansion of ABPs in other local areas. The ongoing processes of policy implementation and evaluation are expected to contribute to truly inclusive ABPs in Korea.

Notes

1 The Korean won (KRW) is a unit of currency in Korea. One US dollar (USD) is roughly equivalent to KRW 1114.
2 The project was originally named Didim Seed Savings Accounts. In this chapter we use the project's primary offerings, CDAs, to refer to the project as a whole.
3 Information on the Seoul Individual Development Account (Hope Plus Account) programme comes mainly from Kim, Lee, and Sherraden (2012).
4 Information on SCDAs is retrieved from Seoul Welfare Foundation (2012).

References

Choi, Hyunsoo, Chang-Keun Han, and Junyoung Choi. 2011. 탈 수급 촉진을 위한 희망 키움통장 참여가구 모니터링 및 평가연구 – 2차 [Monitoring and evaluation study on Hope Building Account for welfare exit – second study]. Research Report 2011-107. Seoul: Korea Institute of Health and Social Affairs.

Choi, Hyunsoo, Chang-Keun Han, Junyoung Choi, and Kyunghee Park. 2011. 탈 수급 촉진을 위한 희망키움통장 참여가구 모니터링 및 평가연구 - 2차 (2011) 탈 수급 촉진을 위한 희망키움통장 참여가구 모니터링 및 평가연구 – 1차 [Monitoring and evaluation study on Hope Building Account for welfare exit – first study]. Research Report. Seoul: Korea Institute of Health and Social Affairs.

Chowa, Gina, David Ansong, and Rainier Masa. 2010. 'Assets and Child Well-Being in Developing Countries: A Research Review.' *Children and Youth Services Review* 32 (11): 1508–1519. doi:10.1016/j.childyouth.2010.03.015.

Clancy, Margaret, Chang-Keun Han, Lisa R. Mason, and Michael Sherraden. 2006. *Inclusion in College Savings Plans: Participation and Saving in Maine's Matching Grant Program*. CSD Research Report 06-03. St. Louis: Washington University, Center for Social Development. http://csd.wustl.edu/Publications/Documents/RP06-03.pdf.

Han, Chang-Keun. 2013. 'A Comparative Study of Asset-Based Policy in Asia: Korea, Singapore, and Taiwan.' *Journal of Comparative Policy Analysis* 15 (1): 54–67. doi:10.1080/13876988.2013.741437.

Han, Chang-Keun, and Agnes Chia. 2012. 'A Preliminary Study on Parents Saving in the Child Development Account in Singapore.' *Children and Youth Services Review* 34 (9): 1583–1589. doi:10.1016/j.childyouth.2012.04.011.

Han, Chang-Keun, and Song-Iee Hong. 2011. 'Assets and Life Satisfaction Patterns among Koran Older Adults: Latent Class Analysis.' *Social Indicators Research* 100 (2): 225–240. doi:10.1007/s11205-010-9613-8.

Kim, Kyo-Seong, and Yun Min Kim. 2013. 'Asset Poverty in Korea: Levels and Composition Based on Wolff's Definition.' *International Journal of Social Welfare* 22 (2): 175–185. doi:10.1111/j.1468-2397.2011.00869.x.

Kim, Jin, Hoesung Kim, and Taeim Ryu. 2011. 희망플러스 꿈나래통장사업 민간지원 연계방안 연구 [Research on public and private collaboration of asset-based policies]. Research Report 9. Seoul: Seoul Welfare Foundation.

Kim, Youngmi, Soonsung Lee, and Michael Sherraden. 2012. *Seoul Hope Plus Savings Accounts: Asset-Building Program for Low-Income Households in Seoul (Third-Year Collaborative Research Report)*. CSD Research Report 12-32. St. Louis, MO: Washington University, Center for Social Development. http://csd.wustl.edu/Publications/Documents/RP12-32.pdf.

Kim, Mihyun, Yunju Nam, Youngmi Kim, Jisung Kwon, Sunwook Chung, Hyunmira Hong, and Eunlye Lee. 2010. *Seoul Hope Plus Savings Accounts: Asset-Building Program for Low-Income Households in Seoul*. CSD Research Report 10-20. St. Louis, MO: Washington University, Center for Social Development. http://csd.wustl.edu/Publications/Documents/RP10-20.pdf.

Kim, Youngmi, and Michael Sherraden. 2011. 'Do Parental Assets Matter for Children's Educational Attainment? Evidence from Mediation Tests.' *Children and Youth Services Review* 33 (6): 969–979. doi:10.1016/j.childyouth.2011.01.003.

Kookmin Bank Research Center. 2012. 한국부자의 소비지출과 노후준비 [Report on expenditures and retirement planning of the Korean rich]. http://media.daum.net/economic/others/newsview?newsid=20120819070205378.

Korean National Consortium of Social Welfare. 2012. 디딤씨앗통장 [Child Development Accounts]. Accessed 5 February 2013. www.adongcda.or.kr.

Lerman, Robert I., and Singe-Mary McKernan. 2008. 'Benefits and Consequences of Holding Assets.' In *Asset Building and Low-Income Families*, edited by Signe-Mary McKernan and Michael Sherraden, 175–206. Washington, DC: Urban Institute.

Ministry of Health and Welfare and Korea Institute of Health and Social Affairs. 2010. 국민기초생활보장제도 10년사 [10 years of the National Guarantee of Minimum Living Act]. Seoul: MHW.

Nam, Yunju, and Chang-Keun Han. 2010. 'A New Approach to Promote Economic Independence among At-Risk Children: Child Development Accounts (CDAs) in Korea.' *Children and Youth Services Review* 32 (11): 1548–1554. doi:10.1016/j.childyouth.2010.04.009.

Rank, Mark R. 2008. 'Asset Building across the Life Course.' In *Asset Building and Low-Income Families*, edited by Signe-Mary McKernan and Michael Sherraden, 67–87. Washington, DC: Urban Institute.

Rothwell, David W., and Chang-Keun Han. 2010. 'Exploring the Relationship between Assets and Family Stress among Low-Income Families.' *Family Relations* 59 (4): 396–407. doi:10.1111/j.1741-3729.2010.00611.x.

Schreiner, Mark, and Michael Sherraden. 2007. *Can the Poor Save? Saving and Asset Building in Individual Development Accounts*. New Brunswick, NJ: Transaction.

Seoul Welfare Foundation. 2012. 희망플러스통장과 꿈나래통장 [Hope Plus Accounts and Seoul Child Development Accounts]. Seoul: Seoul Welfare Foundation. www.welfare.seoul.kr/business/dream/index.jsp?layout=hope.

Sherraden, Michael. 1991. *Assets and the Poor: A New American Welfare Policy*. Armonk, NY: M.E. Sharpe.

Statistics Korea. 2011. 저소득층 부채가 소득의 9배 [Household debt in Korea]. http://media.daum.net/economic/finance/newsview?newsid=20111118190206697.

Williams Shanks, Trina R., Youngmi Kim, Vernon Loke, and Mesmin Destin. 2010. 'Assets and Child Well-Being in Developed Countries.' *Children and Youth Services Review* 32 (11): 1488–1496. doi:10.1016/j.childyouth.2010.03.011.

Wolff, Edward N. 2001. 'Recent Trends in Wealth Ownership, from 1983 to 1998.' In *Assets for the Poor: The Benefits of Spreading Asset Ownership*, edited by Thomas M. Shapiro and Edward N. Wolff, 40–57. New York: Russell Sage.

5 A comparative study on asset-building policy diffusion in Korea and Taiwan

Li Zou, Li-Chen Cheng, Eunlye Lee, Ciwang Teyra, Chun-yi Chen, and Sung Suk Song

Progressive asset-based social policies focus on investing in low-income people through programmes that promote asset accumulation for long-term development. These programmes are generating national policy discussions in many parts of the world. The idea behind the policies is straightforward: it is fundamental and necessary for those with limited income to accumulate assets that can be used for long-term development and economic stability (Sherraden 1991). Research from the large, multi-site American Dream Demonstration (ADD) project shows that even the poorest low-income individuals and households can save towards asset accumulation over time (Sherraden, Schreiner, and Beverly 2003; Sherraden and Zou 2005). Owning assets, even a savings account, can have profound and lasting positive impacts on low-income individuals and families (Bynner and Paxton 2001; Sherraden 1991). According to Sherraden (1991), asset ownership can create economic stability for individuals, establish an optimistic outlook, increase human capital, and improve intergenerational well-being. He suggests that assets can influence the way people think and behave in response to their environments.

A substantial body of applied and basic research focuses on asset building, but how are asset-building innovations adopted in a new country or state? Summarizing the broad literature on policy diffusion, Graham, Shipan, and Volden (2012) use the term to describe the transfer of social policies from one government to another. A government adopts a new programme or a policy because of such internal determinants as social, economic, and political conditions, particularly dissatisfaction with extant policies (Berry and Berry 1990; Dolowitz and Marsh 1996). Policymakers appropriate successful programmes and policies from other places (Braun and Gilardi 2006; Grossback, Nicholson-Crotty, and Peterson 2004; Rose 1993). In fact, policy successes (Volden 2006; Walker 1969), geographic proximity (Berry and Baybeck 2005), and ideological orientation (Grossback, Nicholson-Crotty, and Peterson 2004) can facilitate the policy diffusion process.

Regional economic competition can also influence the policy diffusion process (Bailey and Rom 2004; Shipan and Volden 2008). Simmons and Elkins (2004, 172) suggest that adoptions of foreign policy 'alter the benefits of adoption for others and ... these adoptions provide information about the costs or benefits of a particular policy innovation'. Reputation is a factor in perception of the benefits of adopting a policy, because failed policy can exact a high political cost. Moreover, politicians could build their 'status, credibility, or "modernity"' by emulating trendy policies (Meseguer 2005, 79). Shipan and Volden (2008, 840) analyse the influence of four mechanisms in the process of policy diffusion: 'learning', in which policymakers study other governments' policy adoptions and the impact of these policies; 'economic competition', in which governments weigh economic effects of adopting or not adopting a policy; 'imitation' in which other governments' actions are copied; and 'coercion', in which governments are encouraged or pressured to take expected actions.

This chapter presents a comparative study on asset-building policy diffusion in Korea and Taiwan. We start by evaluating the global landscape in asset-based social policy. We follow this with documentation of the policy diffusion process in Korea and Taiwan, and then we employ the four mechanisms as a framework for analysing policy diffusion in these contexts. We conclude with a discussion of the implications of policy diffusion for Asia and the rest of the world.

The global landscape of asset-based social policy

When Sherraden (1991) first proposed the concept of asset building, he envisioned national social policies that would support low-income individuals and families in their efforts to accumulate resources for investment in such major life assets as post-secondary education, home ownership, and small entrepreneurial business.

Although there is no national asset-building policy in the United States, the Assets for Independence Act of 1998 (AFI) (Pub. L. No. 105-285, 112 Stat. 2759) created a federal programme that 'enable[s] community-based non-profits and state, local, and tribal government agencies to implement and demonstrate an asset-based approach for offering low-income families help out of poverty' (US Department of Health and Human Services 2012). Over the past decade, a number of federal legislative proposals have sought to promote asset-based national policy in the United States. Each has a different focus and maintains a different link to existing social policies and programmes (King 2009).

Many state governments sponsor 529 college-savings plans. These are tax-advantaged investment tools designed to help families save for children's future higher education. For example, Oklahoma sponsors a seven-year initiative called SEED for Oklahoma Kids (SEED OK). The effort seeks 'to determine the economic and educational impact of "seeding" a college savings account for children at birth' (Oklahoma State Treasurer's Office 2008, 1).

In 2001, the Canadian government launched a nationwide demonstration project called Learn$ave to promote saving for education and training. The initiative targeted low-income people between ages 21 and 65, offering them a special savings account with a 3:1 match rate (Social and Enterprise Development Innovations 2013; Social Research and Demonstration Corporation 2010). In addition to Learn$ave, the Canadian government has initiated the nationwide Registered Education Savings Plan to help families save towards children's post-secondary education. Through the Canada Learning Bond, the government provides an initial CAD 500 deposit into savings plans opened on behalf of children in low-income families and a CAD 100 deposit for each subsequent year (Human Resources and Skills Development Canada 2009).

In Asia, Singapore has the world's most comprehensive series of asset-based social policies and programmes. These efforts support every Singaporean citizen from cradle to grave (Central Provident Fund Board n.d.; Loke and Sherraden 2009). The government offers the Baby Bonus scheme for children of age six and younger (Singapore Ministry of Community Development, Youth and Sports 2013). School-goers between ages seven and 20 are eligible for Post-Secondary Education Accounts and the Edusave scheme (Singapore Ministry of Education 2012a). If a balance remains in the Post-Secondary Education Account when the account holder reaches age 30, it can be transferred to the individual's Central Provident Fund (Singapore Ministry of Education 2012b).

There are a handful of asset-based policies and programmes in other parts of the world. The United Kingdom implemented two national asset-based efforts; the Child Trust Fund targeted British children born after September 2002, and the Savings Gateway targets low-income workers (Child Trust Fund 2013). Unfortunately, the Cameron government suspended both programmes due to the budget shortage in mid 2010, according to a *BBC News* article on 24 May 2010. With support from the Australia and New Zealand Banking Group and the Brotherhood of St. Laurence, Australia launched Saver Plus in 2003 to help low-income people develop savings habits (Australia and New Zealand Banking Group Limited 2013). In addition to these established programmes, pilot studies can be found in many Asian countries (Guo *et al.* 2008 'Dual Incentives'; Guo *et al.* 2008 'Asset Based Social Policy'; Hong Kong Polytechnic University 2012; Sherraden and Zou 2010; Zou *et al.* 2011; Zou and Sherraden 2009). Although there are no national, asset-based social policies in Africa, pilots for various efforts to help children and youth accumulate assets through savings can be found in Uganda, Ghana, and Kenya (Center for Social Development 2011; Chowa *et al.* 2012; Ssewamala, Han, and Neilands 2009).

Asset-based policy in Korea and Taiwan

Additional examples of asset-based social policy can be found in Korea and Taiwan. We examine these cases in detail below, and they provide the focus for our current analysis. Demonstrating a growing interest in asset-based social policies, both nations initiated several innovative efforts to enable individuals and families to accumulate assets. This section documents the process by which the policy spread from one city, county, or state to another (Dolowitz and Marsh 2000; Gray 1973).

Korea

In Korea, the first public discussion of the concept of asset building occurred at the 56th Korean Meeting on National Policy Tasks in late 2004, and the idea spread rapidly through all levels of the Korean government. Findings from the research on Individual Development Accounts in the United States contributed to these discussions. In April 2007, the government of South Korea launched Child Development Accounts (CDAs) nationwide as a part of broad efforts to reduce the increasingly large gap between rich and poor and to boost the nation's falling birth rate. Simin Rhyu, then minister of the Korean Ministry for Health and Welfare, believes that the government could use CDAs to deliver financial education to underprivileged children and to provide a means by which these children can accumulate assets for pursuit of life goals (Nam and Han 2010; Kim *et al.* 2011). He spearheaded the policy implementation. Initially, these CDAs focused on children under age 18 who were in the Korean child welfare system (e.g. children in orphanages, group homes, foster care). The Korean government expanded the programme in 2011 to provide accounts for children born only in 2000 and also for children in low-income families that receive welfare benefits. With this expansion, the programme's enrolment increased by 10,030 children (Korean Social Welfare Association 2012) (Table 5.1).

Each child in Korea's CDA programme has two accounts: a savings account into which the child and his or her sponsor (i.e. the primary caregiver) make deposits, and a fund account into which the government deposits matching funds at a 1:1 rate. The government matches up to USD 30 (approximately KRW 1000) in deposits each month, but encourages additional deposits beyond that amount. Children are not allowed to withdraw from the CDA until age 18. The savings can be used only for education, housing, small business start-up, medical costs, and wedding expenses (Nam and Han 2010).

The Seoul Metropolitan Government followed the national government's example in December 2007, launching an asset-development pilot programme that targeted the working poor (Kim, Lee, and Sherraden 2012). Seoul recruited 100 participants who were 18 years or older and whose income was below 150 per cent of the official Korean poverty line. The government provides particip-ants with savings matches at a rate of 1:1.5; it pays the matching funds if the youth completes the programme within a defined time frame. Participants can receive matches for up to USD 200 (KRW 200,000) in savings per month. They can access their own savings at any time but are eligible to receive the matching funds only to spend on housing, higher education, and business start-up.

In October 2008, Seoul unveiled a comprehensive asset-based plan called the Seoul Hope Dream Project. The project's goal is to alleviate poverty and

Table 5.1 Enrolment in Korean Child Development Accounts as of 2012

	Orphaned	Foster care	Child-headed household	Group home	Disabled	Reunified	Under welfare benefits	Total
Enrolled accounts	18,236	15,723	1243	2133	2918	2217	10,030	52,500

Source: data from Korean Social Welfare Association (2012).

integrate people of all backgrounds into the society (Seoul Metropolitan Government 2008). This plan includes five distinctive programmes: Seoul Hope Plus Accounts, Seoul Hope Dream Bank, Financial Education Services, Expansion of Social Employment and Promotion of Social Enterprise, and Kumnarae Accounts. Out of the five asset-based programmes, two (Seoul Hope Plus Accounts and Kumnarae Accounts) promote asset building through savings.

The Seoul Hope Plus Accounts target working-poor households in the Seoul metropolitan area, encouraging saving for higher education, the start of a small business, and housing. After participants meet the three-year participation requirement, the Seoul Metropolitan Government and other private-sector actors, such as corporations, match their savings at a rate of 1:1. As of November 2011, approximately 15,000 participants have been enrolled in the Seoul Hope Plus Accounts (Kim, Lee, and Sherraden 2012).

The second of the two savings options, the Kumnarae accounts, initially targeted children from low-income families under the age of six. Launched in 2009, the accounts encourage families to save for their children's future education. In 2011, Seoul expanded the programme to include children younger than age 12 (Kim, Lee, and Sherraden 2012).

Following the Seoul Metropolitan Government, four other cities – Daegu, Changwon, Pyeungtaek, and Namyangjoo – launched their own asset-based policies and programmes. In March 2009, the City of Daegu implemented two savings programmes to help low-income households save towards specific goals. A three-year programme focuses on saving for housing and small business start-up; a five-year programme focuses on saving towards children's education. Both savings programmes incentivize participants by providing matched funds at the rate of 1:1 (Lee 2010).

In 2009, the city of Changwon initiated a two-year programme designed to enable the working poor to achieve economic independence and self-reliance though matched savings. Participants can save up to KRW 100,000 (USD 100) every month, and savings are eligible for a 1:1 match (Lee 2010).

In August 2009, the city of Pyeungtaek launched a three-year Individual Development Account programme to encourage saving among the city's working poor (Lee 2010). Participants could receive a 1:1 match for up to KRW 200,000 (USD 200) in savings every month. They may use the matched savings to purchase a home, start a small business, and pursue higher education.

The city of Namyangjoo implemented its own Individual Development Account programme in February 2009. The programme is very similar to the two matched-savings programmes implemented in Daegu. One three-year programme focuses on building savings for the purchase of housing or the launch of a small business. It allows participants to receive 1:1 matches for up to KRW 200,000 (USD 200) in savings every month. A six-year programme focuses on accumulating savings for education and allows participants to receive 1:1 matches for up to KRW 100,000 (USD 100) in savings every month. Both programmes offer financial education and some supportive activities to participants (Lee 2010).

In addition, the Korean Ministry for Health and Welfare has offered two asset-building pilot programmes since September 2009: Haengbok Kium Accounts and Hope Kium Accounts. The governments of Incheon, Gyeungki, Jeonbuk, and Pusan recruited residents to participate. Haengbok Kium Accounts target working-poor individuals who are between the ages of 18 and 34 or who have children under 18. During the three-year enrolment period, participants can save for long-term developmental purposes, including housing, higher education, and business start-up. The programme provides matches at a 1:1 rate to encourage participants to save up to KRW 100,000 (USD 100) per month. Launched in 2010, Hope Kium Accounts target welfare recipients who have incomes between 60 per cent and 100 per cent of the official Korean poverty line. The accounts are designed to enable participants to leave welfare through savings (Nam and Han 2010). Participants can commit to saving either KRW 50,000 (USD 50) or KRW 100,000 (USD 100) every month for three consecutive years. If they leave the welfare system when the programme ends, the ministry matches their savings at a 1:1 rate. Participants may use the combination of savings and matching funds to pay basic living expenses, purchase or rent a home, pursue higher education, obtain job training, or start a business (Nam and Han 2010).

Finally, the Do-Dream U Plus Accounts represent a significant departure from the governmental programmes and policies detailed above because funding for the savings matches come from corporate donors. The accounts target disabled youth who are in school between the sixth and ninth grades and who come from low-income families (below 150 per cent of the poverty line). In order to receive a savings match, participants must commit to saving between USD 20 (KRW 20,000) and USD 25 (KRW 25,000) each month for at least two years (they may choose to participate for up to five years). The corporate donors match savings at a 4:1 rate, and the matched funds may be used for college tuition or for job training after high school graduation. As of 2012, 100 youth have enrolled in the programme. This programme represents an interesting development in the process of policy diffusion: the concept of asset building spread beyond government policy and has been appropriated by corporations as part of their corporate social responsibility efforts (Korean Society for Rehabilitation of Persons with Disabilities 2012).

Taiwan

The Taipei City Government pioneered asset-based policy in Taiwan. In 2000, the city launched the three-year Taipei Family Development Accounts project to assist low-income working households in accumulating assets. The launch of the accounts marked the first anti-poverty initiative that incentivizes low-income families to save and accumulate assets as a way to achieve economic self-sufficiency in Taiwan (Cheng 2003). The initiative was also Taiwan's first publicly run anti-poverty programme funded by a private institution. Participants voluntarily joined the programme to save. Upon opening a matched-savings account, they could make the first deposit at a set amount ranging from TWD

2000 to TWD 4000 (USD 1 = TWD 33) and agreed to continue saving for three consecutive years. The firm matches the deposit at a 1:1 rate (Cheng 2003). The programme requires all participants to attend classes that impart fundamental financial knowledge. Participants could not access the savings until the completion of the three-year period. The funds could be used for higher education, small business start-up, or first home purchase.

Pleased with the positive outcomes of the Taipei Family Development Accounts, the Taipei City Government used the accounts as a prototype, subsequently launching several asset-based programmes for poor children and youth. The first of these, the Self-Development Accounts Program, was a three-year programme that started in July 2003. It focused on supporting 100 youth from low-income families by encouraging them to accumulate assets for higher education and preparing them for a future career. Participating youth were students between ages 16 and 23. The programme matched participants' savings at a 1:1 rate. It also required them to attend a minimum of 78 hours of financial education and to participate in 216 hours of service learning (Lin and Hsieh 2007).

In 2007, Taipei City Government launched the Youth Development Accounts Program, which ran through September 2010 and recruited 100 youth from low-income families. The participants were between ages 16 and 20. The programme encouraged youth to save towards higher education and training for employment. The programme matched participants' savings at a 1:1 rate. The unique part of this programme is that it offered an additional .5 match rate bonus from the government-approved private sponsor if youth obtain any job-related licence or training certificate.

In March 2008, the Taipei City Government launched the Children Hope Development Accounts for 300 youth between the ages of 13 and 17. Targeting youth from low-income households, the four-year programme seeks to improve access to education, enhance financial literacy, and create a mutual support network. The programme's design is similar to that of the Self-Development Accounts initiative. It includes matched savings, financial education, and community services.

Informed by the Taipei programmes, a number of local governments in Taiwan launched their own asset-based policies and programmes. For example, the City of Kao-hsiung, a major industrial centre in southern Taiwan, launched the Hope Project for the Second Generation in 2004. This matched-savings project sought to assist 100 low-income youth in escaping poverty and developing good saving habits. It matched savings at a 1:1 rate. The city recruited Kao-hsiung residents attending high school or pursuing higher education. Those youth used the funds to purchase homes, pay for education, and start small businesses (Fu 2008).

In 2004, the central government incorporated the concept of asset accumulation into its revision of the Social Assistance Act (Taiwan Ministry of the Interior n.d., clause 15). The act specifies the legal framework for provision of social assistance to the poor in Taiwan, and a revised clause accommodates asset-accumulation policy by raising the income level at which a household ceases to be eligible for means-tested public benefits; under the revised act, households that participated in government-sponsored asset-building programmes during a three-year programme period were eligible for public benefits if the household's income was at or below 150 per cent of Taiwan's poverty line.

Following the steps of Taipei and Kao-hsiung, the Taipei County Government started a similar two-year programme in 2005. The programme targeted low-income youth in the county and ran from 2005 through 2007. It included matched savings, financial education, and service learning components (Cheng 2007).

Yilan County, near Taipei City, established a seven-year Minority Family Development Accounts programme that uses matched savings to support middle- and low-income households in asset accumulation. Started in 2008 and running through 2015, the programme offers 120 households a generous 1:2 match rate (private donors provide a TWD 2 match for each TWD 1 saved by a participant). The programme imposes eligibility restrictions; participating households must have resided in the county for at least a year and must agree to make monthly deposits of TWD 1000. Also, a member of the household must have been employed continuously for over six months, and households are not allowed to move out of the county while participating in the programme (Yilan County Government Social Affairs Department n.d.).

Ping-Tung County, centred in a rural city south of Kao-hsiung, initiated a three-year Happy Accounts programme in July 2009. The first asset-based pro-gramme operating in rural Taiwan, it provided accounts to 45 low-income rural students and matched their savings at a 1:1 rate. The programme only admitted students enrolled in high school or college and enrolled only one participant from each household. The programme operated through June 2012 (Ping-Tung County Government 2012). Governments in Taoyuan County and Chia-Yi County also started similar matched-savings programmes. These programmes are designed to encourage asset accumulation among youth from middle- and low-income households, offering financial education and matched savings at a 1:1 rate. In addition, several other local governments in Taiwan are preparing to launch asset-accumulation programmes, and asset-building efforts extend beyond the governmental sector.

A key aspect of asset-based policy in Taiwan is the policy's diffusion across sectorial boundaries, and several non-governmental organizations (NGOs) have joined the effort. The Taiwan Fund for Children and Families, a non-profit organization, began Family Life Development Accounts in 2005 with the goal of expanding the educational and vocational opportunities of needy participants (Weng, Zou, and Wang 2007). The programme lasted for 12 months, and the non-repeating cohorts of participants represent 23 areas of Taiwan. The pro-gramme required that participants save between TWD 1000 and TWD 4000 every month. At the end of the one-year programme, the organization matched all savings at a 1:1 rate (Zou 2007). The programme also required that particip-ants join in financial education and service learning (Wang and Chiu 2007). In addition, the Taiwan Fund for Children and Families experimented with

Self-Supporting Youth Accounts in 2006. Specifically targeting low-income youth enrolled in either college or vocational school, the accounts include many features similar to those of the Family Life Development Accounts. The Self-Supporting Youth Accounts programme required participating youth to save at least TWD 3000 (but no more than TWD 12,000) every three months. Financial education and service-learning commitments are also part of the programme (Wang and Chiu 2007).

Asset-based programmes in Taiwan diffuse from north to south and from urban to rural. This pattern influenced the Social Assistance Act amendments in 2011. The amendments continue to encourage asset accumulation as a means to enable economic self-sufficiency. Clause 15 in the amended act states that all income and savings earned from anti-poverty programmes are exempt from means-test calculations during programme years. The act also allows for a one-year extension of the exemption. For example, a household's exemption from the income-means tests may be extended during the year in which the household spends accumulated savings for designated goals (Taiwan Ministry of the Interior n.d.).

Discussion

This section reviews four distinctive mechanisms that Shipan and Volden (2008) contend are determinative in the process of policy diffusion: learning, economic competition, imitation, and coercion. We consider how each applies to the diffusion of asset-building policy in Korea and Taiwan.

Learning

The learning mechanism of policy diffusion focuses on the process by which policymakers learn about a policy adopted elsewhere and assess its effects (Shipan and Volden 2008). Research reveals that larger and wealthier governmental entities are more likely to adopt a new policy (Walker 1969). In both Korea and Taiwan, policymakers initially learned about the concept of asset building through Sherraden's work in the American Dream Demonstration Project. The research demonstrates that even poor people can save limited resources over a period of time (Zou and Sherraden 2009). Policymakers from both the Korean and Taiwan governments were intrigued and motivated to learn from policies and practices that have proven effective.

Economic competition

This mechanism focuses on the consideration of economic effects in governmental decisions on whether to adopt a policy (Shipan and Volden 2008). Economic factors are evident in policy diffusion among different cities and counties in both Korea and Taiwan. In Korea, Seoul launched the 2008 Seoul Hope Dream Project, and four other cities implemented their own asset-based social policies within a year. Viewing such efforts as social policy to increase the well-being of the disadvantaged (Bailey and Rom 2004), local governments compete to adopt the asset-building policy of the capital city. This competition is motivated by fear of being left behind and desire to reap positive economic benefits from serving people. In Taiwan, the Taipei City Government successfully experimented with the Taiwan Family Development Accounts in 2000 and the Self-Development Accounts Program in 2003. The City of Kao-hsiung and Taipei County adopted the asset-building concept. In creating their own initiatives, each considered the positive economic effects of adopting a policy similar to that in Taipei City. Consistent with the theoretical hypothesis, we find that the likelihood of a city adopting the asset-building policy increases with the positive effects experienced by other cities. We see this in both Korea and Taiwan.

Imitation

This mechanism refers to efforts by one government to copy the actions of others (Shipan and Volden 2008). As two of the Four Asian Tigers, Korea and Taiwan have highly developed economies. It is no surprise that the two governments learned about policy successes in other Asian Tigers. This mechanism differs from the learning mechanism by focusing on the actor (here, the governments of Korea and Taiwan) instead of the action (i.e. adoption of the asset-building policy). Evidence of the imitation mechanism can also be found at local levels in Korea and Taiwan. In Korea, Daegu, Changwon, Pyeungtaek, and Namyangjoo adopted asset-building policies a year after Seoul launched the Seoul Hope Dream Project. In Taiwan, Kao-hsiung City, Taipei County, and Yilan County followed suit after the City of Taipei implemented a series of positive asset-building efforts.

Coercion

The coercion mechanism focuses on the encouragement and/or pressure a government receives to meet the expected goals (Shipan and Volden 2008). We find no evidence that coercion played a role in the diffusion of asset-building policy in Taiwan. In Korea, the national government encourages four local governments (Incheon, Gyeungki, Jeonbuk, and Pusan) to implement the Haengbok Kium Accounts project and to recruit participants.

Benefits of the asset-building policy diffusion

The diffusion of asset-building policy in Korea and Taiwan occurred at the level of both state and local governments. These policies and programmes provide an alternative approach to social assistance for the disadvantaged, especially assistance for the poor and the young. They give participants an opportunity to save towards predetermined goals. In the process of asset-building policy diffusion, policymakers, government officials, and policy entrepreneurs (Mintrom 2000) are key actors who initiate dynamic policy change, articulate policy innovations within a government agenda, and energize the diffusion process. They identify problems, network in the policy arena, shape policy debates, and build coalitions to support policy innovations.

In Taiwan and Korea, programmes employ similar financial incentives (matching savings at a 1:1 rate) to induce participation by target populations in the government-initiated programmes and to encourage them to save over a defined time frame. These governments identify new innovations on programmes and policies and emulate regions that are successful, culturally similar, and in close adjacency. Through these policies, they promote access to financial services for the disadvantaged, especially services for low-income families (Zou and Isern 2007).

Conclusion

Asia is fortunate to have so many innovative and dedicated governments that care about their citizens' long-term well-being and development. The 332.3 million children in Mainland China, Hong Kong, and Korea account for the lion's share of the total population of Asian children under age 15 (Population Reference Bureau 2012). It is encouraging to see that a growing number of Asian governments focus on children and youth as the main populations targeted by asset-accumulation policies. If these policies succeed in improving asset ownership among the young, the improvements could lead to positive educational and social outcomes. Once these young people grow up and engage in economic activities, they are likely to be integrated into formal financial systems and to become financially knowledgeable customers (Ledgerwood 2013; Isern, Zou, and Yang 2007; Zou and Isern 2007).

Asian countries share vital values in both economic and social developments. Scholars and policymakers are eager to encounter new policy options if the ideas are empirically proven to be effective. Even in authoritative cultures, policymakers can be actively involved in transforming ideas into policy actions if the ideas are positioned properly. Proper positioning contributes in part to the rapid diffusion of policy from one place to another. In both the Taiwan and Korea cases, policymakers, academic scholars, and programme staff have contributed to the policy diffusion. Future research could consider capturing in detail how these networks and coalitions of interested parties work jointly in policy diffusion.

Given the deep financial difficulty the world is in today, governments could take this unique opportunity to consider increasing investments in their citizens, especially those with the fewest assets: the disadvantaged and the young. Among individuals, in communities, and across nations, there is a growing appreciation of the essential role of savings. Although it is difficult to predict when the economic downturn will change direction, even small amounts of assets can enhance economic security during this stringent period.

The two cases discussed in this chapter illustrate how local and national governments adopt and implement asset-based policies and programmes.

Governments, financial institutions, community organizers, and academic scholars could align their efforts to continuously innovate and generate more asset-based policies and programmes. The pace of advancement in information technology could facilitate this alignment. Ideally, such efforts will come to cover the entire populations of these nations.

References

Australia and New Zealand Banking Group Limited. 2013. 'Saver Plus.' Accessed 13 March 2013. www.anz.com/personal/bank-accounts/help-select-account/concession-card-holders/saver-plus.

Bailey, M.A., and M.C. Rom. 2004. 'A Wider Race? Interstate Competition across Health and Welfare Programs.' *Journal of Politics* 66 (2): 326–347. doi:10.1111/j.1468-2508. 2004.00154.x.

Berry, F.S., and W.D. Berry. 1990. 'State Lottery Adoptions as Policy Innovations: An Event History Analysis.' *American Political Science Review* 84 (2): 395–415. doi:10.2307/1963526.

Berry, W.D., and B. Baybeck. 2005. 'Using Geographic Information Systems to Study Student Interstate Competition.' *American Political Science Review* 99 (4): 505–519. doi:10.1017/S0003055405051841.

Braun, D., and F. Gilardi. 2006. 'Taking "Galton's Problem" Seriously: Towards a Theory of Policy Diffusion.' *Journal of Theoretical Politics* 18 (3): 298–322. doi:10.1177/0951629806064351.

Bynner, J., and W. Paxton. 2001. *The Asset-Effect*. London: Institute for Public Policy Research.

Center for Social Development. 2011. *Broad and Deep: The Extensive Learning Agenda in YouthSave*. Research Agenda, 17 August. St. Louis, MO: Washington University, Center for Social Development. http://csd.wustl.edu/Publications/Documents/YouthSaveLearningAgenda.pdf.

Central Provident Fund Board. n.d. 'Overview.' Central Provident Fund Board. Accessed 8 February 2013. http://mycpf.cpf.gov.sg/CPF/About-Us/Intro/Intro.htm.

Cheng, L.C. 2003. 'Developing Family Development Accounts in Taipei: Policy Innovation from Income to Assets.' CSD Working Paper 03-09, Center for Social Development, Washington University, St. Louis, MO. http://csd.wustl.edu/Publications/Documents/WP03-09.pdf.

Cheng, L.C. 2007. 'Asset-Based Policy in Taiwan: Demonstrations and Policy Progress.' CSD Policy Brief 07-33, Center for Social Development, Washington University, St. Louis, MO. http://csd.wustl.edu/Publications/Documents/PB07-33.pdf.

Child Trust Fund. 2013. 'Child Trust Fund.' Accessed 13 March 2013. www.gov.uk/child-trust-funds/overview.

Chowa, G., D. Ansong, R. Masa, M. Despard, I. Osei-Akoto, A. Richmond, A. Agyei-Holmes, and M. Sherraden. 2012. *Youth and Saving in Ghana: A Baseline Report from the YouthSave Ghana Experiment*. Research Report 12-56. St. Louis, MO: Washington University, Center for Social Development. http://csd.wustl.edu/Publications/Documents/Ghana_Baseline_Report_FINAL.pdf.

Dolowitz, D.P., and D. Marsh. 1996. 'Who Learns What from Whom: A Review of the Policy Transfer Literature.' *Political Studies* 44 (2): 343–357. doi:10.1111/j.1467–9248. 1996.tb00334.x.

Dolowitz, D.P., and D. Marsh. 2000. 'Learning from Abroad: The Role of Policy Transfer in Contemporary Policy-Making.' *Governance* 13 (1): 5–24. doi:10.1111/0952-1895.00121.

Fu, T.H., ed. 2008. Chu xu fa zhan zhang hu tuo pin ce lue zhi shi shi, cheng xiao yu tiao zhan yan tao hui lun wen hui bian [Proceedings of the Forum on the Implementation, Impacts, and Challenge of Savings Development Accounts]. Taipei, Taiwan: Social Welfare Association of Taiwan.

Graham, E.R., C.R. Shipan, and C. Volden. 2012. 'The Diffusion of Policy Diffusion Research in Political Science.' *British Journal of Political Science*. doi:10.1017/S0007123412000415.

Gray, V. 1973. 'Innovation in the States: A Diffusion Study.' *American Political Science Review* 67 (4): 1174–1185. doi:10.2307/1956539.

Grossback, L.J., S. Nicholson-Crotty, and D.A.M. Peterson. 2004. 'Ideology and Learning in Policy Diffusion.' *American Politics Research* 32 (5): 521–545. doi:10.1177/1532673X04263801.

Guo, B., J. Huang, M. Sherraden, and L. Zou. 2008. 'Dual Incentives and Dual Asset Building: Policy Implications of the Hutubi Rural Social Security Loan Programme in China.' *Journal of Social Policy* 37 (3): 453–470. doi:10.1017/S0047279408001992.

Guo, B., J. Huang, L. Zou, and M. Sherraden. 2008. 'Asset-Based Policy in Rural China: An Innovation in the Retirement Social Insurance Program.' *China Journal of Social Work* 1 (1): 63–76. doi:10.1080/17525090701855976.

Hong Kong Polytechnic University. 2012. *Report of Consultancy Study on Child Development Fund Pioneer Projects*. Report, December. Hong Kong: Hong Kong Polytechnic University. www.cdf.gov.hk/english/whatsnew/files/CDF_Final_Report_Eng.pdf.

Human Resources and Skills Development Canada. 2009. 'Frequently Asked Questions: Registered Education Savings Plan.' Human Resources and Skills Development Canada, CanLearn. Accessed 14 September 2013. www.hrsdc.gc.ca/eng/learning/education_savings/public/resp.shtml.

Isern, J., L. Zou, and X. Yang. 2007. 'Highlight on China, Part 1: A View of the Landscape.' Highlights on Access to Finance in China, 7 October. Microfinance Gateway. www.microfinancegateway.org/p/site/m/template.rc/1.26.9145.

Kim, Y., Li Zou, S.J. Young, and M. Sherraden. 2011. 'Asset-Based Policy in South Korea.' Policy Brief 11-22, July, Center for Social Development. St. Louis, MO: Washington University, http://csd.wustl.edu/Publications/Documents/PB11-22.pdf.

Kim, Y., S. Lee, and M. Sherraden. 2012. *Seoul Hope Plus Savings Accounts: Asset-Building Program for Low-Income Households in Seoul*. Research Report 12-32. St. Louis, MO: Washington University, Center for Social Development. http://csd.wustl.edu/Publications/Documents/RP12-32.pdf.

King, J. 2009. *Promoting Saving and Financial Security for America's Working Families: 2009 Legislative Priorities of the Asset Building Program*. Report, January. New America Foundation. www.newamerica.net/publications/policy/promoting_saving_and_financial_security_america_s_working_families.

Korean Social Welfare Association. 2012. '아동발달계좌' [Child Development Accounts]. Korean Social Welfare Association. Accessed 27 December 2012. www.adongcda.or.kr:444/contents/sub0102.php.

Korean Society for Rehabilitation of Persons with Disabilities. 2012. '두드림 유플러스 통장' [Do-Dream U Plus Accounts]. Korean Society for Rehabilitation of Persons with Disabilities. Accessed 27 December 2013. www.freeget.net/intro/notice_view.asp?ctg=notice&seq=317.

Ledgerwood, J., ed. 2013. *The New Handbook of Microfinance: A Financial Market System Perspective*. Washington, DC: World Bank.

Lee, E. 2010. 'The Adoption and Diffusion of Asset-Building Program in South Korea: Individual Development Accounts.' Working paper, Mandel School of Applied Social Sciences, Case Western Reserve University, Cleveland, OH.

Lin, S.E., and Y.J. Hsieh. 2007. 'Tai bei shi chu ren tou di fa zhan zhang hu zhuan an de shi shi yu tiao zhan' [The Implementation and Challenge of Self-Development Accounts Program]. Paper presented at the Chu xu fa zhan zhang hu tuo pin ce lue zhi shi shi, cheng xiao yu tiao zhan yan tao hui lun wen hui bian [Seminar of Self-Development Accounts Program's Implementation, Outcome and Challenges in Tackling Poverty], Chiayi, Taiwan, November.

Loke, V., and M. Sherraden. 2009. 'Building Assets from Birth: A Global Comparison of Child Development Account Policies.' *International Journal of Social Welfare* 18 (2): 119–129. doi:10.1111/j.1468–2397.2008.00605.x.

Meseguer, C. 2005. 'Policy Learning, Policy Diffusion, and the Making of a New Order.' *Annals of the American Academy of Political and Social Science* 598 (1): 67–82. doi:10.1177/0002716204272372.

Mintrom, M. 2000. *Policy Entrepreneurs and School Choice*. Washington, DC: Georgetown University Press.

Nam, Y., and C.K. Han. 2010. 'A New Approach to Promote Economic Independence among At-Risk Children: Child Development Accounts (CDAs) in Korea.' *Children and Youth Services Review* 32 (11): 1548–1554. doi:10.1016/j.childyouth.2010.04.009.

Oklahoma State Treasurer's Office. 2008. 'More Than 1,000 Oklahoma Babies Get $1,000 for College Savings.' Press Release, 3 June. www.ok.gov/treasurer/documents/SEED%20OK%20%20PR%206-3-08.pdf.

Ping-Tung County Government. 2012. 'Yuan fu tui dong xin fu an xin zhang hu ji lian he zhu pin zi li fang an cheng guo.' [Results of the County Government's implementation of Happy Accounts Program.] Ping-Tung County Government, Taiwan. http://web.pthg.gov.tw/tw/News_detail.aspx?s=67325&n=10857&p=2.

Population Reference Bureau. 2012. 'Population Age <15.' Asia data profile from 2012 World Population Data Sheet. www.prb.org/DataFinder/Geography/Data.aspx?loc=355.

Rose, R. 1993. *Lesson-Drawing in Public Policy: A Guide to Learning across Time and Space*. Chatham, NJ: Chatham House.

Seoul Metropolitan Government. 2008. 서울 희망드림프로젝트 계획안 [A plan for Seoul, Hope Dream Project]. Seoul, Korea: Seoul Metropolitan Government.

Sherraden, Michael. 1991. *Assets and the Poor: A New American Welfare Policy*. Armonk, NY: M.E. Sharpe.

Sherraden, M., and Li Zou. 2005. 'Individual Development Accounts: Lessons from the American Dream Demonstration.' [In Chinese.] *Jiangsu Social Sciences* 219 (2): 201–205.

Sherraden, M., and Li Zou. 2010. 'Asset-Based Policy in Hong Kong: Child Development Fund.' CSD Policy Brief 10-38, October, Center for Social Development, Washington University, St. Louis, MO. http://csd.wustl.edu/Publications/Documents/PB10-38.pdf.

Sherraden, M., M. Schreiner, and S.G. Beverly. 2003. 'Income, Institutions, and Saving Performance in Individual Development Accounts.' *Economic Development Quarterly* 17 (1): 95–112. doi:10.1177/0891242402239200.

Shipan, C.R., and C. Volden. 2008. 'The Mechanisms of Policy Diffusion.' *American Journal of Political Science* 52 (4): 840–857. doi:10.1111/j.1540-5907.2008.00346.x.

Simmons, B.A., and Z. Elkins. 2004. 'The Globalization of Liberalization: Policy Diffusion in the International Political Economy.' *American Political Science Review* 98 (1): 171–189. doi:10.1017/S0003055404001078.

Singapore Ministry of Community Development, Youth and Sports. 2013. 'Children Development Co-Savings (Baby Bonus) Scheme.' Singapore Ministry of Community Development, Youth and Sports. Accessed 4 April 2013. www.babybonus.gov.sg/bbss/html/index.html.

Singapore Ministry of Education. 2012a. 'Post-Secondary Education (PSE) Scheme.' 19 September revision. Singapore Ministry of Education. Accessed 4 April 2013. www.moe.gov.sg/initiatives/post-secondary-education-account.

Singapore Ministry of Education. 2012b. 'Overview of EduSave Scheme.' 8 November revision. Singapore Ministry of Education. Accessed 4 April 2013. www.moe.gov.sg/initiatives/edusave.

Social and Enterprise Development Innovations. 2013. 'Learn$ave.' Social and Enterprise Development Innovations. Accessed 8 April 2013. www.sedi.org/html/programs/learnSave.asp.

Social Research and Demonstration Corporation. 2010. 'Learn$ave.' Social Research and Demonstration Corporation. Accessed 8 February 2013. www.srdc.org/en_what_we_do_item.asp?category=623&id=27394.

Ssewamala, F.M., C.K. Han, and T.B. Neilands. 2009. 'Asset Ownership and Health and Mental Health Functioning among AIDS-Orphaned Adolescents: Findings from a Randomized Clinical Trial in Rural Uganda.' *Social Science and Medicine* 69 (2): 191–198. doi:10.1016/j.socscimed.2009.05.019.

Taiwan Ministry of the Interior. n.d. 'She hui jiu zhu fa.' [Social Assistance Act]. Accessed 13 March 2014. http://sowf.moi.gov.tw/10/law/1/law01.htm.

US Department of Health and Human Services. 2012. 'About Assets for Independence.' 26 September revision. US Department of Health and Human Services, Administration for Children and Families. Accessed 12 April 2013. http://archive.acf.hhs.gov/programs/ocs/afi/assets.html.

Volden, C. 2006. 'States as Policy Laboratories: Emulating Success in the Children's Health Insurance Program.' *American Journal of Political Science* 50 (2): 294–312. doi:10.1111/j.1540–5907.2006.00185.x.

Walker, J.L. 1969. 'The Diffusion of Innovations among the American States.' *American Political Science Review* 63 (3): 880–899. doi:10.2307/1954434.

Wang, M.Z., and Z.J. Chiu. 2007. 'Chu xu fa zhan zhang hu zai pin kun ruo shi ja ting da zhuanqing nian zhi fu wu ying yong- yi Taiwan er tong jijia ting fu zhu ji jin hui '95 nian qing nian zi li diao gan' wei li.' [The Application of Development Accounts in College Students from Poor Families: A Case of Self-Supporting Youth Accounts]. Working Paper, National Taiwan University. http://homepage.ntu.edu.tw/~lccheng/taiwan/ccf_2_paper.pdf.

Weng, H.Y., H.S. Zou, and Z.Y. Wang. 2007. 'Zi chan lei ji wei ji chu de tuo pin fang an – yi jia fu ji jin hui wei li' [Escape from Poverty: An Assets-based Case of Taiwan Fund for Children and Families (TFCF)]. Accessed 16 April 2013. http://homepage.ntu.edu.tw/~lccheng/index.html.

Yilan County Government Social Affairs Department. n.d. 'Ruo shi jia ting zi chan lei ji fa zhan zhang hu: Tuo pin fang an' [Minority Family Development Accounts Program]. Accessed 8 April 2013. www. yilanuw.org.tw.

Zou, H.S. 2007. 'Xin shou xiang lian- jia zu fa zhan zhang hu tiao cha ji cheng guo bao gao.' [Family Life Development Account: A Case of Taiwan Fund for Children and

Families (TFCF).] Working paper, Department of Social Work, National Taiwan University, Taipei, Taiwan. http://homepage.ntu.edu.tw/~lccheng/taiwan/ccf_1.pdf.

Zou, L., and J. Isern. 2007. 'Highlight on China, Part 3: Development Partner Perspectives.' Highlights on Access to Finance in China, 27 October. Microfinance Gateway. www.microfinancegateway.org/p/site/m/template.rc/1.26.9147.

Zou, L., and M. Sherraden. 2009. 'From "Dead" Savings to Assets for Life: Perspectives on the Retirement Social Insurance Pilot Project in Hutubi, China.' *Asia Pacific Journal of Social Work and Development* 19 (1): 96–115. doi:10.1080/21650993.2009. 9756056.

Zou, L., M. Sherraden, B. Guo, J. Huang, S. Deng, and M. Jin. 2011. 'Asset-Based Policy in China: Applied Project and Policy Progress.' Policy Brief 11–24, July, Center for Social Development, Washington University, St. Louis, MO. http://csd.wustl.edu/Publications/Documents/PB11-24.pdf.

6 The evolution of Singapore's social security system

Tan Tai Yong and Ho Kong Chong

The goal of building a social security system is embraced by individuals in their quest to live better lives. Non-governmental organizations (NGOs) and governments also embrace it in efforts to improve economic and social well-being. That households, civic society groups, and government share this goal, however, does not guarantee the success of the enterprise. Van Ginneken (2003) notes that more than half of the world's population is not protected by any social security arrangement. To understand the difficulty of creating a social security system, one must consider the logic of government expenditure priorities, the state of a country's development, and the relationship between the government and society.

Education is arguably the most successful of the various social expenditures made by the state. This is not only because spending on education benefits households and individuals. In large part, it is because such expenditures directly support national economic priorities by training citizens to become key contributors to the economy and to innovation. Those contributions drive a country's progress. Other key elements of social security – an affordable housing system, an efficient health system, and a stable retirement income – are more difficult to achieve, because any attempt to provide a comprehensive system at these fronts has the potential to drain state finances.

Peterson (1981) highlights the differential impacts of public expenditures. His empirical analysis of local government spending priorities in the United States shows that economic and developmental expenditures, because they add to the economic vitality of cities by attracting businesses and skilled labour, typically triumph over redistributive welfare expenditures. Although welfare expenditures, such as low-cost housing and free medical care, are worthy of public support, Petersen (1981) argues that these are unproductive expenditures and that they will hurt the city's economic position. Welfare expenditures will only become significant when the city is rich enough to provide 'unproductive' services to those in need (Peterson 1981, 64). Peterson locates the responsibility for welfare spending at the level of the national government, where policymakers can develop social policies to benefit the nation. He suggests that national governments assume responsibility for the provision of welfare because national boundaries allow for provision without spatial concentration. In contrast, growth in a city's welfare expenditure may increase the burden for the city's government if more people flock to the city (Peterson 1981).

Peterson conceives of provision in terms of allocation efficiency, but Castells (1978) looks at state welfare provision as a project to ensure the stability of capitalist economic production by supporting the collective consumption needs of the labour force. He asserts that:

> the intervention of the state becomes necessary ... for the functioning of economic activity and/or the appeasement of social conflicts.... It assures the necessary reproduction of the labour power at a minimum level, [and] it lessens the cost of direct salaries.
>
> (1978, 18)

Like Peterson, Castells focuses on cities, asserting that they are where needs and tensions are greatest:

> Fundamentally the urban question refers to the organization of the means of collective consumption at the basis of the daily life of all social groups: housing, education, health, culture, commerce, transport, etc. In advanced capitalism it expresses the fundamental contradiction between, on the one hand, the increasing socialization of consumption (as a result of the concentration of capital and the means of production), and on the other hand, the capitalist logic of the production and distribution of its means of consumption.... In an attempt to resolve these contradictions and their resultant conflicts, the state increasingly intervenes in the city.
>
> (Castells 1978, 3)

Although Castells presents an intriguing proposal on the relationship between state legitimacy and welfare provisions, the relationship must be elaborated through an analysis of the development experiences of countries. And to the extent that provision does not occur within a static context, such an analysis will uncover the evolving capacity of the state, the development of the social security system, and the changing nature of state–society relations. We examine these relationships in the case of Singapore.

The changing state capacity and state–society relations

East India Company settlement

Colonial Singapore was 'founded' and functioned essentially for trade. As the island colony grew from a small trading settlement to a thriving port city in the late nineteenth century, its commercial functions largely determined its development and character. Singapore's free-trade status gave it an important competitive advantage over rival ports in the region. Free trade was not known elsewhere in the region, and the new East India Company settlement benefited immensely by being the first mover (Lee 2008). Because Singapore lacked natural resources and produced virtually nothing of its own, its economic growth depended almost entirely on *entrepôt* trade. That trade revolved around tranship-ment; packaging; processing; provision of credits; and the maintenance of a trade network that integrated European business houses, British banks, Chinese mid-dlemen, and native traders.

With commerce and trade as Singapore's *raison d'être*, the colony undertook management and development only in so far as they facilitated business activ-ities. The logic of free trade informed the ideology of governance, and the colo-nial government adopted a *laissez-faire* policy on running the economy. It refused to impose taxes on income or profits, or duties on trade, lest they should discourage and encumber the free flow of business. Private enterprise essentially drove economic activity, and the state had minimal involvement in 'industrial, commercial, residential and community developments' (Perry, Kong, and Yeoh 1997, 55–56). The East India Company and later the Straits Settlements Council kept administration of the island and the cost of government to a bare minimum. Administrators came to terms with a local business community that wanted to maintain free trade at all costs and that opposed duties of any sort. Ports carried out activities – cargo handling, pilotage, wharfage, and anchorage – without dues or fees. Tax revenues from income or profits were almost non-existent (Lee 2008; see also Turnbull 1972). Without proper revenues, the settlement ran at a loss. The colony had to provide basic infrastructure and amenities but devoted most of its effort to making trade easier and safer in Singapore (e.g. by suppress-ing piracy or improving port facilities and lighthouses). To defray the costs of expenditures, the company resorted to raising revenue by taxing vices, pleasures, and necessities of the Asian people (e.g. gambling houses, cock fighting, opium, local brew; Turnbull 1989).

Because of the roles played by trade and commerce during the East India Company's rule, the administration had few means and minimal role in govern-ing a mainly immigrant society that grew as rapidly as trade in Singapore. According to the Raffles town plan (Perry, Kong, and Yeoh 1997), the immig-rant communities resided in their ethnic enclaves but interacted in the market-place and formed a key segment of Singapore's early economy. For most, Singapore was a temporary base where they would work hard and live frugally, hoping to save for a better life in their homeland. These migrant communities expected little from the state, which remained 'light and lax, providing a semb-lance of law and order but scarcely touching the lives of the inhabitants' (Turn-bull 1989, 49). For well-being, they looked to their own trade and to ethnic and religious organizations. Many of these organizations fell 'outside the pale of official administration' (Turnbull 1989, 49). Although the population of Singa-pore quadrupled and trade tripled between 1830 and 1867, the size of the administration remained static (Lee 2008). The *entrepôt* trade essentially entailed interaction among British, regional, and local traders, often through intermediaries, with the state playing a very indirect role in the livelihoods of the people.

Crown colony

In 1867, Singapore became a crown colony and part of the Straits Settlements. This brought an end to the East India Company's rule and to management from India. As the colony settled and population increased through further immigration, the colonial state expanded its capacities, introduced executive and legislative institutions, and developed specialized agencies to deal with the social demands of a growing community.

In the last quarter of the nineteenth century, the opening of the Suez Canal, the advent of steamships, and the spread of telegraphic communications boosted Singapore's economic growth. Singapore became an important node in an expanded trading network that connected markets in Europe with those in Southeast Asia, East Asia (Hong Kong and Japan), and Australia. These developments set the stage for a subsequent economic boom driven by three commodities: tin, rubber, and petroleum. As it developed into a major trading hub and staple port, Singapore attracted greater numbers of immigrants and its population continued to grow. In the decade between 1871 and 1881, the population increased by more than 40 per cent (Swee-Hock 1991).

Although the British Colonial Office sought to mould the new crown colony into the colonial pattern, the powerful merchant community in Singapore wanted to maintain the minimal, *laissez-faire* governance that prevailed during the period of the East India Company's rule. The merchants wanted a prospering Malaya to pay the costs of that government and Singapore to be the peninsula's most dynamic part. Rich Europeans and Asians composed the most powerful section of the merchant community and acted as the unofficial opposition to the governor in council (Turnbull 1989). Governor Harry Ord wrote in a dispatch to the Colonial Office that they took 'hardly any interest in anything beyond their own immediate business.... They come here solely to make money' (Dispatch by Governor Ord to Colonial Office; cited in Turnbull 1989, 83).

Indeed, the population grew, and newcomers settled in the colony much as predecessors did during the East India Company's rule. Socially, the inhabitants of the colony continued to function autonomously, within their ethnic enclaves. Non-state social, religious, and charitable organizations looked after their respective communities. Among these organizations were clans (*huay kuans*), trade guilds, temples, missionary groups, churches, and Arab family trusts (*wakafs*). They took care of economic activities, welfare, and other social needs, including education. Although the colonial government set up other community institutions, such as the Chinese Protectorate, these were regulatory mechanisms designed to maintain law and order, not to develop the well-being of inhabitants. The government designed such institutions to break up the triad's stranglehold on immigrant labour and to alleviate criminal abuse of the coolie system. If left unchecked, organized criminal activities would disrupt the labour supply, threatening the economic development of Malaya and Singapore (Lee 1991).

Viewing the population as largely transitory, officials took the position that 'people who drifted in and out did so at their own risk' (Lee 1989, 31). The colony's administrators saw no need to provide social services for inhabitants who settled temporarily in the colony. Although life was generally pleasant and comfortable for the colony's wealthy and influential, the lot of the poor worsened as the population increased. There was overcrowding, and inadequate public social welfare systems could not keep pace with population growth. Living conditions remained dire until the 1950s. Lee's (1989, 40) description of the physical face of late-colonial Singapore illustrates the point well:

> [Singapore] was a city solidly built to facilitate the functions of trading houses, banks, and government offices.... The British understood the need to invest in infrastructure and Singapore was their show-piece, an artefact of colonial design and engineering skill.... [In contrast,] schools, hospitals, and homes for the people were either not enough or not up to standard.

The colonial government ran a number of hospitals, but the mass of the population had no access to medical facilities or relied on free charitable institutions founded by philanthropists from their community. Many public hospitals would not have been established without philanthropic contributions from local businessmen such as Tan Tock Seng (Perry, Kong, and Yeoh 1997).

Opium addiction also was a cause of ill health and mortality. The colonial government allowed opium use because it generated revenue. The sale of opium contributed nearly half of the colony's revenue up to the mid-1920s. By 1934, duties on tobacco, petrol, and alcohol overtook the opium excise, which accounted for about one-quarter of official revenue (Lee 2007, 75).

In the decade following the Second World War, the returning British authorities sought to rehabilitate the economy and society from the ravages of the war and occupation. They adopted an involved approach to improving the welfare of the population, creating the Social Welfare Department in 1946. To help refugees and displaced persons, the department opened people's restaurants (i.e. places that provided meals at controlled, affordable prices), children's feeding centres, and a citizens' advice bureau (Social Welfare Department 1946). Even as normalcy gradually returned to post-war Singapore, the Social Welfare Department continued to expand. The appalling living conditions of large parts of the population contributed to 'a chaotic and unwieldy megapolis [that] has been created ... by haphazard and unplanned growth' (Turnbull 1989, 234). The department's expansion also spoke to the state's long neglect of the population's welfare and to the extent of the problems requiring attention.

Self-government

In 1959, the People's Action Party (PAP), a mass-based, democratic socialist party, won a strong majority in the general elections and formed the first elected government under a self-government arrangement provided by the Rendel Constitution. The new government faced a slew of challenges, and left-wing forces from within the government threatened its political future. Political norms and institutions were not yet fully developed, and this was a period of 'bare knuckle' politics. The stakes were very high: losers in these early political battles would lose parliamentary seats and face political devastation. Between 1959 and 1963, the PAP was locked in mortal combat with its political foes and fought some of the key battles within the party ranks (Yeo and Lau 1991).

In August 1965, following separation from Malaysia, Singapore became a city-state without a hinterland. The PAP consolidated its political position but realized that its political power and authority would quickly melt away if it did not show that it was capable of dealing with many of the social and economic challenges the country faced. Its political survival depended on ensuring Singapore's survival, which required a sustainable economy. In turn, a sustainable economy required political and social stability as well as a committed and disciplined workforce. These were considerable challenges in the 1960s, as the colonial economic structure remained very much intact. The economy was based essentially on trade, which accounted for one-third of the GDP in 1959. In the 1950s, commercial activities, transportation, and communications services employed more than half of the work-force. Manufacturing and construction accounted for nearly 20 per cent. The manufacturing sector in Singapore grew out of the *entrepôt* trade (Cheng 1991, 186–187), and much of the manufacturing involved goods made from raw materials produced in the region (e.g. rubber products, food, beverages). Engineering and machinery shops catered to the needs of the tin, rubber, and petroleum industries. Most manufactured goods were made for the internal market, but some found their way to neighbouring countries. Because Singapore lacked a sizable industrial sector, unemployment grew – the unemployment rate was 14 per cent in the early 1960s – as a young population joined the work-force (Cheng 1991).

The business of *entrepôt* quickly declined in this period. Emerging from colonial rule, new states established national tariffs to protect their domestic markets and industries. Embracing industrialization as a means to economic growth, the government of Singapore saw its role in initiating and sustaining industrialization; it would provide the supporting infrastructure – power, water, transportation – and generate the necessary conditions through education and vocational training. It also had to create an environment that would attract capital investments (Recommendations of International Bank for Reconstruction and Development at the request of the Governments of Singapore, Malaya and Britain; cited in Turnbull 1989, 187–188).

In dealing with all of these challenges, the PAP government adopted a pragmatic approach that emphasized socio-economic development. The logic was compelling: if people saw their livelihood improve, they would develop a sense of ownership in the country and, in all likelihood, would continue to support the ruling party. There were political imperatives as well; unless the PAP government demonstrated its ability to deal with the many social and economic problems facing Singapore in the early days of independence, political opposition, still potent in Singapore in the 1960s, would easily find a host of grievances with which to undermine the government's legitimacy.

It was this particular focus – the choice to gain political legitimacy through the solution of key socio-economic problems of the time – that marked the creation of the interventionist state in Singapore. The generally *laissez-faire* housekeeping style of management in the colonial state had already been marked with sporadic attempts at improving the social conditions of Singapore. In the post-colonial phase, the systematic approach to intervention centred on the creation of new state agencies established to develop and guide key programmes. The Jurong Town Corporation was developed specifically to foster and manage industrial estates in support of the industrial strategy. The Urban Redevelopment Authority was started to manage the central area of Singapore with the task of changing a mixed-use city centre into a modern central business district. For social development, the Housing and Development Board (HDB) expanded the fledging public housing programme. The board also resettled a significant number of households affected by redevelopment of the central area of Singapore, the land used for industrial estates, and the land used for new public housing estates. Because of Singapore's general orientation to trade and commerce, the city-state's small size, and the absence of an effective hinterland, Singapore's industrial sector was underdeveloped. These factors combined to influence an industrial development strategy that focused on exports and was led by non-local companies. With this particular strategy in mind, the Economic Development Board was formed to spearhead investment promotion through the development of a network of offices in the industrial developed nations of North America, Europe, and Japan.

Political stability, social stability, and a disciplined work-force formed the basis of PAP's plan for sustained economic growth. In all this, the limited colonial state gave way to an interventionist, post-colonial, developmental state. The nature of this change is evident in the way Singapore has evolved since 1959. The context explains changes in housing, health, and social security.

Building Singapore's social security system

Retirement income security

When the British returned to Singapore after the war, economic and political reconstruction were the first orders of the day, and these urgent tasks required resources. Over the protests of the governor's advisory council, an unofficial body composed mostly of business and professional elites, the governor enacted an income tax ordinance by decree (Lee 2008, 16).

Despite disagreements on the taxes, the new revenue created policy opportunities. In June 1948, the legislature began discussing a social security scheme. The proposal's mover, Thio Chan Bee, felt that such a scheme was necessary because local workers had no pension comparable to that provided for government service and there were no provident funds like the ones enjoyed by European staff. The Singapore Progressive Party, a party of English-educated elites, supported the proposed social security scheme and pressed the government to adopt it (Lee 2008, 16).

Singapore enacted legislation to create the Central Provident Fund (CPF) Scheme in 1953 (Act no. 34 of 1953) and launched the effort in July 1955. The state-enforced saving programme is based on the principle of equal contribution by employer and employee. Initially, the employee contributed 5 per cent of wages to an account, and the employer matched that contribution (contribution rates have grown over time). The scheme allowed workers to begin withdrawing from their account at age 55. Soon after independence, the PAP government found the CPF's pension scheme to be inadequate and expanded it into a means for citizens to purchase flats built by the HDB. In other words, the scheme offered more than a retirement fund; citizens could use their CPF retirement savings to purchase, by instalments, a government-built apartment. In 1968, just as the HDB launched a revised home ownership scheme, the legislature amended the CPF Act to raise the rate of contribution. Thereafter, workers could use CPF savings to make the 20 per cent down-payment for their flats and to repay the 20-year housing loan in monthly instalments (Lee 2000, 117).

Indeed, beyond survivability, CPF savings became an essential mechanism for stability and nation building when the accumulated savings became the means for ordinary citizens to purchase their own homes. As economic growth boosted incomes, Singapore gradually increased the rate of required CPF contributions, allowing a net increase in the worker's income but also limiting his or her spendable money to control inflation (Lee 2000). Also, allowing workers to purchase homes with their CPF savings contributes to industrial peace and social stability. The CPF forces the working population to pay for its own retirement, health care, and housing through forced savings. It provides 'a comprehensive self-financing social security fund equal to any old-age pension system', and it meets a key social need 'without shifting the burden to the next generation of workers' (Lee 2000, 127). Because the CPF is a government-managed pension fund, it also provides the state with large amounts of relatively cheap funds that can be invested for domestic development.

As a form of social security, the CPF has obvious limitations. It provides security only for those who work and may not provide a sufficient retirement pension if inflation and utilization for home purchase whittle down the savings. But the government maintains its commitment to hold welfare expenditures to the barest minimum, offering assistance only to the handicapped and the aged. Indeed, the government's aversion to subsidies can be seen in the gradual decline of government transfers from 12.8 per cent of government expenditure in 1960 to 1.4 per cent in 1974. However, this decline may also stem in part from economic growth, rising prosperity, and a relatively young population that requires few public welfare services (Lim 1989). Although CPF contributions have grown over the years (from 10 per cent of monthly wages, evenly split between employees and employers, in 1955 to 50 per cent in 1984), it offers only partial social security (Lim 1989); families must play a part in providing for the elderly.

Housing security

As we note above, the rapid population growth in British colonial Singapore led to congestion and a poor housing stock. In the post-war period, inadequate housing manifested itself in the 'black holes' (the dark living cubicles in China-town), in the slums of the central area, and in the squatter settlements around the city's fringes.

The passing of Singapore Improvement Ordinance (Act no. 10 of 1927) led to establishment of the Singapore Improvement Trust, and this ushered in a new era of public planning. Between 1936 and 1941, the trust built the first public housing town, Tiong Bahru, which accommodated 6000 people. However, the poor could not afford to purchase the flats there or to rent the flats at rates deemed affordable (Sennet 1948). Although the trust represented a correct approach to addressing the housing needs of the growing population, it was unable to build units quickly. Inadequate funding, the lack of official backing (roads and other city infrastructure took priority over housing), shortages of professional and technical staff, and poor leadership all hindered the trust's efforts. Between 1947 and 1959, it constructed 21,000 units in the area around Alexandra and Queenstown (Singapore Improvement Trust 1959).

On 1 February 1960, the newly elected PAP government established the HDB to provide low-cost housing for low-income groups. The HDB estab-lished a goal of building 10,000 units per year between 1961 and 1964. The new units would include such essential services as water, electricity, gas, and modern sanitation. The board would rent the units at affordable prices: SGD 20 per month for a self-contained, one-room flat.[1] It subsequently built larger, two- and three-room flats, renting these at SGD 40 and SGD 60 per month, respectively (HDB 1962).

In 1961, the Bukit Ho Swee fire left 16,000 people homeless, and the HDB faced pressure to increase the pace of building. The government instructed the board to construct housing on a 150-acre site within nine months, and the HDB completed most of the units by the end of 1961. Within three years of its estab-lishment, the HDB completed a total of 12,230 flats (HDB 1963) and established several new satellite towns (Queenstown, Alexandra, Toa Payoh, Jurong, St. Michael, MacPherson, and Kallang Airport). The board did not fail to meet the targets for the first five-year plan; it built 51,000 low-cost units at a cost of SGD 192 million. Together, the HDB units and the 23,000 flats built by former gov-ernments housed 400,000 persons – 23 per cent of a population of 1.8 million (Singapore Parliament 1965).

The success of the public housing policy from the 1960s to the 1980s enabled the government to achieve a number of social and political objectives. We have already noted that the home-owning scheme enabled workers to purchase their homes and gave the population a stake in the country. The government solved early problems of overcrowding in the city centre by the planned dispersal of the population into housing estates outside the old municipal area. Rehousing thus became a form of social mobilization (Clancey 2003). Compulsory urban resettlement broke up the urban slums, dissolved latent social hot spots, and undermined potential electoral opposition by dispersing old ethnic, working-class concentrations that were fertile grounds for anti-government agitation (Lim 1989). By resettling inhabitants into orderly, decent, government-managed flats, the government achieved a homogenization of lifestyle and social experience. In these efforts, it used public housing to foster social integration and national identity.

Of the several social policies adopted by the PAP government since it came to power in 1959, housing initiatives have perhaps had the greatest impact in the transformation of Singapore. In 1959, only 8.8 per cent of the population lived in public housing; by 1985, 75 per cent lived in HDB housing. The government achieved its goal of creating 'a nation of homeowners'.[2] In doing so, it transformed a population of migrants into a settled citizenry.

Health security

As recounted above, the colonial state attempted to deal with the social and health challenges posed by a growing population, but inadequate resources and half-hearted legislation left health care in the hands of the community and local philanthropists. As a consequence, and partly because of the hardship caused by the Japanese occupation, health care was a major challenge in post-war Singapore. Typhoid, cholera, malaria, and other infectious diseases were prevalent, and there was a severe shortage of nurses and medical officers.

The PAP government made marked improvements soon after it came to power. Health expenditures accounted for 13.4 per cent of government spending in 1960, but for 19.7 per cent in 1964. Per-capita health spending amounted to SGD 20 per person in 1960 but rose to SGD 195 by 1985 (Lim 1989). This represents a significant increase even if the amounts are adjusted for price inflation. Although the proportion of public funds spent on health fell after 1964, partly because of defence spending, both overall government spending on health and per-capita spending increased steadily in real terms (Lim 1989). The numbers of public hospitals, outpatient dispensaries, and maternal and child health clinics all increased significantly, as did the ratio of doctors to inhabitants. Much of the PAP government's early effort centred on reorganizing public health services. For example, the government combined the City Health Department and the Government Health Department to form the Ministry of Health, thereby bringing all medical and health services under a single authority. It also launched campaigns to combat infectious diseases and promote healthy living. A prominent example is the school immunization programme, which inoculated all students to prevent spread of diphtheria, tetanus, poliomyelitis, and small pox. The state also enacted population planning measures through the Singapore Family Planning and Population Board Act (no. 32 of 1965).

The desire to create a healthier and more productive workforce drove the government's attention to health. Health care became a fundamental right of all citizens. Over time, demographic, economic, and social changes augmented the effects of these early government efforts, further improving the population's health. The economy grew, income rose, and the young population enjoyed a high standard of living (Lim 1989). It gradually came to seem that government health policies were neither necessary nor sufficient conditions for improving the health status of the population (Lim 1989). In the early years, the government saw health expenditures as social welfare; as Singapore prospered and stabilized, it came to see health as a responsibility of the citizen. In 1982, Goh Chok Tong, then the second minister for health, noted:

> Instead of heavily subsidizing medical treatment, in particular where hospitalisation is needed, as we do now, we could reduce the subsidy.... In order that the population can afford to pay the more realistic scale of medical charges, a health saving scheme must be formulated to make every Singaporean save for his own health as soon as he starts work.
>
> (Tong 1982, 85)

This scheme became the new foundation of Singapore's health management system. From 1984 to 1993, the governments implemented three critical elements: Medisave, MediShield, and Medifund. A medical savings programme within the CPF, Medisave is designed to enable citizens to accumulate funds that can be used to pay for hospitalization. MediShield, the government's health insurance scheme, is designed to supplement Medisave in the event of critical illness. Medifund, the third component, provides low-income citizens and the elderly with supplemental assistance for medical expenses not met by Medisave and MediShield. The government set up Medifund in 1993 with SGD 200 million and provides yearly top-ups from government budgetary surpluses. (For a more detailed analysis, see Chiu, Ho, and Lui 2012.) Thinking shifted with the introduction of Medisave; Singapore considered health care to be a right and saw assistance with health expenditures as a form of welfare, but the nation came to see health care and health expenditures through the lens of an ideology that promotes individual responsibility (Barr 2001).

Conditions for developing a social security system

The Singapore story reveals the essential elements necessary for the development of a social security system. The roles and functions of the state are instrumental in defining the scope and nature of social services in a country. In Singapore, the role of the state evolved. During the colonial period, the state played an extremely limited role that centred on supporting commerce. Gradually, the state assumed additional responsibilities, particularly after the Second World War. The war, the British defeat in 1942, and the Japanese occupation caused major disruptions to the state, economy, and society. In an effort to restore legitimacy after the defeat, and to 'tackle the human wreckage left by the war and pestilence of the Japanese Occupation' (Social Welfare Department

1946, 3), the returning British authorities turned to welfarism. This renewed interest in social intervention indicated the colonial state's recognition of the social problems in post-war Singapore and its effort to reclaim lost ground. In this post-war effort, we see a number of factors that drew the state's attention to social expenditures. Social problems are persistent among large urban populations, but the need of British authorities to restore legitimacy with the local population spurred social spending.

Legitimacy was also a pressing concern for Singapore's first democratically elected government. In this post-colonial phase, the national push for industrialization required the state to extract a great toll from the local population. To support the industrialization drive, the state resettled inhabitants, appropriated land for national development projects (industrial estates, public housing, new infrastructure), and refashioned the population into a dedicated, disciplined workforce. Driven by pragmatism, Singapore became an interventionist state. It developed political and social objectives and policies that fed on each other. Many of the social policies that transformed Singapore – social security, public housing, and health care – first developed in this context.

The examination of these three policy areas indicates the roles played by ideology and legitimacy in the state–society relationship. Following Poulantzas, Castells has seen the relationship in terms of state spending on social expenditures to support the reproduction of labour as a way of gaining legitimacy vis-à-vis capital and labour (Saunders, 1986). Holliday's work may be seen as a conceptual extension of this work through his attempt to specify rights, the focus of social policy, and the relationship of provision with market and family (Holliday 2000). Describing East Asian social policy as 'productivist welfare capitalism', Holliday (2000) points out that the array of welfare provisions rolled out in East Asia is closely linked to the economic system.

In the Singapore model, this relationship is certainly emphasized. That is, welfare provision is not associated with a clear notion of the rights of subjects who are entitled to social services. Instead, the ideology behind welfare provision is closely coupled to the economic productivity of the household (or anticipated productivity, in the case of children and youth) and the labour force. An associated reasoning is that the quantum of social expenditures is determined not only by the seriousness of the need, but also by the productivity of the economy. Thus, for example, the amount set aside in the Medifund to meet the needs of those unable to afford medical services (those with low income and the elderly) is linked to the budget surplus, which is generated by the economy.

Individual responsibility is built into the Singapore security system. Thus, the employer and employee both make significant contributions to the income security system. In the public housing scheme, the government subsidizes the production and ultimately the cost of new public housing units by providing land. Additional grants are provided for first-time buyers as well as low-income groups. However, the individual purchaser pays for the unit (often using retirement income funds). Likewise, although the state provides strong support to the

Singapore health system for the existing health infrastructure, the system is also one in which the individual is expected to bear costs, and a vigorous means-testing is required before public funds can be released for the poor.

The system of productivist welfare capitalism (Holliday 2000) and the related notion of oikonomic (household management) welfare states (Jones 1990) are embedded in the economic history of the country. As the chapter shows, there were fledgling attempts at developing the social security system in the colonial period, but the systematic building of the social security infrastructure took place in earnest when Singapore achieved self-government status. At the level of the state, the need to redevelop the economy away from its dependence on trade and commerce toward manufacturing was tempered by the need of the government to secure political legitimacy. This historic moment created the conditions for a social security system in which provision and economic productivity are closely related. The development of the social security system was set against an early post-colonial phase; a plural society that emerged from colonial management of migrant groups was set to change. The system's development presented the individual with an opportunity to visualize citizenship and nationhood. These conditions allowed the new government to press for responsibilities rather than rights.

By successfully implementing all three policies, the government created the legitimacy it needed to continue its mandate. The political, economic, and societal conditions in which the social security system developed have shifted the ideological grounding away from provision as a citizenship right. Instead, retirement savings, housing, and health care are matters of individual responsibility: comprehensive provision involves a partnership between state and society.

Notes

1 The Singapore dollar (SGD) is the primary unit of currency in the city-state. USD 1 is presently equivalent to approximately SGD 1.24.
2 Lee Kuan Yew has used the phrase 'a nation of homeowners' many times. See, Lee 2000, 117.

References

Barr, Michael D. 2001. 'Medical Savings Accounts in Singapore: A Critical Inquiry.' *Journal of Health Politics, Policy and Law* 26 (4): 709–726. doi:10.1215/03616878-26-4-709.

Castells, Manuel. 1978. *City, Class and Power*. Translated by Elizabeth Lebas. New York: St Martin's Press.

Cheng, Siok Hwa. 1991. 'Economic Change and Industrialization.' In *A History of Singapore*, edited by Ernest C.T. Chew and Edwin Lee, 182–215. Singapore: Oxford University Press.

Chiu, Stephen W.K., K.C. Ho, and Tai-lok Lui. 2012. 'Reforming Health: Contrasting Trajectories of Neoliberal Restructuring in the City-States.' In *Locating Neoliberalism in East Asia: Neoliberalizing Spaces in Developmental States*, edited by Bae-Gyoon Park, Richard Child Hill, and Asato Saito, 225–256. Chichester: Wiley-Blackwell.

Clancey, Gregory. 2003. 'Toward a Spatial History of Emergency: Notes from Singapore.' Working Paper 8, August, Asia Research Institute, Singapore. www.ari.nus.edu. sg/docs/wps/wps03_008.pdf.

Holliday, Ian. 2000. 'Productivist Welfare Capitalism: Social Policy in East Asia.' *Political Studies* 48 (4): 706–723. doi:10.1111/1467-9248.00279.

Housing and Development Board. 1962. *Annual Report, 1961.* Singapore: Government Printing Office.

Housing and Development Board. 1963. *Annual Report, 1962.* Singapore: Government Printing Office.

Jones, Catherine. 1990. 'Hong Kong, Singapore, South Korea and Taiwan: Oikonomic Welfare States.' *Government and Opposition* 25 (4): 446–462. doi:10.1111/j.1477-7053. 1990.tb00396.x.

Lee, Edwin. 1989. 'The Colonial Legacy.' In *Management of Success: The Moulding of Modern Singapore*, edited by Kernial Singh Sandhu and Paul Wheatley, 3–50. Singapore: Institute of Southeast Asian Studies.

Lee, Edwin. 1991. *The British as Rulers Governing Multi-Racial Singapore: 1867–1914.* Singapore: Singapore University Press.

Lee, Edwin. 2008. *Singapore: The Unexpected Nation.* Singapore: Institute of Southeast Asian Studies.

Lee, Kuan Yew. 2000. *From Third World to First: The Singapore Story, 1965–2000.* Singapore: Times Media.

Lee, Soo Ann, ed. 2007. *Singapore: From Place to Nation.* Singapore: Pearson/Prentice Hall.

Lim, Linda Y.C. 1989. 'Social Welfare.' In *Management of Success: The Moulding of Modern Singapore*, edited by Kernial Singh Sandhu and Paul Wheatley, 171–200. Singapore: Institute of Southeast Asian Studies.

Perry, Martin, Lily Kong, and Brenda Yeoh. 1997. *Singapore: A Developmental City State.* West Sussex, England: Wiley.

Peterson, Paul E. 1981. *City Limits.* Chicago, IL: University of Chicago Press.

Saunders, Peter. 1986. *Social Theory and the Urban Question.* 2nd edn. London: Hutchinson Education.

Sennet, C.W.A. 1948. *Report of the Housing Committee, Singapore, 1947.* Singapore: Government Printing Office.

Singapore Improvement Trust. 1959. *Annual Report.* Singapore: Government Printing Office.

Singapore Parliament. 1965. 'Agenda, National Development.' Parliamentary debate, 8 December. In *Singapore Parliament Reports*, vol. 24. Singapore: Government Printing Office.

Social Welfare Department. 1946. *Annual Report 1946.* Singapore: Department of Social Welfare.

Swee-Hock, Saw. 1991. 'Population Growth and Control.' In *A History of Singapore*, edited by Ernest C.T. Chew and Edwin Lee, 219–241. Singapore: Oxford University Press.

Tong, Goh Chok. 1982. 'Stay Well for Health.' In *Our Heritage and Beyond: A Collection of Essays on Singapore, Its Past, Present, and Future*, edited by S. Jayakumar, 82–85. Singapore: National Trades Union Congress.

Turnbull, Constance Mary. 1972. *The Straits Settlements, 1826–67: Indian Presidency to Crown Colony.* London: Athlone Press.

Turnbull, Constance Mary. 1989. *A History of Singapore 1819–1988.* 2nd edn. Singapore: Oxford University Press.

Van Ginneken, Wouter. 2003. 'Extending Social Security: Policies for Developing Countries.' *International Labour Review* 142 (3): 277–294. doi:10.1111/j.1564-913X.2003. tb00263.x.

Yeo, Kim Wah and Albert Lau. 1991. 'From Colonialism to Independence, 1945–1965.' In *A History of Singapore*, edited by Ernest C.T. Chew and Edwin Lee, 117–153. Singapore: Oxford University Press.

7 Can Singapore's Central Provident Fund still meet retirement income needs?

Kok-Hoe Ng

In the current climate of welfare austerity that prevails across many of the mature welfare states in Europe, there is a common perception that demographic ageing does not exert the same fiscal pressures on fully funded, defined-contribution old-age pension schemes, like Singapore's Central Provident Fund (CPF), as on pay-as-you-go pension systems. Some argue that, because individuals save for their own retirement in defined-contribution schemes, the increasing number of elderly persons relative to that of working-age adults (an increase due to growth of life expectancies and decline of fertility) does not translate into a public-financing issue. Enforced saving through the CPF is also regarded as a form of asset building that promotes personal financial independence and responsibility.

But within this discourse, the unique vulnerabilities of the CPF model of old-age income provision are sometimes overlooked. First, although demographic ageing does not tilt the fiscal balance of pension financing in Singapore, it has equally serious implications for intergenerational support within the family. Between 1990 and 2010, the average number of children born to women aged 40–49 years fell from 2.8 to 2.0 (Department of Statistics 2012). This implies that there are fewer adult children available to provide financial support for elderly parents, and such support has been a vital source of retirement income security. Second, as CPF contributions are drawn from wages, the scheme is most favourable to individuals who are successful in the labour market. Elderly persons with a history of low or interrupted earnings are likely to have poorer access to CPF benefits during retirement.

This chapter presents empirical evidence and original projections in support of these arguments. It investigates the impact of the CPF on old-age income security within the context of rapid demographic ageing. Focusing on elderly persons aged 65 and above, it shows that, despite the CPF's long tradition as a central pillar of social policy in Singapore, the scheme has not been a major part of retirement financing among recent elderly cohorts. The chapter also argues that demographic ageing and the weakening of family support will require the CPF to play a greater role in old-age financial provision in the coming decades, but that a substantial proportion of future elderly populations may continue to lack access to CPF benefits. The current design of the CPF further suggests that the scheme on its own may not provide adequate retirement income even for those who have access to CPF savings.

Background of the Central Provident Fund

The British colonial administration introduced Singapore's CPF in 1955 to provide retirement income security (Ramesh 2004). In the first few decades, the CPF gradually expanded to incorporate a multitude of other social objectives (Table 7.1). The most important of these is the provision for pre-retirement with-drawals to purchase housing. Such withdrawals support home ownership but also divert savings away from old-age pensions. In addition, the CPF's contribution and interest rates have been subjected to frequent adjustment. Contribution rates rose to a peak of 50 per cent in 1985, but several sharp cuts to employer contributions in 1986, 1998, and 2003 were made to manage labour costs during economic downturns (Low and Aw 2004). The CPF's nominal interest rates, which are administratively determined, have also fluctuated between a high of 6.5 per cent in the 1970s and the current rates: 2.5 per cent per annum for the Ordinary Account and 4 per cent for the Special Account (CPF Board 2013).[1] In recent years, several measures have been introduced to reprioritize retirement income security. Examples include measures to provide additional interest for the first SGD 60,000 of savings,[2] to tighten the partial withdrawal of retirement savings at age 55, and to replace phased payments over 20 years with a compul-sory life annuity.

Currently, employees contribute 20 per cent of monthly wages to the scheme until they reach age 35, and employers contribute an additional 16 per cent. Lower rates apply for older employees (Table 7.2). Monthly savings are alloc-ated to three separate individual accounts: the Ordinary Account for housing and other pre-retirement withdrawals; the Special Account, which is ring-fenced for retirement; and the Medisave Account, which finances health care spending. As Table 7.2 shows, the allocation ratios vary with the individual's age. Savings above a minimum may be invested in approved financial products. Otherwise, the fund as a whole is centrally managed and invested by the state. Total savings, including interest, are paid out as a life annuity from age 65.

Old-age incomes and the CPF, 1995 and 2005

This section discusses the impact of the CPF within the context of old-age income security in Singapore. First, it examines income levels among elderly persons aged 65 years and older, focusing on persons with low incomes. Next, it compares the prevalence of income from the CPF with the prevalence of income from other sources in old age, highlighting the role of financial support from adult children. Finally, it considers the importance of intergenerational co-residence and its role in protecting income. The analysis in this section is based on the datasets from the 1995 and 2005 (the most recent from which microdata are available) rounds of the National Survey of Senior Citizens in Singapore.

Table 7.1 Major policy extensions to Singapore's Central Provident Fund

Year	Scheme
Housing	
1968	Public Housing Scheme: for purchasing public housing
1981	Approved Residential Properties Scheme: for purchasing private housing
Health	
1984	Medisave Scheme: for hospitalization and approved treatment expenses
1990	MediShield Scheme: an insurance scheme for catastrophic illnesses
2002	ElderShield Scheme: a severe disability insurance scheme for older adults
Education	
1989	Education Scheme: allows loans from individual CPF savings to support children through tertiary education
Investment	
1978	Singapore Bus Services Share Scheme: first approved investment scheme using CPF savings
1986	Approved Investment Scheme: for private investment in approved financial products, later expanded and renamed CPF Investment Scheme
Insurance	
1982	Home Protection Insurance Scheme: to assist family members with mortgage payments in the event of permanent incapacity or death
1989	Dependents' Protection Insurance Scheme: to provide financial support for family members in the event of permanent incapacity or death

Source: Adapted from Asher (2004) and Low and Aw (2004).

Note
CPF = Central Provident Fund.

Table 7.2 Central Provident Fund contribution rates by age, 2013

Age	Contribution (% monthly wage)			Allocation (% monthly wage)		
	Employer	Employee	Total	Ordinary Account	Special Account	Medisave Account
Up to 35	16	20	36	23	6	7
36–45	16	20	36	21	7	8
46–50	16	20	36	19	8	9
51–55	14	18.5	32.5	13.5	9.5	9.5
56–60	10.5	13	23.5	12	2	9.5
61–65	7	7.5	14.5	3.5	1.5	9.5
Above 65	6.5	5	11.5	1	1	9.5

Source: CPF Board (2013, Annex A, 3).

To date, this survey is the most comprehensive study of the living arrangements, income security, and social well-being of older adults in Singapore. The survey targets households that include at least one member age 55 years or older. The two rounds reached almost 5000 households each, about .5 per cent of all resident households. The survey employed stratified sampling, choosing respondents based on housing type. Data are weighted by age, ethnicity, and sex. Data from the first round are weighted to be representative of the population identified in the 1990 Census of Population, and data from the second round are weighted to be representative of that from the 2000 Census (Ministry of Community Development, Youth and Sports 1995, 2005).

Individual income levels

The convention in international income studies, such as the Luxembourg Income Study and those by the Organization for Economic Co-operation and Development, is to adopt some point between 40 per cent and 60 per cent of equivalized household income as a threshold of poverty risk. Because equivalized household incomes are not reported for Singapore, the analysis here adopts various proportions of the population's median gross earnings as convenient approximations of these thresholds. The use of these benchmarks reveals that the incomes of elderly persons in Singapore are highly inadequate. More than nine in 10 elderly persons had incomes lower than the population's median gross earnings in 1995 and 2005 (Table 7.3). Over the 10-year period between the survey rounds, incomes among elderly persons worsened at the lower end. The proportion of the elderly with very low incomes – below 33 per cent of median earnings – increased from 64 per cent to 73 per cent. The composition of the low-income elderly population has a strong gender dimension. In 1995, 69 per cent of elderly women and 59 per cent of elderly men had very low incomes. By 2005, women's position deteriorated further relative to men's. The proportion of women with very low incomes increased to 80 per cent, while that of men grew to 65 per cent.

Table 7.3 Percentage of elderly persons (aged 65 and older) in Singapore with low incomes, 1995 and 2005

Relative to median population gross wage	1995	2005
Below median	96	93
Below 60 per cent median	89	89
Below 50 per cent median	82	81
Below 33 per cent median	64	73

Source: author's analysis using data from Ministry of Community Development, Youth and Sports (1995, 2005); median population gross wage from Department of Statistics (2011).

Income sources

In 1995 and 2005, contributions from their children were the most common income source for elderly persons in Singapore (Figure 7.1). Around 80 per cent of elderly persons received some income from their children in both years. In contrast, only 12 per cent of elderly persons received CPF income in 2005. In both years there was very low access to other independent income from such sources as work and private pensions. Eligibility for public assistance is strictly limited to elderly persons in financial destitution, so its role is almost negligible. Thus, the elderly are almost singularly dependent on informal support from their children. An important change between 1995 and 2005 was the increase in the prevalence of CPF income (from 3 per cent to 12 per cent) as the incidence of income from children fell. This reflects an improvement in CPF coverage for successive cohorts of employees as well as a decline in the availability of support from children due to falling fertility rates. A critical policy question with regard to the prospects for old-age income security is therefore whether CPF income will adequately make up for lost support from children in the future. The next section addresses that question.

Evidence indicates that access to CPF income did not improve equally for men and women. Although the proportion of elderly men with CPF income increased from 4 per cent to 19 per cent between 1995 and 2005, the proportion of elderly women with CPF income grew from 1 per cent to 7 per cent. This reflects women's lower participation in the labour market in Singapore (International Labour Organization 2012). In pension systems that feature a tight link between contributions and benefits (e.g. the CPF), elderly women tend to depend more heavily than men on other public and informal income sources. In 2005, children contributed income to nearly 90 per cent of elderly women across all but the highest income brackets. But this proportion ranged between 45 per cent and 80 per cent for the men (Figure 7.2). On the whole, the picture for retirement income sources is more dynamic for elderly men between the two years and became more varied by 2005. Women's income sources are less diverse and become more static over time. The result is a heavy and persistent reliance on income from their children.

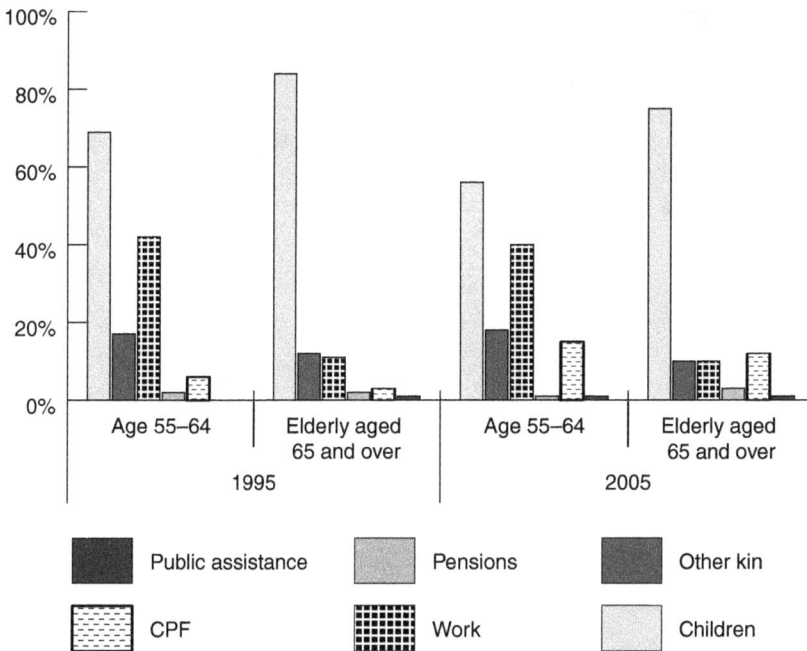

Figure 7.1 Percentage of elderly persons (aged 65 and older) with income from selected sources, Singapore 1995 and 2005 (source: author's calculations using data from Singapore National Survey of Senior Citizens 1995, 2005).

Note: CPF = Central Provident Fund.

As the surveys did not ask respondents to provide a breakdown of income composition across the various income sources, very little can be said about the amount of income support from children. Sociological studies on intergenerational transfers also tend to be silent on this issue. The only recent information on the amount of children's contributions comes from published reports based on a national study of households living in public housing estates (Housing and Development Board 2010). Among persons aged 55 or older with married children, the average amount of contributions received in 2008 from all children was SGD 445 per month. This is equivalent to 18 per cent of the population's median gross earnings of SGD 2450 that year. It is a sizeable amount considering that almost three-quarters of elderly persons in 2005 had total individual incomes that were less than one-third of the population's median gross earnings (Ministry of Manpower 2011).

Intergenerational co-residence as income protection

In Singapore, co-residence with adult children was the norm for the elderly population in 1995 and 2005 (Figure 7.3). Between 1995 and 2005, the prevalence of co-residence with children decreased from 84 per cent to 72 per cent, and the proportions of elderly persons living alone or only with their spouse increased correspondingly. Elderly women are also more likely than elderly men to co-reside with their children. In principle, co-residence does not always mean that the elderly parents' needs are met by children's resources. Equally, children who are not living with their elderly parents may provide financial contributions or in-kind support (Natividad and Cruz 1997). But previous research has found that co-residence often implies access to a range of resources. In Singapore, almost 80 per cent of older adults aged 60 and older have meals with their

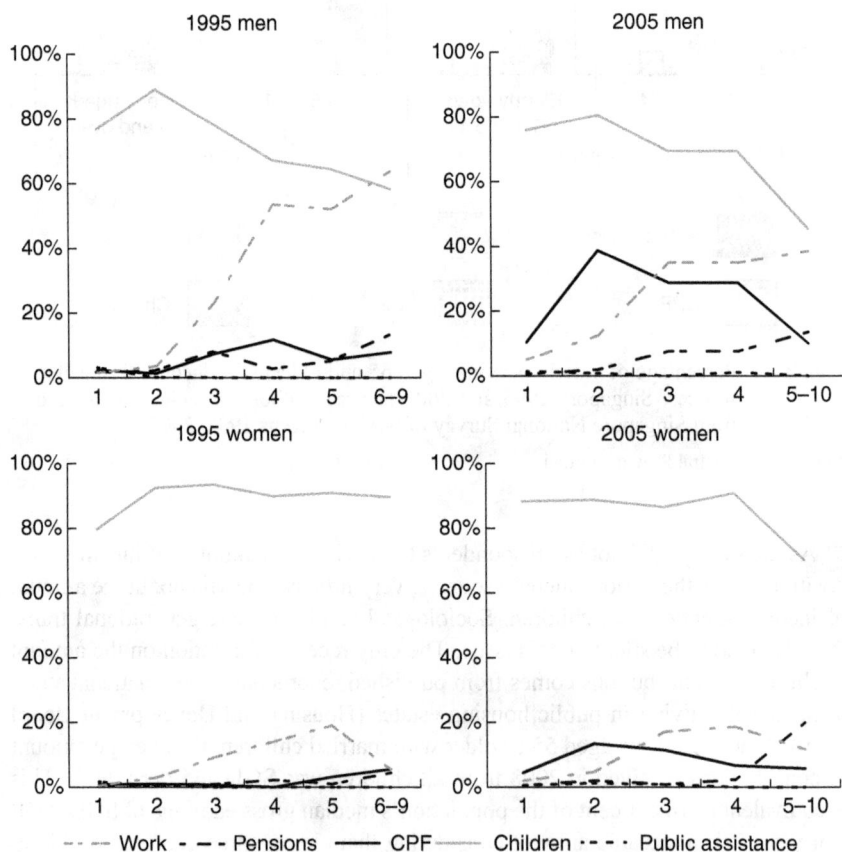

Figure 7.2 Percentage of elderly persons (aged 65 and older) with income from selected sources by income band, Singapore 1995 and 2005 (source: author's calculations using data from Singapore National Survey of Senior Citizens 1995, 2005).

Note: Income bands in SGD for 1995 are (1) <SGD 250, (2) SGD 250–499, (3) SGD 500–749, (4) SGD 750–999, (5) SGD 1000–1249, and (6–9) SGD 1250 or more. For 2005 they are (1) SGD 1–499, (2) SGD 500–749, (3) SGD 750–999, (4)SGD 1000–1249, and (5–10) SGD 1250 or more.

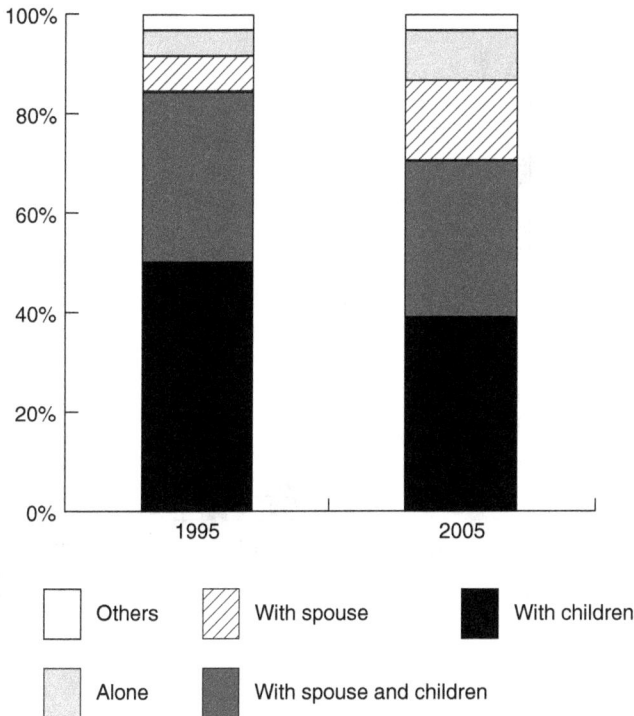

Figure 7.3 Living arrangements of elderly persons (aged 65 and older) in Singapore, 1995 and 2005 (source: author's calculations using data from Singapore National Survey of Senior Citizens 1995, 2005).

co-resident children 'often', and elderly parents are more likely to receive physical care from co-resident children than from children who are not co-residents (Chan 1997; Mehta 1999). In other places, such as Hong Kong, co-residence often means that elderly parents are able to live rent free and do not have to pay for food or utilities (Lee 2004). Two further observations from the survey data point to the income-protective function of co-residence with adult children.

First, the survey data show that elderly persons who live with their children are more likely to have very low individual incomes than are elderly persons who do not live with their children. In 2005, 75 per cent of elderly persons who lived with their children reported individual incomes below 33 per cent of the population's median gross earnings. The same is reported by 67 per cent of elderly persons who did not co-reside with children. Second, elderly persons who co-reside with their children are more likely to receive financial contributions from them and less likely to have income from other sources (Figure 7.4). Elderly persons who did not co-reside with children had more diverse income sources.

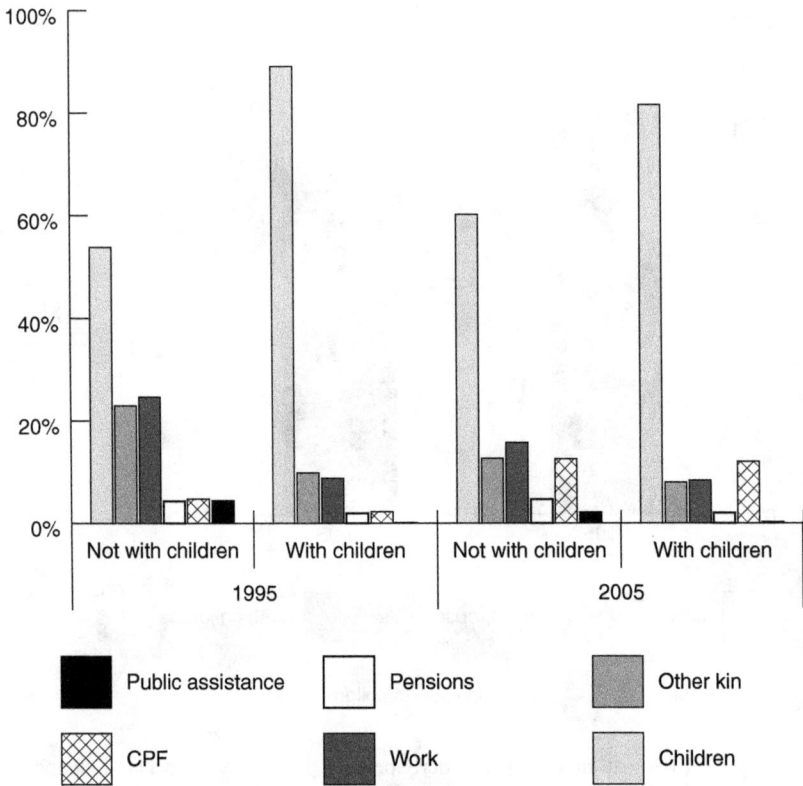

Figure 7.4 Elderly persons' (aged 65 and older) income sources by living arrangements, Singapore 1995 and 2005 (source: author's calculations using data from Singapore National Survey of Senior Citizens 1995, 2005).

The analysis in this section highlights the prevalence of low incomes among elderly persons under Singapore's retirement income system, which is built around the CPF. In fact, most elderly persons rely on children's support through financial contributions and co-residence rather than on their CPF savings. Improvements in access to CPF savings have also been uneven: the gains by elderly men are more prominent than those by elderly women. The next section turns towards future cohorts, their access to CPF savings, and the availability of family support.

Future elderly populations and income sources, 2005–2030

This section examines two key aspects of the prospects for old-age income security in Singapore. First, it presents projections of the future living arrangements of elderly persons in Singapore. The section focuses on the likelihood of co-residence with children because co-residence plays an income-protective function. Next, it models their access to the major categories of income sources.

The projections are made using *macrosimulation,* also known as the cell-based approach. First, a base population is stratified into *cells* that share common characteristics (e.g. sex, age group, and marital status). The incidence patterns of certain events (e.g. living arrangements or social security receipt) – patterns observed in the base population across the cells – are then applied to later cohorts. This technique has been used to study public expenditure (Propper 1993), long-term care financing (Comas-Herrera *et al.* 2006; Pickard 2008; Wittenberg *et al.* 1998), and the living arrangements and health status of older persons (Gaymu, Ekamper, and Beets 2008) in the United Kingdom and other European countries.

Future elderly living arrangements

The macrosimulation model in this study covers the period from 2005 (when microdata were last available) to 2030. The first set of projections estimates the number of elderly persons in each of four different living arrangements: (1) living with neither the spouse nor the children, (2) living with a spouse only, (3) living with children only, or (4) living with children and a spouse. To do this, the elderly population is divided into 48 cells based on sex, age group, labour-force participation, and living arrangements (Table 7.4). The size of the elderly population by sex and age in each year between 2005 and 2030 is drawn from the population projections by the United Nations.[3] Separate projections of labour-force participation (International Labour Organization 2012) are then incorporated to derive the proportion of elderly persons in the work-force within each sex–age category.[4] Next, the distribution of elderly persons by living arrangement in each sex–age–labour-force participation category is taken from the 2005 national survey data. Finally, given the considerable changes in the prevalence of intergenerational co-residence

Table 7.4 Variables used to divide elderly population into 48 cells

Variables	Levels	Values
Sex	Women Men	From United Nations (2011) population projections
Age	65–69 70–74 75+	From United Nations (2011) population projections
Labour-force participation	Not in labour force In labour force	From International Labour Organization (2012) projections
Living arrangements	Neither spouse nor child Spouse only Child only Both spouse and child	From national survey data in 1995 and 2005

as discussed above, the rate at which living arrangements changed for each sex–age–labour-force participation category between 1995 and 2005 is extrapolated and fitted into the projections from 2005 onwards.[5]

Figure 7.5 shows the results of the projections. The absolute number of elderly persons increases steadily across all living arrangements. At the start of the projections, the most common living arrangement is with children only, followed by living with both a spouse and children. But by 2030, living with a spouse becomes the most likely arrangement. During this period, the total intergenerational co-residence rate (i.e. co-residence with children and with a spouse and children) is projected to fall dramatically from 72 per cent to 47 per cent of all elderly persons. There is also a steep rise in the absolute number of persons living with neither a spouse nor children (from 45,000 in 2005 to 296,000 in 2030, an increase of 6.6 times).

The projections anticipate different patterns of intergenerational co-residence by gender between 2005 and 2030 (Figure 7.6). There is a steeper decline in co-residence with children for elderly men. Among men, the total rate of

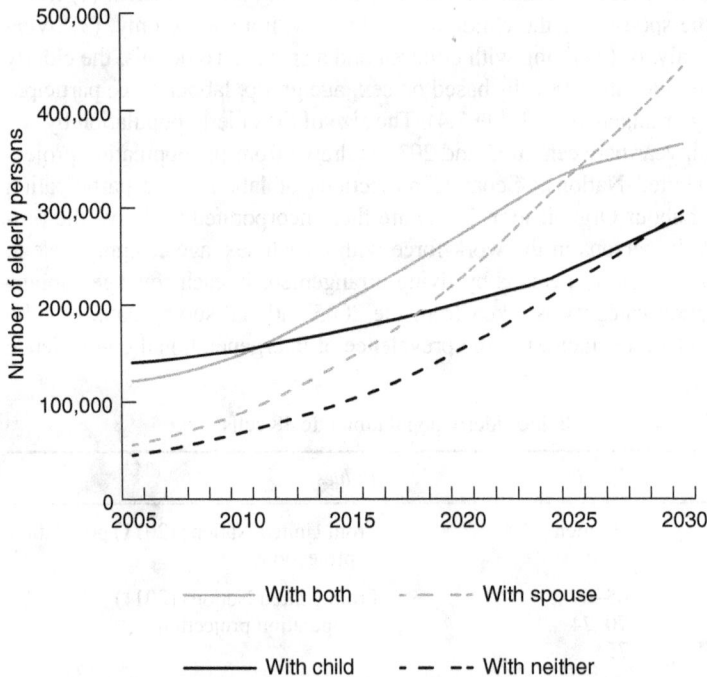

Figure 7.5 Projected elderly persons' (aged 65 and older) living arrangements, Singapore 2005–2030 (source: author's projections).

Note: Projections based on medium variant of United Nations (2011) population projections, International Labour Organization (2012) labour-force projections, and changes to living arrangements by age, sex, and labour-force participation at the same rate as between 1995 and 2005 as observed in the Singapore National Survey of Senior Citizens (1995, 2005).

intergenerational co-residence (with or without a spouse) is projected to decline by almost half, from 66 per cent to 36 per cent. By 2030, just 5 per cent of elderly men will live with their children only. In contrast, 17 per cent did so in 2005. For elderly women, the projected decrease in co-residence with children (with or without the spouse) is less sharp: from 77 per cent in 2005 to 56 per cent in 2030. A striking trend is that the proportion of elderly women living with neither their spouse nor their children is expected to almost double from 14 per cent to 27 per cent, whereas the relative size of this group remains stable among elderly men. Because elderly women tend to have fewer independent sources of income and are more reliant on informal support, including support received through shared living arrangements, this trend represents a particularly worrying prospect for women's income security.

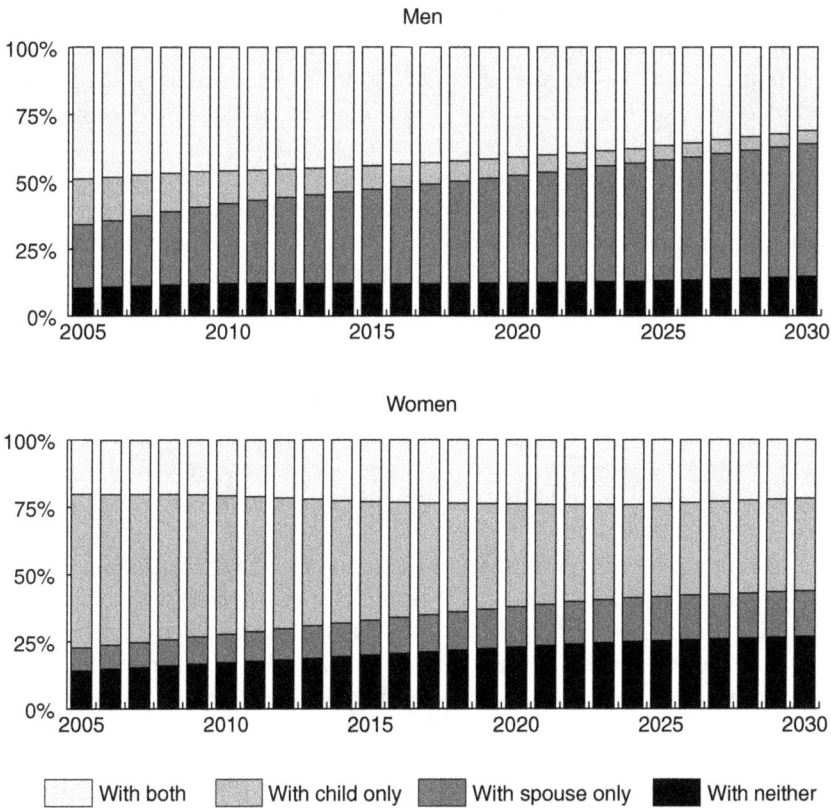

Figure 7.6 Projected elderly persons' (aged 65 and older) living arrangements by gender, Singapore 2005–2030 (source: author's projections).

Note: Projections based on medium variant of United Nations (2011) population projections, International Labour Organization (2012) labour-force projections, and changes to living arrangements by age, sex, and labour-force participation at the same rate as between 1995 and 2005 as observed in the Singapore National Survey of Senior Citizens (1995, 2005).

Future income sources

The second set of projections builds on the results for living arrangements to estimate elderly Singaporeans' access to different income sources. We first ana-lysed data on income sources from the 2005 national survey using multinomial logistic regressions that incorporate the four cell parameters – sex, age group, labour-force participation, and living arrangements – from the first set of projec-tions, which are applied as predictor variables. We coded income sources as the dependent variable using four scenarios: (1) neither market income nor chil-dren's contributions, (2) children's contributions only, (3) market income only, and (4) market income and children's contributions. Market income refers to wages, dividends, rent, pensions, annuities, and CPF benefits. These and chil-dren's contributions are among the most frequently cited income sources for elderly persons. Other possible income sources, such as contributions from other kin and public transfers, are therefore not considered in the projections. The regression model is significant at the .001 level (Table 7.5). We then used fitted probabilities from the regression model as incidence rates to calculate the number of persons from each cell who are projected to experience each of the four income scenarios for every year between 2005 and 2030.

Assuming that the relationships between income sources and personal charac-teristics (i.e. sex, age, labour-force participation, and living arrangements) remain constant from 2005 onwards, the estimates project an increase in access to market income, including income from the CPF, and a decline in the avail-ability of children's contributions by 2030 (Table 7.6). The proportion of elderly persons with any amount of market income increases from 26 per cent to 30 per cent, while the total proportion with children's contributions falls from 75 per cent to about 70 per cent. A particularly striking trend pertains to persons with access to neither market income nor children's contributions. Instead of dimin-ishing, the relative size of this group grows by 1–2 percentage points. By 2030, 222,000 elderly persons in Singapore may have access to neither market income nor children's contributions.

Combining the earlier projections of living arrangements with this analysis of income sources enables us to identify potentially vulnerable groups of elderly persons. Between 2010 and 2030, the projected number of elderly persons who have no access to market income or children's financial contributions and who do not co-reside with their children grows from 34,000 to 158,000. As a propor-tion of the total elderly population, this vulnerable group increases from 6 per cent to 11 per cent, signalling an increase in the risk of income insecurity.

Together, the two sets of projections suggest a steady decline in children's support through co-residence and financial contributions until 2030. Although access to market income, including income from the CPF, is expected to rise, the likelihood of having neither market income nor transfers from children may also increase. This casts new light on assumptions that improvement in CPF coverage among younger cohorts will benefit retirement income security across the elderly population.

Table 7.5 Multinomial logistic model of income sources for elderly (aged 65 and older) in Singapore (*N*=2663)

Income source[a]	B	SE	z	P > |z|
Children's contributions only				
Constant	.353	.179	1.98	.048
Men	−.644	.136	−4.73	.000
Ages 65–69 (ref)				
Ages 70–74	.227	.183	1.24	.215
Ages 75+	−.273	.150	−1.82	.069
In labour-force	−.967	.239	−4.04	.000
Living with neither (ref)				
Living with spouse only	1.635	.217	7.54	.000
Living with children only	1.683	.163	10.33	.000
Living with both	2.183	.196	11.12	.000
Market income only				
Constant	−1.190	.247	−4.82	.000
Men	.573	.199	2.88	.004
Ages 65–69 (ref)				
Ages 70–74	−.013	.235	−.06	.956
Ages 75+	−.681	.215	−3.17	.002
In labour-force	2.173	.227	9.56	.000
Living with neither (ref)				
Living with spouse only	.724	.273	2.65	.008
Living with children only	−.445	.267	−1.67	.095
Living with both	.799	.248	3.22	.001
Both				
Constant	−1.442	.261	−5.52	.000
Men	.493	.173	2.84	.004
Ages 65–69 (ref)				
Ages 70–74	.052	.213	.24	.809
Ages 75+	−.900	.190	−4.73	.000
In labour-force	1.013	.230	4.40	.000
Living with neither (ref)				
Living with spouse only	1.640	.290	5.66	.000
Living with children only	1.568	.250	6.26	.000
Living with both	1.863	.268	6.96	.000

Source: based on data from Ministry of Community Development, Youth and Sports (2005).

Notes
SE = standard error; ref = reference category.
a Reference category is 'neither children's contributions nor market income'.

Expected CPF pension outcomes

For elderly persons who do have access to CPF savings, there is a question about the level of expected pension outcomes. Studies that make theoretical projections based on existing pension rules provide a useful indication of these outcomes, given that the actual amounts of CPF pension payouts are not disclosed. These studies have produced a wide range of results. At the lower end, the OECD (2012)

Table 7.6 Elderly persons' projected access to children's contributions and market income, Singapore 2005–2030 (thousands of persons)

Income source	Men			Women			All (percentage of total)		
	2005	2020	2030	2005	2020	2030	2005	2020	2030
Neither	22	55	98	27	70	124	49(14)	125(15)	222(16)
Child	78	163	256	141	306	493	218(60)	469(55)	748(54)
Market	31	93	151	11	38	64	41(11)	131(15)	215(15)
Both	35	87	136	19	46	72	54(15)	133(16)	208(15)

Source: author's projections.

Notes

Projections are for elderly persons aged 65 and above. *Child* refers to cash transfers from children to elderly parents. *Market* refers to market income (e.g. salary, CPF, private pensions, annuities, rent, and dividends). Underlying projections of living arrangement based on medium variant of United Nations (2011) population projections, International Labour Organization (2012) labour-force projections, and changes to living arrangements by age, sex, and labour-force participation at a rate equal to that of the period 1995–2005, as observed in the Singapore National Survey of Senior Citizens for 1995 and 2005 (Ministry of Community Development, Youth and Sports 1995, 2005). Income sources estimated by regression on selected individual variables in the 2005 national survey dataset. See text for explanation.

estimates that average earners with stable earnings who join the CPF system in 2008 at 20 years old under currently legislated pension rules and retire after a full career will achieve a gross pension income that is 11–13 per cent of net individual lifetime average earnings (i.e. the net replacement rates), compared to an average of around 57 per cent across the OECD countries. But these estimates are likely conservative because the OECD omits the Ordinary Account in the calculations, essentially assuming that it is used entirely for housing and other purposes not related to retirement. At the upper end, a recent study commissioned by the Singapore government that incorporates dynamic wage growth paths and housing purchase arrives at gross replacement rates of 50 per cent to 52 per cent for median earners but notes that these may fall by up to 30 percentage points, depending on the type of housing assumed in the projections (Chia and Tsui 2012). A major challenge in interpreting the results from such theoretical projections is that they are highly sensitive to the underlying assumptions.

An alternative approach to approximate pension outcomes is to make use of the level of the minimum sum set by the government, which establishes a target pension saving that policymakers deem adequate 'to support a modest standard of living during retirement' (CPF Board 2007, 22). Taking the cohort aged 55 in 2009, the stipulated minimum sum translates into a monthly pension upon retirement that is equivalent to 43 per cent of the population median gross work income that year (Ng 2011; Ministry of Manpower 2011). But not everyone achieves this minimum sum. Among individuals from this cohort, the average actual CPF savings are estimated to fund a monthly pension that is just 31 per cent of the population median work income.

The difficulty of accumulating CPF savings to fund an adequate pension, despite very high contribution rates, is partly the result of current policy rules that permit pre-retirement withdrawals for other purposes, especially housing.[6] In 2005, on an aggregate level, withdrawals to purchase public housing made up 38 per cent of the total withdrawals from CPF savings that year, whereas withdrawals for retirement accounted for just 18 per cent (CPF Board 2005). By 2010, the proportion of withdrawals for retirement rose to 32 per cent, but withdrawals for public housing was still equivalent to 36 per cent (CPF Board 2010). Purchasing public housing has been the single biggest usage of CPF savings, rather than old-age pensions.

Conclusion

This chapter is concerned with the impact of the CPF on old-age income security in Singapore within the context of rapid demographic ageing. It analyses elderly incomes using evidence from national surveys conducted in 1995 and 2005, presents projections of future elderly populations and their income sources, and reviews the evidence on expected CPF pension outcomes. Results from these analyses point to four conclusions. First, mandated CPF saving has been in place for a long time, so the prevalence of low incomes among elderly persons is both surprising and worrying. In 2005, 73 per cent of elderly persons in Singapore had individual incomes that fell below one-third of the population's median gross earnings. Second, the CPF was not a prominent source of retirement income for elderly cohorts in the mid 1990s and mid 2000s. Instead, children's contributions were the most common form of income, and co-residence with children may have served a particularly important income-protective function for financially vulnerable elderly persons. Third, results estimated under certain assumptions suggest that future elderly cohorts until at least 2030 will have better access to market income, including from the CPF, but a substantial and rising proportion of elderly persons will have income from neither market sources nor their children. Intergenerational co-residence is also expected to decline, and this may hit vulnerable elderly persons the hardest. Fourth, even among persons with access to CPF benefits, the expected pensions may not be generous despite high contribution rates that limit individuals' capacity for private saving that may otherwise have helped finance retirement.

The disadvantage that women face is a particularly serious concern. The current CPF scheme accentuates rather than compensates for the income disparity that originates from gendered patterns of labour-market performance. Despite gains in the past few decades, women in Singapore still have lower labour-force participation and lower wages at equivalent educational levels than men (International Labour Organization 2012; Ministry of Manpower 2012). These result in poorer access to CPF saving in retirement and leave women more dependent on informal income, mainly children's support. The overall configuration of the retirement income system, with familial provision as a central pillar supported by a savings-based public pension scheme, heightens the risks of financial hardship for women under conditions of demographic ageing, which are expected to erode family support. Their financial vulnerability can already be seen in their poorer individual incomes, less diverse income sources, higher dependence on intergenerational co-residence, and a possible increase in the likelihood of living alone in the future.

The position of women draws attention to the larger issue of the interaction between policy and family that is discussed widely within the modernization and 'crowding out' literature. Modernization theory expects industrialization and development to gradually replace traditional familial care arrangements with solidaristic provisions of the welfare state (Burgess 1960; Cowgill 1972). Likewise, recent debates have considered whether the welfare state will eventually crowd out such family functions as intergenerational exchange within the household. European research suggests that family support even in industrialized societies has not given way entirely to state support and that family members continue to exchange a wide range of resources across generations (Kohli, Künemund, and Vogel 2008). Künemund and Rein (1999) argue that public pensions can in fact help to 'crowd in' family exchange by enabling elderly parents to give financial assistance to their children and grandchildren. But developments in Singapore are following a different chronology. Instead of state encroachment threatening the traditional role of the family, the challenge is one of public provision being slow to respond to retreating family functions. Income security will depend critically on the ability of policymakers to respond to the empirical reality that a shifting demography is changing the capacity and norms of familial obligation.

Notes

1 These are the legislated minimum interest rates (CPF Board 2013). In every quarter, the rate for the Ordinary Account is checked against a weighted sum of 12-month fixed deposit and month-end savings deposit interest rates at major local banks. The account's rate is revised if this weighted sum exceeds 2.5 per cent. The interest rate for the Special Account is compared against the 12-month average yield of 10-year government securities plus 1 per cent, also on a quarterly basis. These rules, though market related, are essentially arbitrary; CPF savings, being held over a much longer time, are not directly comparable to these benchmarks. The government does not fully disclose the actual performance of CPF investments.

2 The Singapore dollar (SGD) is the city-state's primary unit of currency. One US dollar (USD) is equivalent to approximately SGD 1.24.

3 The United Nations makes projections for several different demographic scenarios. The one adopted here is the medium variant: total fertility is assumed to converge on 1.85 for all countries; life expectancy is assumed to continue increasing but at a lower rate for countries like Singapore, where it is already high; and recent rates of international migration are assumed to continue.

4 Because the International Labour Organization projections stop at 2020, the macrosimulation model holds participation rates constant from 2020 to 2030. The projections are not differentiated by age, so the distributions of labour-force participation across elderly age groups are based on the national survey data from 2005. On the whole, labour-force participation is expected to rise for elderly men and women.

5 To account for the unavoidable uncertainty associated with these projections, calculations also were made under an alternative assumption that living arrangements change at a slower rate (i.e. half of the rate observed between 1995 and 2005). In this alternative scenario, (1) the likelihood of co-residence still declines but more gradually, to 58 per cent in

2030 instead of 47 per cent; (2) there is little difference in the projected distribution of elderly persons by income source, with no more than 1 percentage point variance in the prevalence of any of the four income scenarios when compared to projections under the faster rate of change; (3) in absolute numbers, there may be 208,000 elderly persons with access to neither market income nor children's contributions by 2030 instead of 222,000; and (4) the proportion of elderly persons with access to neither income source and who do not live with their children increases to 9 per cent instead of 11 per cent by 2030.
6 Low administered interest rates are another factor. See critique in Asher (2004).

References

Asher, Mukul G. 2004. 'Retirement Financing Dilemmas: Experience of Singapore.' *Economic and Political Weekly* 39, (21): 2114–2120.

Burgess, Ernest Watson. 1960. 'Aging in Western Culture.' In *Aging in Western Societies*, edited by Ernest Watson Burgess, 3–28. Chicago, IL: University of Chicago Press.

Chan, Angelique. 1997. 'An Overview of the Living Arrangements and Social Support Exchanges of Older Singaporeans.' *Asia-Pacific Population Journal* 12 (4): 35–50.

Chia, Ngee Choon, and Albert K.C. Tsui. 2012. *Adequacy of Singapore's Central Provident Fund Payouts: Income Replacement Rates of Entrant Workers*. Report. Singapore: National University of Singapore, Department of Economics.

Comas-Herrera, Adelina, Raphael Wittenberg, Joan Costa-Font, Cristiano Gori, Alessandro Di Maio, Concepció Patxot, Linda Pickard, Alessandro Pozzi, and Heinz Rothgang. 2006. 'Future Long-Term Care Expenditure in Germany, Spain, Italy and the United Kingdom.' *Ageing and Society* 26 (2): 285–302. doi:10.1017/S0144686X05004289.

Cowgill, Donald O. 1972. 'A Theory of Aging in Cross-Cultural Perspective.' In *Aging and Modernization*, edited by Donald O. Cowgill and Lowell D. Holmes, 1–13. New York: Appleton-Century-Crofts.

CPF (Central Provident Fund) Board. 2005. *Annual Report 2005*. Singapore: CPF Board. http://mycpf.cpf.gov.sg/CPF/About-Us/Ann-Rpt/Ann_Report.htm.

CPF (Central Provident Fund) Board. 2007. *Annual Report 2007*. Singapore: CPF Board. http://mycpf.cpf.gov.sg/CPF/About-Us/Ann-Rpt/Ann_Report.htm.

CPF (Central Provident Fund) Board. 2010. *Annual Report 2010*. Singapore: CPF Board. http://mycpf.cpf.gov.sg/CPF/About-Us/Ann-Rpt/Ann_Report.htm.

CPF (Central Provident Fund) Board. 2013. 'Central Provident Fund Board.' CPF Board. Accessed 1 June 2013. www.cpf.gov.sg.

Department of Statistics. 2012. *Population Trends 2012*. Singapore: Department of Statistics.

Gaymu, Joëlle, Peter Ekamper, and Gijs Beets. 2008. 'Future Trends in Health and Marital Status: Effects on the Structure of Living Arrangements of Older Europeans in 2030.' *European Journal of Ageing* 5 (1): 5–17. doi:10.1007/s10433-008-0072-x.

Housing and Development Board. 2010. *Public Housing in Singapore: Well-Being of Communities, Families and the Elderly. HDB Sample Household Survey 2008*. Report, March. Singapore: Housing and Development Board, Research and Planning Department. www.hdb.gov.sg/fi10/fi10297p.nsf/ImageView/Survey2008/$file/Monogram+2+Lores_R1.pdf.

International Labour Organization. 2012. LABORSTA Internet. Labour statistics database. International Labour Organization. Accessed 20 January 2012. http://laborsta.ilo.org.

Kohli, Martin, Harald Künemund, and Claudia Vogel. 2008. 'Shrinking Families? Marital Status, Childlessness, and Intergenerational Relationships.' In *First Results from the*

Survey of Health, Ageing and Retirement in Europe (2004–2007): Starting the Longitudinal Dimension, edited by Axel Börsch-Supan, Agar Brugiavini, Hendrick Jürges, Arie Kapteyn, Johan Mackenbach, Johannes Siegrist, and Guglielmo Weber, 166–173. Mannheim, Germany: University of Mannheim, Mannheim Research Institute for the Economics of Aging.

Künemund, Harald, and Martin Rein. 1999. 'There is More to Receiving than Needing: Theoretical Arguments and Empirical Explorations of Crowding In and Crowding Out.' *Ageing and Society* 19 (1): 93–121. doi:10.1017/S0144686X99007205.

Lee, William Keng-mun. 2004. 'Living Arrangements and Informal Support for the Elderly: Alteration to Intergenerational Relationships in Hong Kong.' *Journal of Intergenerational Relationships* 2 (2): 27–49. doi:10.1300/J194v02n02_03.

Low, Linda, and Tar Choon Aw. 2004. *Social Insecurity in the New Millennium: The Central Provident Fund in Singapore*. Singapore: Marshall Cavendish.

Mehta, Kalyani. 1999. 'Intergenerational Exchanges: Qualitative Evidence from Singapore.' *Southeast Asian Journal of Social Science* 27 (2): 111–122. doi:10.1163/0303824 99X00075.

Ministry of Community Development, Youth and Sports, 1995. *National Survey of Senior Citizens 1995*. Singapore: Ministry of Community Development, Youth and Sports.

Ministry of Community Development, Youth and Sports, 2005. *National Survey of Senior Citizens 2005*. Singapore: Ministry of Community Development, Youth and Sports.

Ministry of Manpower, Manpower Research and Statistics Department. 2011. *Report on Labour Force in Singapore, 2010*. Singapore: Ministry of Manpower, Manpower Research and Statistics Department. www.mom.gov.sg/Documents/statistics-publications/manpower-supply/report-labour-2010/mrsd_2010LabourForce.pdf.

Ministry of Manpower, Manpower Research and Statistics Department. 2012. *Report on Labour Force in Singapore, 2011*. Singapore: Ministry of Manpower. www.mom.gov.sg/Documents/statistics-publications/manpower-supply/report-labour-2011/mrsd_2011LabourForce.pdf.

Natividad, Josefina N., and Grace T. Cruz. 1997. 'Patterns in Living Arrangements and Familial Support for the Elderly in the Philippines.' *Asia-Pacific Population Journal* 12 (4): 17–34.

Ng, Kok-Hoe. 2011. 'Review Essay: Prospects for Old-Age Income Security in Hong Kong and Singapore.' *Journal of Population Ageing* 4: 271–293. doi:10.1007/s12062-011-9051-7.

OECD. 2012. *Pensions at a Glance Asia/Pacific 2011*. Paris: OECD Publishing.

Pickard, Linda. 2008. *Informal Care for Older People Provided by Their Adult Children: Projections of Supply and Demand to 2041 in England*. Report to the Strategy Unit (Cabinet Office) and the Department of Health, March. Kent, England: University of Kent, Personal Social Services Research Unit. www.pssru.ac.uk/pdf/dp2515.pdf.

Propper, Carol. 1993. 'A Cell Based Approach to Modelling Public Expenditure.' *Health Economics* 2 (2): 149–161. doi:10.1002/hec.4730020208.

Ramesh, M. 2004. *Social Policy in East and Southeast Asia: Education, Health, Housing, and Income Maintenance*. London: RoutledgeCurzon.

Wittenberg, Raphael, Linda Pickard, Adelina Comas-Herrera, Bleddyn Davies, and Robin Darton. 1998. *Demand for Long-Term Care: Projections of Long-Term Care Finance for Elderly People*. Report. Kent, England: University of Kent, Personal Social Services Research Unit. www.pssru.ac.uk/pdf/ltcrep98.pdf.

Part II

Asset building and diverse populations

8 A review of features and outcomes of the Hong Kong Child Development Fund

Charles C. Chan, Simon M.K. Lai, Eddie C.W. Ng, and Wendy S.Y. Lau

Policy background

Theories on poverty suggest that intergenerational poverty transmission is associated with poverty-related culture and the handed-down lifestyle (e.g. Lewis 1959). Risk and protective factors in family and community influence children's opportunities for development, and that influence affects whether they can leave poverty (Harper, Marcus, and Moore 2003). The literature proposes two promising approaches to poverty alleviation: mentorship programmes and targeted saving.

Many international studies support the idea that children from families with sufficient financial resources have better personal development outcomes than those with insufficient financial resources. Williams Shanks *et al.* (2010) point out that having sufficient financial resources can have direct and indirect influences on child development through families' ability to afford tertiary education, extracurricular activities and social opportunities, a stable and financial secure environment, and more time to communicate with children and provide non-financial resources.

Formal mentorship programmes facilitate positive youth development and help prevent youth problems (World Health Organization 2002; Centers for Disease Control and Prevention 2002). Mentors are non-related adults who promise to help mentees cope with problems they encounter during development (e.g. academics, relationships, emotions, even physical activity skills). In developing positive relationships with mentees, mentors expose youth to new experiences and provide emotional support. Research evidence indicates that young people benefit in different ways from participating in mentorship programmes. For example, participation may facilitate development of new interests, improve academic performance, reduce drug-related behaviours, or promote social skills (Dubois *et al.* 2002; Herrera *et al.* 2011).

In Hong Kong, the gap between the rich and the poor has been a major concern in recent years, and public awareness of intergenerational poverty is heightened (Gini coefficient in 2011 = 0.537) (Government of the Hong Kong Special Administrative Region [HKSAR] 2012). The former Commission on Poverty (COP), established in 2005, examined existing child development policies and measures. The commission identified developmental needs of children and youth from disadvantaged backgrounds to provide support for helping them break the poverty cycle (COP 2007). After reviewing international studies and considering various factors, the COP recommended the establishment of a Child Development Fund (CDF) to help children from disadvantaged backgrounds develop an asset-accumulation habit and provide long-term support for their personal and career development. The COP recommended gathering resources for participants' accounts from donations by family, the private sector, the community, and the government.

The HKSAR government created the fund and established provisions for its oversight. The government's Labour and Welfare Bureau is responsible for overseeing the implementation of the CDF and managing its long-term value. The Social Welfare Department of the HKSAR government is responsible for vetting the non-governmental organizations (NGOs) that enrol participants. The department also sets programme requirements and supports and monitors the CDF Pioneer Projects. The government also formed a steering committee for the CDF, inviting relevant and involved stakeholders to assist in overseeing, promoting, and monitoring implementation of the CDF.

Youth aged 10–16 comprise the targets for the three-year CDF Pioneer Projects, the main objective of which is to assist children from disadvantaged families through efforts to alleviate intergenerational poverty. All participating children come from families that received Comprehensive Social Security Assistance, accepted full grants from student finance schemes administered by the Student Financial Assistance Agency, or had a household income less than 75 per cent of the median monthly domestic household income in Hong Kong. Comprehensive Social Security Assistance is part of Hong Kong's social safety net, and the grants support students' access to education by providing financial subsidies for textbooks, travel, and internet access. Comprehensive Social Security Assistance and the grants are available only to individuals and households with low incomes.

Traditional service models provide programmes and services to satisfy needs, but the CDF Pioneer Projects introduce a new asset-based model to Hong Kong. The programme encourages children from disadvantaged backgrounds to develop asset-building habits and attempts to help children build a positive mindset, learning ability, sense of responsibility, and values.

Programme description

The CDF Pioneer Projects provide training, community service opportunities, and guidance to participating children to help them build monthly saving habits and achieve their short-term personal development goals. Mentors help participating children plan goals and accumulate non-financial assets. The CDF Pioneer Projects also offer training for parents and mentors to help them provide sustained guidance and support to participating children over a period of three years.

Six operating NGOs managed the first batch of seven CDF Pioneer Projects, each located in a different district of Hong Kong. The three components of the projects – personal development plan (PDP), mentorship programme, and targeted savings – convey the importance of key factors of child development. Social workers help the operating NGOs implement and manage the projects, including recruiting, providing routine administrative duties, monitoring progress, providing support, and reporting to the government.

Plans for personal development

The CDF Pioneer Projects require participating children to create PDPs with short- and long-term goals and specific action targets in the first two years and implement the plan to achieve targets in the third year. Targets must relate to education, vocational training, or skills advancement. The operating NGOs provide training on life and financial planning, voluntary service, and mass and group activities for personal and interpersonal development to assist participants in building a social network, financial literacy, attributes of caring and character, self-worth, and a mindset to plan for the future. They also help youth develop non-financial assets through mentoring relationships with adults.

Mentorship programme

The operating NGOs match each participant with a voluntary adult mentor who guides the participant to create and implement a PDP and helps identify specific action targets (e.g. obtaining a job-related qualification or purchasing learning equipment). In the process, mentors share life experiences and help youth build non-financial assets (e.g. time and resource-management skills). Mentors also help youth obtain support for their PDPs from stakeholders and resource holders. Participating children are encouraged to discuss their plans with their families and other non-familial adults (e.g. social workers and teachers). Mentors can act as mediators and facilitators for such communication by introducing relevant networks and resources.

Targeted savings

Participating children accumulate financial assets to implement their PDPs. Participants commit to saving each month during the first two years of participation. If a family financial crisis arises, the CDF Pioneer Projects provide casework services with the goal of keeping participants in the programme. The operating NGOs seek partnerships with individual and business sector-donors who match the youth's savings at a minimum 1:1 ratio of an amount not to exceed HKD 200. The government provides a special financial incentive of HKD 3000 upon completion of the targeted savings component.

Programme innovations

The CDF Pioneer Projects differ from other asset-based programmes in several key ways. First, they focus on developing and accumulating financial and non-financial assets and the ways in which the two augment one another (e.g. building saving habits through a mentoring relationship to ensure a successful experience in planning and execution of a short-term personal goal).

Another difference is the expected use of targeted savings. Participants in many asset-based programmes are families or individual adults, and programmes often restrict participants' use of matched savings to education, training, home purchase, and small business development. Such programmes are designed to help participants build tangible assets and leave poverty (Cheng 2004, 2007; Grinstein-Weiss, Wagner, and Ssewamala 2006; Mason *et al.* 2009; Ministry of Education Singapore 2009; Schreiner and Sherraden 2007; Sherraden 1991). In contrast, Hong Kong's CDF Pioneer Projects target children and young people from disadvantaged backgrounds and allow them to use savings to achieve short-term and long-term goals related to education, vocational training, or skills advancement, as stated in their PDPs. The projects encourage participants to use the funds for personal and career development purposes. Other matched savings programmes require disadvantaged youth to spend savings on education or training.

The mentorship and targeted savings elements of the CDF Pioneer Projects prepare children to accomplish their PDPs, which are tailored to the personal development expectations and capability of each youth. Each participant's PDP is sensitive to his or her unique developmental environment, stage, and needs. Because the savings are targeted to these individual needs, they are used for more varied purposes than savings in other asset-building programmes. The CDF Pioneer Projects provide plenty of opportunities for participating children to learn how to plan for their own personal and career development.

Most children in the CDF Pioneer Projects enrol at an age immediately before they face the challenge of transitioning 'from school to work'. Setting goals and taking strategic actions to achieve them are pertinent experiences. The projects' design provides the environment necessary to give participants a foretaste of aspiration achieved, matching each with a mentor who guides the youth in choosing and pursuing aspirations. Also, the inclusion of community-matched saving and government financial incentives reinforces that parents have roles to play in saving for their children's futures and in providing guidance. This design orients participants' families, development, and environment in a favourable direction.

Design and methods in the evaluation study

Analyses in this chapter stem from a government-commissioned evaluation study of the CDF Pioneer Projects (Hong Kong Polytechnic University, Department of Applied Social Sciences 2012). Participants' success in relation to the targeted savings component and the PDPs are the main outcome indicators

(Social Welfare Department 2008). Intermediate outcomes covered in the evaluation study to enhance understanding of the effectiveness of the projects included mentoring relationship, saving regularity, and saving patterns. Figure 8.1 presents the framework of the CDF Pioneer Projects. Surveys, focus-group discussions (FGDs), and process data are used to evaluate the effectiveness of the components.

This longitudinal study, which used a quasi-experimental design, lasted for the 42 months from December 2008 to June 2012. It examined various characteristics of participating youth, their parents, their mentors, and the operating NGOs. Specifically, it considered how these parties are affected by the implementation and operation of the CDF Pioneer Projects, which includes 750 participating children. We use data from the 721 participating children (96.13 per cent) who completed all three components of the projects and 208 of 488 matched control group participants who were eligible but did not participate. The CDF Pioneer Projects participants and control group members completed all rounds of the surveys.

Despite a significant age difference between the participant and control groups (t [516]$=-4.75$, $p<.01$; mean difference$=-.79$), we found no significant difference in their baseline performance on all psychosocial outcome measures. Yet, parents' expectations for children's educational attainment in the participant group are significantly higher than parents' expectations for those in the control group (t [379.76]$=-3.32$, $p<.001$), and parents' expectations for children's education are higher among parents of participants than among parents of control group members (t [402.27]$=-2.50$, $p<.05$). The two groups do not differ significantly in the importance (t [515]$=.353$, $p>.05$) and meaning assigned to studying (t [514]$=1.624$, $p>.05$).

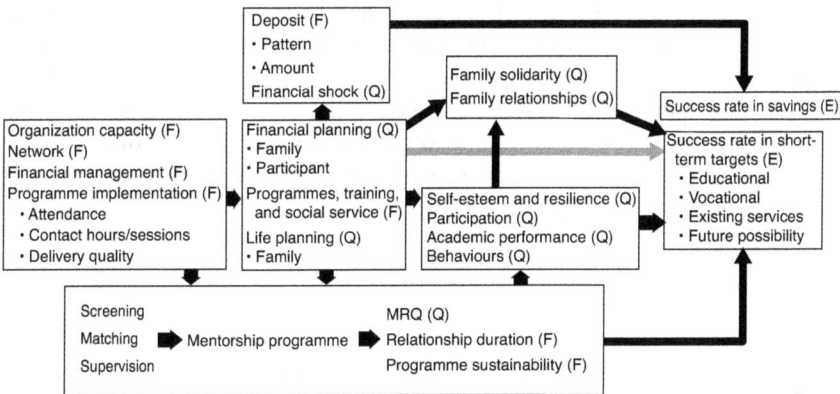

Figure 8.1 Conceptual framework of the CDF Pioneer Projects.

Note: (F) = collected by form; (Q) = collected by questionnaire; (E) = final outcomes; MRQ = mentoring relationship quality.

Surveys

Evaluation surveys were conducted at five different stages during the CDF Pioneer Projects: before the projects began (i.e. baseline), in the sixth month, at the end of the first year, at the end of the second year, and at the end of the third year.

The study designed separate questionnaires for survey participants, parents, and mentors to measure aspects of the three components. Youth's plans for future studies and careers are measured as part of personal development. Scale items on family relationships, interpersonal relationships, relationship with mentors as mentoring relationship quality (MRQ), psychological outcomes, future plans, and resilience were included as non-financial assets cultivated by the mentorship programme.

For the targeted savings component, the survey measured saving behaviours, attitudes towards saving, family saving habits, and financial status of parents.

Focus-group discussion

Three annual rounds of FGDs were conducted separately with each of the four stakeholder groups (i.e. participating children, parents, mentors, and staff from operating NGOs) to provide in-depth data on opinions and comments. Geographical location is the criterion used to select the participants for the first and third rounds of these discussions, whereas the purposive sampling method was used in the second round. This allowed us to investigate differences in participation across the three groups of different levels of performance, identify specific reasons for the low attendance in some activities, and understand the failure of some participants to meet the requirements (Social Welfare Department 2008).

The FGDs took place in a semi-structured format. The study created a discussion outline with questions about the three components of the CDF Pioneer Projects. It allowed discussants to freely share their personal experiences, feelings, and opinions on topics related to the areas identified in the outline. The discussions explored views on the projects and possible factors that contributed to differences in performance. A researcher led each FGD session, acting as moderator and guiding the discussion according to the outline. The duration of each FGD was about an hour to an hour and a half. Researchers audio-recorded each session to ensure accurate analysis of the qualitative data.

Process data

Process data come from the operating NGOs every six months. The data provide regular information on each participant's savings, activities, training record of frequency and duration of activities and content, and attendance at activities and training events. Data on PDP development are collected throughout the second year, and data on the PDP implementation process are collected at six and 12 months in the third year.

Main outcomes of the CDF Pioneer Projects and discussion

Financial asset accumulation: savings and usage

Saving performance

As stated earlier, 721 of 750 participating children (96.1 per cent) completed all three project components. Of those, 702 youth saved according to the specified schedule of HKD 200 per month for two years, received the incentives, and accumulated financial assets in the planned amount of HKD 12,600. The other 19 youth adjusted their saving targets according to their financial ability, either for the whole term or for certain months, and their savings ranged from HKD 7500 to 12,400.

Most parents in the FGDs reported that the HKD 200 monthly saving target was not a financial burden to the family, and family financial status does not affect their saving ability. They indicated that they can save this amount by planning and adjusting daily life expenses. A very low level of emergency fund usage, .69 per cent of the saving records with an average amount of HKD 554.54, shows that participating families were capable of meeting the targeted savings goals to accumulate and develop financial assets for their children's development.

During the 24 months of targeted savings, over 90 per cent of participating families saved every month, with the level missing a monthly saving instalment at approximately 7 per cent throughout this period. In the second year, the operating NGOs implemented different measures as follow-up actions to participants who did not meet the first year expected accumulative saving target (e.g. adjusting saving target and emergency fund). The positive effect of these actions was evident as 95.2 per cent of participants saved the expected amount in the middle of the second year. By the end of the targeted saving period, all youth achieved their corresponding amount of savings. Measures to help families save had a greater influence on completion of savings than financial status or individual factors, which did not correlate with the saving performance indicators.

Use of savings and time

The operating NGOs provided process data on the PDPs of 346 of the 721 participating children. Of these 346 youth, 332 developed their PDPs into 915 specific action targets.[1] A substantial majority (81.63 per cent) of these 332 youth developed and then changed at least one action target. Such adjustments to the PDPs and targets are routine and expected. As youth develop relationships with their mentors and save towards their goals, plans and targets evolve. Most of the modified action targets became more concrete and adequate to meet the needs expressed in the PDPs. Comprehensive data, including amount of money spent and completion rate, are available for 657 of the 915 action targets. Of these, data are available on whether 621 reached completion, and the average completion rate for these action targets is 78.84 per cent. In addition, 79.76 per cent of the 657 action targets involved use of targeted savings: 132 targets spent less than HKD 1000, 83 spent between HKD 1000 and 2000, and 12 spent between HKD 10,000 and 12,600. Amount of savings used varied and comments made during the FGDs suggest several reasons why some participants did not use their accumulated savings. Some discussants reported that they used public and network resources to implement PDPs. Others mentioned time constraints and indicated that school demands conflicted with the programme schedule.

Although the CDF Pioneer Projects allow participants to access and use their savings only in the third year, there is variation among children and parents on the appropriate time to start using targeted savings. There is no majority support among parents and youth for any of the six half-year periods in the three years of the projects as the appropriate time to start using savings. This suggests that preferences in the matter are influenced by differences in the timing of personal development and use of savings.

Understanding of development and targeted savings

Most participants identified clear goals for their savings, and over 95 per cent implemented PDPs relating to education, vocational training, or skills advancement. Such plans enabled youth to prepare for future personal and career development. Participating children who had development goals at an early stage started researching information on their action targets at the beginning of the targeted savings component or before joining the projects. This enabled them to cultivate sufficient understanding of the various aspects of their development goals and better use their financial assets. Other participants who did not have clear goals considered targeted savings to be a contingency plan for meeting unexpected needs, like paying course application fees for alternative education pathways.

In the FGDs, most parents agreed that targeted savings should be used on PDPs, thinking of academic development as a priority. Parents and participants recognized the importance of non-academic skills and interests, and the targeted savings and PDPs enabled participants to develop skills and interests they were unable to afford before joining the CDF Pioneer Projects.

Children and parents have limited communication on their understanding of development, and the CDF Pioneer Projects facilitate this communication. Because this work requires stakeholders to learn, which can take time, it is important to draft PDPs early. Social workers and mentors can act as mediators when children and parents do not agree on goals.

The aim of the CDF Pioneer Projects, instead of providing a short-term financial subsidy, is to equip participants and families with non-financial assets and financial capability to deal with complex and fast-changing financial conditions (Schreiner and Sherraden 2007; Sherraden 1991, 2003, 2005; Sherraden, Schreiner, and Beverly 2003). Participating children and their families must understand the CDF Pioneer Projects' objectives in order to cope with the limitation in achieving ambitious goals and fluctuation in the costs of action targets and avoid expectation on larger monetary support. Flexible implementation schedules for PDPs may be beneficial for participants going through major education or life transition period (e.g. public examination). The savings could be used to prepare them for the changes and taking a break from the programme could allow more time for other demands.

Non-financial asset building

Saving habits and financial training

In the first two years of the CDF Pioneer Projects, the percentage of parents who saved monthly outside of the projects' framework increased from 55.03 per cent (who started saving at the beginning of the programme) to 57.53 per cent (who saved after two years). In the first two years of the project, the proportion of parents who saved for participating children increased from 30.54 per cent to 40.32 per cent, and the proportion of participating youth who saved monthly increased from 69.32 per cent to 76.34 per cent. However, the saving regressed back to levels observed at the end of the CDF Pioneer Projects (35.57 per cent among parents and 68.01 per cent among participants). Only the number of parents who saved for participating children continued to increase by 5 per cent over the project period. The return to the original style of financial management after the targeted savings ended indicates that the targeted savings component can effectively promote parents' awareness of savings, but the effectiveness wears off. This may be related to the fact that parents have difficulties in implementing the effective financial management skills learned through the project-provided training. Clearly, training customized for the financial environment and daily life needs of these parents is necessary (Johnson and Sherraden 2007).

Targeted saving and training in financial planning provide participating children and parents with valuable experience. In addition to tangible financial assets, they develop financial knowledge in areas such as savings, planning, and development. As youth undertake financial planning and use savings for their PDPs, the CDF Pioneer Projects help them and their families develop financial literacy, financial skills, and confidence in handling financial problems. Increasing financial knowledge and literacy are important outcomes of the CDF Pioneer Projects. However, financial and non-financial outcomes can be greatly enhanced and many of the challenges in targeted savings overcome if youth and their families develop financial capability through participation; understand the effects of their financial decisions on themselves, their communities, and society; learn financial rights and responsibilities; access various financial resources in different social circumstances and occasions; and understand demands in different social circumstances and occasions.

Relationships

Various features of the CDF Pioneer Projects facilitate the development of children's relationships and communications with their parents and mentors.

Targeted saving provides parents and youth with a shared goal. In discussing plans, recognizing priorities, and implementing PDPs, youth improve communication and relationships with several stakeholders. Parents come to feel capable of saving a considerable amount of money for their children's development and are able to identify a variety of positive changes in their children. By participating in activities, meetings, and communications, youth and their mentors develop mutual knowledge and understanding. These experiences bring invaluable experience to participating children.

Mentoring relationship

Available data enable us to assess the frequency of 'communication and meetings' between 468 participating children and 265 mentors. The total number of reported communications and meetings are correlated positively with some dimensions of the mentoring relationship, and correlation coefficients increased gradually throughout the three-year period (Tables 8.1 and 8.2). The increase shows that communication and meetings facilitate development of the mentoring relationship.

Results from prospective analyses of the associations between mentoring relationship and children's various psychosocial outcomes confirm that the mentoring relationship exerts positive influences on resilience, future planning, self-esteem, and family relatedness $(0.12 < \beta < 0.17)$ (Table 8.3). The psychological proximity-seeking dimension of the mentoring relationship improves family relatedness psychology: proximity seeking. The trust dimension of the mentoring relationship enhances family relatedness: emotional quality. The estimates also indicate that the positive emotional engagement dimension of the mentoring relationship improves children's resilience through developing personal competence, career life planning, and goal setting. If participating children perceive that their preferences and interests are matters of concern to their mentors, they may increase positive emotional engagement through different modes of interaction. The perception also may promote and strengthen their trust in their mentors and their sense of responsibility for their own development. Such outcomes would further enhance participants' development of resilience, future planning, and family relatedness. International studies support the notion that good mentoring relationships exert positive influences on child and youth development (Allen and Eby 2011; Catalano *et al.* 2004; Chan and Ho 2006, 2008; DuBois *et al.* 2002; DuBois and Karcher 2005). Therefore, the CDF Pioneer Projects should focus on maintaining meetings and communication between mentors and participating children as a way to promote quality mentoring relationships and prepare for the potential challenges in mentoring relationships. Matching mentors with participating children, ensuring the maintenance of quality mentoring relationships, and enhancing the quality of mentoring relationships are all important in building the psychosocial assets of youth. Such non-financial assets are useful to their personal and career development.

Goals, plans, and poverty alleviation

Findings in this area are largely positive. Participating children outperformed control group members in setting life goals. Participating youth also did better in planning for life after graduation, constructing academic and career plans, developing long-term life goals, and formulating means of achieving life goals. Results from analyses that control for the level at baseline suggest that participating children perform better than their control group counterparts in career-life planning, goal setting, and future planning. Participating in the project significantly promotes the probability that youth set long-term life goals and plan for future academic enterprises or careers ($1.47 < ORs < 2.37$). Participation is also positively associated with identifying possible ways to achieve goals ($1.91 < ORs < 3.24$) and parents' understanding of their children's expectations towards the future or a career ($1.53 < ORs < 1.82$). In fact, the CDF Pioneer Projects require participating children to discuss personal development goals with their parents. Therefore, the programme can be expected to have a significant effect on the development of life goals and long-term planning. The findings confirm these expectations. The design of the CDF Pioneer Projects requires the operating NGOs to provide training on life planning and one-on-one guidance from mentors. Although the children develop their PDPs, they must discuss them with mentors, parents, and social workers. In this way, participation increases communication and understanding between children and stakeholders. These interactions enable participating children to use community and social network resources, increasing the channels and means available to implement life goals and plan for the future.

These findings could echo results from international studies on resilience. In those studies, adolescents with life goals exhibit higher academic expectations (Masten 2011; Masten and Wright 2010). In the process of pursuing and achieving goals, adolescents strengthen their self-esteem, and the endeavours promote family relationships. Components of the CDF Pioneer Projects enhance young people's pursuit and attainment of life goals, setting the foundation for participants' long-term development, family relationships, and resilience.

Since the study covers only a three-year period, the current data cannot provide direct evidence to support the hypothesis that participation contributes to the long-term alleviation of poverty. The findings on planning, goal development, and academic expectations demonstrate that the CDF Pioneer Projects provide a good foundation for participating children and create a favourable condition for their departure from poverty. They also exhibit better time management than the control group. Thus, participation is associated with an increase in extra-curricular activity participation and with a decrease in delinquent behaviours.

International studies indicate that people with long-term development goals have higher levels of resilience than those without such goals. They also note the importance of long-term development goals and higher levels of resilience as protective factors in poverty alleviation (e.g. Werner 1995).

Table 8.1 Statistically significant correlations between mentoring relationship quality dimensions reported by mentee and psychosocial outcomes

Psychosocial outcomes	Mentoring relationship quality dimensions						
	Round 2						
	Youth-centred relationship	Positive emotional engagement	Absence of negative emotional engagement	Trust	Psychological proximity seeking	Help to cope	Empowerment and performance standard
Resilience							
Survey round 1. Resilience – personal competence	.18**	.24**	.17**	.13*		.15**	.25**
Survey round 1. Resilience – acceptance of self and life	.15**	.21**	.19**	.13*			.21**
Survey round 3. Resilience – personal competence	.22**	.23**	.16**	.17**	.13*	.17**	.22**
Survey round 3. Resilience – acceptance of self and life	.18**	.20**	.15**	.17**	.14**	.16**	.22**
Survey round 4. Resilience – personal competence	.24**	.26**	.17**	.20**		.17**	.23**
Survey round 4. Resilience – acceptance of self and life	.22**	.22**	.14*	.14*	.11*		.15**
Future planning							
Survey round 1. Future planning		.13*		.19**		.11*	.14**
Survey round 3. Future planning	.15**	.18**	.14**	.22**		.10*	.17**
Survey round 4. Future planning	.18**	.17**		.11*			.15**
Career life planning and goal setting							
Survey round 1. Career life planning and goal setting	.31**	.37**	.18**	.21**	.17**	.26**	.29**
Survey round 3. Career life planning and goal setting	.26**	.29**	.11*	.11*	.17**	.20**	.24**
Survey round 4. Career life planning and goal setting	.27**	.29**	.11*	.15**		.16**	.19**

Self-esteem

	1	2	3	4	5	6	7
Survey round 1. Self-esteem	.14**	.19**		.18**		.13*	.17**
Survey round 3. Self-esteem	.12*	.15**	.11*	.15**		.14**	.16**
Survey round 4. Self-esteem	.14*	.17**	.24**	.26**			.14**

General health questionnaire

	1	2	3	4	5	6	7
Survey round 1. General health questionnaire	.16**[a]	.15**		.15**		.14*	.18**
Survey round 3. General health questionnaire							.13*
Survey round 4. General health questionnaire				.11*			

Family relatedness

	1	2	3	4	5	6	7
Survey round 1. Family relatedness – emotional quality	.30**	.30**	.14**	.13**	.34**	.22**	.28**
Survey round 1. Family relatedness – psychological proximity seeking	.21**	.28**	.21**	.22**	.14*	.20**	.30**
Survey round 2. Family relatedness – emotional quality	.26**	.33**	.12**	.11*	.37**	.18**	.29**
Survey round 2. Family relatedness – psychological proximity seeking	.24**	.29**	.32**	.35**	.17**	.22**	.30**
Survey round 3. Family relatedness – emotional quality	.23**	.22**	.10*	.11*	.29**	.19**	.24**
Survey round 3. Family relatedness – psychological proximity seeking	.19**	.22**	.17**	.24**	.12*	.20**	.27**
Survey round 4. Family relatedness – emotional quality					.22**		
Survey round 4. Family relatedness – psychological proximity seeking	.14*	.17**	.26**	.26**	.16**	.12*	.21**

continued

Table 8.1 Continued

Psychosocial outcomes	Mentoring relationship quality dimensions						
	Round 3						
	Youth-centred relationship	Positive emotional engagement	Absence of negative emotional engagement	Trust	Psychological proximity seeking	Help to cope	Empowerment and performance standard
Resilience							
Survey round 1. Resilience – personal competence	.19**	.21**	.25**	.23**	.14*	.25**	.26**
Survey round 1. Resilience – acceptance of self and life	.20**	.13*	.20**	.21**	.11*	.19**	.23**
Survey round 3. Resilience – personal competence	.25**	.28**	.22**	.17**	.18**	.19**	.32**
Survey round 3. Resilience – acceptance of self and life	.19**	.24**	.23**	.24**	.14**	.14**	.24**
Survey round 4. Resilience – personal competence	.22**	.23**	.14**			.21**	.29**
Survey round 4. Resilience – acceptance of self and life	.17**	.21**	.18**		.15**	.20**	.24**
Future planning							
Survey round 1. Future planning		.12*	.24**	.18**		.11*	.11*
Survey round 3. Future planning	.12*	.18**	.26**	.22**	.18**	.11*	.19**
Survey round 4. Future planning	.13*	.17**	.27**	.13*	.13*	.15**	.17**
Career life planning and goal setting							
Survey round 1. Career life planning and goal setting	.31**	.29**	.19**	.13*	.18**	.22**	.32**
Survey round 3. Career life planning and goal setting	.22**	.24**	.13**	.12*	.22**	.17**	.32**
Survey round 4. Career life planning and goal setting	.27**	.28**	.21**	.11*		.17**	.32**

Self-esteem

Variable							
Survey round 1. Self-esteem	.16**						
Survey round 3. Self-esteem	.15**	.20**		.22**		.15**	.13**
Survey round 4. Self-esteem	.14**	.11*	.12**			.11*	.15**

General health questionnaire

Variable							
Survey round 1. General health questionnaire	.18**	.17**	.21**			.15**	.18**
Survey round 3. General health questionnaire	.11*	.10*		.16**			.14**
Survey round 4. General health questionnaire	.12*				.11*		.11*

Family relatedness

Variable							
Survey round 1. Family relatedness – emotional quality	.24**	.24**	.14**	.17**		.19**	.24**
Survey round 1. Family relatedness – psychological proximity seeking	.20**	.21**	.27**			.20**	.23**
Survey round 2. Family relatedness – emotional quality	.23**	.25**	.29**	.13*	.31**	.23**	.29**
Survey round 2. Family relatedness – psychological proximity seeking	.23**	.24**	.28**	.30**		.23**	.30**
Survey round 3. Family relatedness – emotional quality	.23**	.29**	.19**	.09*	.37**	.21**	.26**
Survey round 3. Family relatedness – psychological proximity seeking	.21**	.25**	.28**	.17**		.18**	.26**
Survey round 4. Family relatedness – emotional quality	.19**	.19**	.14**	.14**		.14**	.16**
Survey round 4. Family relatedness – psychological proximity seeking	.17**	.14**	.27**	.25**		.22**	.23**

continued

Table 8.1 Continued

Psychosocial outcomes	Mentoring relationship quality dimensions						
	Round 4						
	Youth-centred relationship	*Positive emotional engagement*	*Absence of negative emotional engagement*	*Trust*	*Psychological proximity seeking*	*Help to cope*	*Empowerment and performance standard*
Resilience							
Survey round 1. Resilience – personal competence	.12*	.19**	.22**	.17**		.17**	.16**
Survey round 1. Resilience – acceptance of self and life		.11*	.25**	.21**	.15**	.13*	.13*
Survey round 3. Resilience – personal competence	.12*	.23**	.18**	.17**		.18**	.19**
Survey round 3. Resilience – acceptance of self and life	.10*	.18**	.22**	.24**	.14**	.14**	.15**
Survey round 4. Resilience – personal competence	.17**	.23**	.16**	.12*	.12*	.18**	.21**
Survey round 4. Resilience – acceptance of self and life	.13**	.24**	.19**	.21**	.10*	.17**	.20**
Future planning							
Survey round 1. Future planning		.13*	.24**	.25**		.13*	.12*
Survey round 3. Future planning			.25**	.28**			
Survey round 4. Future planning		.10*	.18**	.29**	.10*	.09*	.12*
Career life planning and goal setting							
Survey round 1. Career life planning and goal setting	.22**	.27**	.22**	.16**	.13*	.23**	.20**
Survey round 3. Career life planning and goal setting	.13*	.18**	.20**	.18**	.11*		.13*
Survey round 4. Career life planning and goal setting	.20**	.26**	.18**	.13**		.24**	.27**

Self-esteem

Survey round 1. Self-esteem	.16**			.18**	
Survey round 3. Self-esteem	.12*			.16**	
Survey round 4. Self-esteem	.15**			.22**	

General health questionnaire

Survey round 1. General health questionnaire	.12*	.14*	.20**	.15**	.11*	.15**
Survey round 3. General health questionnaire			.10	.16**	.16**	
Survey round 4. General health questionnaire	.11*		.11*	.14**	.14**	

Family relatedness

Survey round 1. Family relatedness – emotional quality	.13**	.17**	.11*	.16**	.22**	.12*
Survey round 1. Family relatedness – psychological proximity seeking			.23**	.25**		
Survey round 2. Family relatedness – emotional quality		.21**	.14**	.15**	.30**	
Survey round 2. Family relatedness – psychological proximity seeking	.15**	.17**	.19**	.22**	.10	
Survey round 3. Family relatedness – emotional quality	.16**	.21**	.21**	.14**	.26**	
Survey round 3. Family relatedness – psychological proximity seeking	.17**	.12*	.25**	.24**	.11*	
Survey round 4. Family relatedness – emotional quality	.12*	.17**	.22**	.14**	.37**	.12**
Survey round 4. Family relatedness – psychological proximity seeking	.14**	.21**	.39**	.29**	.17**	.11*	.15**

Notes

Round 5 survey data are not included due to representativeness issues from a low response rate.

*p<.05, **p<.01.

Table 8.2 Statistically significant correlations between mentoring relationship quality dimensions reported by mentor and psychosocial outcomes

Psychosocial outcomes	Mentoring relationship quality dimensions					
	Round 2					
	Youth-centred relationship	Positive emotional engagement	Absence of negative emotional engagement	Trust	Psychological proximity seeking	Empowerment and performance standard
Resilience						
Survey round 1. Resilience – personal competence			.13*			
Survey round 1. Resilience – acceptance of self and life				.12*		
Survey round 3. Resilience – personal competence	.14*					
Survey round 3. Resilience – acceptance of self and life						
Survey round 4. Resilience – personal competence						
Survey round 4. Resilience – acceptance of self and life						
Future planning						
Survey round 1. Future planning						
Survey round 3. Future planning						
Survey round 4. Future planning						–.13*
Career life planning and goal setting						
Survey round 1. Career life planning and goal setting	.14*					
Survey round 3. Career life planning and goal setting	.12*					
Survey round 4. Career life planning and goal setting	.12*					–.12*

Self-esteem
  Survey round 1. Self-esteem ... .14*
  Survey round 3. Self-esteem ... .12*
  Survey round 4. Self-esteem ... .15*

General health questionnaire
  Survey round 1. General health questionnaire ... .12* ... .13*
  Survey round 3. General health questionnaire ... .12*
  Survey round 4. General health questionnaire

Family relatedness
  Survey round 1. Family relatedness – emotional quality
  Survey round 1. Family relatedness – psychological proximity seeking
  Survey round 2. Family relatedness – emotional quality
  Survey round 2. Family relatedness – psychological proximity seeking
  Survey round 3. Family relatedness – emotional quality
  Survey round 3. Family relatedness – psychological proximity seeking ... .12*
  Survey round 4. Family relatedness – emotional quality ... .13*
  Survey round 4. Family relatedness – psychological proximity seeking ... .12* ... .13*

continued

Table 8.2 Continued

Psychosocial outcomes	Mentoring relationship quality dimensions					
	Round 3					
	Youth-centred relationship	*Positive emotional engagement*	*Absence of negative emotional engagement*	*Trust*	*Psychological proximity seeking*	*Empowerment and performance standard*
Resilience						
Survey round 1. Resilience – personal competence						
Survey round 1. Resilience – acceptance of self and life						
Survey round 3. Resilience – personal competence						
Survey round 3. Resilience – acceptance of self and life						
Survey round 4. Resilience – personal competence						
Survey round 4. Resilience – acceptance of self and life						
Future planning						
Survey round 1. Future planning						
Survey round 3. Future planning						
Survey round 4. Future planning						
Career life planning and goal setting						
Survey round 1. Career life planning and goal setting						
Survey round 3. Career life planning and goal setting						
Survey round 4. Career life planning and goal setting						

Self-esteem

   Survey round 1. Self-esteem

   Survey round 3. Self-esteem

   Survey round 4. Self-esteem

General health questionnaire

   Survey round 1. General health questionnaire

   Survey round 3. General health questionnaire   -.15*

   Survey round 4. General health questionnaire

Family relatedness

   Survey round 1. Family relatedness – emotional quality

   Survey round 1. Family relatedness – psychological proximity seeking   -.14*

   Survey round 2. Family relatedness – emotional quality   -.14*

   Survey round 2. Family relatedness – psychological proximity seeking   -.15*

   Survey round 3. Family relatedness – emotional quality

   Survey round 3. Family relatedness – psychological proximity seeking

   Survey round 4. Family relatedness – emotional quality

   Survey round 4. Family relatedness – psychological proximity seeking

continued

Table 8.2 Continued

Psychosocial outcomes	Mentoring relationship quality dimensions					
	Round 3					
	Youth-centred relationship	Positive emotional engagement	Absence of negative emotional engagement	Trust	Psychological proximity seeking	Empowerment and performance standard
Resilience						
Survey round 1. Resilience – personal competence					-.15*	
Survey round 1. Resilience – acceptance of self and life						
Survey round 3. Resilience – personal competence	.19*		.18*			
Survey round 3. Resilience – acceptance of self and life	.16*		.15*	.14*		
Survey round 4. Resilience – personal competence						
Survey round 4. Resilience – acceptance of self and life			.18*	.18*		
Future planning						
Survey round 1. Future planning						
Survey round 3. Future planning		-.15*			-.17*	
Survey round 4. Future planning						
Career life planning and goal setting						
Survey round 1. Career life planning and goal setting						
Survey round 3. Career life planning and goal setting						
Survey round 4. Career life planning and goal setting						

Self-esteem
- Survey round 1. Self-esteem
- Survey round 3. Self-esteem
- Survey round 4. Self-esteem

General health questionnaire
- Survey round 1. General health questionnaire
- Survey round 3. General health questionnaire
- Survey round 4. General health questionnaire — $-.15*$

Family relatedness
- Survey round 1. Family relatedness – emotional quality
- Survey round 1. Family relatedness – psychological proximity seeking — $-.20**$
- Survey round 2. Family relatedness – emotional quality — $-.15*$
- Survey round 2. Family relatedness – psychological proximity seeking
- Survey round 3. Family relatedness – emotional quality — $-.14*$
- Survey round 3. Family relatedness – psychological proximity seeking — $.19*$
- Survey round 4. Family relatedness – emotional quality — $-.17*$
- Survey round 4. Family relatedness – psychological proximity seeking — $.15*$

Note
Round 5 survey data are not included due to representativeness issues from a low response rate.
$*p < .05, **p < .01.$

Table 8.3 Summary of regression analyses of the positive influence of mentoring relationship quality on development outcomes of participants

MRQ Predictor	Outcome	β	P for β	R	R^2	ΔR^2	F	P for F
Positive emotional engagement	Resilience – personal competence	.164	.006	.407	.165	.025	12.974	<.001
Positive emotional engagement	Resilience – acceptance of self and life	.128	<.001	.371	.138	.015	10.742	<.001
Youth-centred relationship	Future planning	.120	.034	.401	.176	.016	12.917	<.001
Trust	Self-esteem	.156	.003	.543	.295	.023	28.025	<.001
Psychological proximity seeking	Family relatedness – psychological proximity seeking	.119	.022	.330	.109	.013	11.522	<.001
Trust	Family relatedness – emotional quality	.116	.022	.601	.362	.013	37.514	<.001

Note
All regression models are adjusted for baseline outcome score, sex, and age.

Conclusion

The CDF Pioneer Projects aim to develop financial and non-financial capability of children and youth from disadvantaged families to empower them to improve their future quality of life. The three components of the CDF Pioneer Projects have all achieved different degrees of success. Targeted saving enables participating children to learn to build financial assets with a well defined goal, and PDPs let them use their savings to experience a measure of success in such goals. Mentors provide guidance and support to participating children and youth throughout this journey, promoting participants' psychosocial outcomes along the way. In addition to implementing the components, the operating NGOs deliver financial and human resources. They develop local networks and community partnerships to sustain a programme monitoring system.

As a result of the territory-wide scaling of CDF Pioneer Projects in Hong Kong, the local community has become more prepared to use an asset-building approach and mentoring strategies to address intergenerational poverty. To date, the CDF Pioneer Projects have enabled establishment of creative partnerships among several sectors. Initiated by the HKSAR government, the CDF Pioneer Projects brought together NGOs, corporate and business sectors, philanthropists, and university research and training facilities. The funded CDF Pioneer Projects have encouraged these sectors to contribute to the community and make effective use of society's resources to create a sustainable intergenerational poverty alleviation programme.

Note

1 In the first and second years, participants completed forms on PDPs, which the operating NGOs collected. At the end of the third year, we asked the NGOs for an update on the progress of implementing participants' PDPs and received updates for nearly half of the records. Despite efforts to follow-up, we have not received further updates from the operating NGOs. Also, youth did not develop action targets. Thus, the number of participants with action targets is fewer than 346. We continue to collect data from the NGOs on participants' PDP spending and are considering other ways to complete the data on spending, which we deem important for understanding the function of the savings and its benefits for participating youth.

References

Allen, T.D., and L.T. Eby. 2011. *The Blackwell Handbook of Mentoring: A Multiple Perspectives Approach*. Hoboken, NJ: Wiley-Blackwell.

Catalano, R.F., M.L. Berglund, J.A.M. Ryan, H.S. Lonczak, and J.D. Hawkins. 2004. 'Positive Youth Development in the United States: Research Findings on Evaluations of Positive Youth Development Programs.' *Annals of the American Academy of Political and Social Science* 591 (1): 98–124.

Centers for Disease Control and Prevention. 2002. 'Strategies to Prevent Youth Violence: Social Cognitive Strategy.' In *Best Practices of Youth Violence Prevention: A Sourcebook for Community Action*, edited by T.N. Thornton, C.A. Craft, L.L. Dahlberg, B.S. Lynch, and K. Baer, 117–207. www.cdc.gov/violenceprevention/pdf/chapter2b-a.pdf.

Chan, C.C., and W.C. Ho. 2006. 'Intensive Community Mentoring Scheme in Hong Kong.' *Journal of Intergenerational Relationships* 4 (2): 101–106.

Chan, C.C., and W.C. Ho. 2008. 'An Ecological Framework for Evaluating Relationship-Functional Aspects of Youth Mentoring.' *Journal of Applied Social Psychology* 38 (4): 837–867.

Cheng, L. 2004. 'Developing Family Development Accounts in Taipei: Policy Innovation from Income to Assets.' CASE Paper 83, March, Centre for Analysis of Social Exclusion, London School of Economics, London. http://sticerd.lse.ac.uk/dps/case/cp/CASE-paper83.pdf.

Cheng, L. 2007. 'Asset-Based Policy in Taiwan: Demonstrations and Policy Progress.' Policy Brief 07-33, January, Center for Social Development, Washington University, St. Louis, MO. http://csd.wustl.edu/Publications/Documents/PB07-33.pdf.

COP (Commission on Poverty). 2007. *Report of the Commission on Poverty*. Hong Kong: COP.

DuBois, D.L., and M.J. Karcher. 2005. *Handbook of Youth Mentoring*. Thousand Oaks, CA: Sage.

DuBois, D.L., B.E. Holloway, J.C. Valentine, and H. Cooper. 2002. 'Effectiveness of Mentoring Programs for Youth: A Meta-Analytic Review.' *American Journal of Community Psychology* 30 (2): 157–197.

Grinstein-Weiss, M., K. Wagner, and F.M. Ssewamala. 2006. 'Saving and Asset Accumulation among Low-Income Families with Children in IDAs.' *Children and Youth Services Review* 28 (2): 193–211.

Harper, C., R. Marcus, and K. Moore. 2003. 'Enduring Poverty and the Conditions of Childhood: Lifecourse and Intergenerational Poverty Transmissions.' *World Development* 31 (3): 535–554.

Herrera, C., J.B. Grossman, T.J. Kauh, and J. McMaken. 2011. 'Mentoring in Schools: An Impact Study of Big Brothers Big Sisters School-Based Mentoring.' *Child Development* 82 (1): 346–361.

HKSAR (Government of the Hong Kong Special Administrative Region). 2012. 'The Gini Coefficient of Hong Kong: Trends and Interpretations.' In *Half-Yearly Economic Report 2012*, 86–89 (Box 5.2). Hong Kong: HKSAR. www.hkeconomy.gov.hk/en/pdf/box-12q2-5-2.pdf.

Hong Kong Polytechnic University, Department of Applied Social Sciences. 2012. *Report of Consultancy Study on Child Development Fund Pioneer Projects*. Hong Kong: Hong Kong Polytechnic University, Department of Applied Social Sciences. www.cdf.gov.hk/english/whatsnew/files/CDF_Final_Report_Eng.pdf.

Johnson, E., and M.S. Sherraden. 2007. 'From Financial Literacy to Financial Capability among Youth.' *Journal of Sociology and Social Welfare* 34 (3): 119–145.

Lewis, O. 1959. *Five Families: Mexican Case Studies in the Culture of Poverty*. New York: Basic Books.

Mason, L.R., Y. Nam, M. Clancy, V. Loke, and Y. Kim. 2009. *SEED Account Monitoring Research: Participants, Savings, and Accumulation*. Research Report 09-05, March. St. Louis, MO: Washington University, Center for Social Development. http://csd.wustl.edu/Publications/Documents/RP09-05.pdf.

Masten, A.S. 2011. 'Ordinary Magic: Resilience Processes in Development.' *American Psychologist* 53 (3): 227–238.

Masten, A.S., and M.O. Wright. 2010. 'Resilience over the Lifespan: Developmental Perspectives on Resistance, Recovery, and Transformation.' In *Handbook of Adult Resilience*, edited by J.W. Reich, A. Zautra, and J.S. Hall, 213–237. New York: Guilford.

Ministry of Education Singapore. 2009. *The Education Endowment and Savings Schemes: Annual Report for Financial Year 2007/2008*. Singapore: Ministry of Education Singapore. www.moe.gov.sg/initiatives/edusave/files/edusave-report-2007.pdf.

Schreiner, M., and M. Sherraden. 2007. *Can the Poor Save? Saving and Asset Building in Individual Development Accounts*. New Brunswick, NJ: Transaction.

Sherraden, M. 1991. *Assets and the Poor: A New American Welfare Policy*. Armonk, NY: M.E. Sharpe.

Sherraden, M. 2003. 'Assets and the Social Investment State.' In *Equal Shares: Building a Progressive and Coherent Asset Based Welfare Policy*, edited by Will Paxton, 28–41. London: Institute for Public Policy Research.

Sherraden, M. 2005. 'Inclusion in Asset Building.' Testimony for hearing on *Building Assets for Low-Income Families, Before the Subcommittee on Social Security and Family Policy, Senate Finance Committee*, 109th Cong., 28 April. www.finance.senate.gov/hearings/hearing/download/?id=902252de-38b0-418b-9778-0b616f2260e7.

Sherraden, M., M. Schreiner, and S.G. Beverly. 2003. 'Income, Institutions, and Saving Performance in Individual Development Accounts.' *Economic Development Quarterly* 17 (1): 95–112.

Social Welfare Department. 2008. *Child Development Fund: First Batch of the Pioneer Projects*. Service specification, May. Hong Kong: Social Welfare Department. www.swd.gov.hk/doc/young/CDF_Service%20Spec_E_rev_final.pdf.

Werner, E.E. 1995. 'Resilience in Development.' *Current Directions in Psychological Science* 4 (3): 81–85.

Williams Shanks, T.R., Y. Kim, V. Loke, and M. Destin. 2010. 'Assets and Child Well-Being in Developed Countries.' *Children and Youth Services Review* 32 (11): 1488–1496.

World Health Organization. 2002. 'Youth Violence.' *World Report on Violence and Health*, edited by Etienne G. Krug, Linda L. Dahlberg, James A. Mercy, Anthony B. Zwi, and Rafael Lozano, 23–56. Geneva: World Health Organization. http://whqlibdoc.who.int/publications/2002/9241545615_chap2_eng.pdf.

9 Savings accounts for youth

Initial findings from Nepal

*Sharad Sharma, Li Zou, Lissa Johnson,
YungSoo Lee, and Gyanesh Lama*

Approximately one-quarter of the Nepalese population of 26.6 million has income below the national poverty line, and about one-third of those in poverty are aged 10–24 (Ministry of Health and Population [MOHP] 2012). Around 83 per cent of Nepal's population lives in rural areas and depends on subsistence farming for their livelihoods (Central Bureau of Statistics 2011). Rural people generally live in poor economic conditions. Rates of illiteracy are high, families are large, and inhabitants own very little or no land. Poverty is especially prevalent among indigenous peoples (National Planning Commission, UNICEF Nepal, and New ERA 2010).

Although unemployment data do not reveal the percentage of Nepal's labour-force aged 15–24, the nation's latest Demographic and Health Survey indicates that the unemployment rate among females in this age group is as high as 32 per cent[1] and 26 per cent among males. The search for employment leads two-thirds of Nepalese youth to move to cities or immigrate to neighbouring countries by age 24, many of whom go to India (MOHP, New ERA, and ICF International 2011).

Despite recent growth in Nepal's financial sector, only 26 per cent of households have bank accounts (Ferrari 2007). The percentage of unbanked youth is likely much higher, as account holders are usually older and employed. Even among banked households, younger members are less likely to hold bank accounts.

The YouthSave project, a collaborative effort led by a global consortium with support from the MasterCard Foundation, investigates the potential of savings accounts as tools for building assets for the future and promoting social and economic development among low-income youth in Colombia, Ghana, Kenya, and Nepal. This study presents initial findings on the project's interactions with Nepalese youth.

Literature review

Asset-building theory posits that accumulation of assets has a positive impact on various dimensions of youth development. As Sherraden (1991) points out, assets play a unique, important role in promoting the life chances and long-term well-being of children and families. He identifies nine potential effects, suggesting that assets (1) improve household stability, (2) create future orientation, (3) promote productivity and human capital, (4) enable focus and specialization, (5) provide a foundation for risk taking, (6) augment personal efficacy, (7) improve the welfare of offspring, (8) expand social influence, and (9) increase political participation. A growing body of evidence from asset-building research empirically supports this theory, finding that assets have positive impacts on the economic, educational, and psychosocial development of children and youth, including those from low-income households in developed and developing countries (Chowa, Ansong, and Masa 2010; Scanlon and Adams 2008; Williams Shanks *et al.* 2010).

Promoting savings through formal bank accounts and financial services may be one effective way to encourage and achieve asset accumulation among low-income children and youth. Research in the microfinance field suggests that linking children and youth to formal financial systems accelerates the pace of financial inclusion by integrating them into the formal financial system early, by improving their knowledge of financial services, and by enhancing their experience with such services (Deshpande and Zimmerman 2010).

Asset-building programmes and policies have been implemented in the United States and several other industrialized countries. Empirical evidence shows that low-income, vulnerable youth are able to save and that accumulated savings enhance their outcomes (Nam *et al.* 2012; Schreiner and Sherraden 2006). There is less evidence on the links between savings (especially savings owned by children or youth) and developmental outcomes in developing countries.

Youth savings initiatives and their impacts in Asian countries

In this section, we briefly review the state of youth savings programmes in Asian countries and discuss the potential effects of those efforts on children's developmental outcomes. A growing number of local and national governments in Asia recognize the value of Child Development Accounts (CDAs) to help their young citizens accumulate assets for development (Zou and Sherraden 2010). Singapore, Korea, and Hong Kong offer examples of policies that use CDAs.

The government of Singapore has a comprehensive, asset-based social policy that covers the entire life cycle of its citizens, and youth are the beneficiaries of unique national asset-based programmes from birth until age 20 (Loke and Sherraden 2009; Zou and Sherraden 2010). The government of South Korea launched a nationwide CDA programme in April 2007 as part of a broad effort to reduce intergenerational poverty, narrow widened gaps in assets, boost birth rates, and invest in young generations for national economic development (Kim *et al.* 2011; Zou and Sherraden 2010). All youth in the child welfare system are eligible for CDAs until they reach age 17. In Hong Kong, the government officially implemented the three-year Child Development Fund (CDF) initiative in November 2008. Beneficiaries are children between the ages of 10 and 16 who come from low-income families. The monthly savings target for each participating child is HKD 200 (USD 26).[2] The matching rate is set at a minimum of 1:1 (Zou and Sherraden 2010).

Evaluations of these CDA programmes indicate that they have promising effects on outcomes. In South Korea, for example, 90.3 per cent of children with CDAs save in their accounts. The total accumulated savings is KRW 18.2 billion (USD 18.2 million), and the average total deposit per child is KRW 28,701 (USD 28.7) (Nam and Han 2010; see also Korean Federation of Child Welfare 2009; Zou and Sherraden 2010).

The Nepalese context

In Nepal, no local or national government policy attempts to build the financial assets of children. Financial institutions are underdeveloped and inaccessible by the majority of the population, especially residents in rural areas. Clustered in urban areas and small towns, financial institutions usually are controlled by a few elites.[3] Currently, there are approximately 30 commercial banks and more than six dozen development banks in Nepal (Lama 2012).

In response to the opportunities presented by growth in the number of cash remittances to the country, many of these commercial banks and financial institutions have launched savings products that target youth and other vulnerable groups. In 2005, for example, the Bank of Kathmandu (BOK) began to offer *Kopila Bachat Yojana* (Flowerbud Saving Plan), a savings account for parents who wish to save for their children. More than two dozen other banks offer savings accounts for children age 16 or younger. However, the majority of these accounts require a minimum balance. A review of published reports provides little information about the youth savings in these banks or the effect of those savings on the financial assets of children. To date, no prior academic research has investigated youth savings accounts and outcomes in Nepal. Little is known about children's access to financial institutions there or about whether they experience any developmental benefits from having a savings account.

YouthSave in Nepal

YouthSave's financial partner in Nepal is BOK, a full-service commercial bank. With 45 branches nationwide, BOK provides a variety of products and services. Its strategy of reaching out to low-income clients and its emphasis on bringing financial inclusion to all Nepalese citizens resonate with the goals of YouthSave. The bank's experience in offering savings products to children and youth is also attractive for YouthSave. The bank's widespread national presence, especially in Nepal's most marginalized western and far western provinces, provides a robust infrastructure for marketing and delivering the YouthSave product. New ERA, YouthSave's research partner in Nepal, is a private research institution that specializes in development research and policy analysis. New ERA works in partnership with the Center for Social Development at Washington University in St. Louis to conduct the research.

Officially launched on 26 April 2012, *Chetanshil Yuwa Bachat Yojana* (CYBY) (Conscientious Youth Savings Scheme) is YouthSave's product in

Nepal (Table 9.1). With CYBY, YouthSave aims to bring marginalized and unbanked youth aged 10–22 into the mainstream financial sector. Designed using data from an extensive market research process (Deshpande 2012), CYBY is a savings account that features an interest rate of 5.5 per cent and requires the account holder to maintain a minimum balance of NPR 100. Youth receive free piggy banks when they open accounts. Those who have reached the age of majority (16) may choose to receive a free Visa debit card (available only at certain BOK branches) instead.

Methods

Which youth client, household, and savings product characteristics are associated with positive savings outcomes? This is one of the primary questions of the YouthSave study, and answers will inform decisions regarding savings product development, marketing approaches, and commercial viability of these accounts. The Savings Demand Assessment – an account-monitoring tool used in all four YouthSave countries to answer the research question – not only provides descriptive information on youth savings account data but also assesses how youth and household characteristics influence savings outcomes. This chapter uses savings data collected from the beginning of product rollout (26 April 2012) through the end of first quarter of activity (31 August 2012).

Data collection

The research team developed a short questionnaire to be administered at the time of account opening. Because very little time is allowed for the account-opening process, the research team was strictly limited in the number of questions. The team selected the most salient characteristics to track (e.g. age, gender, school participation, household income, prior experience with formal savings accounts). After vetting the questions with BOK, the team pilot tested and revised them to ensure account holder comprehension and to reduce time required for completion.

The BOK branch staff obtained youth's consent to participate in the research and then posed the Savings Demand Assessment questions. Youth generally provided responses to the questions but sometimes received assistance from an accompanying guardian or BOK staff member.[4] Staff at BOK then transferred the responses from paper to an internal management information system and submitted data electronically to the research team. BOK provided individual-level transaction records that detail each account's deposits, withdrawals, interest, fees, and taxes.

The research team cleaned the data and merged transaction records with demographic records for analysis. The team also restructured transaction records so that each account holder had a monthly transaction record with variables reflecting monthly, quarterly, and total cumulative amounts of deposits, withdrawals, fees, and interest.

Table 9.1 YouthSave financial product features

Feature	Description
Product name	*Chetanshil Yuva Bachat Yojana* (Conscientious Youth Savings Scheme)
Financial institution	Bank of Kathmandu (BOK)
Type of account	Regular savings account
Eligible youth	Aged 10–22
Ownership	Accounts for minors owned by youth's parent/guardian but become property of youth when he/she reaches age 16
Account-opening requirements	Account opening form
	Minors (under 16): photocopy of parent/guardian's citizenship certificate and of document with youth's date of birth (e.g. birth or school registration certificate)
	Majors (over 16): photocopy of citizenship certificate or passport
	Photographs of youth (and in case of minors, parent/guardian)
Deposit/withdrawal requirements	Minors: adult signature and signature of youth required to withdraw, but youth can deposit independently
	Majors: independent transactions
	Monthly deposits of NPR 30 (NPR 1 per day) encouraged but not required
Interest rate	5.5 per cent on savings
Fees	NPR 100 account closure fee (waived if account held for two years or more)
Minimums	Opening and operating: NPR 100
	Balance required to accrue interest: NPR 1
Withdrawal restrictions	Limited to NPR 5000 per transaction for withdrawals made at aggregation points (i.e. schools, youth clubs)
	No limit for withdrawals made at bank branches
Incentives	Free piggy bank
	Majors can instead receive a Visa debit card, and the issuance charge is waived for the first year after account opening (offers are only available at bank branches for the first six months after account opening, but the period may be extended as part of promotions)
Other features	Free customer identification card
Delivery strategy	Periodic service at aggregation points (schools, youth clubs)
	Service at bank branches any time
	Agents carry point-of-transaction terminals (yet to be implemented)
Conversion upon majority	Once youth turns 16, withdrawals are frozen until the youth submits his or her own citizenship certificate
	Account can be retained indefinitely and is not automatically converted to another type of account but can be switched to another BOK product

Source: Save the Children (2012).

Note
NPR = Nepalese rupee; USD = US dollar.

Analytic procedures

Descriptive statistics summarize youth and household characteristics and savings performance. To determine which youth and household characteristics are associated with savings performance, the researchers conducted a multivariate analysis using ordinary least squares (OLS) regression. Youth participants opened accounts in 43 different BOK branches. To control for unobserved heterogeneity across branches, researchers added a series of dummy variables indicating BOK branches to the model.

There are a sizable number of missing observations, especially in the variables for household characteristics (e.g. household income, education of the head of household [HOH] employment status of the HOH). To consider potential bias due to missing observations, the researchers conducted multiple imputation by chained equation, which produces unbiased estimates for datasets from which a moderate number of values are missing (Ambler, Omar, and Royston 2007; Royston 2004). Researchers also ran the model with multiply imputed datasets to examine whether findings are consistent.

Measurement

Dependent variable

The dependent variable in this analysis is average monthly net savings (AMNS), which we measure as the average account balance per month. Our measure also considers the number of months since the account was opened. The formula for AMNS is as follows:

$$\text{AMNS} = \frac{\overbrace{(\text{deposit} + \text{interest} - \text{withdrawal} - \text{service fees and taxes})}^{\text{total net savings}}}{\text{account holding periods (by month)}}.$$

Because the original savings outcomes were measured in the national currency, the team converted amounts into comparable USD using the purchasing power parity factors for 2011.[5]

Independent variables

Independent variables include youth and household demographic characteristics. Youth demographic measures include gender, age, school enrolment, last grade completed, income in the six months prior to account opening, previous formal accounts held by the youth, the source of funds, caste/ethnic status, and reasons for saving. The analyses treat school enrolment dichotomously (1 = enrolled in school at account opening, 0 = not enrolled in school at that point). The variable for last grade completed originally included seven categories. Given the small sample sizes for several categories and to facilitate analysis, researchers recoded it into three categories: primary or below; secondary; and technical school, college, or university. Whether the youth report receiving income in the six months prior to account opening and having previous formal accounts were measured dichotomously (1 = yes, 0 = no). The variable capturing sources of funds also was measured dichotomously (1 = earned income, 0 = others). The caste/ethnicity variable was measured in five categories: Dalit, Brahmin, Chhetri, indigenous group, and others. The indigenous group was not divided further because there are more than 100 indigenous subgroups in Nepal. Reasons for saving were measured in four categories: emergencies, own education, day-to-day expenses, and other reasons. A series of dummy variables indicating each of the original response categories were used in the analysis.

Household demographic measures included information on the HOH such as formal bank account ownership, education level, employment status, and employment in the agricultural sector. Household measures also included the number of household members, household income, and whether the household owns transportation. The HOH's relationship with the account holder was captured in three categories: father, mother, and others. The measures of formal account ownership, employment in the agricultural sector, and household transportation ownership were recorded as dichotomous (1 = yes, 0 = no). Original response categories for the HOH's education were recoded into four categories: no formal education; primary; secondary; and technical school, college, or university. The HOH's employment status was measured in three categories (1 = employed, 2 = retired/pensioner, and 3 = not employed). To provide a clear understanding of means and resources available, the researchers constructed a household income variable based on reported household income and the International Labour Organization's (2010) minimum monthly household income for each country in 2009. Researchers used the organization's minimum income figure to create six income strata. Stratum 1 includes all account holder households with reported incomes lower than the International Labour Organization's minimum monthly income, and Stratum 6 includes all those with reported incomes more than five times the minimum.

Results

Account uptake

A total of 992 account holders opened accounts between 26 April 2012 and 31 August 2012, and no accounts were closed. Of these 992 account holders, 962 agreed to participate in the YouthSave study and are included in the analysis. Figure 9.1 shows the number of accounts opened during each month of the study period. Youth opened 13 accounts in the first week of product rollout, which occurred in the last week of April 2012. The number of new accounts steadily increased over time and was relatively consistent in the last three months of the period: 152 in May, 285 in June, 258 in July, and 254 in August.

Characteristics of youth account holders

Demographic characteristics of youth account holders are presented in Table 9.2. Their ages are distributed almost equally across the range between ages 9 and 22.

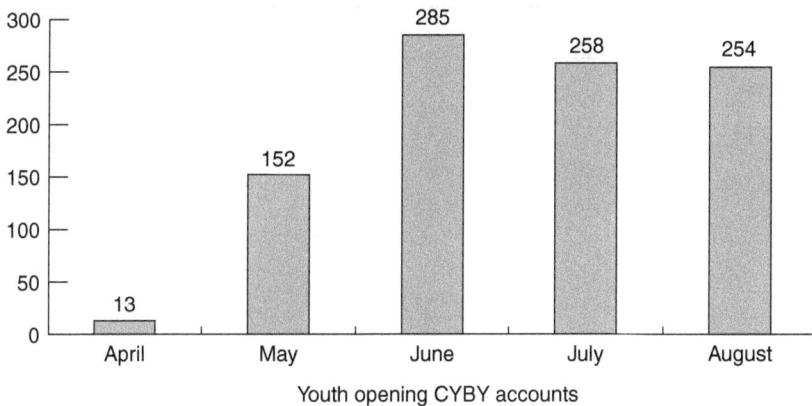

Figure 9.1 Youth account uptake by month (*N*=962) (source: YouthSave Savings Demand Assessment).

Note: CYBY = *Chetanshil Yuwa Bachat Yojana.*

The mean age is 15.59 years, which is near the age of majority (16) in Nepal. The sample includes more young men (65 per cent) than young women (35 per cent). The majority (92 per cent) report being enrolled in school at the time of the survey, while 8 per cent were out of school. Most youth (85 per cent) report that they completed a secondary-level grade (grades 6–10) or higher, which appears to be consistent with the mean age (15 years) of account holders.

Most youth report that the funds for their savings accounts came from their parents or relatives (83 per cent). A small percentage (14 per cent) report that their earned income is the source for the account, which is consistent with the 19 per cent of youth who report that they worked for income during the six months prior to opening the account. Only 16 per cent of youth report that they had previous experience with formal banking. The two most commonly cited reasons for saving in YouthSave accounts are for their own education (61 per cent) and emergencies (27 per cent). The largest proportion of account holders reports learning about the YouthSave product through radio, television, or newspapers (40 per cent), but sizable proportions report learning about it from friends or family (28 per cent) and BOK's fairs, rallies, and meetings (15 per cent).

Household characteristics

Table 9.3 details the characteristics of account holders' households. The average household includes 4.92 people. This is consistent with the preliminary results from a 2011 census, which indicates that household size has decreased from 5.4 to 4.7 people since 1991 (Central Bureau of Statistics 2011). All castes and several ethnic groups are represented among the account holders. To facilitate

Table 9.2 Descriptive statistics of youth characteristics

Variable	n (%)
Categorical	
Age	
Below 10	6 (1)
10–12	229 (24)
13–15	211 (22)
16–18	274 (28)
19–22	241 (25)
Gender	
Male	628 (65)
Female	334 (35)
Currently enrolled in school	
Yes	887 (92)
No	75 (8)
Education level	
No education/pre-primary	8 (1)
Primary (grades 1–5)	136 (14)
Secondary (grades 6–10)	456 (47)
Higher secondary (grades 11–12)	307 (32)
Technical school, college, or university	55 (6)
Income in six months prior to account opening	
Yes	187 (19)
No	775 (81)
Prior experience with formal bank account (youth)	
Yes	150 (16)
No	800 (84)
Source of savings	
Earned income	138 (14)
From parents/relatives	796 (83)
From friends/others	28 (3)
Reason for saving	
For emergencies	259 (27)
For a business	9 (1)
For own education	583 (61)
For relatives' education	7 (1)
For day-to-day expenses	60 (6)
How learned about account	
Radio, TV, or newspaper	392 (40)
Bank fair, rallies, or mass meeting	142 (15)
Financial education workshop	75 (8)
School or college	64 (6)
Friend or family	268 (28)
Comic book, internet, or other	30 (3)
Continuous	
Age[a]	15.59 (3.43)

Note

a Results are presented as means (and standard deviations).

analysis, we divided youth into two broad groups: the indigenous group and the caste group. About 27 per cent of study participants identify themselves as indigenous.[6]

The father is most often reported as the HOH (83 per cent). As such, HOH information generally reflects fathers' characteristics. Eighty-two per cent of HOHs are reported to have had a formal bank account at some prior point. The reported education levels of HOHs are distributed evenly across the spectrum: 32 per cent are reported to have a primary-level education (grades 1–5) or less, 29 per cent are reported to have secondary (grades 6–10) education, and 39 per cent are reported to have higher secondary (grades 11–12) or more education.

Most HOHs (76 per cent) are reported to be employed at the time of account opening, 7 per cent are reported to be retired, and 13 per cent are reported to be unemployed. The majority (63 per cent of the full sample; 48 per cent of those employed) do not work in the agricultural sector. Household income levels are distributed across the six strata, but only 27 per cent of households have incomes that place them in the two lowest income strata. The percentage of households in the bottom three strata (51 per cent) is almost equal to that in the upper three strata (49 per cent).

A potential indicator of wealth is asset ownership. To help assess levels of wealth among households, the survey includes one question about transportation ownership. Although 41 per cent of households own no mode of transportation, 22 per cent own non-motorized transportation, and 37 per cent own some form of motorized transportation. If one assumes that owning motorized transportation reflects a relatively high wealth status, it would appear that 63 per cent of the account holders are in a lower wealth group. However, bicycles and rickshaws are two of the most common forms of transportation in Nepal, and approximately one-fourth of the urban population owns a motorcycle. Therefore, responses to this question alone do not provide a sufficient basis for conclusions about wealth level, and additional information is needed (MOHP, New Era, and ICF International 2011).

Knowing the relationship of the person who signed to open the account may provide useful information. It can indicate whether youth signed up for their own accounts and who answered the demographic questions. For example, a high number (50 per cent) of youth opened accounts on their own, which may reflect the age of the sample (more than 50 per cent are age 16 or over) and the legal age of majority being 16 years in Nepal.

Savings performance

Table 9.4 shows overall savings performance across all accounts during the period from the product rollout (26 April 2012) until the end of the first quarter (31 August 2012). On average, accounts were open for 57 days before the end of the study period. During that time, account holders deposited a total of NPR 9,353,110 (USD 276,850). After interest, withdrawals, taxes, and fees, account holders had total savings of NPR 3,545,647 (USD 104,951). On average, youth

Table 9.3 Descriptive statistics of household demographic characteristics

Variable	n (%)
Categorical	
Head of household	
Father	798 (83)
Mother	125 (13)
Self or other	39 (4)
Prior experience with formal bank account	
Yes (this or other financial institutions)	695 (82)
No	148 (18)
Education level	
No formal education	122 (14)
Primary (grades 1–5)	161 (18)
Secondary (grades 6–10)	254 (29)
Higher secondary (grades 11–12)	135 (15)
Technical school, college, or university	206 (24)
Work in agricultural sector	
Yes	349 (37)
No	595 (63)
Employment status	
Employed	734 (76)
Pensioner/retired	67 (7)
Not employed	120 (13)
Other	41 (4)
Household income	
Strata 1	76 (11)
Strata 2	118 (16)
Strata 3	174 (24)
Strata 4	111 (16)
Strata 5	79 (11)
Strata 6	156 (22)
Household transportation	
No transportation	394 (41)
Non-motorized	216 (22)
Motorized	314 (33)
Both non-motorized and motorized	38 (4)
Caste or ethnicity	
Indigenous group	257 (27)
Dalit	46 (5)
Brahmin	309 (32)
Chhetri	284 (29)
Others	66 (7)
Who signed for account	
Parents	443 (46)
Relatives or others	41 (4)
Self	478 (50)
Continuous[a]	
Household income	3.65 (1.65)
Number of household members	4.92 (1.24)

Note
a Results are presented as means (and standard deviations).

made two deposits and one withdrawal between the time of account opening and the end of the data collection period. Table 9.4 also shows the average amount of savings and withdrawals per account holder. For the study period, each youth saved an average of NPR 3686 (USD 109).

Youth opened accounts at different times during the study period. We calculate AMNS to account for these differences (Schreiner 2001). For the study period, the AMNS is NPR 1912 (USD 57).

The research team conducted a multivariate analysis to identify youth and household characteristics associated with savings performance (Table 9.5). In this OLS model, AMNS serves as the dependent variable. Only one variable, household size, is significantly associated with savings performance at an alpha level of .05 ($b=-45.36$, $t=-3.24$, $p<.001$). That is, the more people in the household, the lower the amount of savings.

Three additional variables are marginally significant at an alpha level of .10: gender, youth's prior experience with a bank account, and caste/ethnicity. Although more males opened accounts, females saved more. Youth who report prior experience with a formal bank account save more than do those who report no such experience. Youth who identify themselves as Brahmin save less than do those from the indigenous group.[7]

As we mention above, this study uses multiple imputation by chained equation to impute values for several household variables. We created five imputed datasets and calculated combined estimates across them. Findings based on the multiple imputed datasets are consistent with those from the raw data, except that analyses of imputed data indicate that gender is significantly associated with savings performance at an alpha level of .05 ($b=-67.39$, $t=-2.54$, $p<.05$).

Table 9.4 Summary of accounts

Savings	NPR (USD)
Account totals	
Total amount of deposits	9,353,110 (276,850)
Total amount of interest	53,197 (1575)
Total amount of withdrawals	5,858,000 (173,396)
Total amount of service fees	2660 (79)
Total net savings	3,545,647 (104,951)
Average activity per account	
Average amount of deposits (including interest)	9778 (289)
Average amount of withdrawals (including fees)	6092 (180)
Average net savings (balance) per account	3686 (109)

Source: YouthSave Savings Demand Assessment, 26 April to 31 August 2012.

Notes
NPR = Nepalese rupee; USD = US dollar. Results are converted into comparable USD using the purchasing power parity factors for 2011. The conversion rates are drawn from the International Monetary Fund's World Economic Outlook dataset: www.imf.org/external/pubs/ft/weo/2012/01/index.htm.

Table 9.5 Youth and household characteristics associated with average monthly net savings

Characteristic	Coefficient	SE
Male	−56.85[†]	35.37
Age	4.72	7.05
Enrolled in school	18.93	73.23
Last grade completed (primary or below)		
Secondary, grades 6–12	26.08	54.05
Technical school, college, or university	17.58	93.64
Income in six months prior to account opening	−26.15	62.21
Youth's prior experience with formal bank account	87.02[†]	47.13
Source of fund (other source)		
Earned income	−29.74	71.43
Reason for savings (for emergencies)		
For education	22.66	40.96
For day-to-day expenses	29.31	79.87
For other reasons	5.21	75.15
Caste/ethnicity (indigenous group)		
Dalit	−72.63	79.76
Brahmin	−83.41[†]	44.52
Chhetri	−44.77	43.97
Others	−19.52	81.54
Head of household (father)		
Mother	−50.39	52.29
Others	−103.56	97.40
Head of household's prior experience with formal bank account	−65.43	46.37
Household size	−45.36*	14.00
Education of head of household (no formal education)		
Primary, grades 1–5	−88.24	59.60
Secondary, grades 6–12	−69.95	56.31
Technical school, college, or university	−25.20	65.87
Agricultural sector (head of household)	19.29	40.07
Employment of head of household (employed)		
Retired/pensioner	−23.41	61.41
Not employed	54.46	58.40
Household income	11.04	12.24
Having transportation	−41.91	38.61

Notes

$N=592$; $R^2=.09$. Reference categories are identified in parentheses in the leftmost column. A series of dummy variables indicating each branch are included in the model to control for unobserved heterogeneity across branches (estimates are not shown in this table).

[†]$p<.10$; *$p<.001$.

Discussion

Initial findings indicate that youth in the targeted age range (10–22 years) are signing up for the account and that the distribution of account holders is nearly equal across the age range. Half of the youth sign up on their own with no guardian as signatory, which suggests that youth choose to manage their savings in a formal banking institution if given the opportunity.

A key question is whether *low-income* youth are signing up for accounts. Although BOK designed a product to attract low-income youth specifically, the CYBY account seems to be equally attractive to youth across the income spectrum. The income range reported by the youth suggests that only 27 per cent are from the targeted low-income households. What might explain this? First, a product designed for youth is likely to be popular regardless of the youth's household income. Also, the product marketing and media efforts have been extensive, reaching the wider population and beyond targeted geographic areas or specific populations.

Are youth saving in their accounts? It is important to keep in mind that only four months passed between the product release and the end of data collection for this analysis. On average, accounts had been open for less than two months at that point. Nonetheless, the youth made an average of two deposits and one withdrawal in the 57 days after opening an account. The average monthly balance is NPR 1912 or USD 57. It is too early to draw conclusions about patterns of saving over time, but youth are opening accounts and saving in them.

Finally, we ask who is saving the most. Because it is so early in the rollout and numbers are still low, it is difficult to identify significant findings. Household size is the only variable significantly associated with savings performance, which is a logical result. Youth from larger households may save less because the available resources are spread across more people. Although only marginally significant, differences in gender, youth's prior experience with a bank account, and caste/ethnic status bear some discussion.

Of interest is the finding that males opened almost twice as many accounts as did females, but that female account holders saved more. One possible explanation is that young men are more comfortable with the financial institution or have more opportunity or mobility to open an account.

Another important focus of the research is the level of experience with accounts at formal financial institutions. The findings indicate that BOK is attracting youth who have not previously used financial institutions and that youth save more when they have some prior experience with the formal financial sector. This latter finding supports theories on financial capability and affirms the purpose of the YouthSave project. Those theories and the project emphasize the importance and potential impact of early exposure to saving opportunities (Johnson and Sherraden 2007; Sherraden 2010).

Brahmin households, on average, save significantly less than indigenous group households. Similarly, savings by indigenous groups do not differ significantly from those by any other caste group, except the Brahmin. The reason for this is not clear. Similarly, there is no significant difference in savings by income level, but it is worth noting that youth who are in low-income categories save as much as those in high-income categories. The findings imply that poorer people may be saving proportionally more. At this stage, however, caution should be exercised in interpreting findings.

Limitations

Some limitations in this study affect the ways in which readers should interpret the findings. First, the data come from the period immediately following the initial rollout of a new financial product and new account-opening procedures. Only four months passed between the product's launch and the end of data collection for this analysis, so it is too early to detect saving patterns or offer strong interpretations of them. Second, BOK implemented new data collection and consent processes during account opening, and bank staff required additional training and time to become comfortable with the processes. Familiarity with the processes varied by branch and across branch staff. Data quality may vary as a result. Third, bank staff collected data on demographic and household characteristics during the account-opening process. A constrained time frame limited the number of questions included in the questionnaire. Therefore, researchers selected questions that prior literature suggests are most relevant to youth savings contexts. Fourth, findings may be affected by variation in whether the respondent is a youth, a youth's parent, or another adult who accompanied the youth to the bank. Respondents' knowledge of household characteristics likely varied and resulted in missing values. Most missing information is related to household questions, which may have been difficult for youth to answer. In collaboration with BOK staff, the research team made an effort to minimize missing data, and the analyses employ multiple imputation to address a potential for bias from missing data. Finally, findings of this study may not be generalizable to all Nepalese youth because the sample consists of those who voluntarily opened bank accounts. The use of mass media and targeted product marketing strategies could have influenced who was exposed to the opportunity.

Conclusion

Although the CYBY product is relatively new to the youth financial market in Nepal, it is encouraging to see that Nepalese youth are able to set aside money in secure formal savings accounts. It is particularly encouraging that low-income youth from all ethnic and caste groups do so. Although the total savings are not large, youth have demonstrated their interest in this financial product. There is little market demand for youth-focused products in the Nepalese financial sector. If the observed rate of account opening continues, we will see more youth of all income groups participating in YouthSave and opening CYBY accounts. The findings suggest that the sooner youth are exposed to formal banking, the more likely they are to save. Future research will build on the general themes and patterns we observe among CYBY youth account holders and will explore in more detail how individual youth view their personal experiences with CYBY.

Notes

1 The Demographic and Health Survey covers a representative sample of 10,826 households across the country.
2 The currency code HKD refers to Hong Kong dollars; USD refers to US dollars; KRW refers to Korean won, and NPR refers to Nepalese rupees.
3 Microfinance institutions and co-operatives are exceptions and not included in this characterization.
4 The data collection and consent processes lengthened beyond the normal amount of time required to open an account. Experience in managing the consent and data collection processes varied by branch and within branch staff. There was variation in who responded to the demographic questions, as there was variation in the people accompanying the youth to the bank. Bank staff had varying levels of knowledge about the research project. Most missing information pertains to the household questions.
5 The purchasing power parity conversion rates for 2011 are drawn from the International Monetary Fund's World Economic Outlook dataset: www.imf.org/external/pubs/ft/weo/2012/01/index.htm.
6 Indigenous peoples represent more than 60 different ethnic and linguistic groups (Lama 2012). This study does not perform a comparison of the indigenous subgroups. Because of the heterogeneity within the caste group, we divide it into three categories: Dalit (5 per cent), Brahmin (32 per cent), and Chhetri (29 per cent). The Dalit are considered to be the lowest in the caste hierarchy, and Brahmin the highest. The size of the sample allows the research team to conduct subgroup comparisons across the caste group.
7 If the model holds all other covariates constant, the AMNS for the Brahmin group is lower by about $83 (i.e. purchasing-power-parity-converted dollars) than that for the indigenous group ($b=-83.41$, $p<.10$). There is no significant difference between the AMNS of the indigenous group and those of the other caste groups.

References

Ambler, Gareth, Rumana Z. Omar, and Patrick Royston. 2007. 'A Comparison of Imputation Techniques for Handling Missing Predictor Values in a Risk Model with a Binary Outcome.' *Statistical Methods in Medical Research* 16 (3): 277–298. doi:10.1177/0962280206074466.

Central Bureau of Statistics. 2011. *Preliminary Results of National Population Census 2011.* Report. Kathmandu, Nepal: Central Bureau of Statistics.

Chowa, Gina, David Ansong, and Rainier Masa. 2010. 'Assets and Child Well-Being in Developing Countries: A Research Review.' *Children and Youth Services Review* 32 (11): 1508–1519. doi:10.1016/j.childyouth.2010.03.015.

Deshpande, Rani. 2012. *What Do Youth Savers Want? Results from Market Research in Four Countries.* Save the Children YouthSave Note. Washington, DC: Save the Children. http://youthsave.org/sites/youthsave.org/files/YouthSave%20Market%20Research%20Report_FINAL.pdf.

Deshpande, Rani, and Jamie M. Zimmerman, eds. 2010. *Youth Savings in Developing Countries: Trends in Practice, Gaps in Knowledge.* YouthSave Consortium Report, May. Washington, DC: YouthSave Consortium. www.youthsave.org/sites/youthsave.org/files/YouthSavingsReportFINAL%20%288.24.2010%29.pdf.

Ferrari, Aurora. 2007. *Access to Financial Services in Nepal*. With the assistance of Guillemette Jaffrin and Sabin Raj Shrestha. Conference edition. Washington, DC: World Bank.

International Labour Organization. 2010. *Global Wage Report 2010/11: Wage Policies in Times of Crisis*. Geneva: International Labour Office. www.ilo.org/wcmsp5/groups/public/---dgreports/---dcomm/---publ/documents/publication/wcms_145265.pdf.

Johnson, Elizabeth, and Margaret S. Sherraden. 2007. 'From Financial Literacy to Financial Capability Among Youth.' *Journal of Sociology and Social Welfare* 34 (3): 119–146.

Kim, Youngmi, Li Zou, Young Sun Joo, and Michael Sherraden. 2011. 'Asset-Based Policy in South Korea.' CSD Policy Brief 11-22, July. Washington University, Center for Social Development, St. Louis, MO. http://csd.wustl.edu/Publications/Documents/PB11-22.pdf.

Korean Federation of Child Welfare. 2009. 디딤 씨앗 저축 예금에 저축 결과의보고 [The report of savings outcomes in Didim Seed Savings Accounts]. Report, March. Seoul: Korean Federation of Child Welfare, Division of Child Development Accounts.

Lama, Gyanesh. 2012. 'Global Poverty: Local Problem – Institutional Determinants of Poverty among Indigenous Peoples in Nepal.' PhD diss., Washington University in St. Louis, George Warren Brown School of Social Work, St. Louis, MO.

Loke, Vernon, and Michael Sherraden. 2009. 'Building Assets from Birth: A Global Comparison of Child Development Account Policies.' *International Journal of Social Welfare* 18 (2): 119–129. doi: 10.1111/j.1468–2397.2008.00605.x.

Ministry of Health and Population (MOHP). 2012. *Nepal Adolescent and Youth Survey 2010/11*. Kathmandu, Nepal: MOHP.

Ministry of Health and Population (MOHP), New ERA, and ICF International. 2011. *Nepal Demographic and Health Survey*. Kathmandu, Nepal: MOHP. www.mohp.gov.np/english/publication/NDHS%202011%20Full%20version.pdf.

Nam, Yunju, and Chang-Keun Han. 2010. 'A New Approach to Promote Economic Independence among At-Risk Children: Child Development Accounts (CDAs) in Korea.' *Children and Youth Services Review* 32 (11): 1548–1554. doi:10.1016/j.childyouth.2010.04.009.

Nam, Yunju, Youngmi Kim, Margaret Clancy, Robert Zager, and Michael Sherraden. 2012. 'Do Child Development Accounts Promote Account Holding, Saving, and Asset Accumulation for Children's Future? Evidence from a Statewide Randomized Experiment.' *Journal of Policy Analysis and Management* 32 (1): 6–33. doi:10.1002/pam.21652.

National Planning Commission, UNICEF (United Nations Children's Fund) Nepal, and New ERA. 2010. *Child Poverty and Disparities in Nepal: Towards Escaping the Cycle of Poverty*. Nepal Report 2010. Kathmandu, Nepal: UNICEF Nepal. www.unicef.org/nepal/Child_Poverty_and_disparities_in_Nepal.pdf.

Royston, Patrick. 2004. 'Multiple Imputation of Missing Values.' *Stata Journal* 4 (3): 227–241.

Save the Children. 2012. 'YouthSave Products Feature Summary.' Internal document, 8 May. Save the Children, Washington, DC.

Scanlon, Edward, and Deborah Adams. 2008. 'Do Assets Affect Well-Being? Perceptions of Youth in a Matched Savings Program.' *Journal of Social Service Research* 35 (1): 33–46. doi:10.1080/01488370802477048.

Schreiner, Mark. 2001. 'Measuring Savings.' CSD Research Background Paper 01-4. Washington University, Center for Social Development, St. Louis, MO. http://csd.wustl.edu/Publications/Documents/73.MeasuringSavings.pdf.

Schreiner, Mark, and Michael Sherraden. 2006. *Can the Poor Save? Saving and Asset Building in Individual Development Accounts*. New Brunswick, NJ: Transaction.

Sherraden, Margaret S. 2010. 'Financial Capability: What Is It, and How Can It Be Created?' CSD Working Paper 10-17, Center for Social Development, Washington University, St. Louis, MO. http://csd.wustl.edu/Publications/Documents/WP10-17.pdf.

Sherraden, Michael. 1991. *Assets and the Poor: A New American Welfare Policy*. Armonk, NY: M.E. Sharpe.

Williams Shanks, Trina R., Youngmi Kim, Vernon Loke, and Mesmin Destin. 2010. 'Assets and Child Well-Being in Developed Countries.' *Children and Youth Services Review* 32 (11): 1488–1496. doi:10.1016/j.childyouth.2010.03.011.

Zou, Li, and Michael Sherraden. 2010. 'Assets for Children: Experiences in Asia and Implications for China.' *US–China Education Review* 7 (8): 87–94.

10 Financial access and economic participation of youth with disabilities in China

An exploratory study

Suo Deng and Yu Meng

Financial independence is seen as an important indicator of adult status for young people transitioning to adulthood. It may affect individual continuous development as well as crucial life events like educational attainment, educational completion, employment, and marriage (Arnett 1998; Wells, Sandefur, and Hogan 2003). Although many find financial security elusive, those with physical, mental, intellectual, and other types of disabilities face even greater barriers to financial security and independence. Thus, they are at higher risk for lifelong poverty and dependency on public programmes. Studies demonstrate that enormous personal, family, and social costs are associated with unsuccessful transitions of disabled youth. These costs include substantial and negative impacts on their economic and socio-psychological well-being (Fraker and Rangarajan 2009; Knapp *et al.* 2008).

A growing policy concern for the economic self-sufficiency of disabled youth coincides with recent efforts to extend financial inclusion to vulnerable children and youth, for whom these efforts seek economic security and long-term well-being (Cramer 2010; Friedline 2012a). One of the most important strategies for enhancing financial inclusion is to augment people's access to mainstream financial services, especially in life's early stages. Evidence suggests that connecting children and youth to formal financial services, such as structural savings programmes, may result in a variety of positive educational and financial outcomes over the life-course (Elliott 2009).

The issue of financial access for the poor and vulnerable populations, including people with disabilities, has attracted increasing attention in China and many other developing countries (Claessens 2006). Amid growing income gaps and inequality, China has shifted strategies towards an inclusive development. The government places new emphasis on promoting active economic participation and on building an integrative social safety net for vulnerable populations (Ali and Zhuang 2007).

People with disabilities are among the poorest and most marginalized in China. They tend to be excluded from such mainstream economic opportunities as employment and financial engagement. In addition to difficulties associated with their disability, adolescents and youth with disabilities often face significant social and institutional disadvantages that impede economic participation, including financial access. There is great theoretical and practical value in investigating how these youth perceive financial services, identifying their options for accessing such services, and examining factors that may facilitate or hinder their financial access. Little research focuses on financial access among adolescents and young adults with disabilities. Thus, little is known about their financial lives. The current study seeks to fill this gap. Based on data collected through a survey of youth with disabilities in Beijing in 2012, this work provides an exploratory quantitative analysis of the status of the target group's financial access in China.

Background

Financial access, broadly described as financial inclusion, is defined as the possibility of having connections to basic, mainstream financial services. The term focuses on access among people in need, especially access among those who are typically underserved by mainstream economic and financial institutions (Friedline 2012a).

Broad access to financial services is an important aspect of national socioeconomic development (Claessens 2006; Friedline 2012b). Although theory holds that inequality is the inevitable consequence of economic growth in the beginning stages of development, scholars indicate that all levels of inequality, including unequal financial access, have adverse effects on the economic growth prospects at the societal level (Imboden 2005; World Bank 2008). Noting the role of a broad-based financial system in advancing a country's development, particularly its role in benefiting the poor, Kumar and Mohanty (2011) contend that financial inclusion is a precondition to inclusive national development.

At individual and household levels, access to financial services can play roles in both development and production. Connection to formal financial services creates opportunities for low-income families to accumulate financial assets that can serve as a cushion in times of crisis. A growing body of literature reveals the positive economic and socio-psychological outcomes produced by asset holding (Lerman and McKernan 2008; Paxton 2001; Zhan and Sherraden 2003). Empirical evidence identifies some particular benefits of extending financial inclusion to children. For instance, a savings account in the name of a child is positively associated with parental aspirations for the child's education and with the child's educational achievement in their later stages of life (Conley 2001; Elliott 2009; Zhan and Sherraden 2003). For children in child welfare systems, lack of saving and financial management skills may increase the risk of experiencing economic hardship, low educational achievement, and employment difficulties when they age out of the system (Keller, Cusick, and Courtney 2007; Nam and Han 2010). Access to basic financial services is seen as a key component of financial capability – one that is significant for a youth's development prospects (Johnson and Sherraden 2007).

Mainstream financial services often are not available or accessible to vulnerable populations, especially people with disabilities. In addition, there are significant gaps in financial access (measured by bank account holding) between the developing and developed countries, between low- and high-income households, as well as between disabled and non-disabled groups. The Global Financial Inclusion (Global Findex) data from the World Bank demonstrate significant disparities in access to financial services across 144 economies and individual characteristics such as race, gender, and income (Demirguc-Kunt and Klapper 2012). Using Panel Study of Income Dynamics data, Friedline (2012b) finds that about 69 per cent of high-income youth have a savings account but only 38 per cent of their low-income counterparts have one. Disability research from the United States shows that individuals with disabilities are significantly less likely than those without disabilities to have a savings account. Estimates suggest that around 30–50 per cent of individuals with disabilities have no banking relationship in their community (Mendelsohn 2006). The financial access gaps between advantaged and disadvantaged populations are more astonishing in developing countries (Imboden 2005; Schmeling *et al.* 2006).

Explanations for inequality in access to financial services fall into two main frameworks: supply–demand explanations and institutional explanations. Proponents of the supply–demand approach view access to finance as the availability of a supply of reasonable-quality financial services at a reasonable cost. Researchers distinguish access to financial services from actual use or consumption of those services; they tend to attribute the prevalence of unbanked households to either inadequate supply – possibly a symptom of relatively high transaction costs – or to low demand – perhaps a symptom of poverty (Claessens 2006; World Bank 2008). Noting that demand for financial services is often low among the poor, Claessens (2006) suggests that not using financial services may be more a problem of poverty than of insufficient supply. However, the supply–demand approach focuses less on explaining the underlying institutional mechanisms that lead to financial exclusion.

By contrast, the institutional approach emphasizes that the lack of institutional infrastructure is an impediment preventing the vulnerable from accessing formal financial services. This includes the lack of institutional eligibility and practicality in accessing mainstream financial services (Beverly and Sherraden 1999). For instance, many low-income individuals and families are not eligible to participate in government programmes, such as the pension plan and college savings that facilitate the building of financial assets and the use of related financial services. From this perspective, unequal access to basic financial services is a structural failure. Such a failure creates an unequal playing field on which those who are vulnerable or have low incomes encounter more difficulties than others in the population. They face difficulty in establishing banking relationships and in accessing other institutional sources that might enable them to develop financial capability (Beverly and Sherraden 1999; Elliott 2012). The institutional approach has attracted increasing attention from scholars concerned with the financial exclusion of disadvantaged groups, including the exclusion of youth with disabilities (Christy-McMullin 2000; Lombe *et al.* 2010).

With a few exceptions (Osili and Paulson 2008; Schmeling *et al.* 2006), the literature rarely examines the multiple demographic, household, or institutional factors that may affect financial access. Even less research focuses on disabled people in the transition to adulthood. Estimates from a nationally representative survey conducted in 2006 suggest that there are about 85 million people with disabilities in China. Children and adolescents younger than age 18 account for around 6 per cent of that population (more than five million) (Zheng *et al.* 2011). The survey does not employ a specific category for young adults, so no specific estimates are available for youth between ages 18 and 25. Although recent policies, including the 12th Five-Year Development Plan, set the goal to promote disabled people's economic participation and development (Wang 2012), the issue of their financial participation is largely neglected in the literature and policy debates. The current study represents a preliminary effort to examine the nature and extent of financial access among disabled youth in China.

Methods

Data for this study come from a survey of youth with disabilities in Beijing in 2012. The survey is part of a research project on disability and youth development. The dataset is one of the few that focus particularly on adolescents and young adults with disabilities. The survey provides an excellent opportunity to comprehensively study the financial lives of the disabled youth in China.

The research team deployed a purposive sampling strategy to collect data (Babbie 2010). Given the low response rate and poor quality of responses from selected youth with other kinds of disabilities (e.g. mental and intellectual disabilities), we focus only on youth with three major types of disability status: visual, hearing and/or speech, and physical disabilities. In a nationally representative survey in 2006, people with these three major disability types accounted for about 70 per cent of the whole disabled population (Zheng *et al.* 2011). Ultimately, the team collected valid responses from 159 cases, and the analytical results of these cases are reported in this paper. While we are aware of the bias embedded in the nonprobability sampling method, we believe that we have taken an initial but significant step into this area and laid an empirical foundation for future verification and modification. To complement inadequate information collected from survey, we also conducted a few in-depth interviews with several respondents and government officials. With the agreement of the participants, we taped (and afterward transcribed) some interviews. All qualitative data are systematically coded for analysis.

Following previous research (Osili and Paulson 2008), this study focuses on two dimensions of financial access: breadth and depth. They are two appropriate, measurable variables that reflect the nature and extent of financial access. Access breadth indicates whether an individual has any relationship with a bank. It is measured by individual account-holding status (i.e. whether an individual has a checking or savings account) and categorized as a dichotomous variable: a coding value of 1 is assigned to this variable if the individual indicates that he or she has a banking account, and a value of 0 is assigned if the individual indicates that he or she has no banking account. The measure of access depth provides additional insights into the extent of access by capturing information on the frequency and type of banking activity. A dummy variable reflecting this concept is created from the responses to a question that inquires about the occurrence of several banking activities (e.g. depositing, withdrawing, borrowing on credit) within the week before they were surveyed. A value of 1 is assigned for this variable if the individual indicates that any banking activity occurred within that week, and the variable takes a value of 0 if the individual reports that none of the banking activities occurred in that period.

The independent variables include those indicating respondents' individual, household, and financial-institution characteristics. Individual characteristics include disability status, age, gender, education, and employment. Disability status is measured through two variables: disability type and disability severity. As previously mentioned, we mainly focus on three disability types, in this study: visual disability, hearing and/or speech disability, and physical disability. According to the 2006 nationally representative survey (Zheng *et al.* 2011), visual disability is defined as 'poor vision or constriction of the visual field in both eyes from any cause and is not correctable' (blindness and weak vision). Hearing and/or speech disability 'refers to permanent hearing loss of varying degrees' and/or 'any type of language disorder' (789). Physical disability is defined as 'a loss of motor function of varying degrees or limitations in movements or activities resulting from deformed limbs or body paralysis', or other damage-caused deformity (789). The severity of disability influences how a given participant perceives his or her disability situation. The survey asks respondents to rate severity in one of three categories: mild, moderate, or severe.

We capture educational attainment with the individual's responses indicating the highest level of education completed by the respondent and his or her parents. We measure this in three categories: middle school and below, any high school, and any college or above. After checking the variance upon each education variable, we find that the largest variance lies along the college level among our respondents and along the high school level among their mothers. Thus, before introducing the education variables into the regression models, we recoded them as dummies: the respondent's education is assigned a value of 0 if the respondent indicates that he or she has less than a college education and 1 if the respondent reports having college or further education; the respondent's mother's education is assigned a value of 0 if she indicates that she has less than a high school education and 1 if she reports having high school and further education.

Household-level factors in the regression models include mother's education, father's monthly income, and household registration type (urban or rural). Research indicates that mother's education is an important factor affecting children's well-being (Currie and Moretti 2003). We consider the father's income to be an approximation of household economic status. The income variable is natural-logarithm transformed to shrink the dispersion of the values. Financial institution factors include two variables: geographic distance from the respondent's residence to the nearest bank and convenience of services. The latter is constructed as a dichotomous variable that captures participants' evaluation of the financial service environment; a value of 1 is assigned for this variable if the respondent indicates that the financial services at the nearest bank branch are convenient to use, and a value of 0 is assigned otherwise.

We present results from two sets of analyses to investigate the nature and extent of financial access among youth with disabilities. First, we present estimates from a descriptive analysis of access breadth and depth. Then, with results from logistic regression models that control for gender and age, we examine the effects of different independent variables on access breadth and depth. We find no alarming collinearity problems in the analytic models.

Findings

Descriptive results

Table 10.1 presents the demographic and household characteristics of disabled youth in this sample. The average age of respondents in this sample is around 21, and the sample is balanced in terms of gender. We purposely include individuals who report three major disability types. To identify these three types, we rely on estimates from a nationally representative survey conducted in 2006 (Zheng *et al.* 2011). Youth with hearing and/or speech disabilities account for the largest proportion of the sample (56.5 per cent); 32.7 per cent of youth report physical disabilities; and 10.9 per cent report visual disabilities. Overall, 45.2 per cent of youth perceive their disability as mild, and 42.9 per cent report that it is moderate.

In terms of educational level, the sample includes both respondents who were enrolled at the time of the survey and those who have exited school. The descriptive statistics show that this particular sample is quite well educated: over half of respondents indicate that they have at least some college-level education. This high proportion may be due to our broad definition of college education (the definition includes enrolment in programmes that allow one to study by oneself at home). About 23 per cent of sampled youth report current employment.

As to the household characteristics, the majority of respondents (87.8 per cent) come from households registered in an urban area. At the aggregate level, these respondents have more education than their parents; only 14 per cent of fathers and 11 per cent of mothers have college-level education. On average, respondents' fathers earn CNY 1086 each month (approximately USD 175).

Table 10.2 reports descriptive statistics characterizing the disabled youth's financial access and connections to financial institutions. Almost three-quarters of sampled youth are connected to a bank through a bank account: 64 per cent hold a checking account but only 11 per cent have a savings account. The results

Table 10.1 Sample characteristics (*N*=159)

Variables	Mean or percentage
Individual characteristics	
Age (SD)	21.4 (2.7)
Female	49.1
Disability type	
Physical	32.7
Visual	10.9
Hearing and/or speech	56.5
Perceived disability severity	
Mild	45.2
Moderate	42.9
Severe	11.9
Individual education	
College and above	53.3
High school	29.6
Middle school and below	17.1
Currently employed	23.0
Household characteristics	
Household registration type	
Urban	87.8
Rural	12.2
Father's education	
College and above	13.8
High school	34.5
Middle school and below	51.7
Mother's education	
College and above	10.5
High school	28.7
Middle school and below	60.8
Father's monthly income (SD)	1086.0 (1177.8)

Note
SD = standard deviation.

on access depth (involvement in banking activities) indicate that less than half of surveyed individuals (40 per cent) are regularly involved in such banking-related activities as account management. Table 10.2 also presents results on the features of banks. The results indicate that the average geographic distance from respondents' residences to the nearest bank branch is about 5 km.[1] The survey also asks respondents whether they feel that the financial services provided by the nearest bank branch are convenient to use. Surprisingly, about 62.1 per cent of respondents give a positive assessment. Nonetheless, it may be necessary to further investigate the gap between the perceived convenience of using financial services and actual financial access, especially between perceived convenience and actual banking activity.

Table 10.2 Characteristics of financial access and financial institutions (*N*=159)

Variables	Mean or percentage
Financial access breadth	
Checking account holding	63.9
Savings account holding	11.4
Either checking or savings	72.2
Financial access depth	
Involvement of banking activity	40.0
Financial institution characteristics	
Distance to nearest bank branch (km)	4.9
Perceived convenience of banking services	62.1

Regression analysis

Additional analyses enable us to further investigate factors that may strongly affect financial access breadth and depth among youth with disabilities in China. We use logistic regression to model the associations among multiple factors, including the relationship of financial access with individual, household, and financial institution characteristics. Gender, age, disability type, and disability severity are clustered as individual characteristics. Registration status, mother's education, and father's income comprise the cluster of household characteristics. The cluster for financial-institution characteristics includes distance to nearest bank branch and perceived convenience of banking services. To detect the different effects of the clusters of factors, we run separate models by entering variables in steps in order. Table 10.3 shows results from regressions on access breadth (measured by bank account holding).

Estimates from Model I suggest that those who are older and employed are more likely to hold a bank account (i.e. to have a connection with a financial institution). The results also suggest that access breadth varies to a statistically significant degree by disability type and severity of disability. Compared with physically disabled counterparts, youth with hearing and/or speech disabilities are more likely to have a bank account. One possible explanation for this is that people with physical disabilities may encounter more difficulties in using brick and mortar bank services because there are few barrier-free facilities. However, disability severity significantly decreases the likelihood of account holding; compared to youth with mild disabilities, those with moderate disabilities are significantly less likely have a bank account.

Although youth with severe disabilities tend to have fewer connections with a bank than do those with mild disabilities, this difference is not statistically significant in Model I. Our field interviews indicate that some youth with highly severe disabilities are provided bank accounts for their public allowance, and this increases the general likelihood that youth with disabilities have a bank account.

Table 10.3 Logistic regression on financial access breadth of youth with disabilities

Independent factors	Access breadth (account holding)		
	Model I	Model II	Model III
Individual characteristics			
Female (ref. = male)	−.689	−1.116*	−.887
Age	.201**	.261**	.189
Visual disability (ref. = physical)	−.639	−1.122	−1.111
Hearing and/or speech disability (ref. = physical)	2.038***	2.314***	2.807***
Moderate disability (ref. = mild)	−1.304**	−1.441**	−1.395*
Severe disability (ref. = mild)	−.976	−1.201	−1.107
College education (ref. = below college)	−.005	.350	−.195
Currently employed (ref. = not employed)	1.848***	1.694**	1.771**
Household characteristics			
Urban household registration (ref. = rural)		−.148	.595
Mother's education above high school (ref. = below)		−.271	.264
Father's income (log)		−.083	−.069
Financial institution characteristics			
Distance to nearest bank branch (km)			.257
Perceived convenience of banking services			−.004
Constant	−2.741	−2.744	−2.524
Pseudo-R^2	.359	.444	.444
N	145	101	90

Notes
ref. = reference category.
*$p < .1$; **$p < .05$; ***$p < .01$.

Model II includes household-level factors. Although the addition of these variables seems to explain some variance (the pseudo-R^2 becomes larger), none of the household variables is found to be significantly associated with bank-account holding.

Model III expands upon preceding analyses to include characteristics of financial institutions, but those characteristics do not change the variance (pseudo-R^2) observed in estimates from Model II. This suggests that the characteristics of the financial institution have a similarly weak effect on the likelihood of opening a bank account.

These findings seem inconsistent with previous studies that report a positive effect of parental resources on youth's connection to financial institutions (Beverly and Sherraden 1999; Elliott 2012). We postulate an explanation for this finding: holding a bank account in China is increasingly commonplace among youth, especially those at a mature age (i.e. age 18 and up). In addition, more and more public welfare programmes (such as cash assistance for the poor and disadvantaged) require recipients to have an account and to receive benefits via automatic transfer. Although holding a bank account is extremely important for maintaining a relationship with financial institutions over the life-course, involvement in regular bank activity is also important and may be even more critical to promote asset-accumulation behaviour. In our in-depth interview, a young adult with physical disabilities said that he received a disability allowance of 800 RMB per month from the government, which transfers the money through a mandated checking account. However, he has to rely on his parents to withdraw his money from the bank. He indicates that he rarely has the chance to deal with banking because of his disability status. Our quantitative data also identify the gap between account holding and account-related banking activity, as the results from the second set of regression models demonstrate (Table 10.4).

Regression results in Table 10.4 show the possible effects of selected variables at multiple levels on access depth, which is measured by involvement in regular banking activity. Estimates from the basic model (Model I) suggest a statistically significant and positive association between individual education and access depth. The disabled youth who are educated at college level are more likely than those without college education to engage in banking activity on a regular basis. In Model II, which adds household variables and holds other

Table 10.4 Logistic regression on financial access depth of youth with disabilities

Independent factors	Access depth (banking activity involvement)		
	Model I	Model II	Model III
Individual characteristics			
Female (ref. = male)	.281	.125	.688
Age	.136	.118	.090
Visual disability (ref. = physical)	.074	−.474	.065
Hearing and/or speech disability (ref. = physical)	.810	.535	−.612
Moderate disability (ref. = mild)	−.523	−.495	−.201
Severe disability (ref. = mild)	.097	.366	1.097
College education (ref. = below college)	1.376***	.977*	1.268*
Currently employed (ref. = not employed)	.376	.517	.065
Household characteristics			
Urban household registration (ref. = rural)		2.020**	2.219**
Mother's education above high school (ref. = below)		−.248	−.553
Father's income (log)		.099	.266
Financial institution characteristics			
Distance to a nearest bank branch (km)			1.308
Perceived convenience of banking services (ref. = not convenient)			.037*
Bank account holding			1.619*
Constant	−4.883**	−6.878**	−10.408***
Pseudo-R²	.261	.306	.396
N	139	98	86

Notes
ref. = reference category.
*p< .1; **p<.05; ***p<.01.

variables at their means, the magnitude of college education's effect decreases and urban registration is found to have a positive, statistically significant association with access depth. In other words, disabled youth who are registered as residents of an urban area are more likely than counterparts with rural registrations to regularly engage in banking activities.

Model III in Table 10.4 adds the characteristics of financial institutions. Some of those characteristics are found to have significant and positive associations with involvement in regular banking activity. The disabled youth who deem financial services convenient are more likely to regularly involve themselves in banking activities. It is not surprising that holding a banking account increases the likelihood of involvement in regular banking activity. The Model III estimates indicate that, except for individual education, the depth of financial access is more strongly associated with household and financial institution factors than with individual characteristics. Although account holding becomes more and more popular in China, being registered in a rural area and external financial institutional constraints (e.g. the convenience of banking services) may impede the further involvement of disabled youth in financial services.

Our field interviews show similar patterns on access depth among the disabled youth. The urban–rural difference in the banking engagement might be explained by the knowledge gap between urban and rural residents regarding banking tools and money management skills. For example, some of the youth from urban areas have learned to manage their bank accounts via mobile phones or the internet, but those with rural background have little knowledge of these innovative tools. Regardless of household background, a bank's characteristics, such as the lack of barrier-free facilities, prevent the disabled youth from physically engaging in banking activities. Many respondents complain that, even in a city as large as Beijing, most banks do not provide disability-friendly services.

Discussion and conclusion

This study is based on survey data collected in China from youth with disabilities who are between the ages of 16 and 25. It presents preliminary but empirical findings on the focal group's access to financial services and suggests factors that may impede group members from developing their financial access. Overall, the disabled youth have a high rate of account holding (checking account or savings account). This suggests that they have established connections (whether voluntarily or not) with financial institutions. Nonetheless, a gap remains between basic account holding and further access to financial services. Research rarely investigates that gap. The regression results suggest that some individual characteristics, especially disability type and severity, are significantly associated with account holding. However, the effects of individual factors on the likelihood of involvement in regular banking activity are weaker in terms of magnitude than are those of household and financial-institution characteristics.

This study is an initial exploration and has some limitations. First, due to the special nature of the study subjects and cost considerations, we are not able to deploy a probability sampling strategy, to collect data country-wide, or to undertake efforts to generate a larger and more representative sample even in Beijing. These insufficiencies limit our ability to generalize the findings for inferences about the population of interest (youth with disabilities) in China. Second, the survey lacks indicators of youth's attitudes, financial knowledge, and financial skills. However, these indicators may be important mediators of the effects of the selected individual, household, and financial-institution factors on financial access in this target group. Furthermore, the quantitative analysis, restricted by its limited number of variables (and cases), may not adequately reveal the situation and reasoning behind financial access. Further research should collect and analyse more in-depth interview data. Despite those limitations, this study is expected to generate interesting research in the future. More important, it makes an actual contribution to the existing literature by extending the financial access research to a special population of disabled youth in China by identifying important implications for forming asset-building programmes to enhance this population's financial access.

Financial inclusion has received growing attention worldwide. Statistics show significant inequalities in access to basic, mainstream financial services across groups with different socio-economic privileges. Basic financial services, particularly some structured savings programmes, provide institutional incentives for the poor and vulnerable to accumulate financial assets towards long-term developmental goals. Mounting evidence implies that having a savings account in early life can bring positive outcomes to children as well as to the whole family (Elliott 2009; Loke and Sherraden 2009). However, less attention has been paid to the gap between holding an account and further involvement in banking-related activities. Our study, by demonstrating the effects of household and financial-institution characteristics on banking, has important implications for government programmes aiming to engage disabled youth fully in accessing and utilizing financial services.

Financial education programmes may offer a critical way to build disabled youth's financial capabilities through enhancing both the breadth and depth of their access. Youth who hold a bank account may need to be further involved in management of their money if they are to build capability (Johnson and Sherraden 2007). One important way of increasing their involvement is training, through which they come to understand the importance of financial activities to their status improvement and gain confidence to engage with sufficient knowledge and skills. Previous studies show that they can learn how to manage their credit and debts and make appropriate financial decisions independently (Atkinson *et al.* 2007; Taylor, Jenkins, and Sacker 2011). A well-designed asset-building programme, modelled to broaden and deepen financial access as well as to build financial capabilities, would be especially beneficial for youth with disabilities and other vulnerable populations.

Inclusive development has been a buzzword in recent years and appears in various policy texts. As it enters a new stage of leadership, the Chinese government places unprecedented emphasis on social and economic justice as well as on the well-being of the whole population. The inclusive development strategy is set to ensure all people, especially the most vulnerable and poorest, have equal opportunity to participate in and benefit from the nation's economic growth (Zhuang 2008). In addition to the transitional income-transfer mechanisms designed to maintain minimum living conditions, the government should also direct policy attention to asset-based programmes that offer participants the prospect of a long-term development (Deng *et al.* 2013). For instance, a structured saving programme, such as Child Development Accounts opened in the name of the disabled child, may steer government and the family's investment towards achieving long-term education and career-development goals. Children may benefit from these programmes in the early stages of life; they may gain access to financial services and education about how to make financial decisions independently. Social policies that target youth during the transition to adulthood may have much greater impacts on their future development and on the whole economy than would policies that only target adults. Youth with disabilities are among the most marginalized. They encounter significant obstacles and are excluded from mainstream institutional opportunities. Expanding their financial access and capabilities remains an important policy challenge; governments can accomplish much through social innovations. By implementing experiential social programmes, governments can help these youth embrace a bright future.

Note

1 The distance to the nearest automated teller machine (ATM) may be a more accurate and influential measure for predicting the involvement of youth with disabilities in banking activities, because simple account management activities (withdrawal or deposit) can be accomplished with only an ATM. Unfortunately, information on the distance to the nearest ATM is not available in these data.

References

Ali, I., and J. Zhuang. 2007. 'Inclusive Growth toward a Prosperous Asia: Policy Implications.' ERD Working Paper 97, July, Economics and Research Department, Asian Development Bank, Manila, Philippines. Accessed 18 April 2013. www.adb.org/sites/default/files/pub/2007/WP097.pdf.

Arnett, J.J. 1998. 'Learning to Stand Alone: The Contemporary American Transition to Adulthood in Cultural and Historical Context.' *Human Development* 41 (5–6): 295–315. doi:10.1159/000022591.

Atkinson, A., S. McKay, S. Collard, and E. Kempson. 2007. 'Levels of Financial Capability in the UK.' *Public Money and Management* 27 (1): 29–36. doi:10.1111/j.1467-9302.2007.00552.x.

Babbie, E.R. (2010). *The Basics of Social Research*. Belmont, CA: Wadsworth Publishing.

Beverly, S.G., and M. Sherraden. 1999. 'Institutional Determinants of Saving: Implications for Low-Income Households and Public Policy.' *Journal of Socio-Economics* 28 (4): 457–473. doi:10.1016/S1053-5357(99)00046-3.

Christy-McMullin, K. 2000. 'An Analysis of the Assets for Independence Act of 1998 for Abused Women.' *Violence Against Women* 6 (10): 1066–1084. doi:10.1177/107780 10022183523.

Claessens, S. 2006. 'Access to Financial Services: A Review of the Issues and Public Policy Objectives.' *World Bank Research Observer* 21 (2): 207–240. doi:10.1093/wbro/lkl004.

Conley, D. 2001. 'Capital for College: Parent Assets and Postsecondary Schooling.' *Sociology of Education* 74 (1): 59–72. doi:10.2307/2673145.

Cramer, R. 2010. 'The Big Lift: Federal Policy Efforts to Create Child Development Accounts.' *Children and Youth Services Review* 32 (11): 1538–1543. doi:10.1016/j.childyouth.2010.03.012.

Currie, J., and E. Moretti. 2003. 'Mother's Education and the Intergenerational Transmission of Human Capital: Evidence from College Openings.' *Quarterly Journal of Economics* 118 (4): 1495–1532. doi:10.1162/003355303322552856.

Demirguc-Kunt, A. and L. Klapper. 2012. 'Measuring Financial Inclusion: The Global Findex Database.' Policy Research Working Paper 6025, April, World Bank, Washington, DC. Accessed 18 April 2013. www.wds.worldbank.org/external/default/WDSContentServer/IW3P/IB/2012/04/19/000158349_20120419083611/Rendered/PDF/WPS6025.pdf.

Deng, S., M. Sherraden, J. Huang, and M. Jin. 2013. 'Asset Opportunity for the Poor: An Asset-Based Policy Agenda Towards Inclusive Growth in China.' *China Journal of Social Work* 6 (1): 40–51. doi:10.1080/17525098.2013.766621.

Elliott, W. 2009. 'Children's College Aspirations and Expectations: The Potential Role of Children's Development Accounts (CDAs).' *Children and Youth Services Review* 31 (2): 274–283. doi:10.1016/j.childyouth.2008.07.020.

Elliott, W. 2012. 'Does Structural Inequality Begin with a Bank Account?' Creating a Financial Stake in College Report II, January. Washington, DC: New America Foundation. http://newamerica.net/sites/newamerica.net/files/policydocs/Elliott_II_final1.4.12.pdf.

Fraker, T. and A. Rangarajan. 2009. 'The Social Security Administration's Youth Transition Demonstration Projects.' *Journal of Vocational Rehabilitation* 30 (3): 223–240. doi:10.3233/JVR-2009-0463.

Friedline, T. 2012a. 'The Case for Extending Financial Inclusion to Children: The Role of Parents' Financial Resources and Implications for Policy Innovations.' Asset Building Program Policy Paper, New America Foundation, Washington, DC. http://newamerica.net/sites/newamerica.net/files/policydocs/CaseforFinInclusionFriedlineMay12.pdf.

Friedline, T. 2012b. 'Predicting Children's Savings: The Role of Parents' Savings for Transferring Financial Advantage and Opportunities for Financial Inclusion.' *Children and Youth Services Review* 34 (1): 144–154. doi:10.1016/j.childyouth.2011.09.010.

Imboden, K. 2005. 'Building Inclusive Financial Sectors: The Road to Growth and Poverty Reduction.' *Journal of International Affairs* 58 (2): 65–86.

Johnson, E., and M.S. Sherraden. 2007. 'From Financial Literacy to Financial Capability Among Youth.' *Journal of Sociology and Social Welfare* 34 (3): 119–145.

Keller, T.E., G.R. Cusick, and M.E. Courtney. 2007. 'Approaching the Transition to Adulthood: Distinctive Profiles of Adolescents Aging out of the Child Welfare System.' *Social Service Review* 81 (3): 455–484. doi:10.1086/519536.

Knapp, M., M. Perkins, J. Beecham, S. Dhanasiri, and C. Rustin. 2008. 'Transition Pathways for Young People with Complex Disabilities: Exploring the Economic Consequences.' *Child: Care, Health and Development* 34 (4): 512–520. doi:10.1111/j.1365-2214.2008.00835.x.

Kumar, B., and B. Mohanty. 2011. 'Financial Inclusion and Inclusive Development in SAARC Countries with Special Reference to India.' *Vilakshan: The XIMB Journal of Management* 8 (2): 13–22.

Lerman, R.I., and S.M. McKernan. 2008. 'Benefits and Consequences of Holding Assets.' In *Asset Building and Low-Income Families*, edited by S.M. McKernan and M. Sherraden, 175–206. Washington, DC: Urban Institute Press.

Loke, V., and M. Sherraden. 2009. 'Building Assets from Birth: A Global Comparison of Child Development Account Policies.' *International Journal of Social Welfare* 18 (2): 119–129. doi:10.1111/j.1468-2397.2008.00605.x.

Lombe, M., J. Huang, M. Putnam, and K. Cooney. 2010. 'Exploring Saving Performance in an IDA Program: Findings for People with Disabilities.' *Social Work Research* 34 (2): 83–93. doi:10.1093/swr/34.2.83.

Mendelsohn, S. 2006. 'Role of the Tax Code in Asset Development for People with Disabilities.' *Disability Studies Quarterly* 26 (1). http://dsq-sds.org/article/view/653/830.

Nam, Y., and C.K. Han. 2010. 'A New Approach to Promote Economic Independence Among At-Risk Children: Child Development Accounts (CDAs) in Korea.' *Children and Youth Services Review* 32 (11): 1548–1554. doi:10.1016/j.childyouth.2010.04.009.

Osili, U.O., and A. Paulson. 2008. 'What Can We Learn about Financial Access from U.S. Immigrants? The Role of Country of Origin Institutions and Immigrant Beliefs.' *World Bank Economic Review* 22 (3): 431–455. doi:10.1093/wber/lhn019.

Paxton, W. 2001. 'The Asset-Effect: An Overview.' In *The Asset-Effect*, edited by J. Bynner and W. Paxton, 1–16. London: Institute for Public Policy Research.

Schmeling, J., H.A. Schartz, M. Morris, and P. Blanck. 2006. 'Tax Credits and Asset Accumulation: Findings from the 2004 N.O.D./Harris Survey of Americans with Disabilities.' *Disability Studies Quarterly* 26 (1). http://dsq-sds.org/article/view/654/831.

Taylor, M.P., S.P. Jenkins, and A. Sacker. 2011. 'Financial Capability and Psychological Health.' *Journal of Economic Psychology* 32 (5): 710–723. doi:10.1016/j.joep. 2011.05.006.

Wang, N. 2012. 'Introductory Statement at the Meeting of the U.N. Committee on the Rights of Persons with Disabilities on Consideration of China's First Compliance Report.' China Disabled Persons' Federation. Accessed 18 April 2013. www.cdpf.org. cn/english/events/content/2012–09/29/content_30416336.htm.

Wells, T., G.D. Sandefur, and D.P. Hogan. 2003. 'What Happens after the High School Years Among Young Persons with Disabilities?' *Social Forces* 82 (2): 803–832. doi:10.1353/sof.2004.0029.

World Bank. 2008. *Finance for All? Policies and Pitfalls in Expanding Access*. Policy Research Report. Washington, DC: World Bank. Accessed 18 April 2013. http://siteresources.worldbank.org/INTFINFORALL/Resources/4099583-1194373512632/FFA_book.pdf.

Zhan, M., and M. Sherraden. 2003. 'Assets, Expectations, and Children's Educational Achievement in Female-Headed Households.' *Social Service Review* 77 (2): 191–211. doi:10.1086/373905.

Zheng, X., G. Chen, X. Song, J. Liu, L. Yan, W. Du, L. Pang, *et al.* 2011. 'Twenty-Year Trends in the Prevalence of Disability in China.' *Bulletin of the World Health Organization* 89 (11): 788–797. doi:10.2471/BLT.11.089730.

Zhuang, J. 2008. 'Inclusive Growth Toward a Harmonious Society in the People's Republic of China: Policy Implications.' *Asian Development Review* 25 (1–2): 22–33.

11 Asset poverty and happiness in urban China

Jin Huang

Policymakers and researchers show increasing interest in the use of happiness as a measure of subjective well-being. Policymakers indicate that measures of happiness provide more balanced estimates of social development than do measures that focus on economic growth or gross domestic product (GDP). The 12th Five-Year Plan of the Chinese central government specifies the state's economic and developmental goals for 2011–2015 (Casey and Koleski 2011). One such goal is to ensure that all Chinese citizens share the benefits of economic growth, and the plan 'has been hailed as a blueprint for a "happy China" ', as noted in an *Economist* article on 17 March 2011. In their own five-year plans, provincial governments also emphasize the idea of promoting happiness. For instance, Guangdong province declared that it would become 'happy Guangdong' between 2011 and 2015, and Beijing claimed that it wants its citizens to lead 'happy and glorious lives', according to the same *Economist* article.

Previous studies examine important social factors that affect happiness, focusing on individual and household socio-economic characteristics as well as inequality. Despite the extensive research concerning the effects of household income and income disparity on perceptions of happiness, little is known about the relationship between happiness and household assets (or wealth). Assets are the stock of wealth-type resources held by households at a certain point in time. They may include a home, a business, savings, stocks, bonds, and other resources of monetary value. Assets function not only as reserves to protect household economic security and future consumption, but also as an important instrument for facilitating long-term economic development and social mobility (Caner and Wolff 2004; Nam, Huang, and Sherraden 2008). Beyond consumption, household assets affect an individual's opportunities for business start-up, education, and home ownership, as well as one's ability to achieve economic aspirations. Research shows that asset effects extend beyond the economic arena; the psychological well-being of individuals and households depends in part on assets owned (Caner and Wolff 2004; Schneider 2004; Sherraden 1991). Therefore, household assets and income may have different effects on personal happiness.

This study fills a knowledge gap by examining the association between household assets and personal happiness in urban China. In particular, this project focuses on the concept of asset poverty – the insufficiency of assets to satisfy basic household needs for a limited period of time (Haveman and Wolff 2004). The study hypothesizes that asset poverty and household income are key determinants of an individual's subjective well-being (happiness). I also hypothesize that four factors mediate the relationship between asset poverty and happiness: precautionary savings, household living standard, perceived fairness of the income distribution, and predicted future income. The findings from this study have important implications for policy efforts that employ asset-building strategies to promote happiness in China.

Background

Happiness and economic inequality

Well-being is increasingly measured not only by economic indicators (such as income and poverty), but also by subjective measures of well-being (such as happiness). Happiness is generally defined as the 'degree to which an individual judges the overall quality of his life-as-a-whole favorably' (Veenhoven 1984, 98). A global term, it represents the result of a self-assessment of life quality and living conditions. It covers various domains, such as marital, work, and social relationships. Recognizing it as the ultimate goal of human beings, Kittiprapas *et al.* (2007) propose that happiness provides a new paradigm for public policy and particularly for development policy. They contend that a key indicator of successful social development is whether it improves subjective well-being, and they indicate that increasing individual happiness should be a specified goal of development.

The literature on the determinants of happiness has come a long way since the 1990s. Research demonstrates that one's subjective well-being depends on various factors, including income, health, employment status, age, gender, social networks (e.g. friendships), social capital, individual adaptation, and democratic institutions (Frey and Stutzer 2002; Layard 2005). In addition, studies suggest that individual happiness is partially determined by the difference between one's actual income and one's income aspirations. Research also indicates that it is partially determined by a comparison of one's actual income with the income of others, especially the income of those who share similar socio-economic characteristics (Easterlin 1995). This 'relative income hypothesis' of happiness implies an association between individual happiness and economic inequality (McBride 2001, 254). Thus, the hypothesis lends theoretical support for an inclusive strategy of economic development, a strategy that focuses on maximizing happiness.

Brockmann *et al.* (2009) draw attention to the decline of individual happiness and life satisfaction during China's economic expansion. Noting that these declines came even as material living standards improved substantially, they suggest that economic inequality explains this seemingly contradictory trend. That is, as the income distribution becomes skewed toward the upper end, those who did not gain much from the economic boom are left behind; financial dissatisfaction grows, and happiness declines. Although this implies a link between happiness and economic inequality, few studies specifically examine how asset distribution and asset poverty (indicators of economic inequality) contribute to perceived happiness and life satisfaction.

Asset distribution and asset poverty in urban China

In China, the widened economic inequality is reflected in the distribution of household assets. Household assets have grown substantially since the late 1970s and especially since the turn of the new century (Zhao and Ding 2008). The economic reform opened opportunities for individuals to accumulate significant assets. Reforms in such areas as land use, housing, state-owned enterprises, and finance allowed people to become owners of property. Estimates from the China Household Income Project (CHIP) show that per-capita net worth, defined as the combined value of all assets less the value of non-housing liabilities, increased by more than twofold, from CNY 13,700 in 1995 to CNY 46,100 in 2002. Between 1995 and 2007, the net worth of a typical household increased from CNY 66,747 (Li, Zhong, and Gustafsson 2000) to CNY 306,000 (Cheng 2008). Housing and financial assets were the two largest categories of assets held by urban households; together, they represented 70 per cent of net worth in 1995 and 90 per cent of net worth in 2002 (Li and Zhao 2007; Zhao and Ding 2008). Asset inequality also widened in the last two decades. The group in the highest decile owned 34 per cent of all net worth in urban households, and those in the two lowest groups owned only 2.8 per cent (Zhao and Ding 2008). In urban areas, the Gini coefficient of wealth distribution was 0.48 in 2002 (Zhao and Ding 2008), 0.56 in 2005, and 0.58 in 2007 (Liang, Huo, and Liu 2010). Liang, Huo, and Liu (2010) show that in 2007 housing and financial assets contributed to 90 per cent of asset inequality in urban China.

Among urban households in China, asset accumulation is highly related to household demographics (Liang, Huo, and Liu 2010; Meng 2007). More importantly, a series of economic reforms and institutional transitions have provided tremendous opportunities for asset accumulation. However, the distribution of such opportunities is extremely unequal. Political and economic elites are the primary beneficiaries of these institutional arrangements, which allow them to accumulate more assets than other groups (Meng 2007). Despite the widely acclaimed institutional changes implemented in China over the past three decades, many Chinese, especially those with low income and low wealth, are excluded from the asset accumulation opportunities in the reform process.

Inevitably, restricting disadvantaged populations' access to asset accumulation opportunities leads to asset poverty. The concept of asset poverty focuses on the low end of the household asset distribution. It can be used to examine the relationship between economic inequality and happiness. Households are considered asset poor 'if their access to wealth-type resources is insufficient to enable them to meet their basic needs for some limited period of time'

(Haveman and Wolff 2004, 149). For example, two US studies (Caner and Wolff 2004; Haveman and Wolff 2004) use the average duration of unemployment in the states to define the period of time as three months. The basic needs are often defined by poverty thresholds adjusted for household size. A specific definition of asset poverty for urban China is discussed in the Methods section below.

Asset poverty as a potential determinant of happiness

Household assets and asset poverty may affect individual happiness through many different approaches (Figure 11.1). First, household assets can protect households from negative income shocks. Asset-poor households are less likely than other households to have sufficient precautionary savings for emergencies, such as unemployment and health issues. Previous literature on happiness in China suggests that lack of security is the most common concern among those with a low level of happiness (Knight and Gunatilaka 2010). Second, asset-poor households are more likely to have low living standards, and this may lead to unhappiness. Household assets can be used for direct consumption (e.g. purchase of housing, a car, and furniture) or transferred into income to improve the quality of life. Third, assets may affect how one perceives one's place in society. More than an indicator of an individual's position in social stratification, asset holding may affect how the individual perceives inequality (e.g. perceived fairness of distribution of economic resources). Such perceptions may be related to self-reported happiness as well. Furthermore, assets provide households with opportunities for future development. For example, a household that has assets on hand is able to make investments as opportunities arise. Asset poverty limits opportunities for social and economic mobility. Also, asset poverty limits the ability of household members to achieve economic development. Thus, asset-poor households are more likely than others to predict that they will have low levels of future income. The absence or dearth of economic development opportunities may lead to low levels of happiness as well.

This study examines the relationship between household asset poverty and individual happiness. Two research questions are of central interest: (1) Does asset poverty correlate with happiness? (2) If there is an association between asset poverty and happiness, is it mediated by precautionary savings, household living standard, perceived fairness of the income distribution, and predicted future income?

Methods

Data and sample

The 2002 CHIP is a nationally-representative dataset collected by the Institute of Economics at the Chinese Academy of Social Sciences. The 2002 CHIP

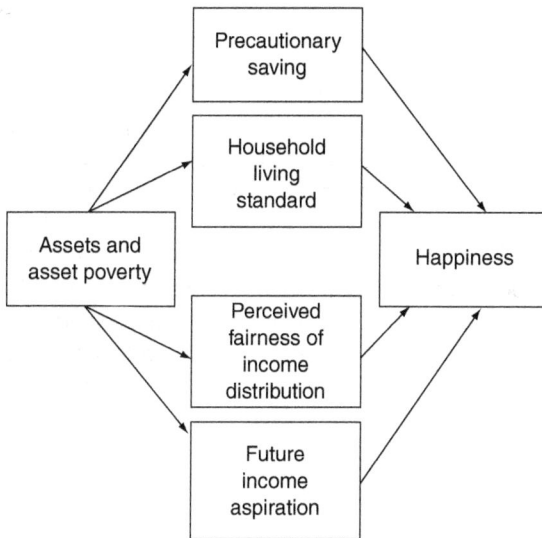

Figure 11.1 Mediation mechanism of asset poverty and happiness.

collected comprehensive information on household demographics, income sources, financial and physical assets, social benefit receipt, individual happiness and life satisfaction, and additional factors. Using a multi-stage stratified probability sampling method, the 2002 CHIP obtained an urban sample that covers 12 provinces from eastern, central, and western regions of Mainland China. The sample includes 6835 households and 20,632 individuals from 77 cities. It is representative of the 502.1 million people in urban areas of China. The study interviewed one participant, the household head, in each of the 6835 participating households. The analytic sample used in this chapter excludes 564 participants for whom data are missing for some variable reported (see Table 11.1). The final sample includes the 6271 CHIP participants for whom no information is missing on the analysed variables.

Measure of happiness

To measure happiness, the study uses responses to the following question: 'Generally speaking, do you feel happy – would you say that you are very happy (5), happy (4), neither happy nor unhappy (3), not very happy (2), or not happy at all (1)?' This is a general question applied in many surveys (e.g. the 1975–1992 Eurobarometer Survey series and the US General Social Survey). Despite the potential limitations of this single, self-reported measure, research using this measure generally has consistent findings (Alesina, Di Tella, and MacCulloch 2004).

Definition of asset poverty

Household assets

As mentioned above, this study adopts the definition of asset poverty developed by Haveman and Wolff (2004); a household is considered asset poor if its assets are insufficient to enable the household to meet its basic needs for three months. The 2002 CHIP provides information on multiple asset categories, including self-reported values for home equity, savings, stocks, bonds, money lent out, investment in enterprises or business, housing funds, commercial insurance, collections, durable goods, productive fixed assets, and other assets. Net worth consists of all the asset categories mentioned above net of total household debts. A second indicator of net worth excludes home equity from the calculation. Liquid assets are the total value of stocks, bonds, and savings in certificates of deposit and regular savings accounts.

Asset-poverty line

The asset-poverty line refers to a minimum level of resources required to meet household consumption needs for a period of three months. Since there is no official poverty line for urban China, this study adopts two approaches to measuring basic household needs. First, the study uses a specific poverty line developed by Khan (2004) to measure basic household needs in urban China. (For examples of other studies that use the measure, see Gao, Garfinkel, and Zhai [2009] and Gustafsson and Deng [2011]). This poverty line is set at CNY 2534 per capita per year, almost double the World Bank poverty line (USD 1.25 per day in 2005 dollars adjusted for purchasing power parity). To calculate the asset-poverty line for a household, I multiply Khan's line (CNY 2534) by the number of household members. Because Khan's line represents an annual level of asset poverty but this study measures asset poverty in three-month periods, I then divide the annual per-capita line by four.

The second approach uses the monthly household minimum expenditure reported by household heads to calculate basic household needs. The 2002 CHIP asked household heads to estimate the minimum amount of economic resources needed to satisfy monthly basic needs. Under this second approach, the asset-poverty line is the product obtained from multiplying the self-reported minimum expenditure by three (i.e. three months). This approach considers poverty from the perspective of consumption rather than income. By using self-reported minimum expenditure, I determine a subjective poverty line that may be especially useful for studying subjective well-being.

Other measures

The study includes three groups of demographic variables as control variables: the characteristics of the household head, the features of the household, and four factors that may mediate the relationship between asset poverty and happiness. The household head's characteristics include gender, age (20–29, 30–39, 40–49, 50–59, and 60 and above), employment status (employed or not), ethnic group (Han versus minority groups), marital status (married versus otherwise), health condition (very good versus otherwise), political party (Communist party versus otherwise), Hukou (urban Hukou or not), and highest education level completed (less than a high school diploma, high school diploma or equivalent, two- or three-year short-cycle college, and four-year college or above). A Hukou is a household registration record that officially identifies a person as a resident of an area.

Household characteristics are household size (the number of people living in the same household), number of children (younger than age 18), number of elderly members (older than 64), and annual household income in 2002 (including salary, bonus, subsidies, unemployment benefits, and so on). Because the distribution of household income in the sample is positively skewed, the study uses a log-transformed income measure in multivariate analyses.

The third group includes four variables that may mediate the relationship between asset poverty and self-reported happiness: precautionary savings, household living standard, fairness of income distribution, and predicted future income. Precautionary savings indicates whether a household's precautionary savings are greater than CNY 10,000. Perceived fairness of income distribution captures the respondent's characterization of the national income distribution (possible responses include 'very unfair', 'not very fair', 'fair', and 'very fair'). The household's living standard is represented by responses in four categories: low, below middle, above middle, and high. Finally, predicted future income represents the respondent's prediction concerning his or her household's future income over the next five years. These predictions are captured in four response categories: decrease, no change, small increase, and rapid increase.

Statistical analysis

The study first reports demographic characteristics, asset distributions, and the distribution of happiness scores for the sample. Using the two asset-poverty lines, the study then assesses asset poverty rates at the household level. This provides an estimate of the share of households living under the asset-poverty line.

To further examine the relationship between asset poverty and self-reported happiness, the study uses ordinary least squares (OLS) regression to estimate two additional models. Although happiness is an ordinal measure in this study, previous literature confirms that it is robust to different regression models, such as OLS, ordered probit, or logit regressions (e.g. Chyi and Mao 2012; Kuroki forthcoming). The study chooses OLS regression because its results are easy to interpret. The first OLS model, Model 1, uses asset poverty and the first two groups of control variables to predict happiness. To examine the four proposed mediation mechanisms, the second regression, Model 2, adds the third group of control variables into the analysis; this analysis considers the four possible mediators to be continuous variables.

Results

Sample characteristics

Table 11.1 reports the distribution of happiness scores and demographic characteristics in this sample. The mean happiness score is 3.49 (SD = .85), and over 80 per cent of households report that they are 'happy' or 'neither happy nor unhappy'.

Of the 6271 households, 33 per cent are headed by females. When the data were collected, most household heads were middle-aged; only 2 per cent were younger than 30. A small proportion of the household heads are members of

Table 11.1 Sample characteristics (*N*=6271)

Variables	Mean (SD) or %
Self-reported happiness	
Mean (SD)	3.49 (.85)
Categorical distribution	
Very happy	6.97
Happy	49.47
Neither happy nor unhappy	31.25
Not very happy	10.11
Not happy at all	2.20
Household head's characteristics (%)	
Gender (1 = female)	32.61
Age	
20–29	2.17
30–39	22.45
40–49	35.37
50–59	23.84
60 and above	16.17
Ethnicity (1 = Han)	96.16
Marital status (1 = married)	94.15
Employment status (1 = employed)	70.52
Hukou (1 = urban)	98.74
Education level	
Below high school	35.91
High school or equivalent	37.00
Two- or three-year college	18.19
Four-year college and above	8.90
Health condition (1 = very good)	20.62
Political party (1 = Communist Party)	38.37
Household characteristics	
Household size	3.02 (.79)
Number of children	.56 (.56)
Number of older adults	.23 (.55)
Household income in CNY	23,836.23 (15,527.59)
Liquid assets in CNY	28,205.20 (41,531.17)

Net worth in CNY without home equity	48,556.30 (66,512.71)
New worth in CNY	128,855.10 (144,399.80)
Mediators (%)	
Precautionary savings greater than CNY 10,000	18.19
Household living standard	
Low	10.86
Below middle	55.83
Above middle	32.55
High	.77
Fairness of income distribution	
Very unfair	32.31
Not very fair	54.35
Fair	12.77
Very fair	.57
Predicted future income	
Decrease	19.01
No change	32.23
Small increase	46.52
Rapid increase	2.25
Asset-poverty lines	
Khan's (2004) poverty line in CNY	1915.35 (500.62)
Self-reported expenditure in CNY	3374.63 (2761.47)

Note
CNY = Chinese yuan.

ethnic minority groups (less than 5 per cent are not Han), and 38 per cent are members of the Communist Party of China. Most household heads were married (94 per cent) and employed (70 per cent) in 2002. Almost all household heads have urban Hukou (99 per cent). About one-third of the householders have education below a high school diploma, and another third had a high school diploma or equivalent. Nearly 20 per cent attended two-year or three-year colleges, and 9 per cent had at least a four-year college degree. Twenty per cent of household heads report that they have very good health. On average, there are .56 children and .23 elders (ages 64 and above) in these households. The mean household income in 2002 was CNY 23,836 (SD = CNY 15,528). The average liquid assets, net worth without home equity, and net worth are CNY 28,205, CNY 48,556, and CNY 128,855, respectively.

Less than 20 per cent of households have precautionary savings greater than CNY 10,000. Nearly nine out of 10 respondents consider the household income distribution to be very unfair or not very fair, and nearly 70 per cent of respondents characterize their household living standard as low or below middle. Only 2 per cent of respondents predict rapid income increase in the next five years, and half of respondents anticipate no income change or even a decrease in income.

Asset poverty and its bivariate association with happiness

Table 11.2 shows asset-poverty rates estimated using the three different asset measures (liquid assets, net worth, and net worth excluding home equity) and the two asset-poverty lines (Khan's [2004] poverty line and the line constructed from the self-reported minimum household expenditure). Among the three asset measures, liquid assets generate the highest estimates of asset-poverty rates: Khan's (2004) poverty line identifies 17 per cent of sampled households as asset poor, and the line constructed from the self-reported minimum expenditure identifies 21 per cent as such. It is perhaps not surprising that asset-poverty rates are lowest in the estimates from the net worth measure, because net worth is an inclusive measure of wealth-type economic resources (Caner and Wolff 2004). Regardless of the poverty line used, less than 3 per cent of households have net worth that is not sufficient to meet consumption needs during a three-month period. If home equity is excluded from household net worth, asset-poverty rates rise to about 5 per cent under Khan's line and about 6 per cent under the line generated from the minimum household-expenditure figure. Overall, these estimates of urban asset-poverty rates are much lower than those in developed countries (Brandolini, Magri, and Smeeding 2010).

Table 11.3 presents mean scores of self-reported happiness by asset-poverty status. The average happiness score is about .3 to .5 lower for asset-poor households than for asset-non-poor households; the bivariate analyses suggest that the difference in mean happiness scores by asset poverty status is highly significant ($p < .001$).

Multivariate results

Table 11.4 presents results from the two OLS regression models. Model 1 includes controls for the characteristics of the household head and the household. Model 2 includes controls for those characteristics and for the four mechanisms posited to act as mediators in the relationship between asset poverty and happiness. The table reports regression coefficients for asset poverty as well as for the four possible mediators. The results are consistent across the three asset measures and the two asset-poverty lines. First, as the

Table 11.2 Asset-poverty rates ($N = 6271$)

Household economic resources	Asset poverty rates (%)	
	Khan's poverty line	Self-reported expenditure
Liquid assets	17.30	21.00
Net worth without home equity	5.17	6.35
Net worth	2.18	2.42

Note
Khan's poverty line is drawn from Khan (2004).

Table 11.3 Mean happiness score by asset poverty (*N*=6271)

Asset poverty lines	Happiness score	
	Asset poor	Asset non-poor
Khan's (2004) poverty line		
Liquid assets***	3.22	3.55
Net worth without home equity***	3.06	3.51
Net worth***	2.94	3.50
Self-reported expenditure		
Liquid assets***	3.27	3.55
Net worth without home equity***	3.12	3.51
Net worth***	2.97	3.50

Note
***$p < .001$.

estimates from Model 1 show, the happiness scores of asset-poor households are significantly lower than those of households that are not asset poor. Regardless of which poverty line is employed, net worth poverty is associated with a reduction in the happiness score by about .4 points, and liquid asset poverty is correlated with a .2-point decline in the score. Second, the four proposed mediators all have significantly positive relationships with happiness in Model 2. Among these four possible mediators, the perceived household living standard has the greatest marginal effect on happiness. The happiness score increases by about .4 points when the perceived living standard increases from one level to the next higher level. Third, the results in Model 2 confirm the hypothesis that the association between asset poverty and happiness is partially mediated by precautionary savings, perceptions of the fairness of the income distribution, perceptions of the relative household living standards, and predictions of income in the next five years. With the inclusion of controls for these four possible mediators, the asset-poverty regression coefficients decline by about 50 per cent for liquid assets and net worth without home equity. They decline by about 25 per cent for net worth.

The study also replicates the preceding analyses with data from a subsample of low-income households. This analysis focuses only on two groups: (1) those with annual household income lower than the product of household size and the poverty line developed by Khan (2004) (i.e. CNY 2534 per capita per year); and (2) those with annual household income lower than the product obtained from multiplying the monthly minimum expenditure by 12 (i.e. 12 months). In this analysis, the Khan poverty line identifies 307 households as low income, and the line calculated from the self-reported minimum expenditure identifies 601 respondents as low income. Table 11.5 presents the results, which are generally consistent with those reported in Table 11.4. Furthermore, estimates in Table 11.5 suggest that asset poverty has a greater marginal effect on happiness for low-income households than for households with higher incomes.

Table 11.4 Results from OLS regression of asset poverty and happiness (N=6271)

Variables	Khan's (2004) poverty line						Self-reported expenditure					
	Liquid assets		Net worth without home equity		Net worth		Liquid assets		Net worth without home equity		Net worth	
	Model 1	Model 2	Model 1	Model 2	Model 1	Model 2	Model 1	Model 2	Model 1	Model 2	Model 1	Model 2
Asset poverty (yes)	-.19***	-.10***	-.31***	-.15***	-.41***	-.32***	-.16***	-.08***	-.27***	-.13***	-.39***	-.31***
Precautionary savings (yes)		.06*		.05**		.05**		.05*		.05**		.05**
Household living standard		.35***		.35***		.35***		.35***		.35***		.35***
Fairness of income distribution		.17***		.17***		.17***		.17***		.17***		.17***
Predicted future income		.17***		.17***		.17***		.17***		.17***		.17***

Notes

OLS = ordinary least squares. Model 1 includes controls for the characteristics of the household head and the household. Model 2 includes controls for those characteristics and for the four mechanisms posited to act as mediators in the relationship between asset poverty and happiness.

$*p < .1$; $**p < .05$; $***p < .01$.

Table 11.5 Results from OLS regression of asset poverty and happiness among low-income households[a]

Variables	Khan's (2004) poverty line (n = 307)						Self-reported expenditure (n = 601)					
	Liquid assets		Net worth without home equity		Net worth		Liquid assets		Net worth without home equity		Net worth	
	Model 1	Model 2	Model 1	Model 2	Model 1	Model 2	Model 1	Model 2	Model 1	Model 2	Model 1	Model 2
Asset poverty (yes)	-.36***	-.24***	-.36***	-.13	-.61***	-.49**	-.15**	-.05	-.34***	-.21**	-.56***	-.53***
Precautionary savings (yes)		-.11		-.03		-.04		-.03		-.02		-.02
Household living standard		.41***		.42***		.42***		.37***		.32***		.33***
Fairness of income distribution		.31***		.30***		.29***		.18***		.17***		.18***
Predicted future income		.26***		.26***		.27***		.18***		.18***		.19***

Notes

OLS = ordinary least squares. Model 1 includes controls for the characteristics of the household head and the household. Model 2 includes controls for those character-istics and for the four mechanisms posited to act as mediators in the relationship between asset poverty and happiness.

a Low-income households refer to those with annual household income lower than four times the asset-poverty lines.

*p<.1; **p<.05; ***p<.01.

Discussion and conclusion

Using survey data from the 2002 CHIP, this study examines the relationship between asset poverty and happiness in urban China. Estimates in models that control for income, education, and other socio-economic characteristics suggest that asset poverty is negatively related to happiness. Asset poverty has a greater marginal effect on happiness for low-income households than for those with higher incomes. The association between asset poverty and happiness is partially mediated by precautionary savings, household living standard, perceived fairness of the income distribution, and predicted future income. The findings have several implications for the development of asset-building programmes that include components to improve happiness.

First, household assets contribute to happiness. When household assets increase from below the asset-poverty line to above it, the happiness score also increases by about 25–50 per cent of its standard deviation (depending on which asset measure is used). Such an influence is not negligible. The result suggests that social policies to help individuals and households accumulate assets can supplement other social assistance programmes designed to promote happiness. It also suggests that such asset-accumulation policies could be a component in the social policy system. At the 17th National Congress of the Communist Party of China in late 2007, President Hu Jintao issued an unprecedented call for the creation of appropriate conditions to enable citizens to generate asset income (Hu 2007). Asset income accounted for only 2 per cent of per-capita disposable income in 2007, and asset-based programmes have great potential as an effective policy tool for reforming income distribution.

Second, because household assets and asset poverty have greater associations with happiness among low-income households than among other households, asset-based programmes should be inclusive and should provide additional institutional support to disadvantaged populations. For instance, asset-based programmes could have an automatic enrolment feature (i.e. Child Trust Fund in the United Kingdom) to achieve the goal of universal participation and could provide additional financial subsidies to disadvantaged populations. In addition, the appropriate conditions for generating asset income are likely to vary because there is heterogeneity in socio-economic background and individual ability. Therefore, policy innovations should consider differences in the need for asset building.

Third, after basic income-assistance programmes are implemented, asset-based programmes may offer an efficient way to promote happiness – more efficient, at least, than additional income-support programmes. For instance, the average Khan poverty line for households in this sample is nearly CNY 2000. That is slightly higher than the average three-month minimum living standard set by the government (about CNY 1700; Huang *et al.* forthcoming). In other words, providing low-income households with less than CNY 2000 can raise the household happiness score by between .2 and .5 points (depending on which asset-poverty measure is used). More importantly, it is likely that this increase in the happiness score can be maintained. Asset building could be an integral part of the new agenda in China to promote happiness.

References

Alesina, A., R. Di Tella, and R. MacCulloch. 2004. 'Inequality and Happiness: Are Europeans and Americans Different?' *Journal of Public Economics* 88 (9–10): 2009–2042. doi:10.1016/j.jpubeco.2003.07.006.

Brandolini, A., S. Magri, and T.M. Smeeding. 2010. 'Asset-Based Measurement of Poverty.' *Journal of Policy Analysis and Management* 29 (2): 267–284. doi:10.1002/pam.20491.

Brockmann, H., J. Delhey, C. Welzel, and H. Yuan. 2009. 'The China Puzzle: Falling Happiness in a Rising Economy.' *Journal of Happiness Studies* 10 (4): 387–405. doi:10.1007/s10902-008-9095-4.

Caner, A., and E.N. Wolff. 2004. 'Asset Poverty in the United States, 1984–99: Evidence from the Panel Study of Income Dynamics.' *Review of Income and Wealth* 50 (4): 493–518. doi:10.1111/j.0034-6586.2004.00137.x.

Casey, J., and K. Koleski. 2011. *Backgrounder: China's 12th Five-Year Plan*. Report, 24 July. Washington, DC: U.S.–China Economic and Security Review Commission. http://origin.www.uscc.gov/sites/default/files/Research/12th-FiveYearPlan_062811.pdf.

Cheng, Y. 2008. 'Zhong guo cheng xiang cai fu fen bu de bi jiao fen xi.' [The comparative analysis of China's urban and rural wealth distribution]. *Jin rong yan jiu* [Journal of Financial Research] 12: 87–100.

Chyi, H., and S. Mao. 2012. 'The Determinants of Happiness of China's Elderly Population.' *Journal of Happiness Studies* 13 (1): 167–185. doi:10.1007/s10902-011-9256-8.

'Don't Worry, Be Happy,' *Economist*, 17 March 2011, www.economist.com/node/18388884.

Easterlin, R.A. 1995. 'Will Raising the Incomes of All Increase the Happiness of All?' *Journal of Economic Behavior and Organization* 27 (1): 35–47. doi:10.1016/0167-2681(95)00003-B.

Frey, B.S., and A. Stutzer. 2002. *Happiness and Economics: How the Economy and Institutions Affect Human Well-Being*. Princeton, NJ: Princeton University Press.

Gao, Q., I. Garfinkel, and F. Zhai. 2009. 'Anti-Poverty Effectiveness of the Minimum Living Standard Assistance Policy in Urban China.' *Review of Income and Wealth* 55 (Special Issue 1): 630–655. doi:10.1111/j.1475-4991.2009.00334.x.

Gustafsson, B.A., and Q. Deng. 2011. 'Di Bao Receipt and Its Importance for Combating Poverty in Urban China.' *Poverty and Public Policy* 3 (1): 116–147. doi:10.2202/1944-2858.1127.

Haveman, R., and E.N. Wolff. 2004. 'The Concept and Measurement of Asset Poverty: Levels, Trends and Composition for the U.S., 1983–2001.' *Journal of Economic Inequality* 2 (2): 145–169. doi:10.1007/s10888-004-4387-3.

Hu, J. 2007. 'Report to the Seventeenth National Congress of the Communist Party of China on Oct. 15, 2007.' Xinhuanet. http://news.xinhuanet.com/english/2007-10/24/content_6938749.htm.

Huang, J., M. Jin, S. Deng, B. Guo, L. Zou, and Michael Sherraden. Forthcoming. 'Asset Poverty in Urban China: A Study Using the 2002 Chinese Household Income Project.' *Journal of Social Policy*.

Khan, A.R. 2004. 'Growth, Inequality and Poverty in China: A Comparative Study of the Experience in the Periods before and after the Asian Crisis.' Issues in Employment and Poverty Discussion Paper 15, International Labour Organization, Geneva, Switzerland. www.ilo.org/wcmsp5/groups/public/---ed_emp/documents/publication/wcms_120689.pdf.

Kittiprapas, S., O. Sawangfa, C. Fisher, N. Powdthavee, and K. Nitnitiphrut. 2007. *Happiness: New Paradigm, Measurement, and Policy Implications; the Synthesis from the International Conference, Happiness and Public Policy, July 18–19, Bangkok, Thailand.* Bangkok: Happy Society Associate.

Knight, J., and R. Gunatilaka. 2010. 'Great Expectations? The Subjective Well-Being of Rural–Urban Migrants in China.' *World Development* 38 (1): 113–124. doi:10.1016/j. worlddev.2009.03.002.

Kuroki, M. Forthcoming. 'Crime Victimization and Subjective Well-Being: Evidence from Happiness Data.' *Journal of Happiness Studies.* doi:10.1007/s10902-012-9355-1.

Layard, R. 2005. *Happiness: Lessons from a New Science.* New York: Penguin.

Li, S., and R. Zhao. 2007. 'Changes in the Distribution of Wealth in China, 1995–2002.' Research Paper 2007/03, United Nations University–World Institute for Development Economics Research, Helsinki, Finland. www.wider.unu.edu/publications/working-papers/research-papers/2007/en_GB/rp2007-03/.

Li, S., W. Zhong, and B.A. Gustafsson. 2000. 'Zhong guo cheng zhen ju min de cai chan fen Ppei' [Distribution of wealth among urban and township households in China]. *Jing ji yan jiu* [Economic Research Journal] 3: 16–23.

Liang, Y., Z. Huo, and K. Liu. 2010. 'Zhong guo cheng xiang ju min cai chan fen bu de shi zheng yan jiu.' [An empirical study of wealth distribution of urban and rural households in China]. *Jing ji yan jiu* [Economic Research Journal] 10: 33–47.

McBride, M. 2001. 'Relative-Income Effects on Subjective Well-Being in the Cross-Section.' *Journal of Economic Behavior and Organization* 45 (3): 251–278. doi:10.1016/S0167-2681(01)00145-7.

Meng, X. 2007. 'Wealth Accumulation and Distribution in Urban China.' *Economic Development and Cultural Change* 55 (4): 761–791. doi:10.1086/516761.

Nam, Y., J. Huang, and M. Sherraden. 2008. 'Asset Definitions.' In *Asset Building and Low-Income Families*, edited by S.M. McKernan and M. Sherraden, 1–32. Washington, DC: Urban Institute Press.

Schneider, M. 2004. *The Distribution of Wealth.* Northampton, MA: Edward Elgar.

Sherraden, M. 1991. *Assets and the Poor: A New American Welfare Policy.* New York: M.E. Sharpe.

Veenhoven, R. 1984. *Conditions of Happiness.* Dordrecht: D. Reidel.

Zhao, R., and S. Ding. 2008. 'The Distribution of Wealth in China.' In *Inequality and Public Policy in China*, edited by B.A. Gustafsson, S. Li, and T. Sicular, 118–144. New York: Cambridge University Press.

12 The Hutubi Model

What have we learned?

Baorong Guo, Xincai Guo, and Li Zou

This study reviews the Hutubi Model, a successful local policy innovation in Hutubi, a remote county in northwestern China. We evaluate the model in the light of asset theory and discuss its broad implications for the development of asset-based social policy in China. The Hutubi Model focuses on asset building, a set of strategies to increase such financial and tangible assets as savings, homes, and businesses of all kinds (Center for Social Development 2012). In its 12 years of operation (1998–2010), this model allowed farmers who participated in a rural retirement-insurance programme to borrow against their retirement-insurance accounts for funds to invest in economic activities such as farming and raising livestock. Because of this model, Hutubi County was able to defy the national trends in China, where rural retirement-insurance programmes lost participants and retirement funds depreciated (Guo *et al.* 2008 'Asset-Based Policy in Rural China'). Exploring the unique features of this model, we examine its extraordinary successes in building assets for business investment, retirement, microfinance, and many other purposes. We also review the model's efforts to build financial inclusion. In examining all of these aspects, we consider the model's implications for the new rural retirement-insurance programme as well as for efforts to develop just and sustainable social policy in China.

A relatively new policy tool, asset-building programmes include low-income people in the process of asset accumulation as a way to tackle poverty and social inequality (McKernan and Sherraden 2008; Sherraden 1991). As is well known, China's urban–rural divide contributes tremendously to the unequal distribution of wealth and social benefits. Social policies and programmes provide urban residents with ways to save for housing and retirement, but most of their rural counterparts are institutionally excluded from such opportunities. As a result, rural–urban inequality in wealth holding continues to grow. According to Zhao and Ding (2008), the average per-capita wealth (net worth) was CNY 12,938 among rural residents in 2002 but CNY 46,134 among urban residents in that year. The rural–urban differences in financial assets and durable consumption goods are even greater (Zhao and Ding 2008).

Despite these gaps, asset-building policies and programmes are emerging in rural China (Zou 2010). Although limited in scale and scope, the programmes signal a new era of policy development in rural China. The Hutubi Model exemplifies such developments.

The Hutubi Model

In 1992, China introduced a rural retirement-insurance programme for farmers. One of the first asset-building initiatives in rural China, this voluntary programme allowed participants to contribute to their individual retirement savings accounts, which would begin remitting annuity payouts when the participant reached the age of 60 years. The policy required low individual contributions and encouraged collective contributions (by villages and village enterprises), though collective contributions were rare. Within a few years of implementation, the programme was unable to attract new participants or to retain existing ones. Although well intentioned, the programme seemed to offer participants little more than a retirement savings account. Fearing inflation, farmers became reluctant to accumulate savings in an account they could not access for decades to come.

The Hutubi Rural Retirement Insurance Office responded by initiating a loan programme in the local area. The programme allowed rural retirement-insurance participants to use their own and other participants' retirement-insurance registration cards as legal collateral for loans. Introduced in 1998, the loan programme was suspended during the following three years due to questions about its legitimacy, but finally was endorsed by the county government in 2002. One of this study's co-authors, Xincai Guo, headed the Hutubi Rural Retirement Insurance Office and launched the initiative.

This initiative involved close co-operation between the office and local banks. A participant seeking a loan surrendered the retirement-insurance registration card (indicating ownership of the retirement savings account) to the administration office. In exchange, the office gave the participant a notice that specified the amount he or she intended to borrow, and then the participant took the notice to a partnering bank (e.g. the rural credit co-operatives or the Bank of Agriculture). In applying for a loan, the participant gave the lender the notice and took out a loan in the amount indicated by the notice. When the borrower retired the debt, the bank issued a notice to him or her. The participant then returned to the administration office and exchanged the bank's notice for the account registration card. The interest rate charged for the loan was the same as that for a bank loan. The loan term varied from three months to three years. If the participant did not repay the loan on schedule, the bank imposed a punitive interest rate. (For a detailed description of the loan process, see Guo *et al.* 2008 'Asset-Based Policy in Rural China').

The Hutubi Model was immediately welcomed by local farmers (Guo *et al.* 2008 'Dual Incentives and Dual Asset Building'; Guo *et al.* 2008 'Asset-Based Policy in Rural China'; Zou 2010; Zou and Sherraden 2009). As of 2006, the Hutubi Model accounted for nearly 1300 loans worth CNY 7.5 million (Guo *et al.* 2008 'Asset-Based Policy in Rural China'). Because access to financial services was limited in rural areas, farmers benefited greatly from this policy innovation. The administrative, survey, and in-depth interview data on the Hutubi Model show that a large majority of participants took out the loans to purchase physical assets for agricultural or pastoral production. Most borrowers used the loans to buy farming supplies such as seeds and fertilizer. Some used them to buy livestock, electrical farming equipment, or transportation (e.g. a truck); others invested in education or a small business (Guo *et al.* 2008 'Asset-Based Policy in Rural China').

Retirement-insurance administrators also deemed the Hutubi Model a success. Although the central government suspended the national retirement-insurance programme in 1998 and participants in many other places dropped out, enrolment in the Hutubi programme remained steady at 8600 for its duration (1998–2010). The insurance fund in the Hutubi programme grew from CNY 170 million in 1998 to CNY 245 million in 2006, and the average annual growth rate of 8.13 per cent far exceeds the 5 per cent rate promised by the government. During the same period, the average savings in each account increased by 57 per cent, from CNY 1798 to CNY 2827 (Hutubi County Retirement Social Insurance Office 2007).

Inspired by the Hutubi Model and a central government directive that encouraged exploration of rural retirement social-insurance systems, governments in the provinces of Sichuan, Jiangxi, Inner Mongolia, and Anhui proposed asset-based retirement social insurance initiatives like the Hutubi Model (Chinese National Development and Reform Commission 2007). In 2006, the Sichuan Tongjiang County Bureau of Rural Social Insurance implemented a retirement-insurance programme for all citizens in its 49 towns. The programme was open to all county residents from newborns to those aged 59. The programme especially welcomed participation of those who lost farm land, worked in cities outside the county, served in the village governments, or followed the national family-planning policy (Tongjiang County Bureau of Rural Social Insurance in Sichuan Province 2007).[1] Like the Hutubi programme, the Tongjiang programme allowed participants to use their retirement-insurance registration cards as collateral for loans. In Tongjiang, borrowers obtained the loans from the rural credit co-operatives for up to 70–80 per cent of the funds in their accounts. They used the loans for health care, children's education, and home repair. The term for all loans was one year, and the programme required borrowers to repay the lending agency by the due date (Tongjiang County Bureau of Rural Social Insurance in Sichuan Province 2007).

Despite the success of the Hutubi Model, it came to an end in 2010. The implementation of the new rural retirement-insurance programme eliminated the policy platform that enabled the Hutubi loan programme. In response to the new policy, the Hutubi government terminated the loan programme, and the Hutubi retirement-insurance programme joined the larger insurance pool operated by the government of the Xinjiang Uygur Autonomous Region.

Previous studies detail the operation, features, and successes of the Hutubi programme (Guo *et al.* 2008 'Dual Incentives and Dual Asset Building'; Guo *et al.* 2008 'Asset-Based Policy in Rural China'; Zou and Sherraden 2009). Below we discuss the programme characteristics as they pertain to lifelong Individual Development Accounts, which have drawn attention from policymakers, practitioners, and researchers worldwide.

Features in light of asset theory

Asset building for multiple purposes

The sole purpose of the 1992 retirement-insurance programme was to help rural people save for later life. With the innovations introduced in the Hutubi Model, it became a multi-purpose asset-building programme. Loans taken from the savings account could be invested for children's education, for purchase of farming equipment and livestock, for economic development, for starting a small business, or for making a down-payment on a home. In other words, the Hutubi Model empowered borrowers to change the form of assets so that they could be used for purposes other than retirement. For example, the model enabled farmers with retirement savings to convert their savings through borrowing activities into seeds, fertilizer, and equipment necessary for farming. When the borrower repaid the loan, the county insurance office returned his or her insurance card, and the assets again became retirement savings. Because the savings continued to grow while held as collateral, the amount of savings at the time of loan repayment was likely greater than the amount at the time of borrowing. In this regard, the Hutubi Model shares some fundamental characteristics with Individual Development Accounts – a single programme feature that can serve an individual's diverse needs for housing, education, economic development, health, and retirement.

Financial inclusion

In Hutubi County, as in many other rural areas of China, financial services are limited and inaccessible to many inhabitants, yet farmers need loans for investment in economic production, especially in the spring (Guo *et al.* 2008 'Dual Incentives and Dual Asset Building'). Before microfinance emerged in rural China in the mid 1990s, those with little or no collateral barely had any access to financial services.[2]

Group lending is a popular form of microfinance in rural China. It changed collateral requirements and borrowing conventions. It involves loans from commercial banks to groups of five individuals who are together liable for repayment. Group lending effectively uses local information and networks to screen potential borrowers and enforce loan repayment without subjecting farmers to collateral requirements (Park and Ren 2001). Although this practice can minimize risk of default by involving multiple parties, it is not as convenient as a direct relationship between borrower and lender. In contrast, the Hutubi Model involves an individual relationship between each borrower and the lender. By connecting farmers with commercial banks and leveraging retirement insurance cards as collateral, the Hutubi Model presents a convenient alternative to group lending, especially when the loan amount is low and the loan term is short.

The Hutubi Model provided local farmers with important opportunities for financial inclusion. Assets essential for farming, raising livestock, and business start-up often exceed a farmer's liquidity; without access to microfinance, farmers have difficulty acquiring new assets (Guo *et al.* 2008 'Dual Incentives and Dual Asset Building'). Microloans not only give farmers the opportunity to build credit, but also increase their access to microcredit and other financial services.

Lifelong asset building

The 1992 rural retirement-insurance programme specified an age requirement: participants must be at an age between 20 and 60 years old to open a retirement savings account. The programme excluded the rest of the rural population, including children. In 2006, Hutubi County lowered the minimum age for parti-cipation in the retirement-insurance programme, allowing parents to enrol their children at any point after a child's birth. Although this age expansion makes the insurance programme a lifelong asset-building programme in theory, the promise of lifelong asset building could not have been attractive to participants without the loan programme.

Even for those who are willing to save for later life, participation in the insur-ance programme would not be an easy decision because it means one has to give up control over his or her retirement savings for a long time horizon. For most rural residents, lifelong saving could be compromised by a legitimate concern over current uncertainties that may necessitate the use of accumulated family economic resources. By enabling farmers to borrow against their retirement savings accounts, the Hutubi Model assured farmers that they could access savings, gave them an incentive to engage in saving for later life, and encour-aged them to begin saving early for their children.

The new policy context: challenges and opportunities

The new rural retirement-insurance programme launched in 2010 improves upon its predecessor in many ways. We mainly focus on improvements in programme access, incentives, and expectations, all of which are identified by Beverly *et al.* (2008) as determinants of asset building. Table 12.1 summarizes the main differ-ences between the new and old programmes in four key areas: eligibility, provi-sion, delivery, and finance.

First, the 2010 programme alters the terms of eligibility for rural retirement insurance. The new programme lowers the minimum age for participation to 16 years and removes the upper age limit. This expansion increases the number of potential participants and, thus, the number of potential beneficiaries. Under this new policy, individuals aged 60 and older who have never contributed to the pool of retirement savings may draw a basic, guaranteed retirement benefit from the programme.

Table 12.1 Comparison of rural retirement-insurance programmes

Category	Rural Retirement-Insurance Programme (1992)	Hutubi Model (1998–2010)	Rural Retirement-Insurance Programme (2010)
Eligibility	Rural residents aged 20–60 years old	Hutubi rural residents aged 0–60 years old	Rural residents aged 16 years or older
Provision	For rural retirement-insurance programme participants aged 60 and older; benefit level varies depending on the level and duration of individual contribution	For rural retirement-insurance programme participants aged 60 and older; benefit level varies depending on the level and duration of individual contribution; participants may use their savings as collateral for loans	To calculate the annual benefit for participants aged 60 and older, the 2010 programme divides the total individual contribution by 139 and adds that result to the basic, government-guaranteed benefit (CNY 55 per year)
Administration and delivery	County government	County government in partnership with local banks	Initially overseen by the county government; will transition to the provincial government
Finance	Individual contribution starts at CNY 2 per year with an increment of CNY 2; contribution maximum is CNY 20; almost fully funded; collective contribution is encouraged	For retirement insurance: individual contribution starts at CNY 2 per year with an increment of CNY 2, and the maximum is CNY 20; almost fully funded; collective contribution is encouraged. For the loan programme: loans from individual retirement-insurance accounts	Individual contribution: participants agree to make annual contributions in the amount of CNY 100, CNY 200, CNY 300, CNY 400, or CNY 500 Collective contributions: decisions made at the village level Government contributions: guaranteed CNY 55 for those eligible to withdraw retirement savings; the local government contributes CNY 30 per participant per year

Second, the benefits provided by the 2010 programme differ from those provided by the old one. A participant's monthly provision level is determined by both the individual contributions and the basic benefit, which is guaranteed by the government. Not only is the provision level of the 2010 programme much higher than that of the old programme, but the benefit's composition is more diversified: benefits paid by the 2010 programme include contributions from the individual participant, collective entities (e.g. villages), the local government, and the central government. The new programme specifies the responsibilities of governments at different levels and fosters social equity by providing a basic, guaranteed benefit to all rural seniors age 60 and over.

Third, the 2010 programme alters the ways in which rural retirement insurance is administered and the benefits are delivered. Although counties initially administered the 2010 programme during the pilot phase, responsibility for the programme's oversight will eventually transition to the provincial government. The shift to provincial administration is expected to broaden the pool of potential participants and, thus, the pool of available retirement funds. As a result, the funds will be less subject to risk than they were in the old, county-administered retirement system.

Fourth, the 2010 programme substantially changed the financing approach. The 1992 rural retirement-insurance programme offered individual savings accounts fully funded by participants' savings. Under the new programme, voluntary individual contribution is combined with mandatory contributions from the central and local governments. In economically developed areas, the new programme also encourages collective contributions (e.g. those made by rural enterprises). By combining a social pool with funds from individual savings accounts, the 2010 programme reduces the risk associated with sole reliance on individual contributions.

However, the 2010 programme appears to share some of the old programme's limitations, which the Hutubi Model attempted to address. In the 2010 programme, both individual and government contributions seem too low to provide benefits at levels that ensure economic security for retirement even by the current standard, and the costs of living continue to grow. Also, the main structural incentive for programme participation – namely, the contributions promised by the central and local governments – does not seem to be very effective in some rural areas. A study of randomly chosen rural residents finds that more than half of those who have not participated in the programme indicate low income as the primary reason for not participating (Fei *et al.* 2010). Finally, the 2010 programme, like its predecessor, does not allow participants to invest their contributions. Individual, collective, and government contributions all have to go into individual retirement savings accounts that generate interest based on the rate set by the People's Bank of China (the central bank in China) for a one-year certificate of deposit. High inflation in prior years and the recent slowing of economic growth raise questions about the security of retirement funds in individuals' accounts.

Although it ended with the enactment of the new rural retirement-insurance programme, the Hutubi loan programme has direct policy implications for today.

As discussed above, the Hutubi Model used the existing policy platform and reinforced incentives that make asset building feasible for rural citizens. A comparison of the 2010 programme with the Hutubi Model suggests that the Hutubi Model has its own advantages (see Table 12.1). The model can inform future asset-building policies and programmes in three key areas.

First, an individual may have competing needs for asset building; therefore, an ideal design would involve individual savings accounts that allow participants to convert assets seamlessly and transfer them for different purposes. In China and other parts of the world, many asset-building programmes are segmented to address different needs. In the United States, for example, 529 college-savings plans allow parents to save for children's post-secondary education; 403(b) and 401(k) plans are designed for retirement savings; there are also health savings plans. In urban China, there are similar savings plans for housing and health, respectively. Created to address a specific need, these segmented asset-building programmes more or less share two problems: high operational costs and constraints upon the free transfer of assets. The Hutubi Model is exemplary because it allows participants to convert assets conveniently and, thus, may be able to serve a greater number of purposes. In fact, the local government in Hutubi once considered developing the Hutubi Model into an Individual Development Account programme but did not succeed because innovation in the existing policy context is tremendously difficult. Nevertheless, the key insight is that there is a need for a single asset-building programme that serves broad purposes.

Second, the goal of asset building is best achieved if a programme also considers the current needs of rural citizens. In Hutubi County and elsewhere, one such need is financial inclusion. It is estimated that at least 45 million rural households in China are in need of microfinancial services (Bedson 2009), and nearly 3000 towns in China have no banking outlet (China Banking Regulatory Commission 2009). Perhaps the biggest obstacles to financial inclusion in rural areas are the lack of collateral and the lack of financial services. In partnering with the local commercial banks, the Hutubi Model expands financial services and brings farmers into mainstream financial services.

Finally, a consideration of lifelong asset building is important. Sherraden (1991) notes that an individual has various needs for development in the course of life. In early adulthood, individuals need college education, which is required for stable employment in many societies. In adulthood, an individual needs a house to raise a family. To satisfy entrepreneurial aspiration, an individual needs to start up a small business. In later adulthood, an individual needs retirement savings to ensure economic security and offset dwindling income. If an individual fails to accomplish a developmental task at a certain life stage, the failure will likely affect later stages. For example, children whose families cannot afford to pay for their college education may later experience difficulty securing a job. Individual failure to meet development needs may have broad social implications that lead to social inequality. Therefore, institutional support is needed to create opportunities for equal and sustainable development across the lifespan. We can find examples in the Child Savings Accounts offered by the United

Kingdom, the United States, and Hong Kong. The programmes automatically open an account when a child is born so that parents can start saving for the child's future. The accumulated savings build an economic foundation for the child's development and transition to adulthood.

Conclusion

This study reviews the Hutubi Model. Built upon the 1992 rural retirement-insurance programme, the model's loan programme allows account holders to use their individual retirement-insurance cards as collateral for commercial loans. It seems clear that rural citizens have a need for asset building, and the need is multi-faceted; they need savings for retirement as well as tangible assets for current development. The Hutubi Model demonstrates a successful asset-building programme that meets these needs, offers a path to financial inclusion, and enables participants to build assets across the life course. Although it came to an end in 2010, the Hutubi Model was successful in meeting the needs of local farmers.

Notes

1 In China, farmland is collectively owned by the state or by local communes. Families obtain the right to use a plot of land and then retain that right by paying rent. Families can lose the right of use by failing to pay rent or by migrating out of the local community (e.g. to work in cities).
2 Chinese law prohibits farmers from using their land as collateral.

References

Bedson, J., ed. 2009. *Microfinance in Asia: Trends, Challenges and Opportunities*. South Brisbane, Australia: Foundation for Development Cooperation.

Beverly, S.G., M. Sherraden, M. Zhan, T.R. Williams Shanks, Y. Nam, and R. Cramer. 2008. 'Determinants of Asset Building.' *Poor Finances: Assets and Low-Income Households*. Series Report, March. Washington, DC: Urban Institute. www.urban.org/url.cfm?ID=411650.

Center for Social Development. 2012. 'Overview.' Washington University, Center for Social Development. Accessed 10 August 2013. http://csd.wustl.edu/AssetBuilding/Pages/Overview.aspx.

China Banking Regulatory Commission. 2009. *Zhong guo yin hang jian du wei yuan hui 2009 nian bao* [China Banking Regulatory Commission Annual Report 2009]. China Banking Regulatory Commission. http://zhuanti.cbrc.gov.cn/subject/subject/nianbao2009/2009zwzz.pdf.

Chinese National Development and Reform Commission. 2007. 'Ge di xin xing nong cun she hui yang lao bao xian shi dian de qing kuang.' [A Pilot Study of the New Rural Retirement Social Insurance in Some Regions of China]. Chinese National Development and Reform Commission. www.ndrc.gov.cn/zjgx/t20070412_128791.htm.

Fei, Y., L. Shi, J. Lei, and Y. Ma. 2010. 'Tong ji xue jiao xue an li.' [Cases for teaching statistics]. Yunnan Institute of Finance and Trade, Kunming, Yunnan, China. http://202.203.192.204/eol/common/fckeditor/openfile.jsp?id=DBCPDHDGDIDGCPMNLDLMMGNBKHLNMMNBKHLALIMAPNCOHDHHGG.

Guo, B., J. Huang, M. Sherraden, and L. Zou. 2008. 'Dual Incentives and Dual Asset Building: Policy Implications of the Hutubi Rural Social Security Loan Program in China.' *Journal of Social Policy* 37 (3): 453–470. doi:10.1017/S0047279408001992.

Guo, B., J. Huang, L. Zou, and M. Sherraden. 2008. 'Asset-Based Policy in Rural China: An Innovation in the Retirement Social Insurance Programme.' *China Journal of Social Work* 1 (1): 63–76. doi:10.1080/17525090701855976.

Hutubi County Retirement Social Insurance Office. 2007. 'Hutubi xian yang lao bao xian ban gong shi dang an.' [Records of the Hutubi County Retirement Social Insurance Accounts]. Records, Hutubi County Retirement Social Insurance Office, Xinjiang, China.

McKernan, S.M., and M. Sherraden, eds. 2008. *Asset Building and Low-Income Families*. Washington, DC: Urban Institute Press.

Park, A., and C. Ren. 2001. 'Microfinance with Chinese Characteristics.' *World Development* 29 (1): 39–62. doi:10.1016/S0305-750X(00)00087-5.

Sherraden, M. 1991. *Assets and the Poor: A New American Welfare Policy*. Armonk, NY: M.E. Sharpe.

Tongjiang County Bureau of Rural Social Insurance in Sichuan Province. 2007. 'Tong jiang yuan nong cun yang lao bao xian shou ce zhi ya dai kuan de tan suo yu si kao.' [Some thoughts on the Tongjiang County Rural Social Insurance Loan Program.] Paper presented at the Seminar on Chinese Rural Social Insurance and Asset Building, organized by East Asian Social Policy Studies Network, Beijing, 14 November. www.easpec.org.cn/upFiles/File/2007_11_19_10_25_08_95.doc.

Zhao, R., and S. Ding 2008. 'The Distribution of Wealth in China.' In *Inequality and Public Policy in China*, edited by Björn A. Gustafsson, Li Shi, and Terry Sicular, 118–144. New York: Cambridge University Press.

Zou, Li. 2010. 'Diffusion of Asset-Based Social Policy in East Asia.' Working paper, Washington University, Center for Social Development, St. Louis, MO.

Zou, L., and Michael Sherraden. 2009. 'From "Dead" Savings to Assets for Life: Perspectives on the Retirement Social Insurance Pilot Project in Hutubi, China.' *Asia Pacific Journal of Social Work and Development* 19 (1): 96–115. doi:10.1080/2165099 3.2009.9756056.

13 Rebuilding cultural assets in an ethnic-minority village in Yunnan Province, China

Hok-Bun Ku

In March 2001, the Department of Applied Social Sciences at the Hong Kong Polytechnic University, the Department of Social Work at Yunnan University, and the Shizhong County government in Yunnan Province, China, conducted a joint action research project. They aimed to develop a model for rural social work that is culturally sensitive to the Chinese context and appropriate for building the capacity of local villagers to alleviate poverty. The project was carried out in Pingzhai, a village largely inhabited by the Zhuang ethnic minority group (though some villagers are of Han origin). The village is located in the northeastern region of Yunnan Province, which is in south-western China. This chapter details an action research pilot project that grew out of the 2001 collaboration.

Pingzhai is an administrative village with a 300-year history. It comprises eight natural villages and covers an area of approximately 23 square kilometres. The village is very remote, and a tractor-ploughed road is the only thoroughfare connecting villagers to the outside world. Census figures indicate that Pingzhai had a total of 347 households and a population of 1469 in 2000. At the time, the county government classified Pingzhai as a 'poor' village because it often encountered shortages of food and clothing. It was common to see more than 20 households suffering from food shortages for 4–6 months every year. According to the cadre from the Pingzhai Village Committee, 44 people in 16 households were exempt from the agricultural tax in August 2005 because of their 'extreme poverty'.[1] Furthermore, 285 people in 62 households relied on food donated by others to live during the same year. When the project began, we found that many villagers, especially those living in mountainous areas where the soil is poor, have to pay an exorbitant amount of interest on the money they borrow to buy food. In addition, many children in the village are denied educational opportunities because they cannot afford to pay fees.

Various attempts have been made to combat poverty in Pingzhai. The local government has encouraged farmers to grow high-tech crops, engage in agricultural development in winter,[2] and make structural adjustments. However, the central government's rural reforms and China's integration into the global capitalist market made the farmers in Pingzhai even more vulnerable, and their financial hardship deepened. They also were losing ethnic and cultural identity.[3]

The plight of villagers in Pingzhai first came to our attention in 2002 during work on cultural preservation projects that grew out of the 2001 collaboration mentioned above. However, it was not until 2005 that, inspired by the idea of fair trade, we began the new, cross-disciplinary pilot project on which this chapter focuses. The pilot is designed to reassess local assets, encourage villagers to employ local resources in producing arts and crafts for urban consumption, and help locals generate additional income. Such efforts seek to help villagers preserve and revitalize their cultural pride and identity, foster community participation, and strengthen community life and cohesion. Ultimately, we designed the project to protect them from the corrosive forces of globalization. This chapter documents our activities and experiences in the village as well as the lessons learned there.

Research design and methods

Our research team, which includes a number of social workers, an anthropologist, and a designer, adopted an interdisciplinary approach to its work (Sanoff 2000). We aim to practice participatory action research in which the women of Pingzhai are research partners, not informants, in our effort to map local cultural assets by recording their life stories and understanding of the meanings of their handicrafts. Empowerment and capacity building are goals of our project, and we see our research work as a transformative process (Park 1993; Small 1995; Vickers 2005). It exposes women in Pingzhai to new knowledge, fosters their awareness of development alternatives, and provides inspiration for action strategies (Park 1993, 1999; Small 1995). The research team believes that we can be transformed by what we learn from the women's participation as co-investigators in the research (Park 1999) and from their engagement in the planning–action–reflection cycle (Gaventa 1988; see also Park 1999; Schruijer 2006; Small 1995; Streck 2007). The resulting insights enable us to become effective reflexive practitioners.

In planning and designing the project and implementing the research, we followed the logic of action research, proceeding cautiously through different phases described below. We began by attempting to establish trust with participants, understand their living experiences, and deduce the meaning of the traditional culture. We pursued these goals by collecting a series of oral testimonies and conducting participant observation. When the research team established personal trust with participants, the research moved into a second phase in which the team worked to help local women form a handicraft group. We used focus groups to explore ideas for the group's business and strategies for poverty mitigation. As they developed the business model, the women felt that they needed to increase their capacity to design and produce handicrafts. As we provided access to instruction on a variety of subjects, we recorded their experiences and our own in log journals and reflective notes. When the time came to sell and market their products, the women conducted campaigns to educate consumers on fair trade and rural development. In field notes, we recorded participant observations and informal feedback during these steps. When the women finally consolidated the group, they held a public meeting to allow participants to share their sentiments. Again, members of our team kept notes. The qualitative written documentations are the main sources of our data.

The making of a cultural identity crisis

After spending several years working in Pingzhai we realized that, like other villages in China, it is at a crossroads. Modernization and change are occurring rapidly. Many have left the village to seek better educational and employment opportunities and have been exposed to new urban cultures and commodities. New patterns of consumption have emerged, profoundly affecting traditional ways of thinking, lifestyle, and social relationships. Changes in government policies and modern technology have had additional effects. The traditional economic foundation and cultural fabrics have disintegrated, poverty has deepened, and villagers have lost respect for their cultural identity.

New information technology allows villagers to access the ideas and lifestyles of the wider world. Life portrayed in television programmes is reinforced in the dominant discourse and sets the standard of modernity and progressivity. This prompts people to re-evaluate what they think of as good, bad, basic, insufficient, modern, and antiquated. The value and significance of traditional cultural practices are entirely overlooked. Villagers consider time-honoured lifestyles to be backward and poor, and have experienced a loss of identity and self-esteem as a result (Hairong 2008; Ku 2003, 2011).

Several other developments have eroded the tranquillity of everyday life in Pingzhai. Although some villagers are employed as casual labourers on farms, many men are engaged in mining and factory work. Children leave the village to pursue education in townships, and the growth of tourism has led to an influx of visitors from urban areas. The traditional culture has been invaded in a sense. During 2001, our first year in the village, young people gathered in front of the village leader's house every night after dinner to listen to the stories of those who work outside Pingzhai. That fascination with modernity persists. They discuss mobile phones, movie celebrities from Hong Kong and Taiwan, fashion, high-rise buildings, pop music, and other aspects of contemporary urban life. Some young people wear jeans and bleach their hair blonde. Many believe that a happy life can only be achieved by pursuing affluence in the city. As a result of these conversations, they begin to yearn for life outside the village and feel embarrassed by their own culture. Gradually, they become disillusioned (Pun 2003).

The Zhuang people once expressed their attitudes towards life, their feelings, and particularly their love for one another through traditional folk songs. They rarely sing these songs anymore. Instead, they sing love songs by Hong Kong and Taiwanese pop singers and cover the walls of their rooms with posters of their idols. They look down on traditional cultural ceremonies, folk songs, medicine, and other customs.

In recent years, many young people in the village have refused to wear traditional costumes, which they consider unattractive symbols of backwardness and ignorance. Pop music and fashionable clothes from the outside world represent progress and modernity to them, and they ridicule village girls who still wear old-fashioned Zhuang costumes and make-up. The girls are even ridiculed for their inability to speak Putonghua.[4]

This lack of regard for the indigenous culture contributes to low self-esteem and temerity. Although deeply attracted to the affluent life outside the village and frustrated by their own hard circumstances, villagers are fearful to leave because of their sense of inferiority and feelings of powerlessness. Moreover, those who leave are not guaranteed a better life. Unable to cope with the intense competition in the cities, most of the young men who leave the village are forced to return. In some cases, their wages do not cover their travel expenses. Upon their return, they do not embrace their old lifestyle of tilling the land and doing household chores. Instead, they continue to emulate the urban lifestyle and try to persuade others to follow their lead. Without the means to make their dreams come true, these young people suffer from a painful frustration and tend to resign themselves to hopelessness. They show off their knowledge of fashion as a way of masking their sense of loss.

Marginalized by mainstream culture, these villagers nevertheless maintain a blind faith in the world outside the village, which they consider to be far superior. This is the challenge facing China's rural social workers. How can they encourage the cultural confidence of local people and combat poverty simultaneously?

Rebuilding cultural assets and local strength

Social work has a long tradition of focusing on strengths and assets. Social workers believe that the poor and marginalized have many capacities that they and others sometimes do not recognize (Saleebey 1997; Sherraden 1991; Templeman 2005; Tice 2005). Asset- and capacity-building perspectives allow us to see that local communities contain a wide range of resources and strengths and discourage us from dwelling on deficiencies, problems, or disabilities. The practice models that keep us focused on strengths, assets, and capacities are critical for social work practice in rural communities (Cheers, Darracott, and Lonne 2005; Collier 2006; Ginsberg 2005; Lohmann and Lohmann 2005). As Scales and Streeter (2003) note, the role of the rural social worker is to uncover and reaffirm people's abilities and talents and communities' assets and resources. We are committed to empowering rural communities to use their resources in innovative ways to create new assets. We help them determine their own direction, set their own priorities, and leverage internal and external resources. We focus on discovering capacities and developing potentialities to promote individual and communal change. Capacity building involves a long-term investment in people and organizations and a commitment to changing the various processes and forces that affect people's lives negatively. While spending time with the

Pingzhai women, we identified rich cultural assets that could be leveraged to build capacity, enhance income, and restore cultural identity. The following sections describe the stages of the project during the period from 2005 to 2010.

Rediscovering cultural assets through oral testimonies

Because it is of primary importance to listen to the voices of the women and help them take control in the development process, we decided that our first act should be to collect oral testimonies to discover the meaning of their weaving and embroidering. Oral testimony is a method of participatory rural appraisal, which is an effective means of mobilizing community participation and discovering community needs (Grele 1991; Ku 2011; Ku and Luk 2002; Perks and Thomson 1998; Portelli 1998; Slim and Thomson 1995; Yow 1994) and gives us access to voices outside the mainstream discourse. It reveals personal experiences and aspects of life that are buried or hidden in the public realm. Oral testimony also offers those in minority groups an opportunity to speak for themselves, tell their own stories, recall their life experiences, and express their own views regarding their circumstances. For members of the local community, it is a means of empowerment. For social workers, oral testimony provides an opportunity to discover the common experiences of community members. It also offers us deeper insight into the community's relation to its past and its cultural heritage.

Due to language barriers and our unfamiliarity with the local community and its culture, we recruited local doctoral students and villagers as research partners. Local villagers have been participants in our work since 2001 and had no difficulty conducting interviews and using tape recorders. In 2005, together with villagers, we began visiting the older women in the various natural villages, encouraging them to tell us about their personal experiences, the strategies they adopt to deal with financial hardship, the history of the village, and their pride in their culture. They demonstrated how to weave cloth and showed us samples of their handmade textiles. After collecting oral testimonies for six months, we understood the process of producing traditional handicrafts and the cultural meaning of the women's art. The oral testimonies enabled us to assess the feasibility of a handicraft project. Through the visits, we found the women with the embroidery skills to produce unique and desirable handicrafts and identified the necessary tools and materials.

In the past, local women wove and dyed all of the cloth used for needlework in Pingzhai. Zhuang women trained young girls to do traditional embroidery. They made their own colourful costumes and bedding. The older generation remembers planting cotton and spinning yarn with a traditional spinning machine, but cotton has not been a crop in Pingzhai for a long time. The women typically buy variously coloured cotton thread from the market. In the past, they used dyes from natural flowers and plants to colour the woven fabric, but most now use a chemical dye. They arrange the thread with help from their neighbours and relatives, weaving the cloth on a hand loom. With this fabric, they make clothes and other goods. They cut a paper pattern and then embroider it. Thus, the satchels and other products are entirely handmade according to local traditions.

The patterns and colours tell the story of Pingzhai and its culture. Most of the pictures they embroider are related to their daily life and farming. One of the women, Qin,[5] commented:

> When I was a child, seeing the adults doing the needlework, I admired it so much. I took my mother's scissors with me when I was going to graze the cattle. I learned to cut the pattern for sewing. At the time, leaves were my paper. The wild flower and nature were my inspiration.[6]

The patterns represent mainly flowers and other common objects. One member of the women's handicraft group, Feng, explained to us why they usually design and embroider flowers:

> We very seldom design other things like animals. The reason is that we often see flowers on the hill. We rarely meet animals. In earlier days, the plant life on the mountain was lush: we want to keep the flowers in our imagination. We designed various patterns of flowers when we were young. Girls embroidered the flowers that grew in the fertile fields. We did not use the chemical fertilizers in those days. When the fields were allocated, we looked for the fields that grew certain kinds of flowers. Everyone competed for those fields. The rice growing in those fields didn't need chemical fertilizer. Rice grew well. However, in recent years, the flowers were damaged by pesticides, so they do not grow any more.

While collecting oral testimonies, we established strong friendships and developed an exceptionally close partnership with the young villagers who participated in the collection. We became a cohesive group with common goals and concerns and came to share a deep respect for the village traditions and the villagers who struggled to preserve their homes and cultural heritage in the context of deep poverty. The young villagers listened to the stories of older villagers and learned the meaning of traditional embroidery. These interactions became a process of education, empowerment, and reconciliation. The process encouraged youth to rediscover their cultural roots, re-establish relationships, and strengthen social cohesion among the villagers. The youth began to appreciate the elder villagers and respect their cultural heritage. In sharing the history of their own lives and the history and cultural practices of the village, the older people regained confidence and rediscovered their abilities. By discussing how the village overcame numerous difficulties in the past, young and old villagers rediscovered their past strengths and developed confidence in their ability as a community to overcome future challenges.

After collecting the oral testimonies, we organized sharing sessions to go through the stories with local participants and other villagers. Our purpose in these sessions was to help villagers discover their needs and aspirations, identify their cultural heritage and community strengths, and make plans for improving their livelihood through a communal decision-making process.

Forming the women's handicraft group

As mentioned above, our visits with women enabled us to assess the feasibility of a women's handicraft project. Some active women proposed the formation of such a group. However, in early 2006, when during a working meeting with the women we raised the issue of forming a co-operative women's group, they expressed hesitation. The villagers, especially the older ones, were hostile to and suspicious of collectivism because they experienced the failure of Mao's Great Leap Forward and suffered from it. A villager named Feng explained that it was difficult to form a large co-operative and gain the co-operation of women from different villages.[7] She suggested: 'If we want our project to go smoothly, we're better to start from a small scale. We don't need to mobilize too many women. If we can earn the money, then most women will actively join our group.'

Feng's reminder also helped us recognize that co-operation is the key to capacity building and empowerment in this project. It is important to challenge the mainstream model of development – which champions individualism and competition – by promoting a new form of collectivism based on mutual help, pooled resources, and active participation. After our discussion with the members of the project, we established the group's objectives as follows:

- To enhance the women's income to support their children's schooling.
- To promote a new form of collectivism.[8]
- To build the capacity of Pingzhai women.
- To protect Pingzhai's traditional culture, strengthen cultural identity, and bolster cultural confidence.
- To raise consumer consciousness of green consumption and fair trade.

Accompanied by Feng, the leader of the women's group, our staff visited all households in the natural villages that comprise the Pingzhai administrative village to mobilize women with embroidery skills to participate in the group. In 2006, we convened several meetings to determine how the women's group would function. However, women worried about the market and had no confidence that their products would be attractive to consumers. We tried our best to convince them that a co-operative enterprise would enhance their income and protect their traditional culture. At this stage, only seven women were willing to join the group.

Capacity building in design and production processes

Playing the role of facilitators, we encouraged women to develop their own initiative and momentum. We helped organize a plan for the first year of the project and provided a start-up loan for purchasing materials and tools. Because group members were poor and could not afford travel expenses, we financed their visits to the market in Kunming, the capital city of Yunnan Province, and other tourist sites so they could assess the potential market for their products.

In September 2006, we arranged for the group to visit the Stone Forest, a popular tourist site in Yunnan Province. Most of the products for sale there are made by a nearby ethnic minority group, the Yi. The Pingzhai women looked at the style and craftsmanship of the tourist products and compared their needlework with that of the Yi. They discussed market prices and other concerns with the staff of Yi Women's Embroidering Handicraft Association. After this initial market research, they drew several conclusions: the quality of the tourist handicrafts was poor; the market price was too low; their own style and embroidery skills were distinctive and unlike the Yi; and the tourist products they saw were made by machines, while theirs were entirely handmade.

In October 2006, project staff took samples of the Pingzhai group's embroidery to Kunming and conducted a market investigation. They found that the embroidery designs could be applied to a range of products popular with consumers. We invited a designer from Hong Kong to suggest ways to apply the embroidery patterns. We instructed the designer not to change the pattern, colour, or style of the women's embroidery but stimulate the women's creativity by designing some useful products that could be decorated with the embroidery. The designer came up with four products: a cloth book cover; a greeting card; a hanging, embroidered picture; and a cushion cover. We took these samples back to Pingzhai and encouraged the women to reject design ideas that did not appeal to them. We tried to assure them that the designer's input did not suppress their creativity and imagination. The women were very excited because they had never imagined their needlework could be adapted to home décor or stationery. They were attracted to the idea of the cloth book cover, the cushion cover, and the hanging picture, but they were not drawn to the greeting card. In Zhuang tradition, they told us, one buys useful gifts for special occasions, and they did not consider cards to be useful. They reminded us that cultural sensitivity is important for rural social workers who must learn to listen carefully and respect local voices.

In November 2006, we began to plan for the start of production. However, after purchasing embroidery thread and cloth from the market, the women were suddenly at a loss and told us they did not know how to proceed. We realized they lacked confidence and encouraged them to draw inspiration from the Yi Women's Embroidering Handicraft Association in the Stone Forest. In January 2007, we took the women on another visit to exchange views. The Yi Association was three years old and had 3000 members at that time. It obtained orders from embroidery factories and distributed jobs to its members. The products were sold in Shanghai, Beijing, Guangzhou, and other major cities, as well as in Korea, Japan, and Southeast Asia. The average annual income of the association's members was CNY 2000 to 5000 in 2007.[9] The Yi Association's success gave the Pingzhai women confidence, enlarged their perspective, strengthened their confidence in co-operation, and enhanced their organizational skills. They developed their own methods of organization and co-operation.

The Pingzhai women also undertook visits to learn about marketing and networking. In November 2006, we visited the manager of a garment company in Kunming to explore the possibility of co-operation. For creative inspiration and to determine what products would be popular, we visited some ethnic handicraft shops and Flower-Bird Street (the biggest street market). We introduced the women to Mr. Lin, the owner of a high-quality craft shop in Kunming. He conducted a workshop in which he shared marketing expertise and described his experiences in running a business. Mr. Lin inspired and encouraged the women. He promised to help them by displaying their products in a window cabinet. Keen to learn about running a business, the Pingzhai women discovered that there are three types of markets for handicrafts: popular, high-quality, and fair trade. The women felt that this visit was extremely useful and gave them many ideas about possible products and marketing strategies.

Participating in alternative trade

After returning to the village, the Pingzhai women had an intense and lively discussion to determine which markets to target. They finally decided that they preferred the high-quality and alternative markets. They considered the price for popular market goods to be too low and felt that such goods were of poor quality. If they produced substandard embroidery work, they would feel unhappy and ashamed. Because they expected the quality of their embroidery would be highly appreciated by consumers, they felt that the price should reflect their labour and effort and the value of their traditional culture.

To test the market, strengthen the group's confidence in its ability to sell products, and encourage publicity about the group, we decided to market the work at two international conferences. Drawing inspiration from samples produced by the designer and products in the markets they visited, the women designed their own goods, and their creativity was astonishing. For these conferences, the Pingzhai women produced many handiworks, including cellphone holders, tablecloths, cushion and pillow covers, tissue box covers, book covers, name-card holders, cotton pen cases, lovers' cotton bracelets, and hanging, embroidered pictures.

The first conference, the 15th symposium of the International Consortium for Social Development, took place 16–20 July 2007, at Hong Kong Polytechnic University. We set up a counter and exhibition booths to introduce our project and display the women's handicrafts. It was highly encouraging that the goods were appreciated by the delegates and sold well. Many were interested in the production processes and the cultural meanings of the handiworks. They also wanted to know more about how the women's group organized itself.

A week after the first conference, the Pingzhai women showcased their products at another international conference on Rural Social Work and Development in China at Yunnan University. On this occasion, the Pingzhai women participated in the conference, giving a presentation and answering questions from conference participants. They also introduced and sold their products to delegates, explaining how they produced their embroidery and calculated the price. Some of the Pingzhai women initially felt shy and were reluctant to interact with strangers, but they quickly overcame their nervousness when they saw that the delegates appreciated their products and were willing to buy. Many delegates, particularly local ones, recognized that the prices were much higher than those of the general tourist market but purchased items anyway. The women became brave and empowered.

Consolidating the development

With products sold and orders placed at the two conferences, the Pingzhai women earned about CNY 23,700 and needed to decide how to consolidate their organization and plan future development. We had no confidence that the women would distribute the income fairly or that they were capable of building a management system. However, they proved themselves and showed us their agency by collectively deciding how to apportion the money they earned and asking us to teach them book-keeping and accountancy. After deducting CNY 10,000 for materials, they decided to allocate income to each member based on working hours. More importantly, they decided to invest CNY 7000 in a collective development fund. As this process unfolded, we came to see our own bias.

To help the women consolidate their project and better understand the meaning of collectivism, we contacted a famous embroidery organization run by women from the Miao ethnic minority developed to preserve the traditional Miao culture and enhance the income of local women. It also provides embroidery training and job opportunities for young Miao women. More importantly, the organization is concerned with not only generating income but also empowering the women and reinforcing their dignity and self-confidence. The Miao women have been very successful in promoting their products and have created markets in large metropolises and foreign countries, including Taiwan and Japan.

Our project staff and the group members visited Guizhou in December 2007. The Pingzhai women and the Miao women had a productive exchange of views on their embroidery skills and experiences forming a women's group. For the Pingzhai women, this visit presented a vision of the future and strengthened their faith in the enterprise. They were moved and encouraged by the Miao women. They began to understand the meaning of preserving traditional culture.

After returning to Pingzhai, the women outlined a plan for 2008, developed a management system and regulations, and began to recruit new members from other natural villages. They clearly established a division of labour: one woman is responsible for book-keeping and accounting, one for quality control, one for pattern and product design, and so forth. Their regulations reflect their goal of collectivism based on mutual help, trust, pooling of resources, and active participation.

As of this writing, the group has met some of the goals outlined in the 2008 plan. In July 2008, the women set up a web site to introduce their project, share their stories, and promote their products. They have successfully explored the fair trade network and alternative markets. For example, they received orders to produce embroidered souvenirs for Hong Kong University's student union and other institutions. The women discussed the benefits of entering into co-operation with Hong Kong Fair Trade Power, a non-profit social enterprise. They began to collect the traditional Zhuang embroidery work in preparation for the creation of a Zhuang embroidery gallery or museum and set up a window cabinet to exhibit their handiworks at the China Research and Development Network of the Hong Kong Polytechnic University. The women also participated in a public forum on gender and development in Beijing and held an exhibition at Peking University in December 2010.

Discussion

After nine years in development, this rural social work project is moving towards our intended goals of building the capacity and enhancing the financial situation of Pingzhai women. Our most gratifying achievements are the establishment of a core group of committed and motivated women who are keen to develop the project, increase a sense of solidarity and social cohesion among the local villagers, and promote their confidence and pride. Through this highly participative and empowering process, the women have regained their sense of control over their own destinies and have developed a much stronger sense of identification with their cultural heritage.

The women involved in the project were transformed from passive recipients of outside funding assistance to active participants in community development. At the outset, the women thought they were working for the project organizers and were concerned only with what they could receive from us. However, they now clearly understand that it is their own project. Responsibility for the group's development falls on its members.

During the process of establishing the group, the Pingzhai women discovered their own capacity and potential. At first, they wanted professionals to teach them product design or give them a sample to copy. However, when they had the opportunity to observe the handicraft market and compare their skills with those of other ethnic minorities, their confidence grew. As their creativity and capacity to generate designs developed, the intervention of professional designers ceased to be necessary. The Pingzhai women became designers, experimenting with patterns, colours, and types of products.

The women also have become active in public affairs and earned respect from locals. In the 2010 grassroots election, one of the women was elected to serve as village vice-head. A villager said that he voted for her because she not only improved her own household economic situation but also sacrificed her time to serve the community by becoming an activist in our project.

The project broke down barriers established by household individualism and overcame socio-cultural hostilities and suspicion towards collectivism in the village. At the outset, when we emphasized the importance of building a collective organization, the women were suspicious. However, as the project developed, they began to realize the advantages of mutual help and co-operation.

Now there is a clear division of labour in the group, and each woman is assigned a duty consistent with her particular talents and abilities. The project focuses on building capacity in marketing and trade. After two years of training, the women have acquired basic business knowledge (e.g. the ability to calculate costs, set prices, and merchandise).

The cultural identity crisis is an obstacle to the development of rural China. Under the influence of a market economy, the value of a good is measured by its market price. Pingzhai villagers lost appreciation for their traditional culture because their skills and knowledge appear to have no market value. Traditional costumes have become unpopular. Young people prefer to wear T-shirts and jeans. Young girls are reluctant to learn embroidery skills because the process is time consuming and the products seem to have no market value.

However, the project led to a renewal of appreciation for the value of tradi-tional culture. Recognizing that their traditional costumes and linens can be a source of supplementary income, the villagers have revitalized their traditional skills. They have organized training lessons and invited young people to join their group. In 2010, three girls in their late teens returned to the village from the city and decided to join the group. Three other young married women also joined the group, which now comprises 13 members. Their average age is 36 years. Older members are encouraged by the participation of new members.

The women are now aware of the importance of cultural preservation. They have begun to collect old embroidery and fabrics in preparation for opening a museum. They also co-operate with the older women at the village's senior association and have returned to traditional fabric production and colouring prac-tices. They want to ensure that their traditional embroidery skills will be pre-served, revitalized, and improved.

Conclusion

In working with the villagers in Pingzhai, we found that the primary cause of rural poverty is not a low level of education, poor quality of land, remoteness of villages, lack of technological expertise, or unfamiliarity with the market economy. Instead, it is the villagers' sense of lost control in the development process. Development has brought new ideas, resources, and technologies to local communities, but it also has created unrealistic expectations, inequalities, social exclusion, and a crisis in cultural identity. This identity crisis leaves vil-lagers cynical and erodes faith in development.

Another obstacle to rural development is the disappearance of the spirit of collectivism and co-operation. When the people think that *collectivism* is just a euphemism for *sacrifice*, they eschew mutual co-operation. Competition and individual gain become the overriding principles.

To create sustainable rural development, we should focus on not only increasing productivity and villagers' income, but also building assets and local empowerment. We should make an effort to encourage cultural pride and confidence by revitalizing traditional cultural practices. We should help people understand and treasure those traditions and their meanings. Our work in Pingzhai was an attempt to encourage people to think of alternative ways of development and new forms of collectivism so that economic development is not planned by the government from the top down. Villagers can fully participate in decision-making and are able to take control of the development process. We believe that there is no single path to development. What is necessary is that the locals – the subjects of development – make their voices heard, avoid assimilation into the mainstream culture, and resist marginalization.

Development, as it is now understood, is not purely economic but includes advances in peace, justice, human rights, health, education, and the environment. We believe that cultural identity and self-confidence can be fully restored in an era of globalization and modernization only if the individuals involved desire such a restoration. Efforts to gather local assets and improve people's circumstances are only possible if there is vigorous community participation. The development of an alternative model of growth can only be meaningful if it protects the community from the negative impact of market forces (Pun and Ku 2011). The various facilitators – social workers, designers, and other social scientists – must work in, with, and for the community. Social workers in China are increasingly asked to work with the people in rural settings. How will our experiences in rural areas affect social work? How can social workers foster rural development? These questions require our attention.

Notes

1 According the World Bank, extreme poverty is defined as average daily consumption of USD 1.25 or less and means living on the edge of subsistence (Ravallion, Chen, and Sangraula 2008). The agricultural tax was eliminated with the launch of the new agricultural policy in 2006.
2 Under a local policy, the government encouraged the villagers to farm in winter. In traditional farming practice, the villagers let the field lie fallow in winter. The government regarded this traditional practice as unproductive and backward.
3 Similar situations are observed in other developing countries (see Wilson and Dissanayake 1996).
4 Putonghua is the official language in China. In the village, people speak Zhuang dialect or Yunnan dialect. In China, language differences are connected to differences in ethnicity.
5 Here and below, some subjects' names and details have been changed to protect the anonymity of research participants.
6 All quotations are translated by the author.
7 Feng was an active participant at the beginning and later became the group's leader.
8 The phrase 'new form of collectivism' here means a form of economy that is people-centred, community-based, co-operative, democratic, and defined by harmony between

people and the environment. It is a societal system in which production is not for consumption but for servicing the needs of the people. It is different from the old form of collectivism. Premised on a state-planned economy, the old form limited democratic participation through high levels of centralization and bureaucratic management. Under that form, producers lacked motivation and autonomy in the production process.

9 The Yuan renminbi (CNY) is a unit of currency in China. One US dollar is equivalent to approximately CNY 7.7.

References

Cheers, Brian, Ros Darracott, and Bob Lonne. 2005. 'Domains of Rural Social Work Practice.' *Rural Society Journal* 15 (3): 234–251. doi:10.5172/rsj.351.15.3.234.

Collier, Ken. 2006. *Social Work with Rural Peoples*. 3rd edn. Vancouver, Canada: New Star.

Gaventa, John. 1988. 'Participatory Research in North America.' *Convergence* 21 (2–3): 19–48.

Ginsberg, Leon H., ed. 2005. *Social Work in Rural Communities*. 4th edn. Alexandria, VA: Council on Social Work Education.

Grele, Ronald J. 1991. *Envelopes of Sound: The Art of Oral History*. 2nd edn. New York: Praeger.

Hairong, Yan. 2008. *New Masters, New Servants: Migration, Development, and Women Workers in China*. Durham, NC: Duke University Press.

Ku, Hok-bun. 2003. *Moral Politics in a South Chinese Village: Responsibility, Reciprocity, and Resistance*. Lanham, MD: Rowman & Littlefield.

Ku, Hok-bun. 2011. '"Happiness Being Like a Blooming Flower": An Action Research of Rural Social Work in an Ethnic Minority Community of Yunnan Province, PRC.' *Action Research* 9 (4): 344–369. doi:10.1177/1476750311402227.

Ku, Hok-bun, and Tak Chuen Luk. 2002. 'Koushulishi yu Fazhan Xingdong de Fanxing: yi Zhongguo Pinkundiqu Jichujiaoyu Fupinxiangmu Weili' [Oral history and the rethinking of developmental action: a case study of poverty eradication programmes in China's impoverished regions]. *Hong Kong Journal of Sociology* 3: 181–210.

Lohmann, Nancy, and Roger A. Lohmann, eds. 2005. *Rural Social Work Practice*. New York: Columbia University Press.

Park, Peter. 1993. 'What is Participatory Research? A Theoretical and Methodological Perspective.' In *Voices of Change: Participatory Research in the United States and Canada*, edited by Peter Park, Mary Brydon-Miller, Budd Hall, and Ted Jackson, 1–20. Westport, CT: Bergin & Garvey.

Park, Peter. 1999. 'People, Knowledge, and Change in Participatory Research.' *Management Learning* 30 (2): 141–157. doi:10.1177/1350507699302003.

Perks, Robert, and Alistair Thomson, eds. 1998. *The Oral History Reader*. New York: Routledge.

Portelli, Alessandro. 1998. 'Oral History as Genre.' In *Narrative and Genre*, edited by Mary Chamberlain and Paul Thompson, 23–45. London: Routledge.

Pun, Ngai. 2003. 'Subsumption or Consumption? The Phantom of Consumer Revolution in "Globalizing" China.' *Cultural Anthropology* 18 (4): 469–492. doi:10.1525/can.2003.18.4.469.

Pun, Ngai, and Hok-bun Ku. 2011. 'China at the Crossroads: Social Economy as the New Way of Development.' *China Journal of Social Work* 4 (3): 197–199. doi:10.1080/17525098.2011.618445.

Ravallion, Martin, Shaohua Chen, and Prem Sangraula. 2008. *Dollar a Day Revisited.* Policy Research Working Paper 4620. Washington, DC: World Bank Development Research Group. www.wds.worldbank.org/servlet/WDSContentServer/WDSP/IB/2008 /09/02/000158349_20080902095754/Rendered/PDF/wps4620.pdf.

Saleebey, Dennis, ed. 1997. *The Strengths Perspective in Social Work Practice.* 2nd edn. New York: Longman.

Sanoff, Henry. 2000. *Community Participation Methods in Design and Planning.* New York: Wiley.

Scales, T. Laine, and Calvin L. Streeter, eds. 2003. *Rural Social Work: Building and Sustaining Community Assets.* Belmont, CA: Brooks/Cole/Thomson Learning.

Schruijer, Sandra G.L. 2006. 'Research on Collaboration in Action.' *International Journal of Action Research* 2 (2): 222–242.

Sherraden, Michael. 1991. *Assets and the Poor: A New American Welfare Policy.* Armonk, NY: M.E. Sharpe.

Slim, Hugo, and Paul Thomson. 1995. *Listening for a Change: Oral Testimony and Community Development.* London: New Society.

Small, Stephen A. 1995. 'Action-Oriented Research: Models and Methods.' *Journal of Marriage and the Family* 57 (4): 941–955. doi:10.2307/353414.

Streck, Danilo R. 2007. 'Research and Social Transformation: Notes about Method and Methodology in Participatory Research.' *International Journal of Action Research* 3 (1–2): 112–130.

Templeman, Sharon B. 2005. 'Building Assets in Rural Communities through Service Learning.' In *Social Work in Rural Communities*, edited by Leon H. Ginsberg, 123–138. 4th edn. Alexandria, VA: Council on Social Work Education.

Tice, Carolyn J. 2005. 'Celebrating Rural Communities: A Strengths Assessment.' In *Social Work in Rural Communities*, edited by Leon H. Ginsberg, 95–108. 4th edn. Alexandria, VA: Council on Social Work Education.

Vickers, Margaret. 2005. 'Action Research to Improve the Human Condition: An Insider–Outsider and a Multi-Methodology Design for Actionable Knowledge Outcomes.' *International Journal of Action Research* 1 (2): 190–218.

Wilson, Rob, and Wimal Dissanayake, eds. 1996. *Global/Local: Cultural Production and the Transnational Imaginary.* Durham, NC: Duke University Press.

Yow, Valerie Raleigh. 1994. *Recording Oral History: A Practical Guide for Social Scientists.* London: Sage.

14 Asset building and livelihood rebuilding in post-disaster Sichuan, China

Wai-fong Ting

A horrendous earthquake struck China's Sichuan Province in May 2008. In early 2009, a social work station opened to assist with recovery efforts in the rural, disaster-stricken community of Qingping County. The station launched a wide range of community-based programmes theoretically and practically underpinned by the concept of asset building. This chapter assesses the state of theoretical models on asset building, examines the asset-building projects in Qingping County, and discusses the role of those projects in developing four kinds of assets: financial, social, cultural, and human.

The evolution of asset-building policy and practices

Sherraden (2005) points out that income is an essential component of economic security, but is not sufficient to ensure security. He distinguishes income, which is mainly used for short-term consumption, from assets, which are accumulated for long-term goals. An asset, according to Oliver and Shapiro (1990, 131) 'is a more stable indicator of status or position in society and represents stored-up purchasing power ... it reflects savings and investments that can be drawn on in times of need.' Assets can enhance efforts to maintain resources and be used to develop other forms of assets. For example, financial assets can pay for tertiary education (a human asset), provide a down-payment on a home, or maintain a standard of living in retirement. Assets also can provide liquidity to a family in times of economic stress (Wolff 2001) and a cushion against sudden income shocks (Sherraden 1991).

Sherraden (1991) also points out that assets can benefit family stability and lead to positive psychosocial outcomes for adults and positive educational and economic outcomes for children. Moreover, family stability can stimulate the development of human capital, planning for the future, risk taking, and active engagement in the community (Sherraden 1991). Bynner and Despotidou (2001) suggest that assets have lasting independent effects. Finally, Wolff (2001, 34) notes that, 'in a representative democracy, the distribution of power is often related to the distribution of wealth', and people with assets are most likely to have trust in the political system (Bynner and Despotidou 2001). Thus, the evidence indicates that assets can improve the economic and social outcomes of low-income families and foster trust in a society (Bynner and Despotidou 2001; Bynner and Paxton 2001; Shapiro 2004; Yadama and Sherraden 1996; Zhan and Sherraden 2003).

Asset-based policy and the first-generation model of asset development

Despite the evidence that assets have positive effects, many current income-based welfare policies prevent the poor from saving by imposing restrictions to saving. As Beverly and Sherraden (1999) indicate, saving and asset accumulation are shaped by institutions, and they suggest that institutionalized saving mechanisms could promote secure and convenient ways for the poor to save. In addition, they note that financial education could allow the poor to understand the processes and benefits of asset accumulation (Figure 14.1). Incentives like attractive rates of return and saving-related subsidies could facilitate saving behaviour (Beverly and Sherraden 1999). Evidence suggests that assets help participants in asset-building programmes create goals and road maps to reach those goals (Sherraden *et al.* 2004).

International examples of asset-based policy and applied projects

Since the early 1990s, asset-based policy innovation has been led by the Corporation for Enterprise Development in Washington, DC, and the Center for Social Development at Washington University in St. Louis. Various asset-based welfare policy initiatives and social programmes have been implemented in different countries. In 1993, Singapore launched the Edusave Scheme.[1] In the United States, the American Dream Demonstration (ADD) Project began in 1997.[2] Taipei initiated Family Development Accounts in 2000 (Cheng 2004), and the United Kingdom launched two initiatives: the Saving Gateway in 2003 (Harvey *et al.* 2007) and the Child Trust Fund in 2004.[3] Canada began two others: Learn$ave in 2003 and the Canada Learning Bond in 2004.[4]

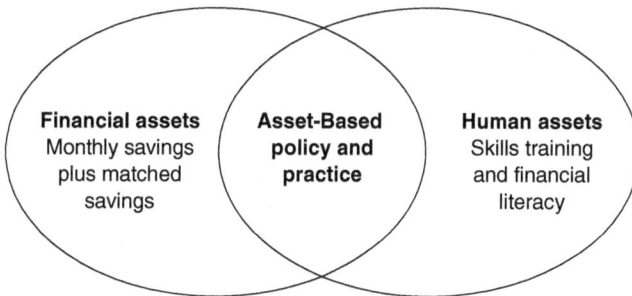

Figure 14.1 Two forms of assets generated in asset-based policy and practice.

Two main types of asset-based policy initiatives exist. The first provides a matched savings account (e.g. an Individual Development Account [IDA]) designed to help low-income individuals and families accumulate short-term savings to meet a specific goal. These programmes normally last from 12 to 36 months and participants are provided with financial literacy training and other support (Mills *et al.* 2004). The second type provides a universal saving programme (e.g. the Child Trust Fund in the UK). The programmes are usually for children, and often the government makes an initial contribution to an interest-earning account for each child (and may match contributions for children in households that receive social benefits). Family members and relatives make additional contributions. The children can only withdraw money from those accounts after they reach a certain age (usually 18), and the programmes do not include financial literacy training.

The development of asset-building programmes in Hong Kong

In 2007, the Tung Wah Group of Hospitals, a Hong Kong-based non-governmental organization (NGO), launched a pilot asset-building project, the Hope Development Accounts (HDAs), with funding from the ZeShan Foundation and the Citi Foundation. In structuring these accounts, the HDA programme adopted several components from IDAs. For example, the programme provides funds to match the account holder's savings, and it designed the accounts to help individuals (primarily adult females) from low-income families save for long-term goals. During the saving period, the programme provides financial planning and related training programmes to enhance both the financial and human capital of participants. Moreover, the accounts rely heavily on the small-group approach featured in microfinance programmes that employ the Grameen Bank model (Yunus and Jolis 2003). Recently, the Tung Wah Group of Hospitals expanded the individual HDAs into Family Development Accounts for low-income families in Hong Kong. At this writing, nearly 200 individuals and families have participated in the two types of accounts. Over 95 per cent of participants remained in the programme for the 30-month duration and accumulated assets.[5]

Since 2008, the government of Hong Kong Special Administrative Region (HKSAR) has provided NGOs with funding to manage the Child Development Fund (CDF), an asset-building programme to combat intergenerational poverty. In the last four years, more than 5000 children between the ages of 10 and 16 have participated. The CDF programmes have three major components: personal development plans, a mentorship programme, and targeted savings. The government expects that these three components will enhance children's abilities to manage resources and plan for their own future.[6] Each participating child has a monthly savings target of HKD 200 and agrees to save that amount each month for two years. Private foundations or businesses match those savings.

The role of social assets in addressing poverty

The preceding appraisal discusses international asset-building programmes designed to develop financial and human assets. However, the literature on these initiatives tends to overlook their role in the development of participants' social assets, the virtuous social relationships that exist within and between groups of people. In this chapter, I use the terms *social assets* and *social capital* interchangeably. A sizable literature examines social capital, its benefits, and efforts to cultivate it (OECD 2001; Policy Research Initiative 2005; Putnam 2000; Ting 2010; Woolcock and Narayan 2000).

Asset-building programmes in Hong Kong deliberately sought to develop bonding and bridging forms of social capital, broadening the social horizon of the participating individuals and families. Strategies to combat poverty are insufficient if they help the poor get by but not ahead (de Souza Briggs 1998). Thus, bridging social capital that forges social connections among different community sectors is crucial if the goal is to increase the resources and opportunities available for people from disadvantaged backgrounds. Efforts to broaden social connections could prevent further social and economic isolation of poor people and disadvantaged communities (Ting 2010).

Second-generation asset building: an integrated model for developing three types of assets

As the preceding discussion suggests, a comprehensive model to address poverty should focus on the integrated, simultaneous development of the three forms of assets – social, financial, and human – among the disadvantaged. That model represents the second generation of asset building (Figure 14.2).

Financial assets refer both to the savings that programme participants deposit during a specified period of time and to the savings match provided by sponsoring organizations. *Social assets* refer to the interpersonal connections and social networks built during the course of programme participation. *Human assets* refer to the knowledge that the programme participants gain from the training, which is designed to enhance their personal capabilities. *Cultural assets*, a fourth form of assets, have not been articulated or pursued in the previous asset-building efforts. However, I will discuss them in greater detail below, as they are one of the four types of assets developed in the post-disaster (re)development project in Qingping County.

Asset-building policy, research, and projects came to China in 2004. In 2005, an asset-building demonstration project began in Xinjiang Uygur Autonomous Region.[7] These early efforts fuelled asset-building policy discussion and research, but there have been few practice projects other than the one in Xinjiang. Inspired by these asset-building ideas and based on practice experiences in Hong Kong, a team of social work educators from the Department of Applied Social Sciences of the Hong Kong Polytechnic University adopted asset building as the overarching theme in efforts to help Qingping County. Funded by ZeShan

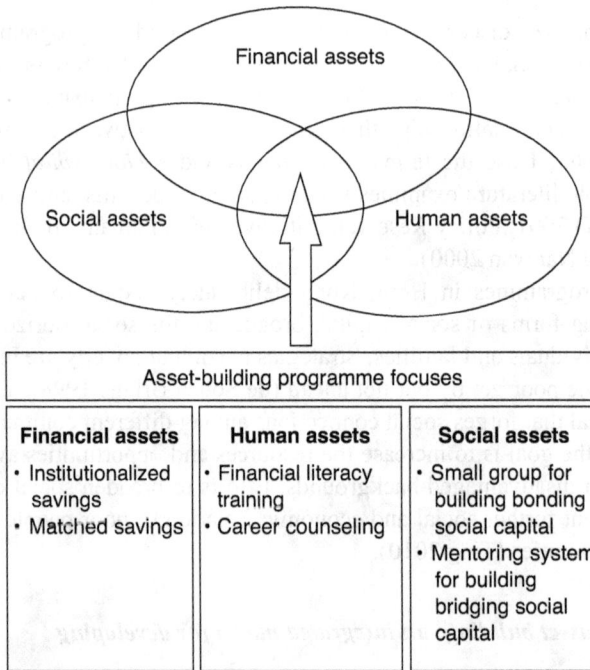

Figure 14.2 An integrated model for the development of three types of assets.

Foundation, the effort seeks to help the disaster-stricken rural community in Sichuan Province recover from two disasters: the Wenchuan earthquake in 2008 and the massive mudslide in 2010.

The 2008 Wenchuan earthquake and reconstruction efforts

On 12 May 2008, a major earthquake struck Wenchuan County in Sichuan province. The earthquake measured 8.0 on the Richter scale and, as of 17 June 2008, affected 46.2 million people. Of these, 15 million were evacuated from their homes and five million were homeless. The death toll was 69,227, the number of injured was 374,176, and 17,923 were missing. The earthquake also destroyed 21 million buildings, including 7000 schools (Argueta Bernal and Procee 2012). The Chinese government responded immediately and efficiently to mitigate the devastating effects on people and property.

China completed 93 per cent of the planned reconstruction by May 2011, three years after the earthquake (Ting and Chen 2012). These efforts included a school, a hospital, a water supply facility, and a cultural centre in every rural county (*xiang zhen*), underscoring the government's intention to elevate the living standards in earthquake-stricken communities. However, such macro-level reconstruction had only indirect effects on efforts to rebuild the lives of villagers

(Ting and Chen 2012). In early 2009, the previously mentioned social work team established a social work station in Qingping County to help this rural community recover and (re)develop.[8]

Qingping County's second disaster and its road to post-disaster (re)development

Before the 2008 earthquake, Qingping County was home to more than 6000 villagers. The county is located in the mountainous area 32 km northwest of Mianzhu City. Qingping County reports that 367 died in the earthquake and another 1000 sustained serious injuries. Villagers also suffered great losses to their houses and other property. A second disaster – a massive mudslide – struck Qingping County on 13 August 2010. It intensified inhabitants' pain and suffering by destroying many newly reconstructed buildings. The mudslide rendered one-fifth of the villagers homeless.

Asset-building policy and projects focus on the alleviation and prevention of poverty in different parts of the world, but there is little literature on the use of asset building as a strategy for redevelopment in disaster-stricken communities. Informed by models of alternative development (Brocklesby and Fisher 2003; Harriss 2006; Helmore and Singh 2001; Pieterse 2010; Sen 1999; Wright 2010), I suggest that the asset-building approach can provide a framework for efforts to rebuild the disaster-stricken community. As I mentioned above, Qingping suffered from multiple losses, and the reconstruction of infrastructure does not measure up to a comprehensive (re)development. By 'comprehensive', I mean the (re)development of multiple assets (e.g. financial, social, cultural, and human) in addition to the necessary 'brick-and-mortar' reconstruction (Figure 14.3).

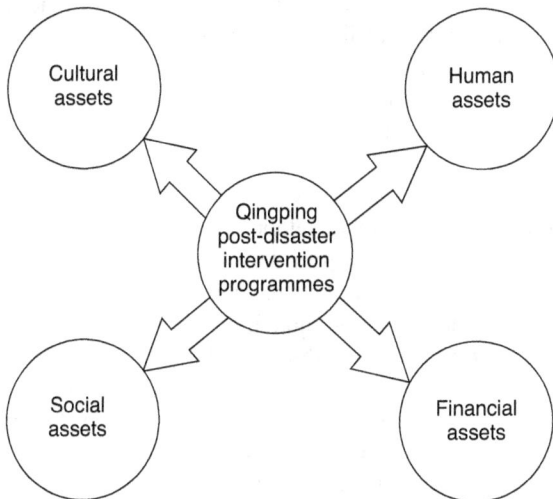

Figure 14.3 Model of multi-asset development in post-disaster Qingping.

The comprehensive (re)development effort launched by the Qingping social work station reckoned that economic recovery was not the only concern (Ting and Chen 2012). The villagers also needed to rebuild lost social relationships, reconnect with their cultural and traditional roots, and be liberated from the spell of disastrous fate. The team of social workers, of which I was a member, started from where the villagers were, where they wished to be, what they possessed, and what they could reasonably expect to repossess. The team incrementally developed a comprehensive, multi-asset intervention for the entire county.

Developing a multi-asset intervention in post-disaster Qingping County

As mentioned, the previous two generations of the asset-development model integrated efforts to develop financial, social, and human assets. However, the literature on asset building seldom mentions cultural assets, the fourth kind of asset to be developed in this post-disaster intervention. Therefore, the incorporation of this new form of asset introduces a new dimension to the asset-building model. The following discussion details the effort to develop all four assets in Qingping County during the four years from 2009 through 2012.

Financial asset (re)development

Qingping County was affluent before the 2008 earthquake. Encouraged by the local government, villagers engaged in various tourism businesses. For instance, some villagers took out bank loans to build guest houses, many of which were demolished in the disasters. Others engaged in the local mining business, which provided gainful employment and stable income to many families until the earthquake struck. These two major means of livelihood were no longer viable after the earthquake, and many villagers were economically devastated. Despite the Chinese government's efficiency in co-ordinating different sectors of society to help in the aftermath of the disaster, the efforts focused primarily on the reconstruction of infrastructure rather than on the task of rebuilding livelihood.

According to Pieterse (2010), participation by the local community and NGOs is critical to the success of any community development effort. In other words, a top-down approach to development (or to post-disaster redevelopment, in this case) is bound to fail because it grossly neglects the contribution of local people and their wisdom. The social-transformation model, which Pieterse (2010) suggests as the alternative to the dominant growth-oriented model, provided useful guidelines for the Qingping social work station in its endeavours to support redevelopment for villagers in Qingping County (Ting and Chen 2012). Moreover, the station saw the villagers not as victims but as survivors who have a personal agency that could enable them to reshape their lives and future. The model emphasizes the resilience of local people as a factor that enables them to withstand past trauma and rebuild capacity.

By late 2009, most of Qingping County's survivors returned to their villages. The social workers formed a co-operative (i.e. co-op) comprising 20 villagers (mostly females) who had known each other throughout their lives but never worked together in socio-economic pursuits. This rural co-op endeavours to facilitate the development of multiple types of assets via the operation of a microenterprise in Qingping County. The co-op, the social work station, other NGOs, local officials, and villagers formed a collaborative network, which co-op members believed they could leverage to obtain the precious resources, both material and non-material, needed for the microenterprise.

This microenterprise provides ecotourism services to visitors from different parts of the country and overseas. Through these services, the co-op generates income and financial assets. Several key principles guide the operation of the co-op and this ecotourism microenterprise: local ownership, equitable venture, equal participation and democratic decision making, holistic development as an indicator of success, process-oriented evaluation, endogenous development (Ting and Chen, 2012). Guided by these principles, the microenterprise began in early 2010. However, the co-op's members lacked the financial assets needed to set-up guest houses and catering facilities. Thus, the Qingping social work station gave microloans to half of the co-op's 20 members first (each of the 10 members received a loan of RMB 5000) to be repaid within one year. However, the August 2010 mudslide postponed the ecotourism project for almost a year, making it impossible for the 10 co-op members to repay the loans, rendering the 10 remaining co-op members unable to take out loans. The social work station and the co-op subsequently devised an IDA-like asset-building plan to resolve the impasse.

The new plan replaces the original microloan with a saving mechanism and requires all 20 members to save income generated from the ecotourism microenterprise (expected to be around RMB 3000 per year). The Qingping social work station provides funds to match these savings. The plan requires the 10 original borrowers to use their own savings and matches to repay the loans, whereas the 10 remaining co-op members can keep their savings and the matched funds. The savings accumulated by the co-op members provided the necessary resources to restart the ecotourism microenterprise in the last quarter of 2011. Between then and December 2012, each participating member received an average income of RMB 3500, which provides a cushion for the families in the disaster-stricken community. Other pressing demands inevitably arose, requiring financial commitments from these families. However, the built-in matched savings mechanism provided an attractive incentive for these families to give high priority to saving and to continue saving regularly.

Social asset (re)development

Social assets differ from other kinds of assets because they are embedded within the unique attributes of social relationships that cannot be separated from other actors and community structures (Ting 2010). In other words, social assets can be seen as the connections among individuals and as the norms of trust and reciprocity that are embedded in those connections (Putnam 2000). These norms govern social relationships and enable people to work together for collective good (Fukuyama 1995). Social relationships, together with human and environmental assets, are essential elements of national wealth (Serageldin 1996; Serageldin and Steer 1994).

Social capital (i.e. social assets) also plays a significant role in alleviating poverty. As Brisson and Usher (2005, 651) note, 'Antipoverty programs and community change initiatives must address the isolation experienced by some families in the poorest neighborhoods and should develop programs that build connections in these neighborhoods.' Moreover, because a social asset is a 'public good – non-excludable and non-rivalrous – the market will underprovide such good' (Dowla 2006, 102). Thus, there is cause for a purposive intervention programme to develop social assets. Gittell and Thompson (2001, 133) also assert that 'social capital is a key resource for community economic development because it can be used to aggregate and leverage other development assets'. This suggests that social-asset development should go hand in hand with efforts to develop other forms of assets.

In communities like Qingping County, villagers live alongside each other for decades. In disasters, the destruction of homes separates villagers and forces them to relocate. An unfortunate and inevitable consequence is that the disaster also destroys social connections built on geographic proximity and social interaction. Thus, post-disaster redevelopment efforts should pay particular attention to rebuilding these precious social assets. Moreover, it is also crucial to revitalize the norms of trust and reciprocity in these social relationships. Without such norms, the social relationship will lack altruism and cannot be considered an asset.

Since its establishment in early 2009, the Qingping social work station has implemented a wide variety of programmes to redevelop social assets among the villagers. For example, the ecotourism microenterprise, though primarily intended to help villagers accumulate financial assets, redeveloped the participants' social assets as co-op members co-ordinated with different groups of villagers. For example, members made arrangements with villagers skilled at hiking and knowledgeable of the county's landscape. Others established connections between the microenterprise and elder villagers well-versed in local folklore (Ting and Chen 2012). These collective activities enabled villagers to reconnect and to rebuild mutual trust and support.

The oral history project represents another effort to redevelop social assets in Qingping County. In Qingping, elderly villagers recall the local cultural stories, but illiteracy prevents many from sharing and documenting these cultural treasures. Designed to resurrect the cultural and traditional stories that used to circulate in Qingping, the project also provided opportunities for in-depth interaction among villagers, especially between the young and their elders. Social workers trained young villagers to interview elders about these cultural stories. Very active, close, cross-generational interactions developed during the interviews. As the young interviewers accumulated stories, youth and elders developed valuable social assets.

The Qingping social work station also organized several community-based social and recreational activities. The events provided villagers with reasons to gather for sharing joy instead of indulging in sorrow. The station formed groups of women and youth, training them to become organizers of these programmes. For instance, volunteers with the women's groups practised day and night to sharpen their singing and dancing skills so they could teach them to other villagers during nightly activities in the county's civic square. In doing so, these women built social connections with each other and with other Qingping County villagers who participated in their lessons. Through teaching and mentoring others, these volunteers built more than a cheerful and pleasant atmosphere in Qingping; they also helped to rebuild the mutuality subsided by the disasters.

Cultural asset (re)development

Cultural assets can be understood in part as cultural heritage, which Jokilehto (2005, 4–5) defines as the 'entire corpus of material signs – either artistic or symbolic – handed on by the past to each culture and, therefore, to the whole of humankind'. According to this definition, the cultural assets of a given society include physical and non-physical features. Physical cultural heritage refers to the human and natural environment and archaeological sites in rural and urban areas (Jokilehto 2005). The non-physical or intangible aspects of a given culture or society's cultural assets include the 'signs and symbols passed on by oral transmission, artistic and literary forms of expression, languages, ways of life, myths, beliefs and rituals, value systems and traditional knowledge and know-how' (Jokilehto 2005, 5). The preservation and presentation of cultural assets are pivotal if a culture is to survive and sustain itself (Jokilehto 2005).

The oral history of Qingping County

The 2008 Wenchuan earthquake inflicted tremendous damage on the human lives and material cultures in Sichuan Province. Amid such loss, constant mourning was inevitable and understandable. The villagers' suffering was understandable, but it became apparent that many of their resources survived the earthquake. Their rich cultural heritage is one of these. Preservation of these assets required dedicated and collective efforts to make explicit the implicit stores of memory and tradition. It required articulating, circulating, and continuing the county's cultural and historical heritage amid massive collective lost and despair. The economically inactive and physically frail elderly villagers were mobilized to develop an oral history project.

This project is significant for several reasons. First, it resurrected local culture and history as assets that hold value for the local population, promoting the notion that these assets cannot be destroyed. This gave a sense of pride and power to the otherwise despairing community. Second, the oral history project gave those unable to contribute to physical reconstruction a chance to make other contributions. In the tradition of social work, it is crucial to instil survivors with a sense of competence and mastery after natural disasters (Mathbor 2007). The opportunity to contribute to the reconstruction empowered the elderly and affirmed their value in the community. Thus, this project was therapeutic for elders who survived the earthquake. Finally, cultural heritage, in both physical and non-physical forms, represents the most valuable resource of a social group. The resurrection of that heritage was vital in helping Qingping County to redevelop into a tourist destination.

Qingping County's elderly contributed stories during interviews conducted by young villagers, and together they collected cultural artefacts for display when the stories were presented later. Between late 2009 and the end of 2012, the project included 33 stories based on the narratives of the elderly that were published in two books. The first book contains stories concerning the various cultural and traditional customs of Qingping County. They record cultural heritage on temple matters and worship, the history of buildings and architecture, marriage and funeral rituals, and the folk music and songs (*shange*) of the Qiang Zu ethnic group. The second book documents Qingping villagers' stories about surviving the two major disasters. It is arranged in subsections devoted to the land, the people, and the relationship between them (*qing*). The elderly villagers presented these stories in community-wide gatherings and invited other villagers' responses for enrichment of these stories.

Rural living as cultural heritage

Rural living as a non-physical form of cultural heritage is gradually dying out because of rapid economic development and urbanization in China. The co-op's ecotourism programme, which invites urban dwellers to experience rural ways of living, represents another effort to resurrect and preserve cultural heritage. This programme advocates for rural–urban collaboration, ecological conservation, and alternative development, and promotes understanding of rural lives by encouraging urban participants to 'live, eat, work, and relax in the rural way' (Ting and Chen 2012). Through these practices, rural organizers and urban participants could enjoy equal status; urban visitors take on the role of their rural counterparts, gaining new perceptions of the rural culture, ecology, and lifestyle. At the same time, these interactions enhance the self-image, confidence, and cultural identity of the rural organizers, possibly fostering fairer rural–urban collaboration.

Co-op members take turns providing accommodation, catering, and organizing activities for ecotourists. These activities include sight-seeing, hiking, learning traditional dances, and working in the fields (e.g. feeding livestock and picking wild vegetables) for the food they consume at meals. One of the sightseeing programmes takes guests to visit examples of the destruction caused by the earthquake and mudslides. During these visits, survivors recount their experiences and tell touching stories of bravery. After these activities, the social workers debrief the visitors, encouraging them to share reflections on their experiences. The social workers hope to promote in-depth understanding and foster long-term harmony between rural and urban people and between humans and the natural environment.

Although this ecotourism microenterprise provides needed income, its most important benefits are cultural. It restores rural life as a form of cultural heritage, enhances solidarity among the villagers, and strengthens their cultural identity.

Finally, daily public efforts facilitate the development of Qingping County's cultural assets. The public, villagers and visitors alike, gather in the county's civic square to sing traditional songs and dance the traditional steps of the Han and Qiang Zu. There is probably no better way to restore a quickly dying cultural heritage than to engage the active participation of the culture's bearers in the performance of their own culture on a daily basis.

Human asset (re)development

The two disasters deprived many in Qingping County of more than their material possessions. Human assets, including skills developed from working in the mines and fields, became useless in helping survivors to secure the jobs available after the disasters. Villagers reckoned that jobs provide not only 'bread and butter' but also the sense that one is useful. The Qingping social work station lacked the resources to launch large-scale livelihood programmes, but the social workers organized meaningful social engagements in the community and encouraged villagers' participation. Some of the station's programmes attempt to develop villagers' human and financial assets at the same time.

Training the microentrepreneurs

The ecotourism microenterprise provides villagers with important opportunities to develop human assets. Although villagers have known each other for many years, few have experience collaborating to operate business ventures. It was and remains crucial for co-op members to learn how to work in a team with fellow villagers and workers from other NGOs. Moreover, the ecotourism microenterprise is not profit driven and does not run on pure business principles. Instead, it underscores the importance of social benefits. Furthermore, co-op members share equally in the financial gains generated from this project or reinvest the gains into the project. All these principles were novel to members, and it was necessary to inculcate them as collectively held core beliefs. The co-op held numerous group meetings and discussions to enable the members to internalize the principles. Members of the co-op also visited other NGOs to learn from the successes and failures of similar social enterprises.

Finally, human assets come into play as co-op members make preparations to receive visitors and provide amicable services in members' homes. Members develop simple, instrumental knowledge and skills in hospitality. In introducing visitors to the scenic landscape, rural lifestyle, and cultural heritage, they learn courtesy and pride.

Training the participants in the oral history project

Participants in the oral history project received training to be able to work in the various stages of production, collecting, developing, and writing stories before presenting them in community gatherings. For example, young villagers were trained to conduct interviews with elderly villagers, and the elderly were trained to tell the stories during public gatherings.

Project participants also acquired skills in compiling the collected materials and presenting them in publishable format. As few villagers had experience in this area, the social workers taught them skills in gathering relevant artefacts, including old pictures, pieces of traditional costumes or headwear used during weddings, and old furniture.

For the villagers, presenting the Qingping stories in community gatherings was the most challenging task. The presenters performed the stories on a stage in front of a few hundred audience members and re-enacted portions of the tales. After recounting the stories, presenters invited the audience to ask questions, enrich the stories with supplementary information, and tell new but related stories unknown to the oral history project team. Together, the participants and social workers have produced several public performances since 2010. Through these occasions, participants preserve the traditional cultural assets of Qingping County and develop new human assets.

Training organizers of social, cultural, and recreational activities

Since the late 1990s, every city and town in China builds a civic square for communal use and promotion of local culture. Post-disaster Qingping created the Felicity Garden as part of reconstruction after the 2008 Wenchuan earthquake. But the square sat unused for some time because the government and county residents did not organize activities. The social workers from the Qingping social work station have been instrumental in bringing cultural and recreational life to the square.

Qingping County was home to the Qiang Zu, one of China's 56 ethnic groups, for more than 3000 years. Many villagers with this ethnic background are proficient in traditional Qiang songs and dances. The social workers were delighted to recruit Qiang Zu descendants to become organizers and performers in the square. As many of them had no experience in producing performances or leading activities, it was essential for social workers to help them develop skills in event organization and co-ordination to eventually assume lead roles as hosts. In late 2010, the Performing Arts of Qi Dian Sisters, a group consisting of around 20 Qiang female villagers between the ages of 20 and 50, was formed. These women learned leadership concepts and related skills in regular meetings and practised applying them in real-life situations. As the group practised traditional singing and dancing skills during the subsequent six months, it also became increasingly capable in leading and co-ordinating public activities within the civic square.

Conclusion

This chapter reviews the concepts of asset-building policy and examines an applied asset-building project in a rural Chinese community that has suffered tremendously from two major natural disasters. As I suggest, asset-building models evolved from an original emphasis on enabling constituents to accumulate financial and human assets to a second-generation model that includes social assets. Such assets are crucial in helping low-income families improve their long-term quality of life, but little scholarship discusses the role that cultural assets might play in helping distressed individuals and communities regain vitality. This chapter theorizes a place for cultural assets in the asset-building model and illustrates that expanded model by detailing efforts to rebuild cultural assets in the devastated rural community of Qingping County.

Rather than seeing members of the disaster-stricken community as victims, the asset-based model advocates a perspective that emphasizes strengths and resilience. It sees people as disaster survivors who, despite multiple losses, possess precious assets that can be mobilized and developed further. As this study demonstrates, the community in Qingping County possesses a number of assets and is capable of (re)developing others. Through a range of community-based programmes, including an ecotourism microenterprise, an oral history project, community volunteering projects, and the civic square cultural and recreational project, the social work station identified and developed all four types of assets. These experiences demonstrate that, despite the devastation, villagers remain hopeful for a better life. With carefully planned intervention programmes, these hopes could come to fruition.

Notes

1 Ministry of Education, Singapore. 2013. 'Edusave Scheme.' Ministry of Education, Singapore. Accessed 10 January 2013. www.moe.gov.sg/initiatives/edusave.
2 Center for Social Development. 2012. 'GAP Projects.' Center for Social Development. Accessed 18 February 2013. http://csd.wustl.edu/AssetBuilding/Pages/gapprojects.aspx.
3 See UK Government. 2013. 'Child Trust Funds.' GOV.UK. Accessed 1 January 2013. www.gov.uk/child-trust-funds/overview.
4 See Government of Canada. 2013. 'Education Savings for your Child.' CanLearn. Accessed 23 January 2013. www.canlearn.ca/eng/saving.
5 The author conducted evaluation research for the HDAs, but the results of that research are not yet published.
6 See the website of Child Development Fund, HKSAR Government. Accessed 13 February 2013. www.cdf.gov.hk/eindex.htm.
7 See Center for Social Development. 2012. 'GAP Projects.' Center for Social Development. Accessed 18 February 2013. http://csd.wustl.edu/AssetBuilding/Pages/gapprojects.aspx.
8 I use *(re)develop*, *(re)development*, and the like to indicate that development and redevelopment are intertwined in complex ways in this context.

References

Argueta Bernal, V., and P. Procee. 2012. 'Four Years on: What China Got Right When Rebuilding After the Sichuan Earthquake.' ReliefWeb. http://reliefweb.int/report/china/four-years-what-china-got-right-when-rebuilding-after-sichuan-earthquake.

Beverly, S.G., and M. Sherraden. 1999. 'Institutional Determinants of Saving: Implications for Low-Income Households and Public Policy.' *Journal of Socio-Economics* 28 (4): 457–473. doi:10.1016/S1053-5357(99)00046-3.

Brisson, D.S., and C.L. Usher. 2005. 'Bonding Social Capital in Low-Income Neighborhoods.' *Family Relations* 54 (5): 644–653. doi:10.1111/j.1741-3729.2005.00348.x.

Brocklesby, M.A., and E. Fisher. 2003. 'Community Development in Sustainable Livelihoods Approaches: An Introduction.' *Community Development Journal* 38 (3): 185–198. doi:10.1093/cdj/bsg002.

Bynner, J., and S. Despotidou. 2001. *Effect of Assets on Life Chances*. London: Centre for Longitudinal Studies, Institute of Education.

Bynner, J., and W. Paxton. 2001. *The Asset-Effect*. London: Institute for Public Policy Research.

Cheng, L.C. 2004. 'Developing Family Development Accounts in Taipei: Policy Innovation from Income to Assets.' Research Paper No. CASE083, March, London School of Economics and Political Science, Centre for Analysis of Social Exclusion, London. http://papers.ssrn.com/sol3/papers.cfm?abstract_id=1159314.

de Souza Briggs, X. 1998. 'Brown Kids in White Suburbs: Housing Mobility and the Many Faces of Social Capital.' *Housing Policy Debate* 9 (1): 177–221. doi:10.1080/10511482.1998.9521290.

Dowla, A. 2006. 'In Credit We Trust: Building Social Capital by Grameen Bank in Bangladesh.' *Journal of Socio-Economics* 35 (1): 102–122. doi:10.1016/j.socec.2005.12.006.

Fukuyama, F. 1995. *Trust: The Social Virtues and the Creation of Prosperity*. New York: Free Press.

Gittell, R., and J.P. Thompson. 2001. 'Making Social Capital Work: Social Capital and Community Economic Development.' In *Social Capital and Poor Communities*, edited by S. Saegert, J.P. Thompson, and M.R. Warren, 115–135. New York: Russell Sage.

Harriss, J. 2006. 'Social Capital.' In *The New Development Economics After the Washington Consensus*, edited by K.S. Jomo and B. Fine, 184–199. London: Zed.

Harvey, P., N. Pettigrew, R. Madden, C. Emmerson, G. Tetlow, and M. Wakefield. 2007. *Final Evaluation of the Saving Gateway 2 Pilot: Main Report*. Research Study, May. London: HM Treasury, Department for Education and Skills. www.hm-treasury.gov.uk/d/savings_gateway_evaluation_report.pdf.

Helmore, K., and N. Singh. 2001. *Sustainable Livelihoods: Building on the Welfare of the Poor*. West Hartford, CT: Kumarian.

Jokilehto, J. 2005. 'Definition of Cultural Heritage: References to Documents in History.' Working Paper, International Centre for the Study of the Preservation and Restoration of Cultural Property, Heritage and Society Working Group, Rome. http://cif.icomos.org/pdf_docs/Documents%20on%20line/Heritage%20definitions.pdf.

Mathbor, G.M. 2007. 'Enhancement of Community Preparedness for Natural Disasters: The Role of Social Work in Building Social Capital for Sustainable Disaster Relief and Management.' *International Social Work* 50 (3): 357–369. doi:10.1177/0020872807076049.

Mills, G., R. Patterson, L. Orr, and D. DeMarco. 2004. *Evaluation of the American Dream Demonstration: Final Evaluation Report*. Cambridge, MA: Abt Associates. www.abtassociates.com/reports/Final_Eval_Rpt_8-19-04.pdf.

OECD (Organization for Economic Co-operation and Development). 2001. *The Well-Being of Nations: The Role of Human and Social Capital*. Paris: OECD Publishing. www.oecd.org/site/worldforum/33703702.pdf.

Oliver, M.L., and T.M. Shapiro. 1990. 'Wealth of a Nation: A Reassessment of Inequality in America Shows that at Least One Third of Households Are Asset-Poor.' *American Journal of Economics and Sociology* 49 (2): 129–151. doi:10.1111/j.1536-7150.1990. tb02268.x.

Pieterse, J.N. 2010. *Development Theory*. 2nd edn. London: Sage.

Policy Research Initiative. 2005. *Social Capital as a Public Policy Tool*. Project Report. Ottawa, Canada: Policy Research Initiative.

Putnam, R.D. 2000. *Bowling Alone: The Collapse and Revival of American Community*. New York: Touchstone.

Sen, A.K. 1999. *Development as Freedom*. Oxford: Oxford University Press.

Serageldin, I. 1996. *Sustainability and the Wealth of Nations: First Steps in an Ongoing Journey*. Washington, DC: World Bank.

Serageldin, I., and A. Steer, eds. 1994. 'Making Development Sustainable: From Concepts to Action.' Environmentally Sustainable Development Occasional Paper 2. Washington, DC: World Bank.

Shapiro, T.M. 2004. *The Hidden Costs of Being African American: How Wealth Perpetuates Inequality*. New York: Oxford University Press.

Sherraden, M. 1991. *Assets and the Poor: A New American Welfare Policy*. New York: M.E. Sharpe.

Sherraden, M. 2005. 'Assets, Poverty, and Public Policy.' Address to the United Nations Association of Australia International Year of Microcredit Conference 2005, entitled 'Towards an End to Global Poverty: Empowering Communities and Individuals through Financial Inclusion', Melbourne, Australia, 29–30 August.

Sherraden, M., A.M. McBride, S. Hanson, and L. Johnson. 2004. 'The Meaning of Saving in Low-Income Households.' Paper presented at the annual meeting of the Eastern Economics Association, Washington, DC, 20–22 February.

Ting, W.F. 2010. 'The Praxis of Social Capital.' In *Social Capital in Hong Kong: Connectivities and Social Enterprise*, edited by S.H. Ng, S.Y.L. Cheung, and B. Prakash, 37–74. Hong Kong: City University of Hong Kong Press.

Ting, W.F., and H.L. Chen. 2012. 'The Alternative Model of Development: The Practice of Community Economy in Disaster-Stricken Sichuan.' *China Journal of Social Work* 5 (1): 3–24. doi:10.1080/17525098.2012.658609.

Wolff, E.N. 2001. 'Recent Trends in Wealth Ownership, from 1983 to 1998.' In *Assets for the Poor: The Benefits of Spreading Asset Ownership*, edited by T.M. Shapiro and E.N. Wolff, 34–73. New York: Russell Sage.

Woolcock, M., and D. Narayan. 2000. 'Social Capital: Implications for Development Theory, Research, and Policy.' *World Bank Research Observer* 15 (2): 225–249. doi:10.1093/wbro/15.2.225.

Wright, E.O. 2010. *Envisioning Real Utopias*. London: Verso.

Yadama, G.N., and M. Sherraden. 1996. 'Effects of Assets on Attitudes and Behaviors: Advance Test of a Social Policy Proposal.' *Social Work Research* 20 (1): 3–11. doi:10.1093/swr/20.1.3.

Yunus, M., and A. Jolis. 2003. *Banker to the Poor: Micro-Lending and the Battle Against World Poverty*. New York: PublicAffairs.

Zhan, M., and M. Sherraden. 2003. 'Assets, Expectations, and Children's Educational Achievement in Female-Headed Households.' *Social Service Review* 77 (2): 191–211. doi:10.1086/373905.

15 Social innovations on land use in rural China

An asset-based analysis

Deyu Zhao and Minchao Jin

Land is a crucial asset to Chinese peasants, just as it is to peasants in other countries. Rural Chinese achieve food security by producing resources from the land (Gale *et al.* 2005), and income from farming has always been a major part of rural household income. The most recent National Bureau of Statistics (NBS) of China's *China Statistical Yearbook* (2012a) indicates that agricultural yield accounts for nearly 30 per cent of household income. In addition, land and the housing built on it make up a significant portion of the wealth of rural Chinese families. Gustafsson, Shi, and Sicular (2008) estimate that, for rural residents, the mean per-capita value of land and housing combined was CNY 9539 in 2002. That sum represents over 70 per cent of the total per-capita wealth.

However, land in China is also an incomplete asset, as rural families only have the right of use, not the ownership of it. The state or the collective (usually villages) owns rural land. The state prohibits or strictly regulates the ability of the individual household to transfer, rent, or bequeath the right of use.

Since China entered the era of the market economy, many rural labourers have left farms to seek seasonal or permanent employment in urban areas. In addition, urbanization has rapidly claimed sizable portions of rural areas. These developments and the legal separation of ownership from the right of use have significantly affected rural China; many young workers have left, much farmland is idle, and many peasants are landless. The present study examines two social innovations advanced to resolve these issues: the Land Shareholding Cooperative Model and the Land for Social Security Model.

Asset-based approaches offer promising tools for tackling the challenge of development. As a stock of wealth, assets can protect consumption against economic shock, enhance capability to invest for development, promote future aspiration, and lead to positive behavioural change (Oliver and Shapiro 1995; Sherraden 1991). Asset-based approaches focus on achieving long-term goals of development and empowerment (Midgley 2003; Schreiner and Sherraden 2007). They pursue these goals by motivating and helping people, especially the poor, to accumulate assets. The two innovations examined in this study do not primarily focus on building assets for rural residents, but they can be viewed as prototypes of an asset-based development strategy for rural residents. This chapter begins by discussing the context of the innovations and analysing each from an asset-based perspective. We then suggest ways to improve the innovations.

Background

Land regulation in rural China

Over time, the regulation of rural land has undergone both centralization and decentralization. In the first three decades of the People's Republic of China, communes organized and managed agricultural production. Communes had both ownership of land and the right of use. Since the 1980s, the commune system has been replaced by villages, and the land is operated through a household contract responsibility system (*jia ting lian chang cheng bao ze ren zhi*). Although rural land is still collectively owned, either by the state or by villages, the right of use is decentralized, and the landowner grants the right to rural households. Rural land is classified by three categories of purpose: land reserved for agriculture (*nong yong di*), land reserved for housing (*zhai ji di*), and unutilized land (*wei li yong di*). The state owns part of the unutilized land and that reserved for agriculture. Village councils and villagers' autonomous organizations control the remainder.

Most of the land reserved for agriculture is contracted to households through the contract responsibility system. Rural households pay rent for the right of use and own the crops, livestock, and tools located on the land. The size and the quality of land contracted to a household are usually based on the household's size, the number of labourers, the household's willingness to engage in farm work, and its ability to do so. In some cases, the village allocates land by invited bid and auction. The length of contract is generally 30 years.[1]

In addition, some of the land reserved for agriculture, a maximum of 15 per cent, is allocated in private plots (*zi liu di*). Households use the plots to ensure the adequacy and diversity of their food supplies as well as to earn additional income, according to a *People's Daily Online* article of 30 March 1981. Brandt *et al.* (2002) show that contracted land accounts for most of the land reserved for agriculture and that private plots represent only about 5 per cent. Rural households pay no rent for the right to use private plots.

The agricultural land can only be used for agricultural production, and tenants may not change the purpose of land (e.g. building houses on agricultural land) without proper authorization from landowners; in many cases, such authorization comes from village councils. In addition, the law prohibits tenants from trading the right of use or offering it as a guarantee for credit.[2] Although households have contracts that grant them right of use, landowners have the authority to reallocate agricultural land assigned to a household. In a study of land use by 215 villages in eight provinces, Brandt *et al.* (2002) found that, between 1983 and 1995, owners reallocated 57.6 per cent of agricultural land. These changes affected 74.4 per cent of the households in those villages (Brandt *et al.* 2002).

Similar provisions govern land reserved for housing. Households given the right to use housing land have full ownership of any structures built on the land, can accumulate equity in that property, and can sell what they own, but they must transfer the property and the right of use together (Huang 2007). This kind of trade is also strictly regulated. For example, only people in the same collectivity (usually the same village) are eligible to buy (Huang 2007). Like agricultural land, housing land and the construction on it cannot be offered as a guarantee for credit, as specified by the Guaranty Law of People's Republic of China. Land reserved for housing also can be reallocated to meet changing needs. Villages grant or reassign the land as people move in or out and households split or merge.

Migration of rural labourers and land expropriation

According to the NBS (2012a), the rural population has declined each year since 1995, though China's total population continues to increase. Labour migration and rapid urbanization are important factors in these continuing declines. In 2011, over 250 million workers migrated to cities for permanent or seasonal off-farm jobs. That number represents about half of the total rural labour force (NBS 2012b). About 33 million of these migrants brought their families with them to the urban areas. Most migrants are males between the ages of 20 and 50 (NBS 2012b). An important if not determinant incentive to migration is off-farm income, which is much higher than income from farm production. Zhu and Luo (2008) find that farmers with low returns from farm production are more likely to seek off-farm employment than are those with high returns. In 2011, the average monthly salary for migrant workers was CNY 2049 (NBS 2012b), which is almost equal to the average annual earnings from a farm (NBS 2012a).

Regulation of land use in rural China contributes to the farm–non-farm income disparity by making it difficult to increase on-farm earning. Reardon and Vosti (1995) note, for example, that land reallocations limit the security of tenure and could discourage rural households from making investments, especially long-term investments. Together, these factors impair the future productivity of land.

The departure of young people from rural areas has resulted in a shortage of farm labour, and the ageing of Chinese society exacerbates the problem. Of those left behind – mainly the elderly, women, and children – many are incapable of farm labour but must continue working the farms because there is no alternative source of labour. An analysis of nationally representative data leads Chang, Dong, and MacPhail (2011) to report that elderly people (aged 51 and above) in the rural households with migrants work 100–200 more hours on farms per year than their counterparts in households without migrants. Girls between the ages of seven and 14 from households with migrants also work twice the number of hours on farms as do those from households without migrants (Chang, Dong, and MacPhail 2011). Because of this labour shortage, a considerable amount of land is idle (He 2004; Jiang 2004; Yang and Wang 2003). Although there is no empirical evidence on whether or how the departure of rural labour affects agricultural production, scholars list it as one of the factors that threaten production (Peng, Tang, and Zou 2009).

If migrant workers actively seek off-farm employment but attempt to retain the right to use the farmland, the owners of the land may revoke the right of use or assign it to another party. A sizable number of rural residents migrate to cities because the household loses a key source of income when the migrant leaves for the city and the owner expropriates the household's right to use the land. In some cases, land expropriation is not connected to migration; landowners also expropriate right of use from tenant farmers so that the land can be reallocated for commercial or industrial development. From 1991 to 2004, the state and villages reassigned 3.23 million hectares of agricultural land for other purposes (Po 2008). In 2011 alone, Chinese landowners allocated .41 million hectares of formerly agricultural land for construction, and that represents a 26.3 per cent increase over the amount of agricultural land converted for construction in 2010 (Ministry of Land and Resource of People's Republic of China 2012). There were over 40 million landless farmers in 2011, and the number is expected to increase by at least three million each year (Huang 2011). These landless farm households, especially the dependents, lose the main sources of income and are very vulnerable to economic shocks. Because they hold only incomplete rights to the land they farm, rural residents have little power in negotiating the amount of compensation they receive from the landowners when their farmland is expropriated.

Urban–rural wealth gap

The unequal distribution of wealth between urban and rural households is remarkable. The mean value of total, per-capita wealth for rural residents was CNY 12,938 in 2002. This is CNY 33,196 less than that of their urban counterparts (Gustafsson, Shi, and Sicular 2008). Two-thirds of the urban–rural difference lies in the value of land and the associated housing. Although the unit price of urban real estate is usually higher than that of rural real estate, the size of the average living area is larger for rural residents ($26.5 \, m^2$) than for urban residents ($22.8 \, m^2$) (NBS 2003). The incomplete property right over land and the strict control of real estate trading contributes to the considerable urban–rural difference in wealth. The value of rural land and rural home equity are likely underestimated, but cashing in home equity is also very difficult for rural households. Home equity is the major asset owned by rural households. In addition, the ban on using land for collateral blocks another way of liquidizing the asset. Viewed from an asset-based perspective, the current regulation on rural land devalues the wealth of rural households, impedes the ability of these households to build capacity for long-term growth, and thus impairs the asset function of land.

Social innovations on rural land

This study focuses on the Land Shareholding Cooperative Model and the Land for Social Security Model, two innovations designed to address the rural land issues discussed above. The Land Shareholding Cooperative Model offers a way to increase the flexibility of rural land use, and the Land for Social Security Model is designed for landless farmers.

Land Shareholding Cooperative Model

The rural Land Shareholding Cooperative Model originated in Nanhai, a district of the Guangdong Province, and then launched widely in coastal areas during the 1990s. Because of its success, the model gained support from the central government. With the development of inland areas, the model has spread into the middle and western provinces. The forms of this model vary (Tang and Zeng 2009), but they share some core features. Rural households, usually within the same village (the village is the collective landowner), form or join a shareholding co-operative by converting their right of land use into shares. Shareholders do not pay rent to retain their shares. The co-operative is administered by shareholder meetings and a board. In some cases, shareholding co-operatives are initiated and administered by village councils. The co-operative then redevelops the land and rents it out for agricultural production or other purposes, such as industry. The co-operative is not bound by a requirement to rent the land to a member of the same collective. Renters can be business enterprises or individuals outside the co-operative. Because of rapid economic changes, demand for land is increasing, and the co-operatives can charge rents that are relatively higher than those paid by the former tenants.

The co-operative collects the rent and other related fees, distributing the profits to shareholders. In some cases, especially when the shareholding co-operative is formed by a village as a whole, the entity retains part of the revenue in a collective fund used for public service projects, such as constructing local roads and maintaining a local library. In general, co-operatives prohibit members from trading, bequeathing, or gifting shares, and the shareholders may not use shares as collateral or withdraw the right of land use from the co-operative. Under some circumstances, however, co-operatives permit shareholders to buy shares from other members (Sui and Wang 2010).

The Land for Social Security Model

The second model examined here seeks to provide social security, particularly pension insurance, for farmers who lose their right of land use through expropriation. In general, there are three institutional variations in the design of this model.

The first variation, Shanghai's Town Social Insurance, provides the elderly and labourers from landless households with social security at a level close to that received by urban residents. When the state or a village expropriates land, the former tenant households receive monetary compensation. Some of that compensation is used to pay the insurance premium, which is relatively low (Chang 2004; Shanghai Municipal Government 2003). The insurance covers medical care, provides income during maternal leave, and pays a benefit during spells of unemployment. It also provides a pension for the elderly. Although the beneficiary pays monthly premiums to maintain the insurance, Shanghai Municipal Government and the employer (if the beneficiary is employed) proportionally match the premium to contribute to a pool of funds. Therefore, the benefit from this insurance is relatively higher than that from the rural scheme of social insurance. If any of the pool remains after the insurance premium is paid, the funds are used to purchase supplemental insurance (Shanghai Municipal Government 2003). Benefits from this supplemental insurance subsidize living expenses and provide additional support for both medical care and retirement. The Shanghai Municipal Government deposits the premium paid for the supplemental insurance into a personal account for the beneficiary. Both the principal and interest in the personal account are fully owned by the beneficiary. The funds in the personal account can only be used for purposes related to social security and cannot be withdrawn freely by the beneficiary (Shanghai Municipal Government 2003).

Jiaxing, a city in Zhejiang Province, designed the second variation on the Land for Social Security Model, and it is similar to the pension insurance for urban employees. The premium is paid by the beneficiary, by collectivities that own the land expropriated from the beneficiary, and by the municipal government of Jiaxing (Song 2007). Beneficiaries usually pay less than 30 per cent of this premium. All of the funding for the premium comes from the compensation paid to the former tenant for land expropriation (Song 2007). All landless labourers are required to enrol in this insurance.

The third design variation is the commercial insurance programme tried out in Yiwu, a city in Zhejiang Province. Designed by the China Life Insurance Company, the commercial pension policy provides group annuity dividend insurance to the landless peasants in Yiwu. Whole villages participate in the insurance, and premiums are paid from the compensation fees paid for rural land expropriation. The municipal government of Yiwu specifies a ratio for the distribution of the compensation: 2:4:4. The village collectively keeps 20 per cent, and 40 per cent is distributed to villagers individually. The other 40 per cent is used for the insurance premium. The principal – that portion of the compensation fee paid for the insurance premium – is collectively owned by the village. China Life Insurance Company is committed to using at least 2.5 per cent of the principal and 70 per cent of the investment gains for pension payments. As it is a commercial insurance, enrolment is voluntary and the benefit is inheritable (Shen and Gao 2007). If a rural family is not willing to take this insurance, they instead receive direct compensation for the land expropriation. This institutional arrangement is special because landless farmers receive commercial pension insurance instead of the social pension insurance for urban employees.

Asset-based analysis of the social innovations

Sherraden (1991) proposes the theory of asset building in his book, *Assets and the Poor*. Studies find that holding assets and the behaviours of asset accumulation have positive effects on well-being (Lerman and McKernan 2008). For example, the assets of parents are valid predictors of children's educational outcomes (Aaronson 2000; Kane 1994; Zhan 2006; Zhan and Sherraden 2003).

Research also documents a statistically positive effect of inheritance on health (Meer, Miller, and Rosen 2003). Assets like home equity provide people with the feeling of self-sufficiency, enhance their future aspirations, and lead to positive behavioural change (Lerman and McKernan 2008).

The significant benefits associated with assets suggest that institutional designs to encourage and facilitate asset building offer promising approaches to empowering people and tackling development challenges; such approaches may be especially effective for the poor (Midgley 2003; Sherraden 1991). A successful example in China is the Hutubi Rural Retirement Social Insurance Loan Programme. More than 2000 peasants in Hutubi County enrolled in the programme by surrendering their social security cards as collateral for loans. In doing so, they turned their pension accounts into a collective fund for loans (Zhang 2007), and most participants used the loans to purchase productive assets (Zhang 2007). This programme provided rural residents with access to credit, built up their assets, and increased their ability to undertake future development (Guo *et al.* 2008). The Hutubi programme establishes a model for the use of institutional innovation to benefit participants by enabling them to build assets. Although the two innovations in this chapter did not begin as asset-building initiatives, they could enable rural households to accumulate assets.

Building assets through the Land Shareholding Cooperative Model

The Land Shareholding Cooperative Model loosens the legal restriction on the land transfer and adds some flexibility to land use by converting land into shares. It benefits both the landowner (the collectivity) and land users (rural households). The co-operative claims the right of use, especially over the land that is idle because of migration. The model could also increase the efficiency of land use, as the new tenants, especially business enterprises, are more market oriented and capable of making significant investments.

In this model, shareholders have weaker control over their land asset and its returns than they would as tenants, because the right of use becomes collectively administered. However, as land usage and transfer rules become flexible, the rural household's incomplete asset – land – becomes functional. Although the law continues to prohibit tenants from trading the right of use over rural land, this innovation allows them to convert land rights into shares and then to rent the land. Thus, the Land Shareholding Cooperative Model can be considered an alternative way to trade the right of use, and the trade happens in a market that is larger than the village collectivity. In addition, transferring shares within the same co-operative is less restricted by law than trading home equity and the housing land.

There is also the matter of risk. Land is a relatively low-risk investment if it is held as shares within a co-operative. In addition, the model resolves the labour shortage faced by families with migrant workers. Moreover, if rent provides shareholders a basic, fixed, annual income, the possible dividends for a household are greater than the income the household would earn from farm production. Rural households actually trade a source of low and unstable income for a source of higher and more stable earnings. Although no direct evidence is available yet on the model's effects, Ma *et al.* (2012) find that the per-capita income of rural residents gradually increased from CNY 9508 in 2004, the year in which the Land Shareholding Cooperative Model began, to CNY 16,439 in 2010. The increase is more than twice the national average and more than twice the average of Guangdong Province. In addition, income increases are reported in several sites (Jia and Ge 2012; Lin and Wang 2010; Yu and Li 2004). Through the model, land – the major asset owned by rural households – becomes a virtual savings account. The 'interest' is very stable and can protect consumption better than can on-farm earning. The model also raises the possibility that the value of land and return from it will increase together. If that is so, the increase in value will add to the total value of assets held by individual shareholders and will reduce the gap in wealth between urban and rural households.

In sum, the Land Shareholding Cooperative Model has the potential to restore part of the property right of land (by restoring the right of sale), to increase the land's value, and to enhance the returns from this asset. Thus, the model may help rural households build their assets. However, rural households might still feel incapable of making big investments for long-term goals. The model can be improved in two ways.

First, the model can be expanded to extend the market for trading shares. A market that is open and bigger could reduce the difficulty shareholders encounter when they cash in shares and could help to achieve a reasonable price for those shares. Under the current model, only shareholders can trade shares, and they must obtain permission from the co-operative in order to do so. Because of the current regulations governing land use, co-operatives may be able to begin such expansions by opening the market to rural residents from the same town, county, or city.

Second, the model could be improved by allowing the shares to function as collateral for credit. Participants enthusiastically welcome efforts to incorporate the right of guaranty in this model, and households with migrant workers are especially enthusiastic about the expansion (Chen 2011; Yu and Li 2004). If formal institutions cannot provide services due to government regulation, land shareholding co-operatives could take the first step and use a portion of their revenues as a pool of funds for loans. Several land shareholding co-operative organizations might collaborate to increase the size of the fund. Borrowers who cannot pay off their loans would forfeit the shares, which the co-operative could then resell by auction or invited bidding. The operation could refer to the Hutubi Rural Retirement Social Insurance Loan Programme, an established and successful predecessor with an asset-based institutional design. The repayment rate for the Hutubi programme suggests that there is little risk in allowing borrowers to use shares as collateral. If given the flexibility to exchange shares for cash, rural households could use the biggest part of their wealth – land – to fund long-term growth.

Building assets through the Land for Social Security Model

All three of the design variations in the Land for Social Security Model exchange the land for some form of social insurance. In other words, they convert a present asset into a long-term asset. As the market for rural land is not fully mature and the current price could be lower than the land's true value, it remains difficult to evaluate whether the Land for Social Security Model is fair for rural households. The following discussion assumes that the compensation for land expropriation is equal to the land's true value.

Among the three designs, the second one, the pension designed by Jiaxing, could instantly add to the value of the land; rural residents pay no more than 30 per cent of the premium, and collectivities (i.e. landowners and the government) pay the rest. In the long term, the first design, Shanghai's social insurance, promises the greatest increase in the value of the land, as it provides a relatively higher level of security. When farmers reach the age of retirement, they can receive more than CNY 1000 per month. That sum is much higher than the payment from any other form of rural social pension insurance because the pooled fund is partly supported by revenue from the local government. The third design, the commercial pension insurance programme in Yiwu, is different from the first two, as neither government nor the co-operatives match the individual contributions. The increment of the assets depends on the market, which can add uncertainty. The advantage of the third design is that enrolment is voluntary. In addition, both principal and interest are clearly inheritable, and that may not be the case in the first and second designs.

The Land for Social Security Model differs from a direct compensation model in that government or co-operatives match the premium, and the initial premium comes fully or partly from the compensation. Both the principle and interest can be used only for welfare purposes. The design is much like that of Individual Development Accounts, an asset-based approach tested in the United States. Individual Development Accounts prompt asset accumulation by matching savings, and the funding in the accounts can only be used for development purposes (Schreiner et al. 2005). To make the Land for Social Security Model more asset based, authorities might allow greater flexibility in the use of compensation fees. The model might also be improved by allowing landless farmers to use funds in their accounts to build capacity. For example, they might use the funds for job training or to start a small business.

Our interest in asset-building initiatives leads us to suggest a final way to improve both models, and this suggestion would also enable rural households to build additional assets. Each model might be expanded so that it includes a personal or household-based development account for each rural resident. The savings vehicles would operate like Individual Development Accounts, and account holders would receive matches for their deposits. Funds for the matches could come from the collective revenue of the land shareholding co-operatives or from the entity subsequently granted the right of use for the expropriated land.

Conclusion

Two social innovations, the Land Shareholding Cooperative Model and the Land for Social Security Model, address new issues arising from the remarkable migration of rural labourers, the rapid pace of urbanization, and the regulation of rural land. Both of the models are helpful for building the assets of rural households and may reduce the gap in wealth between rural and urban residents. The Land Shareholding Cooperative Model builds assets by partially restoring the land's asset function, and the Land for Social Security Model does so by replacing the incomplete asset with a matched savings account. Because neither model is primarily designed as an asset-based intervention, this study offers asset-based suggestions on ways to improve them. Asset-based approaches could be one of the best ways to help the rural residents achieve long-term development. The inspiration provided by the two models can improve asset-based institutional design and facilitate a macro-level policy change that will favour rural households. Both of these developments would fuel strong growth in rural China.

Notes

1 Specified by *Zhong hua ren min gong he gong tu di cheng bao fa* (Law of the People's Republic of China on the Contracting of Rural Land) (promulgated by Standing Committee of National People's Congress [NPC], 29 August 2002, effective 1 March 2003) 2002 NPC Gazette, No. 5, 347, Presidential Order 73.
2 Specified by *Zhong hua ren min gong he guo tu di guan li fa (2004 xiu zheng)* (Land Administration Law of the People's Republic of China [2004 Amendment]) (promulgated by NPC, 28 August 2004, originally effective 1 January 1999) 2004 NPC Gazette, No. 6, 566. Presidential Order 28; and by Zhong hua ren min gong he guo dan bao fa (The Guaranty Law of the People's Republic of China) (promulgated by NPC, 30 June 1995, effective 1 October 1995) 1995 NPC Gazette, No. 5. Presidential Order 50.

References

Aaronson, D. 2000. 'A Note on the Benefits of Homeownership.' *Journal of Urban Economics* 47 (3): 356–369. doi:10.1006/juec.1999.2144.

Brandt, L., J. Huang, G. Li, and S. Rozelle. 2002. 'Land Rights in Rural China: Facts, Fictions and Issues.' *China Journal* 47: 67–97. doi:10.2307/3182074.

Chang, H.Q., X.Y. Dong, and F. MacPhail. 2011. 'Labor Migration and Time Use Patterns of the Left-Behind Children and Elderly in Rural China.' *World Development* 39 (12): 2199–2210. doi:10.1016/j.worlddev.2011.05.021.

Chang, J. 2004. 'Cheng shi hua jin cheng zhong shi di nong min he li li yi bao zhang yan jiu.' [How to Ensure the Rational Benefit of Land-losing Farmers in the Process of Urbanization]. *Zhong guo ruan ke xue* [China Soft Science Magazine] 8: 5–10.

Chen, H. 2011. 'Fen gong yan jin he tu di cheng bao jing ying quan gu fen hua: yi xiang tu di gu fen he zuo she de diao cha ji zheng ce qi shi.' [Evolution of Labour Division and Stock-transforming of Contractual Management Rights of Land]. *Cai mao yan jiu* [Finance and Trade Research] 22 (3): 50–55.

Gale, F., P. Tang, X.H. Bai, and H.J. Xu. 2005. *Commercialization of Food Consumption in Rural China*. Economic Research Report 8. Washington, DC: US Department of Agriculture, Economic Research Service.

Guo, B., J. Huang, M. Sherraden, and Li Zou. 2008. 'Dual Incentives and Dual Asset Building: Policy Implications of the Hutubi Rural Social Security Loan Programme in China.' *Journal of Social Policy* 37 (3): 453–470. doi:10.1017/S0047279408001992.

Gustafsson, B., S. Li, and T. Sicular, eds. 2008. *Inequality and Public Policy in China*. New York: Cambridge University Press.

He, W. 2004. 'Nong cun tu di pao huang yan jiu.' [A Positive Research on Deserting Rural Land]. *Hengyang shi fan xue yuan xue bao* [Journal of Hengyang Normal University] 25 (5): 35–37.

Huang, S. 2007. *Zhong Hua Ren Min Gong He Guo Wu Quan Fa' Tiao Wen Li Jie Yu Shi Yong* [Application and Explanation of the Property Law of the People's Republic of China]. Beijing: People's Court Press.

Huang, W. 2011. 'Nong min de tu di he fa quan yi gai ru he wei hu' [How Can Farmers' Property Right of Land Be Protected?]. *China Land* 12: 34–36.

Jia, C., and Y. Ge. 2012. 'Nong di gu fen he zuo zhi de nong min zeng shou xiao ying yan jiu: Ji yu 1992–2009 nian fo shan si shi (Qu) de shi zheng fen xi.' [Can Rural Land Stock Cooperation Increase Peasants' Income? A Case Study of Four County-level Cities in Foshan during 1992–2009]. *Nanjing shi da xue bao* [Journal of Nanjing Normal University] (*She hui ke xue ban* [Social Sciences Edition]) 1: 58–65. http://d.wanfangdata.com.cn.

Jiang, L. 2004. 'Nong cun geng di pao huan de yuan yin fen xi.' [The Analysis on the Reasons of Abandoning Land]. *Zhongguo tong ji* [China Statistics] 12: 38–39.

Kane, T.J. 1994. 'College Entry by Blacks since 1970: The Role of College Costs, Family Background, and the Returns to Education.' *Journal of Political Economy* 102 (5): 878–911. doi:10.1086/261958.

Lerman, R.I., and S.M. McKernan. 2008. 'Benefits and Consequences of Holding Assets.' In *Asset Building and Low-Income Families*, edited by S.M. McKernan, and M. Sherraden, 175–206. Washington, DC: Urban Institute Press.

Lin, L., and J. Wang. 2010. 'Nong hu dui nong di gu fen he zuo she man yi ren ke ji ying xiang yin su fen Xi: Yi zhe jiang yu yao shi yao jie long cun chang hui tu di gu fen he zuo she wei li.' [On the Rural Households' Satisfaction and its Affecting Factors for the Rural Land Shareholding Cooperatives]. *Nanjing nong ye da xue xue bao* [Journal of Nanjing Agricultural Normal University] (*She ke ban* [Social Sciences Edition]) 10 (4): 28–34.

Ma, Y., J. Lin, H. Jiang, and F. Zou. 2012. 'Tu di gu fen he zuo zhi dui yu nong min zeng shou de ying yiang yan jiu: Ji yu Guangdong Dongguan Humen zhen de diao cha.' [Land Shareholding Cooperative System's Impact on Farmers' Income: A Study based on the Case of Humen Town]. *Guangdong nong ye ke xue* [Guangdong Agricultural Sciences] 39 (4): 201–204. http://d.wanfangdata.com.cn.

Meer, J., D.L. Miller, and H.S. Rosen. 2003. 'Exploring the Health–Wealth Nexus.' *Journal of Health Economics* 22 (5): 713–730. doi:10.1016/S0167-6296(03)00059-6.

Midgley, J. 2003. 'Assets in the Context of Welfare Theory: A Developmentalist Interpretation.' *Social Development Issues* 25 (1–2): 12–28.

Ministry of Land and Resource of People's Republic of China. 2012. *2011 Zhong guo tu zi yuan gong bao* [2011 Report on Land Resource of China]. Ministry of Land and Resource of People's Republic of China. www.mlr.gov.cn/zwgk/tjxx/201205/P020120516305280627517.pdf.

NBS (National Bureau of Statistics of China). 2003. *Zhong guo tong ji nian jian 2003.* [China Statistical Yearbook, 2003]. National Bureau of Statistics of China. www.stats. gov.cn/tjsj/ndsj/yearbook2003_c.pdf.

NBS (National Bureau of Statistics of China). 2012a. *Zhong guo tong ji nian jian* [China Statistical Yearbook 2011]. National Bureau of Statistics of China. www.stats.gov.cn/ tjsj/ndsj/2011/indexch.htm.

NBS (National Bureau of Statistics of China). 2012b. '2011 nian wo guo nong min gong tiao cha jian ce bao gao.' [2011 Report of Migrant Workers in China]. National Bureau of Statistics of China. www.stats.gov.cn/tjfx/fxbg/t20120427_402801903.htm.

Oliver, M.L., and T.M. Shapiro. 1995. *Black Wealth/White Wealth: A New Perspective on Racial Inequality.* New York: Routledge.

Peng, S.B., Q.Y. Tang, and Y.B. Zou. 2009. 'Current Status and Challenges of Rice Production in China.' *Plant Production Science* 12 (1): 3–8. doi:10.1626/pps.12.3.

Po, L. 2008. 'Redefining Rural Collectives in China: Land Conversion and the Emergence of Rural Shareholding Co-operatives.' *Urban Studies* 45 (8): 1603–1623. doi:10.1177/0042098008091493.

Reardon, T., and S.A. Vosti. 1995. 'Links between Rural Poverty and the Environment in Developing Countries: Asset Categories and Investment Poverty.' *World Development* 23 (9): 1495–1506. doi:10.1016/0305-750X(95)00061-G.

Schreiner, M., and M. Sherraden. 2007. *Can the Poor Save? Savings and Asset Building in Individual Development Accounts.* New Brunswick, NJ: Transaction.

Schreiner, M., M. Sherraden, M. Clancy, L. Johnson, J. Curley, M. Zhan, S.G. Beverly, and M. Grinstein-Weiss. 2005. 'Assets and the Poor: Evidence from Individual Development Accounts.' In *Inclusion in the American Dream: Assets, Poverty, and Public Policy*, edited by M. Sherraden, 185–215. New York: Oxford University Press.

Shanghai Municipal Government. 2003. 'Shang hai shi xiao cheng zhen she hui bao xiao zan xing ban fa.' [Interim Regulation of Shanghai Social Insurance in Small Towns]. Shanghai Municipal Government. www.shanghai.gov.cn/shanghai/node2314/ node3124/node3125/node3131/u6ai1206.html.

Shen, L., and Z. Gao. 2007. ' "Tu di huan bao zhang" de liang zhong yang lao bao xian mo shi yan jiu.' [Comparison on the Two Designs of Land for Social Security Model]. *Nong cun jing ji* [Rural Economy] 5: 73–75.

Sherraden, M. 1991. *Assets and the Poor: A New American Welfare Policy.* Armonk, NY: M.E. Sharpe.

Song, M. 2007. 'Shi di nong min "Tu di huan bao zhang" mo shi ping xi.' [The Analysis of the Model 'Land for Social Security' for Landless Farmers]. *Fujian lun tan* [Fujian Tribune] (*Ren lei she hui ke xue ban* [Humans & Social Sciences]) 7: 30–33.

Sui, W., and J. Wang. 2010. 'Nong cun tu di gu fen he zuo zhi te zheng he mo shi yan jiu.' [Reviews on the Fea|tures and Forms of Land Shareholding Cooperative Model]. *China Collective Economy* 18: 5–9.

Tang, H., and F. Zeng. 2009. 'Nong cun tu di gu fen he zuo zhi yan jiu ping shu.' [Research Review of the Rural Land Stock Cooperative System]. *Jiangxi nong ye da xue xue bao* [Journal of Jiangxi Agricultural University] 8 (1): 20–27.

Yang, T., and Y. Wang. 2003. 'Nong cun geng di pao huan yu tu di liu zhuan wen ti de li lun tan xi.' [The Analysis on Idle Land and Land Transferring]. *Diao yan shi jie* [World of Survey and Research] 2: 15–19.

Yu, P., and S. Li. 2004. 'Zhong guo fa da di qu nong di shi yong quan liu zhuan xing wen ti yang jiu.' [Changing Hands of Land Tenure Rights in China's Developed Areas]. *Zhong guo ruan ke xue* [China Soft Science Magazine] 6: 18–21. www.cssm.com.cn.

Zhan, M. 2006. 'Assets, Parental Expectations and Involvement, and Children's Educational Performance.' *Children and Youth Services Review* 28 (8): 961–975. doi:10.1016/j.childyouth.2005.10.008.

Zhan, M., and M. Sherraden. 2003. 'Assets, Expectations, and Children's Educational Achievement in Female-Headed Households.' *Social Service Review* 77 (2): 191–211. doi:10.1086/373905.

Zhang, S. 2007. 'Zhong yi li zhong zi, jie ji ge gua: Hutubi xian yang lao bao xian zheng zhi ya dai kuan de fu li xiao ying' [One Seed Yields Abundant Harvests: The Welfare Effects of the Hutubi Rural Social Security Loan Programme]. In *She hui zheng ce ping lun* [Social Policy Review], vol. 1, edited by T. Yang and D. Ge, 4–17. Beijing: Social Sciences Academic Press.

'Zhong gong zhong yang Guo wu yuan zhuan fa guo jia nong wei "guan yu ji ji fa zhan nong cun duo zhong duo zhong jing ying de bao gao" de tong zhi' [Bulletin on Promoting a Diversified Economy in Rural Area]. 1981. *People's Daily Online*, 30 March 2013, http://cpc.people.com.cn/GB/64184/64186/66701/4495423.html.

Zhu, N., and X.B. Luo. 2008. 'The Impact of Remittances on Rural Poverty and Inequality in China.' Policy Research Working Paper 4637, May. World Bank. https://openknowledge.worldbank.org/handle/10986/6597.

16 Asset-building innovations

Editors' note

Innovative asset-based policies and programmes have been created and tested by many governments in Asia. Most of these efforts target underprivileged populations, such as low-income adults and children. In this chapter, we highlight three case studies, one from Mongolia and two from Thailand, that showcase innovative asset-building programmes designed to reach disadvantaged populations.

The first case, by Toivgoo Aira and colleagues, details a pioneering pilot programme for female sex workers in Mongolia. Combining a matched-savings component, financial-literary education, business development training, and sexual risk-reduction classes, the Undarga programme helps women develop empowering alternatives to sex work and reduce financial pressures that force them into it.

The second case focuses on the Light of Hope Saving Program, an effort to address obstacles facing vulnerable children in Rimping, a municipality in northwest Thailand. Youth who participate in the programme and open a free savings account receive a seed deposit and savings are matched. Light of Hope also provides scholarships, mentorship, HIV/AIDS education, and other supportive activities to foster positive development and life perspectives. Wimonmat Srichamroen also describes an ongoing study to evaluate the programme.

The third case examines Thailand's secure housing (*Baan Mankong*) programme by focusing on its effects in one slum community on the outskirts of Bangkok. Nong Kaem began as a squatter's community, filled with shanties built by garbage pickers who found materials in the nearby dump run by the Bangkok Municipal Authority. Parichart Valaisathien details collaborations that enabled Nong Kaem residents to secure ownership of land, build safe housing, and obtain 15-year mortgages for their homes. She emphasizes the programme's organic development process, which integrates community work, family work, and case work.

We hope that readers will glimpse the challenges faced every day by these socially marginalized people, appreciate the great efforts of these innovative asset-based programmes, and feel inspired to generate other cutting-edge ideas that allow more people to benefit from the asset-building programmes and policies across the world.

A savings-led HIV-prevention intervention for women engaging in sex work in Mongolia[1]

Toivgoo Aira, Susan S. Witte, Laura Cordisco Tsai, Marion Riedel, and Fred M. Ssewamala

This project emerged from narratives of participants in an HIV risk-reduction efficacy trial targeting sex workers in Ulaanbaatar, Mongolia. In post-trial focus groups, women explained that, to achieve real risk reduction, they had to acquire the skills and resources to secure both alternative employment and freedom from the necessity to engage in sex work. Their input informed the creation of Undarga, a savings-led microfinance intervention tailored to female sex workers.[2] This case highlights opportunities and challenges identified during a feasibility test of Undarga. Lessons from this pioneering experience may inform future approaches with vulnerable populations.

Building on prior work by the research team (Witte *et al.* 2011) and funded by the US National Institute of Mental Health, Undarga employed a targeted sampling strategy in Ulaanbaatar. Women were eligible to participate in the Undarga pilot if they reported that they (1) were at least 18 years of age, (2) engaged in sex for money or goods in the prior 90 days, (3) did not use condoms 100 per cent of the time during vaginal or anal sex in the prior 90 days, and (4) were interested in learning more about financial literacy and how to start a small business. Of 204 women screened and deemed eligible to participate, 107 enrolled in the study and were randomized into one of two conditions: an HIV sexual risk-reduction condition (SRR) (Witte *et al.* 2011) or a sexual risk-reduction plus microsavings condition (SRR-plus). The study offered four sessions of sexual risk-reduction training to participants in the SRR group (*n*=50). To women in the SRR-plus group (*n*=57) it offered the same four sessions of sexual reduction plus 30 additional sessions of a multifaceted intervention. The additional sessions consisted of three parts: financial-literacy education, business-development training, and a series of groups mentored by a business woman. Designed to assist women as they attempt to establish new businesses, the mentored groups help participants in implementing lessons learned during the training. Participants in this condition were also invited to participate in a microsavings programme with a matched savings component (Tsai *et al.* 2013).

Participants received financial compensation for each training session attended. Those in the SRR-plus condition were invited to consider setting this income aside in the matched microsavings component, which gave them the opportunity to open a savings account with a local bank partner. The project provided a 2:1 match for any savings that participants deposited and held in their Undarga savings accounts. Participants could use the matched savings funds for vocational education or business development (Sherraden 1991).

To ensure that the project did not create any incentive to engage in sex work, we planned the number of sessions and incentives so that the total amount of incentives, if saved and matched, would be adequate to enable the participant to make some substantial purchases for new business start-up. If women did not attend a session, they received no incentive, could not save it, and did not receive the corresponding match. To build additional motivation for participation in the sessions, we specified that participants would receive savings matches only if they completed nine of 12 financial-literacy education and business-development training sessions as well as eight of 10 mentoring sessions.

In all, the team will conduct four sets of interviews with participants: one before the start of the intervention, another following the fourth HIV risk-reduction session, and additional ones at three and six months after the intervention. To date, we have conducted three-month follow-up surveys with 60 out of 107 women: 38 in the SRR condition and 22 in the SRR-plus condition. The initial assessment collected information on demographic variables, risk for sexually transmitted diseases, alcohol use, general health, financial literacy and business development skills, income, savings and debt status, intimate partner violence, social support, and other potential mediators of risk-reduction outcomes. Because the study is ongoing, we report only preliminary results on the primary aims.

Preliminary savings results

At the time of the baseline interview, most Undarga participants were between the ages of 25 and 44, had a secondary school education or some college, were divorced or widowed, and had one or more children. Roughly half of the women have been engaged in sex work for five years or less. About half had trusted partners; most had no pimp or boss.

At baseline, 20 out of 107 women (18.69 per cent) reported having any money in a savings account. Of the 60 women who completed the three-month follow-up survey, 31.67 per cent ($n=19$) reported that they had money in a savings account; 11 of those 19 are in the SRR-plus condition, and eight are in the SRR condition.

Challenges

The current state of the study enables the research team to offer a preliminary assessment of the challenges and opportunities encountered in fielding the Undarga intervention. Recruitment has been one such challenge. The project began amid rapid growth in Mongolia's burgeoning mining sector and political tensions surrounding national elections. Changes in government leadership and the growth of the international mining community led to heavy policing of traditional sex work venues. This policing drove women to alternative locations, and arrests led to incarceration for extended periods of time. All of these factors impeded our efforts to find and recruit eligible women. In addition, many women indicated that a savings-led intervention initially seemed to be 'too good to be true'. Despite our prior work with the population, the changing landscape of sex work in Ulaanbaatar contributed to a set-back. It took nearly six months to re-establish some level of presence and trust among women engaged in street-based sex work.

Although the team identified many eligible women, few showed up for the first session of the intervention, and regular attendance proved challenging for many of those who did attend the session. Staff attributed participants' absences to fear of the unknown; participants confirmed this in anecdotal discussion with staff and in follow-up surveys. They expressed fear of showing up in an unknown environment, fear of meeting someone they might know and being discovered (as sex work is highly stigmatized), fear of being together with other unknown women in one group, and fear of being arrested for prostitution. Alcohol use, police action (raids, arrests, and detainment), the location of the sessions, injury, and illness are additional reasons given for missing sessions.

Challenges also arose during the sessions. Participants possess varying levels of education. Low levels of literacy and comprehension impede some participants' ability to learn. Others are highly literate, and some possess university degrees. Because of this variation, facilitators found it difficult to present information in a consistently effective manner. Facilitators indicated that some participants struggled to understand the session topics because they worked through the prior night and others might have had hangovers. Facilitators described simplifying materials and delivering concepts in small chunks.

Some unique challenges arose in developing and following standardized protocols for the savings-led intervention. The savings-led protocols include when and how to make incentive payments, how to obtain the savings match, managing accounts, checking account status, and monitoring accumulation of matched savings. There are also procedures for spending down (paying out) matched savings. Although we adapted protocols from prior work by study team members (Ssewamala et al. 2008), we found that many areas require flexibility as we worked out how to create protocols that are both manageable and standardized. For example, this included creating a way for the women to withdraw funds from their personal savings (often for emergencies) then giving them the option to replace personal savings and monitor their accumulated matched savings over time.

Despite advance planning, we encountered a number of bank-specific issues that future studies should address early. High service charges are a key challenge. For instance, banks apply a charge to close an account. In addition, the bank does not offer the option to use subaccounts, which would have allowed the team to keep all matched proceeds in one account and yet to segregate matches for each individual participant. The bank's decision to discontinue use of account passbooks generated concerns among participants, as they prefer passbooks to simple paper statements, finding the passbooks to be more substantial proof of an updated record of their savings. Given the previously mentioned concerns about trust, this issue proved to be particularly important. Additionally, using traditional financial services presents particular challenges for high-risk and vulnerable populations. For example, the bank requires customers to present photo identification when opening a bank account and some participants found that acquiring such identification took time.

Competing priorities and survival needs pose the greatest challenges in a savings-led intervention. Child-care, transportation, health-related needs – all the participants' needs as well as those of dependent children and parents – are everyday priorities that claim the time and resources available to participants. Such priorities prevented many from attending all of the intervention sessions.

Opportunities

Notwithstanding the challenges, there have been many opportunities and successes. In Mongolia, most microcredit programmes target existing entrepreneurs, so Undarga provides a 'levelled playing field' for poor women who possess entrepreneurial impulses but lack business experience and face social stigma. Undarga is the first intervention in Mongolia to offer women engaged in sex work an opportunity to gain financial literacy, learn business-development skills, and participate in a matched-savings programme. It gave participants their first exposure to microfinance-related training. The 2:1 savings match also offered entrepreneurial women the opportunity to build start-up capital more quickly than would otherwise be possible. To date, a few women have successfully launched businesses, including small farming, street vending, and sewing.

Participants reported that the intervention enhanced their financial knowledge and skills. Many articulated goals related to saving and money management. An anecdote illustrates Undarga's influence in this area. A participant reported that she visited the home of another woman from her group and saw the following list written on a note on the refrigerator: '(1) Save money even in a small quantity instead of waiting for big money some day; (2) put money away to reach a goal; and (3) paying debts is a priority.' The women also indicated that they became 'aware of other potential options to earn money'. They said things like 'I just need to work on it', and, 'I can do it.'

Many participants also talked about the intervention's non-economic benefits, indicating that it increased their self-confidence and gave them a new sense of capability. Some reported perceiving an emotional openness that they did not feel in themselves before. Through the intervention, others found courage and a fearlessness that allowed them to make changes in their budgeting and saving behaviours.

Implications

Despite multiple challenges encountered in the implementation of this savings-led intervention among women engaged in sex work, practical solutions also emerged. Preliminary results suggest that the circumstances of the sessions (e.g.

location, timing) are important determinants of attendance. It is critical to identify the safest, most effective, and most convenient circumstances for participants. Findings also suggest practical strategies to help women survive as their main source of income shifts from sex work to an alternative. As we await the final quantitative of the study, these findings on implementation challenges and opportunities may inform future savings-led interventions.

An asset-building pilot for vulnerable children

Light of Hope Saving Program in Lamphun Province, Thailand

Wimonmat Srichamroen[3]

The Light of Hope Saving Program is a pilot initiative designed to build the assets, well-being, and positive life perspectives of vulnerable children in Thailand. Implemented by the Rimping Municipality Office in Lamphun Province, the programme's primary feature is a free savings account with a seed deposit and savings matches. The initiative also provides scholarships, a mentoring programme, and supportive interventions related to reproductive health, drug-abuse prevention, financial literacy, and empowerment. This case study describes the target population, the Light of Hope Saving Program, and a study to evaluate the programme.

Vulnerable children in Thailand

Thailand is home to 6.4 million vulnerable children (International Organization for Migration 2012; Quality Learning Foundation 2012).[4] The government classifies 2,978,770 children as vulnerable because they live in poverty (i.e. live in families with annual income below THB 20,000, or USD 637; Quality Learning Foundation 2012).[5] More than 300,000 Thai children have lost one or both of their parents to HIV/AIDS (UNICEF Thailand 2004).

Each group of vulnerable children requires assistance in different facets of development, but all share the need for educational opportunities to support their self-development, future self-sustainability, and independence (Quality Learning Foundation 2012). Encouraging saving in the family is one way to enhance the livelihoods and rights of vulnerable children, but most vulnerable children in Thailand are members of low-income families or live in poverty (Sumitanant 2012). Such families have limited financial resources, and multiple barriers prevent them from developing their financial assets (Sherraden 1991). Without an effective intervention, low-income families find it almost impossible to accumulate assets, improve their financial condition, and exit poverty (Hogan *et al.* 2004).

Rimping Municipality

Rimping Municipality, the primary site for this study, lies 4 km from the centre of Lamphun Province in northern Thailand (Rimping Municipality Office 2012).

Ten villages comprise the municipality, which stretches over an area of 14.14 km². The municipality has 2621 households and a total population of 6917 people. Eighty per cent of land in the municipality is used for agriculture, and 2080 of its households are engaged in agricultural industry. The municipality has three community schools; two offer classes from kindergarten (two years) to Grade 6, and the third offers secondary-level classes (Grades 7–9).

The Rimping Municipality Office provides several social welfare and community development programmes. In addition to financial assistance, occupational training, and shelters for homeless individuals, the municipality offers recreational programmes for elderly persons with disabilities, HIV-positive residents, children affected by HIV/AIDS, orphaned children, and other vulnerable people (Rimping Municipality Office 2012). The office also offers financial consultation, village funds, and saving advice through Rimping's community bank. Within the municipality reside 38 children who are registered as vulnerable.[6] Among these, 45.5 per cent live in poverty, 32.26 per cent are father orphaned, 9.68 per cent have lost both parents to HIV/AIDS, and 3 per cent are infected with HIV/AIDS (Rimping Municipality Office 2012). All 38 of these children are participants in the Light of Hope Saving Program. Their ages range from 9 to 17 years (median age is 13).[7]

The Light of Hope Saving Program

The pilot programme described in this case study combines an asset-building initiative for vulnerable children with other supportive interventions. The Rimping Municipality adopted the Light of Hope Saving Program in January 2012. In May 2012 the 38 children and their parents attended a meeting about the programme. The Rimping Municipality's community bank then opened Light of Hope savings accounts free of charge for all of the children. On 30 September 2012, each account received a seed deposit of THB 500 (USD 16) funded by the Center for Social Development at Washington University in St. Louis. Participants regularly deposit their money on Wednesdays – the day when the community bank opens for business. Participants stay in the programme at least one year. They have an option to leave the programme after that year but are encouraged to stay in it until they graduate from secondary school (Grade 12), complete the third year of vocational school, or enter a university. In all cases, the participants' age will be approximately 17–19 years old at the time they leave the Light of Hope Saving Program.

To encourage the children to save in the accounts, the Municipality Office provides annual matches at a 1:1 rate; at the end of the school year, each participating child receives THB 1 for every baht held in the account. The annual match is capped at a maximum of THB 365 (USD 12). The match cap is necessary to ensure that children (and their low-income families) do not forgo other expenses (e.g. for food and other necessities) in order to accumulate savings. The cap also enables the Rimping Municipality Office to plan its annual budget and to reserve an amount of money to fund the savings matches.

Because vulnerable children may be unable to save as much as their non-vulnerable counterparts, Light of Hope accounts also receive preferential interest rates from the municipality's community bank. Interest on the accounts accrues at a rate of 3 per cent, but funds in accounts held by non-vulnerable children accrue interest at a rate of .75 per cent. The higher interest rates may help vulnerable children to accumulate their savings quickly.

The programme imposes some restrictions on children's access to their accounts. During the school year, children can withdraw no more than 80 per cent of their own savings. This restriction ensures that the account holds the initial seed deposit and 20 per cent of any savings by the child when the municipality calculates and pays savings matches at the end of the school year. In addition, the programme allows youth to use the accumulated savings only for health care, transportation (e.g. local bus fares, gas for a scooter, and van pooling, which has to be paid monthly to the driver), or education purposes. To ensure that the children use the savings for permitted expenses, the programme requires them to obtain their parents' signed permission or to present a receipt before making withdrawals.

As mentioned, the combination of an asset-building component with several supportive interventions is a distinguishing feature of the Light of Hope programme. The interventions are designed to enhance children's development and lifelong well-being. Once in the academic year, a drug-abuse prevention class and a lecture about drugs are given together with a lecture on reproductive health and HIV/AIDS education. A financial education class is also offered once in the pilot year (April 2013) along with a lesson on household budgeting. To encourage academic achievement and continued saving, Rimping Municipality and private donors offer scholarships to participating children who earn high marks. Although the tuition fee is waived in public schools, students still have to pay for school maintenance (two semesters per year), school uniforms, transportation to school, food at school, and stationery. Children participating in this programme can use their scholarship to cover those costs or save it for their post-secondary education. The Municipality Office determines the qualifications for these scholarships, which are awarded at the end of the school year. In June 2013, during the pilot's first year, eight THB 1000 scholarships were given to programme participants who had a grade-point average between 3.50 and 4.00 on a 4.00 scale.

Educational classes and activities comprise a substantial portion of the programme's intervention efforts. The participating children receive instruction on reproductive health and HIV/AIDS through existing community development programmes provided for villagers and children by the Ministry of Health's provincial office. Although any community member may attend, the municipality ensures that Light of Hope Saving Program members have the opportunity to attend and participate in these classes, which are designed to increase awareness at an early age. If children are knowledgeable about the HIV virus and reproductive health, they can share correct information with their peers at school and people in the community. Light of Hope also offers classes and activities that focus on drug-abuse prevention at the Rimping Municipality Office. The classes feature lessons about prevalent drugs, where to seek advice in stressful situations, how to avoid drug use, effects of drug abuse, and where to report drug abuse. Sports competitions form an important part of these prevention efforts. They are designed to encourage children to utilize their free time and to stay away from drug use.

A financial literacy and self-empowerment class provided at the Rimping Municipality Office complements the programme's asset-building component. Through it, participants learn how to set goals, save, and use their money effectively. The class also focuses on the significance of saving. It emphasizes that participants can achieve such goals as higher education or make investments that improve health and other aspects of well-being.

The final supportive intervention is a mentoring programme offered in collaboration with the schools and funded through the municipality budget system. Designed to enhance the confidence and capacity of vulnerable children, the sessions provide one-on-one interactions with mentors who will help children to develop personal, social, cognitive, and environmental skills. The sessions also encourage students to avoid drug use and violence. Mentors provide advice to the children but also are knowledgeable about community and government services. The children can ask these adults for support when needs arise.

Evaluation of the Life of Hope Saving Program pilot

To assess the merits of this pilot, an evaluation study is examining the programme's effects on saving behaviour, well-being, and participants' expectations for the future. The study uses data from quantitative surveys and administrative sources. The study's population is selected by purposive sampling. Youth registered as vulnerable children with the Rimping Municipality Office comprise the experimental group ($n=38$). The control group includes a similar number of children from Tontong Municipality. The experimental and control groups have similar characteristics with respect to community income and distance from the city.

Data

Three sets of primary data are collected for the evaluation. Set A comes from quantitative surveys of the participating children in the experimental and control groups. Set B comes from surveys of those participants' parents or guardians. Set C provides data from surveys of the participants' homeroom teachers.

Data in Set A provide information on personal characteristics, vulnerability, saving behaviour, programme participation, understanding of HIV/AIDS, activities supporting community learning about HIV/AIDS, and expectations for the saved funds when the programme is complete and the savings have been matched. Personal information includes the child's gender, age, school level, latest grade-point average, parents or guardians' occupation, and reason for participating in the programme. Participants' vulnerability is measured according to the categories of vulnerability used by the Rimping Municipality Office. The survey assesses whether the youth lives in poverty, has been affected by HIV/AIDS, is orphaned, and has a disability. (As a note mentions above, Rimping Municipality recognizes these four categories of vulnerability because local services are available for affected youth.)

Spending behaviour is assessed with questions about regular expenses, sources of stipends, and management of stipends. Young Thai children receive stipends from their parents; given daily, weekly, or monthly, they can be any amount of money and are typically used for such expenses as snacks when the children go to school. There is variation in the amount of money given and in spending behaviour, but some children have unspent stipend funds at the end of the school year and may save the remaining money in a bank account. The survey examines saving behaviour and programme participation by measuring saving frequency, participation in the supporting activities, and saving methods. The survey also asks children about their expectations for the future (e.g. concerning educational attainment and plans for the accumulated savings).

To assess children's knowledge of HIV/AIDS, the survey queries the community's perspectives towards HIV/AIDS and self-esteem. In Thai culture, community members stigmatize HIV/AIDS patients and their family. The stigmatization may affect children's self-esteem if they are affected by the disease. The survey also asks about activities in support of community learning about HIV/AIDS.

Data in Set B provide information on the personal characteristics of parents and guardians as well as on their observations concerning the participating children. Personal characteristics include the parent or guardian's gender, age, educational degree, occupation, and relation to the programme member, as well as the number of children in the individual's household. The survey also investigates parents' observations concerning the child's academic performance, learning behaviour, spending habits, saving behaviour, and academic interests at home. Data in Set C include teachers' personal information (gender, age, grade level taught) as well as their observations on the child's actions (e.g. interactions with classmates), academic performance, spending habits, and saving behaviour.

Secondary data for the evaluation come from documents provided by agencies participating in the programme. These include advertising pamphlets of the Light of Hope Saving Program and its supporting intervention programmes, documents requesting collaborations with other agencies, evaluation forms completed by participants after the supporting intervention activities, and savings records of the programme participants.

Data analysis

Statistical frequency distribution will be used to describe the population and such characteristics as average income, expenses, and savings per month. Descriptive statistics will be used to study saving behaviour and its relationships with academic performance, self-esteem, and expectations in life.

In August 2012, the baseline surveys were disseminated to and collected from children in the programme, their parents, and their homeroom teachers. The data collected from the experimental and control groups before the programme started will be compared with the data collected in 2013, one year after the programme implementation. Because data collection continues at the time of this writing, results from the evaluation are not yet available.

Conclusion

Asset building and disciplined saving behaviours enhance self-development, life well-being, and positive life perspectives of vulnerable populations (Page-Adams and Sherraden 1997; Scanlon, Buford, and Dawn 2009; Sherraden 1991). The Light of Hope Saving Program's developer and the Rimping Municipality Office hope that this programme will produce positive outcomes for the group under study. Positive outcomes would include increases in the children's motivation to pursue higher education and improvements in their perspectives concerning their ability to achieve life goals. It would also be positive if the programme provided evidence to support the implementation of the programme model in other municipalities or communities in Thailand and with other groups of vulnerable populations in the country. However, if the programme is found to have no effect or to produce negative outcomes, the programme developer and the Rimping Municipality will use the results to improve the programme model, or go in a new direction, if that is indicated.

Asset building for home ownership in the Nong Kaem community, Thailand

Parichart Valaisathien[8]

In 2003 the Thai government launched the *Baan Mankong* (secure housing) programme, an initiative to address the problem of insecure housing in urban slums. The programme departs from previous policies by employing a community-driven approach to local development. The programme started with efforts to launch savings activities in communities throughout Thailand. It then registered savings groups as community co-operatives in order to establish legal entities that can access housing loans from the government. Thus, the communities are able to plan and carry out improvements to housing, environment, basic services, and tenure security. Participants manage the budgets themselves (Boonyabancha 2009). This case examines the initiative's influence in a poor community.

The Nong Kaem community

A low-income community on the outskirts of Bangkok, Nong Kaem is located near the Bangkok Metropolitan Authority's garbage dump. Originally a squatter community, Nong Kaem grew as garbage pickers migrated into the area and built one-storey shelters from wood, zinc sheeting, and other materials discarded in the dump. A 2004 study by Ampai describes conditions in Nong Kaem:

> Household equipment, such as water containers, working tools, hose pipes, linoleum, shoes and household extensions cluttered the public roadsides, making it difficult to get through. Most foot-paths were made by dumping discarded garbage materials, such as shoe uppers, rubber sheets, plastic bags, tire, pieces of wood and concrete bricks, the remains of which were piled haphazardly in any empty space between houses. Apart from being unsightly, it was a fertile ground for flies, cockroaches, rats and disease.[9]

These living conditions point to other problems. Drug abuse has been prevalent in the community. In 1995, 40 families, one-quarter of the community, included a member who had been arrested and jailed for drug-related offenses (Juchareon, Ung, and Ritnetikul 2011, 4).

Land rights also are a matter of concern. The original settlement occupied unused land. As Bangkok expanded, building new roads in the area, the value of land rose around Nong Kaem. Landowners wanted to make use of their hold-ings, and evictions became common.

As the inhabitants of Nong Kaem struggled with these problems, community leaders and organizations emerged, establishing relationships with a variety of charities and non-profit organizations. The community began to address some of the issues. Nong Kaem was prepared to join the Baan Mankong programme at its outset in 2003 and was granted approval to participate in 2005.

The Baan Mankong programme

Administered by the Community Organizations Development Institute (CODI) (2004), a public organization established in 2000, the Baan Mankong initiative facilitates collaborations among local governments, non-governmental organiza-tions (NGOs), planning professionals, and residents in poor communities. Through these exchanges, the poor play an important role in developing their communities and their own housing. Community residents plan, secure funding for, and execute improvement projects so that the outcomes are relevant to the lives and needs of community members. According to CODI (2004), Baan Mankong has 11 programme goals: (1) to solve problems and develop housing for the poor in urban slums; (2) to secure tenure of land and housing; (3) to develop public-service and utility-delivery systems and a good environment; (4) to improve and develop the security of house construction; (5) to encourage the formulation of integrated plans and directions for community development; (6) to empower poor communities so that they will be acknowledged by the society at large; (7) to create effective community administration systems; (8) to create a database that identifies squatter settlements throughout the country and tracks their development plans; (9) to create multi-party development mechanisms; (10) to adjust regulations and conditions to create flexibility and relevance to development; (11) to formulate new roles for educational and academic institu-tions to participate in development and to link learning in local communities and universities in order to create new bodies of knowledge among communities, local organizations, and academic institutions.

In public forums, Nong Kaem's community leaders explained Baan Mankong to the community. The inhabitants were enthusiastic about having their own houses and about an exchange of learning with partner organizations that would help them in designing the houses, utility system, and other project plans. In addition, study trips to visit communities in the programme enabled a group of residents to relate what they learned to others in Nong Kaem. Staff from CODI worked to build community understanding of Baan Mankong. Partner organiza-tions came later, providing skilled assistance and additional support.

Prior to the launch of the Baan Mankong projects in Nong Kaem, the com-munity recognized the need for a capital fund, and residents formed a savings group comprised of 116 families. From July 2003 onward, each family paid THB 500 into the fund every month, and most other families joined later. A year after its formation, the savings group registered as a co-operative. The Nong

Kaem Housing Cooperative, and particularly its leadership committee (hereafter, the co-operative's committee, or committee), plays a central role in the Baan Mankong programme's Nong Kaem projects. As Boonyabancha (2009, 313) notes, 'The savings groups and the community co-operatives are two key mechanisms that help communities deal with all aspects of the project – as well as many other development issues – as a group.' The co-operative co-ordinates the community's collaboration with CODI and other partners. It also manages loans, provided through Baan Mankong by public sources, for housing and community infrastructure. With such funds, the co-operative purchases land and pays for construction projects, allocating housing and housing rights to members, who are responsible for retiring the co-operative's loans.

The projects in Nong Kaem provide a model of co-operative living. Instead of delivering homes to individual families, the co-operative develops members' housing in a collective way. Members share the collective land title to prevent speculators from buying individual housing units from the poor and selling the units to higher-income groups. Members sign a common agreement that specifies the rights and obligations of membership. Each is only allowed to sell the house back to the co-operative and can ask only the same price he or she paid for it (not the market price). Thus, this collective method offers a powerful way to expand home ownership among the poor.

To be eligible for a home through the housing co-operative, a family must hold membership, attend its meetings regularly, comply with project regulations, and make regular deposits into the co-operative's savings. Families that joined the co-operative after its establishment must make additional deposits so that their savings equal those of other member families. When the family receives a home, it must make monthly payments to the co-operative, which retires the loans used to purchase the land, build the house, and provide infrastructure. Each family makes such payments for a 15-year term. The co-operative allocates housing in order of membership: priority is given to families that joined the co-operative early. Priority is also determined by members' level of participation in community work and activities.

The Baan Mankong plans for Nong Kaem anticipate the construction of 125 two-storey town houses (THB 170,000 per unit, about USD 5440), 20 one-storey town houses (THB 85,000 per unit, about USD 2720), a multi-purpose building for use in a community recycling business, an office building for the housing co-operative, and a variety of common spaces (e.g. a garden, a children's playground, an exercise area, and roads). All homes are formally registered as residences and have utility services.

Mid-term outcomes

In the first seven years of operation (2005–2012) the Nong Kaem Housing Cooperative supported the acquisition of property for all but two of its 143 member families. This is the most effective implementation of the Baan Mankong programme. It illustrates the principle that 'development work is not about having good rules and regulations and good figures in the accounts, or problem-elimination, but finding ways to solve problems, understanding each member's situation, and developing their capacity during the process' (Banjong Ung, chair of Nong Kaem Housing Cooperative, interview with author, 20 August 2012).

The co-operative's committee openly admits that the co-operative did not operate smoothly or achieve success in all aspects of its work.[10] Irregular loan repayments remain a problem for 20 per cent of members. This includes both people with real money constraints as well as those who lack the discipline to meet their obligations. Although a common agreement binds all members, the co-operative also developed procedures for dealing with problems and makes adjustments to accommodate each family's situation.

For example, a particular member missed loan repayments for three months in a row without providing a good reason. The co-operative's committee decided, in accordance with the agreement, to revoke the family's right to property. However, the head of the family tried to make a contribution to the community by volunteering to sort garbage for the community's recycling business. At the beginning, the committee gave her a per diem of THB 50 (USD 1.60), and the member continued to work diligently with good results. Her work was even better than that of the co-operative's own employees. The co-operative therefore hired the member to work permanently on wages at the level specified by law (THB 215 per day, the minimum wage from 2011 through March 2013) and reinstated the family's membership in the housing co-operative. The committee deducts the required repayments from the member's wages.

Since 2005, members have repaid THB 11 million (about USD 351,970) of the THB 23 million loan the co-operative received from the government through CODI. Each member family with a two-storey town house still owes about THB 90,000 (USD 2870), and those with one-storey houses owe about THB 40,000 (USD 1280). The market value of their houses has risen to three times the original purchase price. Therefore the committee considers missed payments to be a periodic deficit concern but does not deem overdue repayments to be a serious problem for the co-operative.

The co-operative committee employs several measures to deal with deficits resulting from non-payment by members. If the member agrees to pay a fine and the missed payment (in accordance with regulations), the committee covers the family's missed payment with funds from the co-operative's reserve. In 2013 the co-operative launched โครงการทำงานวันละ 2 ชั่วโมง ผ่อนบ้านได้ (*Two hours a day gets you a housing mortgage*; author's translation), a programme to promote occupations and income. If a member agrees to participate in the programme by working two hours per day in the co-operative's business, the co-operative pays the member THB 50 per day, and the member uses this sum to make a daily mortgage payment: THB 25 for a one-storey town house or THB 45 for a two-storey town house. The member may keep the money that remains after the mortgage payment. The committee also finds low-interest loans from sources like the Department of Cooperatives Promotion. Members use the low-cost loans to repay their existing housing loans; because the new loans cost less, families have less difficulty making payments and avoid the high fines for missing them. Finally, the co-operative promotes saving among children and established a children's savings group, which has 30 members.

The practices above show that the Nong Kaem Housing Cooperative's co-operative committee pursues its work through what can be described as an organic development process (Ife 2002). In this flexible process, the committee makes concessions based on a deep understanding of members' lives and livelihoods. The metaphor of organic growth illustrates the theory behind the process: each plant produces fruit only if various environmental conditions are in place.

In the Nong Kaem community, the process of building assets for home ownership corresponds to the Triangle That Moves the Mountain model proposed by Prawase Wasi (2000). Wasi (2000) posits that managing a complex situation (analogous to the task of moving a mountain) requires one to work with three types of forces: politics, people, and knowledge.

It is undeniable that the political realm created an important enabling factor: the policy on secure home ownership. But one cannot measure the success of this initiative only by the number of housing units completed. Additional measures can be found in members' compliance with the initiative's requirements. Individuals must secure ownership of their home by repaying a loan for 15 years, by managing their affairs, and by participating fully in community life.

Success has also depended upon the willingness of the co-operative's committee to listen to the community and communicate with members on a regular basis. In addition to appropriate government policies and the active participation of the people, success depends upon knowledge of the appropriate methods of practice. The co-operative committee operates at the macro level through the consensus of a majority of members and the common agreement. It also considers each family and individual's situation. This represents a suitable integration of the methods of community work, group work, family work, and case-work.

Notes

1 This study was made possible by grant R34MH093227-02 to Principal Investigator Witte from the National Institute of Mental Health.
2 In Mongolian, *Undarga* means 'natural spring' or 'fountain'. It can also be used figuratively to mean an outflow of something good and solid, a water source, or a spring of good things. In choosing this as the programme's name, the research team aims to demonstrate that the programme invites a new beginning for participants.
3 I thank the Center for Social Development for its contribution of seed deposit money for the 38 accounts of Light of Hope Saving Program members. I also thank Michael Sherraden, Li Zou, and CSD staff for providing research resources for the development of the programme. I extend my gratitude to Rimping Municipal Office, Lamphun, Thailand, for adopting the programme design and for their work in making this programme happen and continue.
4 Quality Learning Foundation, an independent agency within the Thai government, reviewed several organizations' assessments of the standard measure of vulnerability

and concluded that several groups should be classified as vulnerable: street children, stateless children (i.e. children with no registered nationality), children of migrant workers, HIV-positive children, neglected and orphaned children, child labourers, child prostitutes, children addicted to drugs, children living in poverty (i.e. those whose family's income does not exceed THB 20,000 per year), children living in remote areas, and children with autism and other disabilities. Issues experienced by these groups of children must be addressed by related government agencies in order to enhance the development of the country's human resources (Policy and Planning Office of the Permanent Secretary of Interior 2011).

5 The Thai baht is a unit of currency in Thailand. One US dollar is equivalent to approximately THB 31.

6 Disabled persons, including children with disabilities, are encouraged to register as a person with disability through the Department of Social Development and Welfare (in Bangkok) or through a provincial office of the Ministry of Social Development and Human Security. Registration entitles them to receive disability benefits; disabled children receive special education services (Ministry of Social Development and Human Security 2013; Office of Welfare Promotion, Protection and Empowerment of Vulnerable Groups n.d.). Local government authorities, such as sub-district municipality offices, use information collected from the annual census to automatically register children with other types of vulnerability for whatever services are appropriate and available in their area. For example, Rimping Municipality's annual census asks whether a child is (1) disabled, (2) living in poverty, (3) orphaned, and (4) affected by HIV/AIDS (Bureau of Promotion and Protection of the Disadvantaged 2013).

7 The age data come from the baseline survey conducted in 2012.

8 The author acknowledges support from the Center for Social Development in the Brown School of Social Work at Washington University in St. Louis, USA and the Faculty of Social Administration at Thammasat University, Thailand.

9 Author's translation.

10 The co-operative committee is responsible for preparing each community housing project through a participatory process that involves co-operative members, and the committee then proposes the project for the government's approval. In collaboration with CODI and other partners, the committee carries out housing projects and manages finances in a transparent way.

References

Ampai, Titirat. 2004. วิถีชีวิตการทำงานกับภาวะสุขภาพอนามัย ของผู้มีอาชีพเก็บขยะ กรณีศึกษา ชุมชนกองขยะหนองแขม [Working life and health conditions of garbage collectors: a case study of Nong Kaem garbage landfill]. MA thesis, Thammasat University, Faculty of Social Administration, Labour Development and Welfare Programme, Bangkok.

Boonyabancha, Somsook. 2009. 'Land for Housing the Poor – by the Poor: Experiences from the Baan Mankong Nationwide Slum Upgrading Programme in Thailand.' *Environment and Urbanization* 21 (2): 309–329. doi:10.1177/0956247809342180.

Bureau of Promotion and Protection of the Disadvantaged. 2013. ยุทธศาสตร์ส่งเสริมการพัฒนาศักยภาพและคุ้มครองพิทักษ์สิทธิผู้ด้อยโอกาส (พ.ศ. 2556–2559) [Strategies to promote capacity and protect the rights of vulnerable populations (2013–2016)]. Bangkok: Bureau of Promotion and Protection of the Disadvantaged. Accessed 30 August 2013. www.oppd.opp.go.th/download_files/28-30-04-56.pdf.

Community Organizations Development Institute. 2004. *Baan Mankong Handbook: Implementing the Baan Mankong Community Upgrading Program in Thai Cities.*

Bangkok: Community Organizations Development Institute. www.codi.or.th/downloads/english/Paper/Implementing%20the%20Baan%20Mankong.pdf.

Hogan, M. Janice, Catherine Solheim, Susan Wolfgram, Busisiwe Nkosi, and Nicola Rodrigues. 2004. 'The Working Poor: From the Economic Margins to Asset Building.' *Family Relations* 53 (2): 229–236. doi:10.1111/j.0022-2445.2004.00013.x.

Ife, J.W. 2002. *Community Development: Community-Based Alternatives in an Age of Globalisation.* 2nd edn. Sydney, Australia: Longman.

International Organization for Migration. 2012. 'Thailand.' Facts and Figures table, April. International Organization for Migration. Accessed 20 September 2013. www.iom.int/jahia/Jahia/thailand.

Juchareon, Prapapun, Banjong Ung, and Natanabhat Ritnetikul. 2011. บทเรียนครอบครัวเข้มแข็ง ชุมชน เข้มแข็ง [Strong family and community: a case study of the Nong Kaem Community]. Nakhonpathom, Thailand: Mahidol University, ASEAN Institute for Health Development.

Ministry of Social Development and Human Security. 2013. การจดทะเบียนคนพิการ [Registration for persons with disabilities]. Accessed 30 August 2013. www.uthaithani.m-society.go.th/Downlonddocument/Registerdisabled.html.

Office of Welfare Promotion, Protection and Empowerment of Vulnerable Groups. n.d. พระราชบัญัติการฟื้นฟูสมรรถภาพคนพิการ ปีพ.ศ. 2534 [Rehabilitation for Persons with Disability Act 1991]. Bangkok: Office of Welfare Promotion, Protection and Empowerment of Vulnerable Groups. Accessed 30 August 2013. www.opp.go.th/km/other/law2_09_01_50.pdf.

Page-Adams, Deborah, and Michael Sherraden. 1997. 'Asset Building as a Community Revitalization Strategy.' *Social Work* 42 (5): 423–434. doi:10.1093/sw/42.5.423.

Policy and Planning Office of the Permanent Secretary of Interior. 2011. แผนปฏิบัติการปฏิรูปประเทศไทย ด้านการสร้างอนาคตของชาติ ด้วยการพัฒนาคนเด็กและเยาวชน [Thailand reform action plan 2011 in building the future of the nation by the development of human resources, children, and youth]. Bangkok: Policy and Planning Office of the Permanent Secretary of Interior, Assembled Policy and Plan Division. Accessed 30 August 2013. www.ppb.moi.go.th/midev02/upload/x1.pdf.

Quality Learning Foundation. 2012. สถานการณ์เด็ก เยาวชน และ ผู้ด้อยโอกาสทางสังคม [The situations of children, youth, and the social-vulnerable populations]. Bangkok: Quality Learning Foundation. Accessed 20 September 2013. www.qlf.or.th/Home/Details?contentId=147#.

Rimping Municipality Office. 2012. ข้อมูลด้านเศรษฐกิจของเทศบาลตำบลริมปิง [Economic information of the municipality]. Rimping, Thailand: Rimping Municipality Office. Accessed 10 October 2013. www.rimping-lp.org/default.asp?content=mpagedetail&id=9515.

Scanlon, Edward, Andrea Buford, and Kenneth Dawn. 2009. 'Matched Savings Accounts: A Study of Youths' Perceptions of Program and Account Design.' *Children and Youth Services Review* 31 (6): 680–687. doi:10.1016/j.childyouth.2009.01.003.

Sherraden, Michael. 1991. *Assets and the Poor: A New American Welfare Policy.* Armonk, NY: M.E. Sharpe.

Ssewamala, Fred M., Stacey Alicea, William M. Bannon, and Leyla Ismayilova. 2008. 'A Novel Economic Intervention to Reduce HIV Risks among School-Going AIDS Orphans in Rural Uganda.' *Journal of Adolescent Health* 42 (1): 102–104. doi:10.1016/j.jadohealth.2007.08.011.

Sumitanant, Rungpetch. 2012. มาตรฐานส่งเสริม-พิทักษ์สิทธิ เด็ก เด็ก เยาวชน ผู้ด้อยโอกาส ผู้สูงอายุ และครอบครัว [Standards of support and protection for the rights of children, youth, vulnerable people, elderly, and family]. Chiang Mai, Thailand: Ministry of Social Development and Human Security, Department of Social Development and Welfare, Technical Promotion Support Office. Accessed 1 October 2013. www.tpso10.org/index. php?option=com_content&view=article&id=138&Itemid=201.

Tsai, Laura Cordisco, Susan S. Witte, Toivgoo Aira, Marion Riedel, Hyesung Grace Hwang, and Fred M. Ssewamala. 2013. '"There is no other option; we have to feed our families … who else would do it?" The Financial Lives of Women Working in Sex Work in Ulaanbaatar, Mongolia.' *Global Journal of Health Science* 5 (5): 41–50. doi:10.5539/gjhs.v5n5p41.

UNICEF Thailand. 2004. เอชไอวี/เอดส์ ภาพรวม [HIV/AIDS, Overview]. UNICEF Thailand. Accessed 25 September 2012. www.unicef.org/thailand/tha/hiv_aids.html.

Wasi, Prawase. 2000. '"Triangle That Moves the Mountain" and Health Systems Reform Movement in Thailand.' *Human Resources for Health Development Journal* 4 (2): 106–110.

Witte, Susan S., Batsukh Altantsetseg, Toivgoo Aira, Marion Riedel, Jiehua Chen, Katie Potocnik, Nabila El-Bassel, *et al.* 2011. 'Reducing Sexual HIV/STI Risk and Harmful Alcohol Use among Sex Workers in Mongolia: A Randomized Clinical Trial.' *AIDS and Behavior* 15 (8): 1785–1794. doi:10.1007/s10461-011-9984-0.

Reflections and conclusions

Michael Sherraden

Asset-building policies and programmes appear to be in a period of emergence and testing around the world. This is part of a larger pattern of strain and adaptation in social policy, a pattern that continues to evolve as societies adjust to the transition from the industrial era to the information era. It may be that asset-based policies will play a more important role in social policy going forward, as part of a growing 'social investment' strategy (Midgley 1999), though that potential role is impossible to predict.

As asset-based policies continue to unfold, experience and knowledge will increase. Scholars, policymakers, and development organizations in Asia will decide how and to what extent asset-based innovations, research, and policy insights are relevant and helpful. This book can be viewed as part of that effort – one step on a long path of overall assessment. As always, appropriate adaptations to particular nations and contexts are fundamental. In this reflection and conclusion, I review and offer a few observations on asset-building policy strategies that are emerging in the Asia region.

It is fitting that Part I of the book on asset-building policies begins with James Lee's focus on housing. Professor Lee lives in Hong Kong, where residential real estate is scarce and the market is largely controlled by wealthy developers. As Lee observes, housing in Hong Kong is subject to speculation and often inflated prices; it is an enormous social issue. Lee is also very familiar with the cases of Singapore, Mainland China, and other countries in Asia. In Singapore, housing is a primary mechanism for asset building in the Central Provident Fund (CPF). In other words, housing is a social policy strategy. The Singapore government controls swings in prices for publicly sponsored housing and provides subsidies at the bottom, so speculation is more contained there than in Hong Kong, and ownership is more widespread. Mainland China, as much as or more than Hong Kong, is also subject to speculative housing bubbles, sometimes putting prices out of reach for ordinary people. Government action on housing in Mainland China operates primarily at the macro level through banking regulation, and prices can be subject to outright bubbles. In each of these cases, as in many other countries, housing is a central focus of asset building at the household level. In addition, housing is often understood in terms of security, belonging, and place in the community and society. In most countries in Asia, it would be almost impossible to conceive of an effective asset-based policy in which housing did not play a large role. Integration into successful social policy, however, may require a public strategy for housing availability – a strategy that is more purposeful than the current ones in many countries.

The chapters by Ross Clare and Siew-Yong Yew present two contrasting examples of asset-based policy oriented primarily towards retirement savings in Australia and Malaysia, respectively. The Australian example of superannuation – or 'the Super' as Aussies sometimes call it – is important because of its relative newness, rapid growth, and increasing effectiveness. The Super was implemented in the last half of the twentieth century and, although still far from perfect, has already grown to become an important source of retirement security for a diverse population in Australia. It is important to emphasize that superannuation in Australia, like the CPF in Singapore, is broadly inclusive. In contrast, the 401(k) system in the United States serves people at the top but not those at the bottom. In addition, superannuation is a 'pay as you go' system, so it avoids large, unfunded 'entitlement' obligations to ageing populations. The Australian example demonstrates that a new asset-based policy can be implemented and become effective within a few decades. What is required is the strategic foresight and political will to begin.

The Employees Provident Fund in Malaysia is an understudied yet important example of a surviving 'provident fund' from the British colonial era. Not wanting to incur large social spending obligations in the colonies, the British created more than two dozen colonial provident funds in Asia and Africa (Dixon 1989). Most of these funds encountered difficulties over time – macroeconomic stresses, especially inflation, and political challenges ranging from ineffective leadership to outright corruption. Consequently, few continue to operate today. Malaysia's Employees Provident Fund is a notable exception. As Professor Yew describes, the fund has some challenges but remains an important source of retirement security for many Malaysians. This asset-based strategy in Malaysia is a story of policy survival and adaptation across political eras and over a long period of economic development.

As Professors Chang-Keun Han and Youngmi Kim document, the Korean story is very different. South Korea is a wealthy country today. For the most part, its social policy has followed Western traditions in relying on social insurance and means-tested income support. Only in the early twenty-first century have asset-building innovations been introduced. These innovations were influenced by research on Individual Development Accounts in the United States (Sherraden and Han 2007). In the past dozen years the national government in Korea has implemented a Child Development Account policy, beginning with an effort to reach the most disadvantaged children in institutional care. Data indicate that this policy has been successful. The innovation was originally planned to reach the bottom half of the income distribution, building assets for child development. Due to regime changes, policy expansion has been put on hold. Over the same period, political and social welfare leadership in Seoul initiated Child Development Accounts for impoverished children there. Leaders in Seoul also launched a version of Individual Development Accounts. These Hope Plus Accounts won a United Nations Public Service Award in 2010. Altogether, the asset-based innovations in Korea have been sincerely implemented as steps towards larger policies but, due primarily to political changes, have remained small-scale initiatives. Whether these small beginnings grow over time or gradually fade away remains to be seen. In any event, the dominance of traditional social policies based on income support is very likely to continue into the foreseeable future.

The chapter by Li Zou and colleagues on policy diffusion in Korea and Taiwan is illuminating in providing concrete examples of how local (usually city-based) innovations of Individual Development Accounts and similar policies have spread to other cities. The Center for Social Development was involved in the initial local innovations in Seoul and Taipei but had little to do with the spread of these innovations to other cities in Korea and Taiwan. This is perhaps an example of 'seeding' local policy innovations that are then copied and spread. Another observation on these innovations is that when Family Development Accounts were first introduced in Taipei, then Mayor Ma Ying-jeou was very supportive, hosting a working conference and press conference at the city hall to support the idea. With his later election to the Taiwan presidency, we had hoped that President Ma would take steps towards a broader asset-building policy across Taiwan, but this has not happened. He is quite busy with economic and political challenges, especially those related to managing relationships with the Chinese mainland and the independently minded population of Taiwan. It is safe to say that social policy innovation and reform are not high on President Ma's list of priorities. Again, we can draw the lesson that getting policy traction is seldom an easy process. Many factors have to come together, and if this occurs at all, it may be over a very long period of time.

Professors Tan Tai Yong and Ho Kong Chong provide an insightful history of Singapore's social policy, with considerable focus on the backbone policy: the CPF. The CPF in Singapore, like the Employees Provident Fund in Malaysia, is a legacy of British colonialism. Singaporeans, however, have done something altogether different with it. The CPF is by far the most successful adaptation of a provident fund, and through purposeful policy innovations has become the most extensive and consequential example of asset-based policy in the world (Sherraden *et al.* 1995). Today, the CPF is a comprehensive social policy system, covering major components of retirement security, home ownership, health care, education, insurance, and investments – all based on a paternalistic policy of asset accumulation. The policy is mandatory and highly inclusive. As a result, more than 90 per cent of Singaporeans own their residences, and with home price appreciation over time, even the bottom quintile of the population holds meaningful assets. (In an interview during the early 1990s I asked then Senior Minister Lee Kuan Yew why the CPF was used so much for housing, and his primary answer was not about social welfare but about national security. He said that if Singaporeans owned their homes, they would be more likely to defend the small and vulnerable nation.) In addition, Singapore now provides each child with an account and an initial deposit at birth. The city-state also provides matching deposits for savings set aside in these accounts. Those potential contributions total more than USD 30,000 per child. It would be hard to overstate the scope of these asset-based policies and government subsidies for inclusion of the whole population. They are much broader than the initiatives in other countries.

However, CPF policy has its shortcomings. As the chapter by Kok-Hoe Ng describes, a substantial number of participants in CPF face a threat to retirement security because they do not have much money remaining in the accounts, and impoverished individuals receive very minimal public income support prior to retirement. Ng questions why such a rich country cannot take care of its poorest people more effectively through greater use of social insurance and, where needed, means-tested benefits. These are important questions. Indeed, Singaporean policy has moved over time to expand social supports. How these policies evolve in the future will be very interesting to see.

Turning to Part II of the book, addressing asset building and diverse populations, Professor Charles C. Chan and colleagues begin with a chapter on Hong Kong's innovative Child Development Fund. This innovation stemmed from high-level discussions in Hong Kong over a decade. The Child Development Fund provides a saving component, mentorship, and a development plan. As indicated, early evidence is promising, though much remains to be sorted out and understood. Regarding innovation, a version of the Child Development Fund is now being implemented with youth from migrant families around Beijing. This is another example of policy innovation transfer. It may or may not lead to further policy development on the Chinese mainland.

Sharad Sharma and colleagues summarize early data from the YouthSave project in Nepal. YouthSave is testing saving and asset building among youth in four developing countries: Columbia, Ghana, Kenya, and Nepal. The overall findings from YouthSave are that very poor youth can save and accumulate assets for education and development when a suitable saving product and service are available. In particular, we are finding that 'taking the bank to the youth' in some form is associated with more positive results (Johnson *et al.* 2013, 78). Although YouthSave is a commercial banking strategy, there is growing recognition that there may be a role for public partnership and subsidy, especially to support asset building for the poorest children and youth.

The concept of asset building was introduced in Mainland China during a 2004 conference, Asset Building and Social Development, held at Shandong University (Zou *et al.* 2011). Washington University's Center for Social Development co-organized this meeting, and I was invited to deliver speeches at subsequent conferences organized by Tsinghua University and the Chinese Academy of Social Sciences. At the 21st Century Forum's 2005 conference, Sustainable Development: China and the World, Wen Jiabao, then the Chinese Premier, spoke positively about the potential of asset-based policy in China. Over the past 10 years, asset-based projects and policy discussion have drawn the attention of the Chinese central government and the nation's mainstream media.

Turning to assets research in Mainland China, Suo Deng and Yu Meng begin with an empirical investigation of financial access and youth with disabilities. Jin Huang's research on asset poverty and happiness adds further to this body of work. These early studies are beginning to appear in academic journals and are entering policy discussions in China. The academic route to policy innovation is never a fast track, but this research is a fundamental part of the effort to inform future policy discussions.

As Baorong Guo, Xincai Guo, and Li Zou note, the Center for Social Development team and the Chinese Academy of Social Sciences jointly conducted a three-year research project from 2005 to 2008 to study asset-building effects in an innovation within the Rural Social Insurance programme (actually a savings and annuity policy – a form of self-insurance) in Hutubi County, located in the Xinjiang Uygur Autonomous Region (Guo *et al.* 2008). The innovation allowed participants to borrow from their retirement savings for pre-retirement investments in agricultural and other productive activities and then to repay the fund.

As indicated, the project was largely successful. One very interesting feature of this innovation is its independent origin: it began in the creativity and initiative of a local administrator. The central government in Beijing watched the policy and, seeing its success, allowed it to continue, even permitting other Chinese provinces to copy the innovation. This looked very promising and continued until another local administrator of the same policy – this time far away in eastern China – was charged with stealing funds. The scandal put a halt to all innovations in China's rural retirement policy.

Of course, after so much good work and progress in Xinjiang – an area of China that has been slower to develop and troubled by ethnic conflict – this policy pitfall in eastern China was very disappointing. What are we to learn? Policy innovation and testing is seldom easy. So much depends on individual initiative, accepting context, and good fortune. Even when successful, innovations may not thrive for political reasons. Nevertheless, the Hutubi project in China was important in that it embodied the asset-building concept, received quite a lot of publicity across the country, and sparked policy interest and discussions that continue. At the present time, revival of the Hutubi concept seems unlikely in Mainland China, but the larger concept of asset building found its footing in this project and continues to generate interest.

Asset building also has been used as a theme in social work community practice. As Hok-bun Ku describes, cultural assets in crafts are a cornerstone of development in projects in Yunnan and Sichuan Provinces. As Wai-fong Ting details, social work faculty and students from the Hong Kong Polytechnic University and Sichuan University have employed asset-building theory to enable families and communities to recover from the devastating 2008 earthquake in Sichuan. These projects indicate a broader understanding of the word 'assets' and are very welcome efforts to conceptually link a range of development initiatives under a common theme.

Deyu Zhao and Minchao Jin make conceptual contributions regarding the social welfare effects of assets. Together with the empirical work discussed above, these academic contributions help lay the groundwork for policy innovations currently under discussion in China. One likely direction is to begin the concept of lifelong asset building in China by testing child and youth development accounts, which is now being considered by the Ministry of Civil Affairs, with international interest on the part of UNICEF. (For an overview of Child Development Account policy, see Loke and Sherraden 2009.)

The final substantive chapter, on case studies in emerging practice, has all the positive energy of newly implemented local strategies that show promise. In these three examples by Toivgoo Aira and colleagues, Wimonmat Srichamroen, and Parichart Valaisathien, we are introduced to savings innovations with sex workers, vulnerable children, and low-income community residents. Most important in these projects will be research that carefully documents both successes and challenges. The social entrepreneurship in each of these innovations is highly appealing, but at the end of the day it is evidence that will matter. Research requires extra effort, and we can be grateful that these authors have taken the trouble to document the innovations thus far.

Overall, the concept of inclusive asset-based social policy and programmes, seldom discussed 20 years ago, seems to be ascendant today in Asia and other parts of the world. Asset-based social policy is now the subject of a broad discussion, and there is a growing emphasis on inclusion – bringing in the whole population, including low-income households and those facing challenging circumstances or conditions that may put them at a disadvantage. This is almost a sea change in thinking, yet we do not know as yet whether and to what extent this thinking will yield more inclusive policies that are responsive to changing social and economic realities.

Taking the broader view, it seems possible – indeed likely – that the years ahead will bring continued questioning and reformulations of social policy. Although it will take decades to evolve, we should anticipate that a renewed social contract in the twenty-first century will retain effective features of current social policies, including universal social insurance, but will also chart new directions. A future social contract might place less emphasis on income maintenance for the poor and more emphasis on social investment. Building assets as a foundation for future family and community development represents a promising social-investment strategy. Experience and evidence to date are encouraging. The chapters in this volume mark the recent progress of this policy concept in Asia. Given the current policy interest in Asia and policy histories that often differ from traditional welfare states in the West, it seems possible that Asia may lead in asset-based policy innovations going forward. We are, very fortunately, living in a period when experience and knowledge in social policy are being generated in many parts of the world, and we all learn from each other.

References

Dixon, John E. 1989. *National Provident Funds: The Enfant Terrible of Social Security*. Belconnen, Australia: International Fellowship for Social and Economic Development.

Guo, Baorong, Jin Huang, Michael Sherraden, and Li Zou. 2008. 'Dual Incentives and Dual Asset Building: Policy Implications of the Hutubi Rural Social Security Loan Programme in China.' *Journal of Social Policy* 37 (3): 453–470. doi:10.1017/S0047279408001992.

Johnson, Lissa, YungSoo Lee, Michael Sherraden, Gina A.N. Chowa, David Ansong, Fred M. Ssewamala, Margaret S. Sherraden, Li Zou, Moses Njenga, Joseph Kieyah, Isaac Osei-Akoto, Sharad Sharma, Jyoti Manandhar, Catherine Rodriguez, Federico Merchán, and Juan Saavedra. 2013. *Savings Patterns and Performance in Colombia, Ghana, Kenya, and Nepal*. YouthSave Research Report, CSD Publication 13-18, 23 August. St. Louis, MO: Washington University Center for Social Development. http://csd.wustl.edu/Publications/Documents/RR13-18.pdf.

Loke, Vernon, and Michael Sherraden. 2009. 'Building Assets from Birth: A Global Comparison of Child Development Account Policies.' *International Journal of Social Welfare* 18 (2): 119–129. doi:10.1111/j.1468-2397.2008.00605.x.

Midgley, James. 1999. 'Growth, Distribution, and Welfare: Toward Social Investment.' *Social Service Review* 73 (1): 3–21. doi:10.1086/515795.

Sherraden, Michael, and Chang-Keun Han. 2007. 'The Social Investment State and Asset-Based Policy: Implications for Korean Social Policy.' In *Proceeding of International Symposium*, 29–50. Seoul, South Korea: Seoul Welfare Foundation.

Sherraden, Michael, Sudha Nair, S. Vasoo, Ngiam Tee Liang, and Margaret S. Sherraden. 1995. 'Social Policy Based on Assets: The Impact of Singapore's Central Provident Fund.' *Asian Journal of Political Science* 3 (2): 112–133. doi:10.1080/02185379508434064.

Zou, Li, Michael Sherraden, Baorong Guo, Jin Huang, Suo Deng, and Minchao Jin. 2011. 'Asset-Based Policy in China: Applied Project and Policy Progress.' CSD Policy Brief 11-24, Center for Social Development, Washington University in St. Louis, St. Louis, MO. http://csd.wustl.edu/Publications/Documents/PB11-24.pdf.

Index

Page numbers in *italics* denote tables, those in **bold** denote figures.

For Product Safety Concerns and Information please contact our EU
representative GPSR@taylorandfrancis.com
Taylor & Francis Verlag GmbH, Kaufingerstraße 24, 80331 München, Germany